POSITIVE CLASSROOM DISCIPLINE

POSITIVE CLASSROOM DISCIPLINE

Fredric H. Jones, Ph. D.

McGRAW-HILL BOOK COMPANY

New York   St. Louis   San Francisco   Auckland   Bogotá   Hamburg
London   Madrid   Mexico   Milan   Montreal   New Delhi   Panama
Paris   São Paulo   Singapore   Sydney   Tokyo   Toronto

This book was set in Times Roman by Compset, Inc.
The editor was Thomas H. Quinn;
the jacket and cover were designed by Laura B. Stover.
Project supervision was done by The Total Book.
R. R. Donnelley & Sons Company was printer and binder.

POSITIVE CLASSROOM DISCIPLINE

4 5 6 7 8 9 0   DOCDOC   8 9 4 3 2 1 0 9

ISBN 0-07-032830-7

Library of Congress Cataloging-in-Publication Data

Jones, Fredric H.
  Positive classroom discipline.

  Includes index.
  1. Classroom management. 2. School discipline.
3. Behavior modification. I. Title.
LB3013.J65   1987   371.1'024   86-18607
ISBN 0-07-032830-7

CONTENTS

ACKNOWLEDGMENTS

I credit my wife Jo Lynne with much of my interest in classrooms. Throughout graduate school she was a teacher, and every night when she got home from work we had a 1-hour "debriefing"—like the astronauts have when they return from outer space. During our debriefings I got to relive every trauma and gratification of the day, and by Thanksgiving, the students were, for better or for worse, members of the family. After 5 years of debriefings you either get very curious about what goes on in a classroom or you get entirely turned off by the whole subject. When I began to do classroom management research, Jo Lynne was a collaborator, and she has been my partner in this endeavor ever since.

Jo Lynne was the kind of teacher who came home and did several hours of work in the evening to prepare for the next day. Knowing how hard good teachers work has been a crucial aspect of my awareness that has influenced every aspect of the development of the classroom management methods contained in this book. It is not enough for a technique to succeed. It must also be affordable in terms of time and energy.

I must also acknowledge my debt to my family. I come from a family of teachers. Not only was my mother a teacher, but also aunts, great-aunts, cousins, and my sister. Both parents taught me a lot about effective discipline before I ever got close to a classroom. Perhaps the most important lesson was that strength and firmness could also be gentle and loving.

I am grateful as well to my teacher, colleague, and friend, William Hansford Miller of the faculty of the Neuropsychiatric Institute at the UCLA Medical Center. Hans taught me the basics of behavioral management, supervised my clinical work with parent training, and collaborated on my first piece of classroom management research. Working together we came to understand limit-setting in the classroom and performance-oriented methods of teacher training. More importantly, Hans was available for hours of brainstorming during which time he helped me see how behavioral incentive systems worked at all times in both the home and the classroom. I am indebted as well to Michael J. Goldstein and Eliot H. Rodnick of the UCLA psychology faculty for teaching me to understand psychopathology in family systems from a psychodynamic framework. Together they supervised my dissertation in the area of developmental psychopathology.

I am also indebted to the Bureau of Cooperative Educational Services #1, Fairport, New York, for supporting much of the research necessary for perfecting the methods presented in this book. It is rare that a school system or educational center will undertake the basic research and developmental work required to perfect solutions to everyday classroom management problems. I am also indebted to the excellent students with whom I have had the pleasure of working in this and other settings: Robert C. Eimers, Ph.D.; William Fremouw, Ph.D.; Aden A. Burka, Ph.D.; Herbert Weis, Ph.D.; Richard J. Cowen, Ph.D.; Kenneth Docteur, Ed. D.; and Steven Carples, M.B.A.

And, finally, I am indebted to the many teachers over the years who have opened their classrooms to our work, who have tried new techniques, and who have enriched those techniques with their own ideas and feedback. I have never trained teachers without myself learning at the same time, and I always come home with several pages of notes that enlarge my understanding of classroom management and improve subsequent teacher training. Although I have spent a decade and a half in careful research and development, in teaching there is nothing new under the sun. To a considerable extent this book represents the collected oral tradition and professional wisdom of the teachers with whom I have had the good fortune to work.

Fredric H. Jones

FOREWORD

In *Positive Classroom Discipline,* Dr. Fredric Jones contributes to educational practice his rich background in psychology, and his excellent work in the real world of classroom discipline. Dr. Jones is acutely aware that the control and "sterility" of the laboratory is not possible in the complexity and "pollution" of the classroom. Nevertheless, psychology has much to say to education and Dr. Jones says it in a clear, interesting, and workable way.

"Rather than having mature technology at its command, education tends to stumble and stagger in the dark, relying repetitively on its time honored home remedies, perpetually off balance and perpetually unprepared" is his only too accurate diagnosis of many present situations.

While stressing the importance of the preventative power of effective teaching, Dr. Jones provides alternatives for those inevitable occasions when additional measures are needed. He emphasizes that while no discipline management system comes with a guarantee, procedures must be low key, easy to use, reduce teacher stress, protect the student, and, most importantly, *self eliminate.* Negative techniques such as punitives, put downs, and humiliation are replaced by teaching strategies which encourage and reward positive behaviors from students.

Use of the book in pre-service and inservice programs will contribute much to illuminate, prepare, and stabilize successful teaching practice.

Madeline Hunter

POSITIVE
CLASSROOM
DISCIPLINE

INTRODUCTION

INTRODUCTION

Positive Classroom Discipline is the first half of a two-volume work describing the fundamental skills of classroom management as they are integrated into the day-to-day functioning of a classroom teacher. The second volume, *Positive Classroom Instruction,* integrates instructional aspects of classroom management with discipline. Together the two volumes provide a guide to effective practice which allows the teacher to see how the whole classroom functions as a social system and to see how to manage it as a whole. Indeed, the two volumes were originally prepared as a single work, and both are needed to provide a thorough understanding of the subject.

The present volume deals primarily with the remediation of classroom disruptions as a means of creating time on task within the context of a positive and affirming classroom atmosphere. Many of the procedures described do, in fact, prevent discipline problems rather than remediate them. But the focus is still on methods of generating cooperation and appropriate behavior as opposed to methods of instruction. *Positive Classroom Instruction* covers advanced instructional methods with attention, for the first time, to many subtle and normally invisible transactions that inadvertently cause most of the discipline, motivation, and learning problems in a typical classroom.

The two books contain detailed descriptions of many specific procedures for use by teachers in the field, but the focus of the books is on fundamentals—the generic processes of teaching the proper execution of which is indispensable for success. Only the thorough understanding of the fundamental skills of our profession (their context, their interrelationship, and their proper application) will produce the improvements in classroom discipline and achievement to which we aspire. General notions or specific skills poorly executed do not succeed in the natural environment. Only "knowing how to" in addition to "knowing about" will spell success for teachers once they are standing in front of a classroom full of young people.

For the past decade and a half, my colleagues and I have attempted to analyze the classroom as a social system in order to understand the subtleties by which success and failure take place. We have combined extensive observation, systematic research, and years of teacher training and experience in all kinds of settings to develop classroom management procedures that are fundamental, practical, successful, flexible, and cost-efficient. During that time we have come to understand, with an increasing level of precision, the interrelatedness between techniques of classroom discipline, instruction, and motivation. All three must be studied together for any to be adequately understood.

The classroom management methods presented in both this volume and the next do not adhere rigidly to any single theoretical framework. Life in the classroom is far too complex for that. Rather, I have drawn upon the sum total of my experience in both psychology and education. This experience includes child psychotherapy, family therapy in a humanistic and psychodynamic framework, and parent training within an operant-conditioning framework, as well as years of work in child development, developmental psychopathology, and the study of communication disorders between adults and children. In addition, my colleagues and I have spent thousands of hours in classrooms where the school of hard knocks fashions theory into practice. Thus, we have invented, extrapolated, borrowed, and, perhaps most important, simply kept working until we got it right.

At all times *whole children* have been at center stage—not only the appropriateness of their behavior but their caring about themselves, their classmates, their teachers, and their priceless opportunity to learn. We have focused not only on the management of behavior but also on the meanings of those behaviors—the many aspects of emotion, self-esteem, values, and relationship building that are not just the by-product of behavioral change but its true goal.

Squarely behind our concern for the student has been our concern for the teachers whose caring, skill, and effort are the indispensable transmitters of the educational process. Through the understanding of children and the mastery of their craft, teachers make young people successful in the most important environment the child will experience outside home. Teachers who have been trained to use the methods of *Positive Classroom Discipline* and *Positive Classroom Instruction* typically express a sense of joy and amazement that a topic as complex and vexing as classroom management could become so clear and "doable." Teachers express satisfaction primarily in their increased success and happiness with their students and in the marked reduction of job-related stress. Indeed, many teachers who were previously facing burn-out or medical disability have found that the classroom can be a therapeutic environment both for themselves and for their students. When teachers and their students enjoy growing together, the practice of one's profession becomes an energizing rather than a debilitating experience.

Positive Classroom Discipline examines, above all else, the *relationship* between adults and young people in an area that has always defined the valence of that relationship at its most basic level—positive/negative, cooperation/antagonism, love/hate. Any systematic treatment of discipline management, therefore, is a treatise on values: the ethics of child rearing. We must choose from among the means and ends available to us those which maximize the humanity of adult-child relations. If not clearly done, the long-term well-being of the child will usually be sacrificed to the short-term well-being of the adult in the heat of the moment.

Yet, values do not stand by themselves in the real world. They are tied to procedures. In the often fleeting interactions between adult and child, values either take on validity or they are revealed as only platitudes. To blind ourselves to the value-laden nature of discipline management procedures is to blind ourselves not only to the meaning of our own behavior but also to the continual need to find a better way. The values embedded within *Positive Classroom Discipline* do not jump out at you, but they do emerge gradually as the procedures fall into a pattern.

It is my hope that this book will serve not only as a guide to teachers in the field but also as a text for teachers in training. Yet there is always a desire to have textbooks that look like textbooks and sound like textbooks with empirical studies piled upon empirical studies. Such a state of affairs, however, is not possible now in the study of classroom management and especially in the study of classroom discipline. Although our efforts have been guided by key empirical studies, much of what we know about successful practice comes from extensive observation, the sharing of ideas among professionals, and trial and error in the field. We must accept this state of knowledge as our text for now. To attempt to write a traditional-appearing text would force one to focus on the research already available on all the subject areas surrounding classroom discipline, such as time on task, traditional behavior modification, communication and problem-solving skills, school climate, the effective schools' literature, leaving nearly untouched the "how to" of day-to-day discipline management in the classroom. Such a text would be a pseudo text, an exercise in appearing to be knowledgeable.

In describing effective procedures in classroom discipline, therefore, I found myself in a position similar to that of the Phi Delta Kappa Commission on Discipline, who in the introduction to their recent *Handbook for Developing Schools with Good Discipline* wrote:

> The desire to be scientific has also frustrated our writing this handbook. Because of limited data, we were confronted time and again by the irrefutable fact that we had to go beyond the data if we were to produce anything of value to our readers. . . . The Man of LaMancha's insightful cry that "facts are the enemies of truth!" is difficult to accept when one has been trained to be concerned with sample size and statistical tests of significance to verify what are essentially commonplace and intuitive truths. We had to overcome the notion that we could support every idea or recommendation when offered by citing repeated observations from objective sources. Any effective educator has to win the same battle, else little school improvement will ever occur. For much of what passes for science in our field is more a blindfold than a lens—and all the more dangerous because it has the stamp of authority that prevents us from seeing what otherwise might be obvious.[1]

Yet, although there are not scientific data for every aspect of the procedures presented here, there are enough theory and data available within the scientific literature to guide us so that our experience can form a unified picture. There is precious little data presented in this volume, however, including my own. The primary objective was to communicate with teachers and their administrators—to describe the "how to" of teaching in plain English. Whenever I would start citing the research literature during preliminary drafts of the various book chapters, the language would become turgid and the primary objective would be lost. For this reason the language has been kept straightforward, and a reference bibliography has been provided for those wishing to pursue the scientific literature in specific topic areas.

Good science, however, begins with deep observation about the nature and meanings of things. Hypothesis testing, where all too many graduate students begin, is well past the halfway point of understanding. The relationship between theory and practice, empirical experiment and the trial and error of field work, might best be viewed as a dialogue with a constant give and take that resembles a winnowing process more than a clear and step-by-step program of research. With the guidance of theory and research at critical junctures, more can be learned from working with teachers in their classrooms that can ever be tested as research hypotheses in a dozen lifetimes. To gain a meaningful and useful picture of the way in which discipline management works in the classroom, therefore, we must combine all levels of science from the earliest stage of systematic observation to the final stage of confirmed hypothesis. "State of the science" may be something of an overstatement for this book at the present time, but "state of the art" is certainly not.

Finally, I must talk about the training function of the companion volume to *Positive Classroom Discipline, Positive Classroom Instruction. First,* effective discipline management within the classroom will fail to achieve its potential unless combined with effective instructional practice. Indeed, most teachers using what has traditionally been accepted as effective instructional practice will typically generate most of their own discipline problems quite inadvertently. Thus, effective discipline and instruction must be integrated in classroom management in order to produce successful classrooms. *Second,* effective classroom discipline techniques, unless they are properly taught, will fail in the hands of all but the most talented individuals. Indeed, skills of any kind improperly implemented typically fail. *Positive Classroom Instruction,* therefore, is a book dealing not only with effective classroom instructional procedures but also with effective staff development procedures. The basics of effective teaching hold true for both little and big people. Unless effective instructional procedures are used in the dissemination of *Positive Classroom Discipline,* disillusionment will be one of the most predictable outcomes.

In setting down on paper the procedures described in this book, I make myself vulnerable, and I am anxious about it. Now I am in control of the dissemination of these methods; I can see that they are properly taught. If I make them public, I lose control of dissemination by placing my methods in the public domain. Yet, if I do not make them public, you would probably never know about them even if I were to spend the rest of my life traveling. With the publication of these books dissemination is up for grabs, and while I will continue to train teachers and to travel, the foolishness of the past as regards staff development will surely be repeated in many school districts. Teachers will be herded into auditoriums in various locales to hear somebody give a talk about some classroom management procedure contained in this book, accompanied by neither adequate background nor skill practice nor follow-through and support at the school site. It is my hope that *Positive Classroom Instruction,* the second volume of this series, will be used to provide guidance not only in the instructional aspects of classroom management but also in teacher training so that the procedures contained in these volumes will find their way into the hands of teachers who have been prepared to succeed.

REFERENCES

1 The Delta Kappa Commission on Discipline. *Handbook for developing schools with good discipline.* Bloomington, Indiana: The Delta Kappa, 1982.

KEEP IT POSITIVE

Classroom discipline, simply stated, is the business of enforcing classroom standards and building patterns of cooperation in order to maximize learning and minimize disruptions. Every teacher is a "disciplinarian" by necessity. Discipline begins before the students are seated in the morning and does not end until the room is empty in the afternoon. It comes as part of the territory.

The way in which discipline is managed in the classroom will govern to a large extent the amount of time that is spent working and the amount of time that is spent "goofing off." Any classroom has the potential of being a "problem classroom." Whether the class develops its full potential depends primarily on how it is handled. A junior high or high school student will act one way with the first-period teacher, another way with the second-period teacher, and yet another way with the third-period teacher. A group of elementary students will act one way with their regular teacher and an entirely different way with a substitute teacher. Although groups of students vary in the extent to which they will stress any management system, one can assume for the most part that student disruption will be equal to *whatever the market will bear*.

In dealing with the wide range of squirrelly behaviors that may come from a room full of young bodies, a skilled teacher needs a *wide range of management techniques*. There is no such thing in classroom management as a panacea or miracle cure. No single, simple method will keep you tranquil until retirement. Teachers must have options that allow them to deal with the wide range of management situations which might be crammed into a single hour. In managing discipline, teachers might best think of themselves as skilled craftspeople who, like a violin maker, must have many tools with specialized purposes so that the right tool can be used to do a particular job cleanly and efficiently. The objective of this book is to provide the teacher with an expanded range of extremely efficient management skills—powerful tools perfected by years of research and classroom use.

There is no assumption, however, that this book will ever begin to describe all the possible discipline management techniques available to the teacher. Nor is there the arrogant assumption common to many workshops that the methods described in this book should *replace* everything that you are presently doing. If you are using a technique that is succeeding for you, *keep it!* You will need it soon enough. Rather, this book is highly *selective* in its choice of discipline management techniques. Instead of being encyclopedic in nature, a relatively few distinct procedures are described in great detail.

In the 15 years of continual research, classroom observation, teacher training, and feedback from the field that have gone into the development of the methods described in this book, two objectives have been foremost.

• First, the classroom management procedures must be positive—they must affirm the student. They must set limits and build cooperation in the absence of coercion. They must be gentle.

• Second, they must be economical—practical, simple, and easy to use once mastered. They must ultimately *reduce* the teacher's work load.

It is no great service to teachers in the field to provide management systems that require great expenditures of time and effort. To serve the teacher, classroom management methods must, in fact, represent a *net savings* in time and energy over the long run. Teachers and administrators cannot afford to invest large amounts of time and energy on an hour-by-hour, day-by-day, week-by-week basis to operate a classroom management system even if the methods are working.

During the past 15 years many techniques have been developed and field-tested, but most have been discarded. Techniques were discarded usually when they were found too cumbersome or expensive, or too much trouble or too failure-prone under specific conditions to merit general or widespread use. Over time, however, the constant dialogue between theory and practice, between experimentation and implementation has produced a management system of depth, breadth, and simplicity.

The writing of this book represents closure. Certainly, we will never stop learning and growing in the topic of classroom discipline. But, most of the things that used to seem complicated are finally beginning to seem simple. It is time to write.

THE LEGACY OF THE PAST

Discipline has been the bastard child of education—a topic nobody wants to own. It has gone noticed but unattended. It has remained an area of concern but not an area of methodological development. Administrators want teachers to take care of it, teachers want administrators to take care of it, and the universities ignore it as though the study of it would ruin their humanistic credentials.

Nearly every recent poll of parents or teachers lists discipline as the number one concern in most classrooms. Yet educators typically approach the subject of discipline with caution and ambivalence. The terms "discipline," "disciplinarian," and "rule enforcement" have a negative, distasteful ring to many. In decades past, to be overly concerned with discipline placed your educational mentality somewhere between the "authoritarian personality" and a "storm trooper."

Finally, discipline is coming out of the closet. It is once again becoming respectable to talk about it directly, to plan for it, to study it, and to strive to become good at it.

Discipline Means Punition

If you were to ask fifty people on the street to describe what it means to "discipline children," fifty would probably answer, "That's punishing them for doing something wrong." Punishment or punition in this context typically means the use of painful or distasteful consequences to control behavior. The equation of discipline and punition is easily one of the most pervasive and damaging stereotypes concerning child management in our culture and in most other cultures. Professionals who deal with children (teachers, social workers, and child psychologists), no less than the parents they serve, commonly equate discipline in schools with reprimands, scoldings, losing privileges, being kept after school, or being sent to the principal's office.

This negative stereotype of discipline has historically led educational researchers and teacher trainers to avoid the topic of discipline. What professor wants to offer a course on coercing children or to be known as the "discipline specialist"? This self-imposed blind spot has unwittingly contributed to today's crisis of discipline in the classroom by limiting the study, development, and dissemination of effective management techniques. We are, in effect, victims of our own desire to avoid the topic. We have never learned how to do it right.

You Will Learn It on the Job

Avoiding the topic of classroom discipline as though it were taboo is nowhere more evident than in teacher education. It is a sobering exercise to look through the catalogs of teacher training programs at colleges and universities in an attempt to find a course entitled "Discipline." It is even more sobering to speak with teachers in the field about what teacher training they received concerning the management of classroom discipline. The responses are most commonly accompanied by either laughter or anger. The three most common replies are, "The subject was never brought up," "We had two lectures on the token economy," or "They told us we would pick it up on the job."

The notion that teachers will somehow, magically, spontaneously learn how to keep thirty kids from going thirty different directions once the teachers are "on the job" is amazing—a cruel hoax used to cover up a major deficiency in teacher training. Mastery of the intricate skills and sophisticated techniques required to succeed at classroom discipline comes neither naturally nor easily. After years on the job even the best teachers still function at a level far below that which could have been achieved with focused training on the use of some advanced management techniques.

Without the training, teachers are left to sink or swim. Perhaps it is not too surprising, then, that over the years classroom discipline has become associated with punition. When you are out of options and your back is against the wall, you must do what you must do to put the lid on.

Love Is Not Enough

It is the undying hope of young teachers and parents that if they just love children hard enough and try hard enough, everything will turn out fine. If you care for them, they will care for you. If you respect them, they will respect you. If you give to them, they will give to you. What the child experiences from you is more important than what they are told by you. They will model themselves after your life. You must parent by example, and you must teach by example.

All these statements may be true, but collectively they do not begin to scratch the surface of the topic of discipline management with young people. One important statement that was left out was: If you give good discipline, you will get self-discipline. But how do you give good discipline?

What do you do when some students are a persistent pain, and nothing seems to work? How do you get them to take responsibility for doing what you want them to do? How do you deal with dawdling and goofing off in a myriad of forms throughout the day? What do you do when they keep talking to each other instead of listening? What do you say when you want to scream? Now that we have our backs against the wall, we fall victim to that selective ignorance that left us unprepared. In the real world the words "discipline" and "punition" do, in fact, tend to go together by default. Most people have difficulty believing, much less understanding, how discipline could be powerful and yet nurturant and supportive at the same time.

Yet, how can you deal with clearly unacceptable behavior, even persistent or severe or provocative or intransigent or nasty behavior, while being nurturant and supportive? If you have one child, it's difficult enough. If you have two children, your skill and energy have to be squared. But, if you have a third child, it takes all that skill and energy cubed. A classroom teacher has a family of thirty, none of whom has a deep relationship with the teacher before the first day of class. Yet the teacher will be with the students for as much of the day as the parents are and will make many more demands.

A teacher cannot afford to walk into a classroom of thirty young people and "wing it" with their favorite home remedies. Home remedies will not make it in this league. They will only make you old and tired at an early age. Unless you learn to do it right—to use a cost-effective set of high-level professional skills—you will become tired and frustrated and ultimately lose your capacity to be nurturant or even to care. The advanced state of this exhaustion and exasperation, which is epidemic, is called burnout.

Discipline is not only a matter of simple caring or wanting to be good with children. In addition to caring you will buy the luxury of caring for many years by your mastery and technical proficiency of specific management skills.

NATURAL DEFENSES

I'm good with kids. I don't have any real discipline problems. I'm not one of these people who goes around yelling and screaming. I know a lot of colleagues who need training, but I don't. Besides, my class is interesting. If it were boring, I might have problems.

Teachers approach no area of professional functioning with more ambivalence, misgiving, and misconception than the area of classroom discipline. As an area of professional development and mastery, it is in the dark ages. Before we can even look at the topic clearly, we must deal with our feelings about it. We must drag some of our private fears and superstitions kicking and screaming out into the light. Although it is not worth our while to spend too much time dragon slaying, it will be useful to list some of the more common misconceptions voiced by teachers which, if taken too seriously, relieve us all of having to worry any further about discipline management.

1 If your curriculum is good enough, you will not have discipline problems. This misconception guarantees that conscientious teachers become depressed as soon as they realize that they have discipline problems that will not go away. You are obviously a failure with curriculum.

2 It is a gift that some teachers are just born with. Any teacher who cannot get thirty squirmy, easily distracted bodies to respond with the precision of a symphony orchestra should be further depressed with the knowledge that he or she suffers from a genetic deficiency. Nobody is born with effective discipline. This "genetic hypothesis" is simply a magical explanation for something that teachers as a group find hard to understand—the fact that a rare few of their colleagues make discipline management look effortless.

3 Some kids are truly unmanageable. This is something of an overstatement. To be accurate, it should read, "Some kids are truly obnoxious." Some are even emotionally, behaviorally, and culturally handicapped, but these conditions do not necessarily make kids discipline problems. All young people, however, are capable of being a complete pain if given the chance. And, all can be quite decent under the proper circumstances.

4 Discipline thwarts creativity and spontaneity. This statement does not say too much for the well-behaved child. It may, however, be partly true. I find it bizarre to think that effective classroom management may stifle creativity in learning, but children are never more creative and spontaneous than when goofing off in a classroom. Good discipline may, therefore, reduce the range of their life experiences somewhat.

5 The longer you teach, the better at discipline you become. "I've been teaching for 25 years, I must be good at it by this time!" Maybe, but if you are, you were probably good at it over 20 years ago too. When it comes to discipline, most teachers patch together some means of survival during their first few years on the job and then repeat their "method" until retirement. The only consistent correlation between age and the disciplining of children that I have ever found is that the older you get, the easier you tire. If it is them against you, you will ultimately lose.

6 I've known some teachers who really needed help. Wrong! Everybody needs help. You can either wing it with your native intuition, home remedies, and undying flow of adrenalin, or you can learn advanced methods and make it easy on yourself.

7 It's just this class that I have this year! Maybe, but there is always next year. Yet for most teachers, every year is as tough as the last.

In spite of the fears and rationalizations welling up from within, we all know that discipline management is inescapable and that our home remedies are costing us too much in effort, frustration, and stress. Yet, if we are all to become disciplinarians, certain humane conditions must be met. In addition to being powerful, new methods must be positive. They must ultimately enhance our relationship with the student. They must support the student even in difficult and stressful situations. They must create a safe learning environment, a classroom environment that both we and our students look forward to in the morning.

BUILDING METHODS OF POSITIVE CLASSROOM DISCIPLINE SLOWLY

Developing positive methods for dealing with disruptive student behavior is a tricky business. It is easy to be positive up to a point. But the point always seems to come when either the energy or the expertise gives out. It is also fairly easy to discover methods that turn a particular situation from bad to good if you work hard enough at it. But how do you build an entire methodology for dealing with all kinds of disrupting, dawdling, and goofing off while being positive and not working too hard?

The methods described in this book and its companion volume, *Positive Classroom Instruction,* took many years of systematic experimentation, trial and error, ideas from some very clever teachers, and many trips back to the drawing board to develop into a coherent system. These techniques comprise the state of the art and vary in scope from self-relaxation to lesson planning. They cover the points a teacher must cover to survive and thrive—to get all the basic management jobs done positively at a price he or she can afford. These methods form a *management system,* an integrated whole in which each part gains strength from every other part.

Methods described in this book deal with positive classroom discipline, getting kids to quit goofing off, to cooperate, to behave responsibly and get on task. *Positive Classroom Instruction,* in contrast, examines methods of getting kids, once they are on task, to learn much more efficiently and enjoyably while working diligently, carefully, and independently. In addition, the second volume examines the process of creating change in education, producing extensive and lasting organizational change that will support the quest for excellence by everyone concerned with the educational process.

It will be helpful in understanding the objectives and nature of the classroom management methods contained in this book if we share something of their evolution and design before launching into a detailed treatment of specific methods. In many ways the evolution of our management system parallels the experience of many teachers who have walked onto a job cold and have had to invent it all "by the seat of their pants." We began by trying to succeed at one job at a time. The system came later.

Getting Your Feet Wet

Go On, Jump In, You Can Swim!   As with most teachers, I began learning about discipline on my first day on a new job. I was consulting with a private, special school for emotionally, behaviorally, and learning handicapped children aged 7 through 14. They had all been kicked out of the Los Angeles City School system. Unbeknownst to me, I had a free ticket to an all-star game—an all-star game of classroom goof-offs.

I was told to help two teachers who were about to lose their jobs because of discipline problems. When I walked into the first classroom, I saw only half the class, and they were standing on top of the coat closet. Then I found the other half. They were hiding in the coat closet. I saw them when the doors of the closet flew open and they began throwing hats and jackets at the kids on top as a clothing war raged before my eyes. The teacher stood in the front of the room in quiet, angry desperation, arms folded, teeth clenched, looking grim, while he said, "Class, I am simply going to *wait* until you *all* settle down!" I knew I had a tough assignment. It was almost December and he was still waiting.

I had lived around universities long enough to know what to do. I was no dummy. My first instinct was to retreat to academia as fast as possible. The next step, of course, would be to offer a graduate course in classroom discipline in which I would have the students read all the literature and tell me about it. Little did I know that there wasn't any literature. Being tough, however, I stuck it out past lunch.

Watching Two "Old Pros"   In the afternoon of the first day I received an incredible stroke of luck. I watched two different groups of students who had mauled two different teachers in the morning enter the classrooms of two *other* teachers in the afternoon. The teachers in the afternoon, however, knew what they were doing. In both cases I watched kids who had been monsters in the morning walk (not run) into a classroom, take their seats, and get to work. I watched teachers give a lesson that was received, and I watched them help students who were on task. I saw discussions where the students took turns, and I watched fifth and eighth graders line up and leave as nicely as any regular classroom. Either the teachers were doing something right, or the students had undergone brain transplants during lunch.

I returned to these classrooms many times to observe, but I didn't see much in terms of recognizable management techniques. Rather, I saw two "old pros" making it look easy. As with any pro who has mastered their craft, the fine points of their technique did not stand out. I did, however, observe three characteristics that I would never forget:

1 They were not working hard at discipline (in fact they were not doing anything that I could see).

2 They were relaxed.

3 They were emotionally warm.

At least I had learned that you could have excellent classroom discipline even with very difficult students without acting like a drill sergeant. The question was, "How did they do it?".

In addition to observing, I spent a lot of time talking to the two old pros about what they were doing and why they were doing it. They could not have been more generous and helpful, but unfortunately they did not help very much. In fact, they could not have described exactly what they did and why if their lives had depended on it. Since there is no formal technology of discipline management, we have no analytic language to describe what we do. Instead, the old pros give me answers like: "Well, you just have to mean business, that's all" or, "Well, you know, as soon as you let the kids get the idea that they can get away with things, they'll run all over you."

Yogi Berra once said, "You can see a lot by looking." I regard that as timeless wisdom. Unfortunately, it didn't help. I observed for hours and saw nothing. What does he know about classroom discipline?

Talking with craftspeople about their craft should also help one to understand. All I learned was that you have to "mean business." Strike two. I was driven to desperation.

Limit-Setting

Decoding Limit-Setting   Finally, the two old pros plus my wife, Jo Lynne, my professor and colleague at the UCLA Neuropsychiatric Institute, Dr. Hans Miller, and I started acting out the roles of teachers and rotten kids in reconstructions of classroom management dilemmas that we had observed during the day in the classroom. Day after day on our feet we began to pick apart and decipher the skills that the effective teachers had been using so effortlessly in their classrooms. Finally we began to learn how, by the way the teachers *physically* responded to disruptions with a minimum of verbiage, they had *trained their classes* early in the year that they "meant business." We were, in fact, decoding a foreign language—*"body language."*

"Limit-setting" is the label that I will use for those subtle, interpersonal skills by which teachers convey to their classes that they mean business. It is the teacher's physical "presence" and emotional tone that conveys to every student that this teacher's rules are *for real*. Limit-setting goes well beyond telling the class what the rules will be; it also trains the class to follow them. Limit-setting is therefore rule enforcement. When done properly, however, rule enforcement is slow, relaxed, supportive, and incredibly strong.

Teaching Limit-Setting   Soon after we gained some confidence in our understanding of limit-setting, Hans Miller and I decided to offer a workshop to the entire faculty of the school so that the rest of them would know how to do it. We offered a 10-week workshop, 1½ hours every Thursday after school. We covered everything from general theory of behavioral management to demonstration of technique. We described, we modeled, we shared anecdotes, we answered questions, and we even had a video clip of limit-setting in action. Our 10-week workshop got rave reviews: "it's practical," "it's down to earth," "it's usable," "we can see that you've spent time in the classroom!" We were not smart enough to leave well enough alone. We took data.

Our data informed us that, in spite of our rave reviews, 10 weeks of workshops had produced *no change* whatsoever in student behavior or teacher behavior. Once again, necessity was the mother of invention. We had to figure out how to teach this stuff.

Hans and I devised a method of skill training which, based on our experience in higher education, seemed revolutionary. It was called practice. After two 1½-hour practice sessions in which the worst teachers in the school were carefully coached by us to set limits, the worst teachers *matched* the performance of the best teachers in reducing their classroom disruptions and getting things under control.[1]

I was thrilled. I could not have imagined a better outcome. It is amazing how much can be learned when it is properly taught. I took 2 years learning how to write a research article and then had it published in 1974. I felt that I had just laid a blessing on the entire teaching profession. Little did I know that nobody reads those journals.

By 1974 when the first article on limit-setting appeared in the research literature, additional research was already being carried out to test the limits of limit-setting.[2,3] These studies demonstrated that, even in extremely difficult classrooms, a fairly simple management technology which centered around limit-setting could consistently produce reductions in classroom disruptions averaging around 75 percent. Additional gains were achieved by the use of individualized behavior modification programs. The largest reductions were in the most disorderly classrooms, since their higher base rates of disruption gave us more room for improvement.

Responsibility Training

The Limits of Limit-Setting   Limit-setting was to meet its match in a regional special education center near Rochester, New York, the Bureau of Cooperative Educational Services (BOCES) #1 in Fairport, New York. Research and development work on discipline management continued during the 6 years I was on the faculty of the University of Rochester. This work, however, was with a new population of students. Most of the classrooms were populated by emotionally, behaviorally, and learning handicapped students, and at the secondary level approximately one-third of the students had felony records. At the secondary level we would be pushed to the wall and forced once again by necessity to invent. How do you produce cooperation and a positive classroom atmosphere with alienated teenagers—the worst discipline problems of a ten-district feeder area?

By the mid-1970s the state of the art in managing classroom discipline problems consisted of (1) clear classroom rules, (2) limit-setting, (3) negative sanctions or "back-up responses" such as time-out or sending a student to the office to "put the lid on" if limit-setting failed, and (4) individualized incentive systems (behavior modification programs) for extremely oppositional or unmotivated students.

The characteristic of our alienated teenagers that made them difficult was not the severity of any single behavior but, rather, the degree of their emotional alienation. We were forced to "put the lid on" repeatedly using our back-up responses. While our back-up responses worked beautifully in putting the lid on, they extracted far too high a price in time and stress from everyone involved. Worse yet, any teacher who had difficulty using limit-setting effectively would usually end up relying heavily on the negative sanctions of their back-up system.

The individualized incentive systems designed for the most oppositional students were often fairly exotic programs: costly, one-of-a-kind inventions requiring extensive planning that could hardly be considered general classroom management procedures. We avoided group incentive programs such as the "token economy" because they were costly and failure-prone at the secondary level, especially with our population of students.

The limits of a classroom incentive technology are ultimately defined by cost, not success. If you have unlimited resources, control of the environment, and some sophistication in managing behavior, you should succeed. You can always arrange the contingencies in students' worlds so that they would be absolute idiots for not doing what you want them to do. But the price has to be right. We reached the limit of our old technology *not* when it failed but when we found ourselves and our teachers putting too much time and effort into succeeding.

Incentive Systems: A Second Generation   The next three years were spent at the Bureau of Cooperative Educational Services perfecting *group* incentive systems for the classroom that relied on inexpensive, learning-related activities as rewards for the class as a whole. I concluded that if we could not generate cooperative and responsible behavior on the part of an entire classroom full of these alienated teenagers without a primary reliance on back-up responses or expensive individualized programs, the quest to manage discipline in the classroom would ultimately be lost from sheer exhaustion. The staff would tire, and over time the use of negative sanctions to manage misbehavior would become the norm with a built-in demand for ever larger negative sanctions— as is the case in most secondary schools today, regular or special.

We had to develop a group incentive program that was so sophisticated that it could get just about any student to do just about anything that was required at just about any time with almost no effort to the teacher. It had to deal with the whole class at once, rely primarily on learning for its rewards, systematically train responsible and cooperative behavior, and have the full backing and participation of the students.

The outcome of this research and development work was "responsibility training." Responsibility training, which has been perfected in field use over a 9-year period, provided us with the high-power, low-cost, broad-spectrum management system we were looking for. We refer to responsibility training and related incentive programs as "second generation" incentive systems since they replaced the expensive "first generation" of individualized incentive systems typically referred to as behavior modification.

It is the objective of second generation incentive systems to free the teacher from the continual drain of managing incentive systems. Cost efficiency, power, and student affirmation have been the criteria of development. Second generation incentive systems attempt to set everyone free to enjoy the process of teaching and learning.

Back-up Systems

In managing classroom discipline, no technique comes with a guarantee and no simple combination of management methods will prove adequate for all situations. Limit-setting and responsibility training gave us the management leverage to succeed almost all the time even with extremely alienated teenagers. But a kid whose life is turning inside-out can still walk into class determined to "go all the way" regardless of your management system. What do you do when push comes to shove?

If the student turns his or her back on relationship, on limit-setting, and on the rewards and peer affirmation offered by responsibility training, the student has then removed all your reward-based options and has left you with negative sanctions. A back-up response is a negative sanction. A back-up response is a response to crisis, a management option to use when everything else fails. The negative sanctions operating at a school site arranged in sequence from small to large to deal with crises of increasing magnitude comprise the back-up system of that school site.

As mentioned earlier, the state of the art of back-up systems within behavior management circles in the mid-1970s was to use time-out in the classroom backed up by larger negative sanctions if necessary, such as being sent to the office. In most regular school sites, especially secondary sites, the use of a far more formidable array of negative sanctions is the norm. A heavy reliance on reprimands, docking grades, detention, loss of privilege, in-school suspension, suspension, and expulsion is largely due to a lack of knowing exactly how to respond to severe discipline problems before they get out of hand.

Our growth in the intervening years has been to learn how to put the lid on a budding crisis swiftly, gently, and tightly in order to protect both the teacher and the student. How do you put the lid on a crisis situation in such a low-key fashion that the rest of the students in the classroom may not even know that the management situation is occurring? Exactly what are the first things you say and do under the stress of crisis—your agenda, your body language, your first words, your successive moves— that short-circuit the growing confrontation without stressing the teacher or humiliating the student?

Classroom Structure

The enforcement of classroom rules rests upon a clear understanding by students of what is expected of them and a shared understanding by them that these are "our rules," not just "your rules." How do effective teachers create a clear, shared sense of purpose within the classroom that embodies a communal value system of respect for learning and respect for each other? This task of clarifying the goals, standards, and rules of the classroom must precede any successful attempt either to enforce rules or to enlist the students' cooperation in attaining shared goals.

Yet the topic of classroom structure extends beyond the boundaries of the classroom. The behavior of a student in school, be it in the area of discipline or motivation to learn, is a product of both the home environment and the school environment. Teachers need parents to get optimal results. They not only need the support of a home value system that affirms learning and appropriate behavior, but they also need constructive collaboration with parents from time to time to prevent small management problems from growing into big ones. The foundation for this constructive collaboration must be systematically built early in the school year so that the parents will respond helpfully rather than defensively when asked to play their role. Teachers must reach out to the community as part of their classroom structure. But this outreach must be affordable—a simple, logical extension of the shared understandings developed with the students in the classroom.

Finally, some aspects of classroom structure simply involve arranging the classroom environment so that discipline management and the development of a sense of group responsibility are made easier. This collection of topics ranges from the arrangement of furniture (and the selection of furniture in the first place) to seating arrangements to the mechanics of assigning chores and seeing that they get done. If teachers heed some of the basic logistics of classroom structure, the effort that they have to expend in management will be reduced during every hour that they ever spend in the classroom.

The first section of *Positive Classroom Discipline,* "Classroom Structure," includes a chapter on rules, routines, and standards (Chapter 3) as well as a chapter on arranging the learning environment to your advantage (Chapter 4). The clarification of structure prior to the management of discrete behaviors is, perhaps, the aspect of discipline management that is typically done most hastily by teachers—as though the topic of classroom rules represented nothing more than one of the preliminaries that must be dealt with on the first day of school before instruction begins. Such a cavalier approach to classroom structure will stress the management system and the teacher's body throughout the remainder of the school year, a brutal price indeed for having shortchanged a crucial topic.

The Plan of *Positive Classroom Discipline*

Positive Classroom Discipline deals with the technology of managing *group* behavior within the classroom in order to reduce disruptions and increase cooperative and responsible behavior on the part of students. The objective of this book, rather than "law and order," is the internalization of discipline or self-discipline. The book deals with four major topics of discipline management, plus a final section entitled "Synthesis," which brings the various management methods together to form a coherent and tightly knit system. The four major topics are:

1 Classroom structure
2 Limit-setting
3 Responsibility training
4 Back-up systems

The topic "back-up systems," however, takes us from the management of behavior *inside* the classroom to the topic of managing behavior *outside* the classroom. Our treatment of behavior management outside the classroom must be brief since to get into it deeply would produce another full-length book. Chapter 16, "Back-Up Responses beyond the Classroom," discusses the collaboration of the teacher and administrators in dealing with a crisis of *classroom* management. Chapter 17, "School Site Management Procedures," deals with the collaboration of teachers and administrators in managing problems which accompany large group gatherings within the school. Such problems include rowdiness in all-school assemblies, noise in the halls, unruliness in the lavatories, and mess in the cafeteria. The main focus of Chapter 17 is on chronic management dilemmas at the secondary level, although all methods apply to the elementary level as well. This chapter serves as a bridge of understanding between the teacher's role in classroom management and her or his role in producing an orderly school environment. Most aspects of school site management, however, that deal with consensus building and team building needed to elevate school standards and improve a school's learning climate will have to wait for another day.

POSITIVE CLASSROOM INSTRUCTION

Problems of the Well-Managed Classroom

By the mid-1970s enough of the discipline management technology was developed so that we could look at regular classrooms that were almost free of discipline problems to see what the "final product" looked like. It did not look like a final product. The classrooms would have been described as functioning beautifully by most observers, but I was preoccupied with the handful of students who never seemed to do anything.

Why was there always a handful of students who did almost nothing in the classroom unless the teacher was standing over them helping them? Why were there always so many students with their hands raised waiting for help? Why were they the same students day after day? Why was there always a large group of students who did only what was required of them? Why was goofing off the predominant indoor sport? Why did teachers have to work so hard to get diligence and excellence out of students?

Once discipline became "old business," learning became our "new business." Why was this pattern of student dependency, helplessness, and mediocrity so consistent from one classroom to another regardless of the teacher's personality, style, subject area, grade level, or even general competence? There had to be some process indigenous to the classroom as a social system to explain this uncanny similarity between otherwise dissimilar learning environments. Something in our basic way of doing things had to be producing this consistent stratification of ability and motivation among students.

Learning How to Teach Positively

From the mid-1970s to the present our classroom management program and our teacher training program has stressed instructional skills and discipline skills equally under the umbrella of Classroom Management. In the area of instruction one insight and innovation has led to another as necessity has once again forced us to learn.

Years of experimentation, observation, and troubleshooting with teachers provided preliminary answers as to the causes of the chronic classroom problems we were observing. We found that most of the chronic motivation problems, most of the discipline problems, and almost all the failure experiences of students in school were a by-product of one of the most unexamined aspects of classroom management—the way in which a teacher helps a student who is "stuck." Ironically, failure was being produced most systematically at the very moment when the teacher was most directly attempting to help the student learn.

The instructional portion of our program, referred to as *Positive Classroom Instruction,* is the second volume of this two-volume work. This title was chosen primarily for its descriptive value. The skills of *Positive Classroom Instruction* systematically remove negative feedback and failure experiences from learning. The topics dealt with in *Positive Classroom Instruction* include (1) the giving of corrective feedback, (2) lesson design, (3) lesson presentation, (4) incentives for diligence and excellence, and (5) creating change in education.

Positive Classroom Instruction, however, does not attempt a comprehensive treatment of instructional methods. Rather, it includes only those *fundamentals* of teaching that we have found critical to any lasting success in classroom management in general and in the management of discipline problems in particular. Indeed, *Positive Classroom Instruction* might best be thought of as the primary prevention component of a comprehensive program of classroom discipline since it prevents the initial occurrence of most discipline problems. *Positive Classroom Discipline* might be thought of as secondary prevention since it represents effective, early remediation that prevents repetition of a problem once it has occurred.

Creating Change in Education

The final section of *Positive Classroom Instruction,* "Creating Change in Education," focuses on the process of disseminating advanced classroom management procedures. As mentioned earlier, our first attempt to train teachers to do limit-setting was not successful. Ten weeks of seminars produced very little change in the classroom. My first response as a teacher, like the response of many teachers who confront a failure in learning, is to blame the students. They just aren't trying! They're unmotivated! You can't teach an old dog new tricks!

We reflected on the notion, however, that teaching is largely a collection of skills, and that every skill we had ever mastered had been learned in the same way—practice, practice, practice! What if we coached the teachers through management dilemmas similar to those encountered every day in the classroom so that the skills of limit-setting could become automatic before their use in class?

When we approached classroom management as a set of skills rather than as a collection of concepts and built our program of teacher training around performance practice, we found that our teachers could achieve a high degree of proficiency rapidly and that they would use the skills in class. When we began teaching properly, we found, to our amazement, that teachers were not resistant to change at all. Rather, they were simply smart. They were smart enough not to stand up in front of a class to "wing it" with some new skills that they had only seen in a workshop.

Good staff development is good teaching. Each skill is a structured lesson to be taught as carefully as any other structured lesson. When you cut corners, you induce failure. When you teach correctly, you produce mastery.

In the decade and a half that has passed since that first learning experience, my colleagues and I have systematically studied the process of producing *deep and lasting change* in teachers, within schools, and within districts. It is one thing to develop a sophisticated classroom management technology, but it is quite something else to have it consistently and correctly implemented. Similarly, it is one thing to have that technology accepted by the members of a faculty, and it is something else again to have it actively supported by the administration.

Each step in producing lasting change in a school district represents an entire methodology unto itself, and the fine points are learned only in the school of hard knocks. A second generation technology of classroom management must be accomplished by a second generation technology of change or no change will occur. The development of methods of classroom management had to be accompanied by the development of a quality *delivery system*.

Training teachers properly with extensive skill practice, while highly successful, has one obvious limitation. Adequate skill practice takes a lot of time, and time costs money. As a result, parallel with the development of classroom management methods, I began developing methods of training teachers to train other teachers. Our first systematic research in the area appeared in the *Journal of Applied Behavior Analysis*[3] and was entitled "Pyramid Training of Elementary School Teachers To Use a Classroom Management 'Skill Package'." This effort demonstrated that teachers who had been well trained to use the classroom management methods and who had received additional training in peer coaching skills could produce excellent results. With adequate training and preparation a quality "trainer of trainers" program was feasible.

In addition to quality skill training, however, a successful delivery system requires the development of a *support network* to help build continuing growth and renewal into the fabric of school life. The key element of this support network is the formation of an enjoyable, ongoing process of review, sharing, and problem solving at each participating school site. Over an extended period of time teachers relearn basic skills and resolve problems of implementation so that techniques can be successfully integrated into classroom life one at a time within a context of collegial support and affirmation.

The staff development program that is the delivery system for *Positive Classroom Discipline* and *Positive Classroom Instruction* is named the Classroom Management Training Program (CMTP). Since the combined technology of *Positive Classroom Discipline* and *Positive Classroom Instruction* is powerful enough to enable motivated teachers to succeed within their own classrooms independent of what is going on around them, the strength of CMTP is measured primarily in terms of *penetration* and *longevity* at the school site rather than in terms of individual success. The most important question in staff development (once an adequate technology of classroom management and teacher training exists) is the degree to which the program will penetrate the total faculty at a school site or district and the degree to which it becomes a permanent part of school life.

OVERVIEW

Positive Classroom Discipline sets forth the fruits of a decade and a half of work to be shared with fellow educators. While specific procedures are described in detail, this book also attempts to present a conceptual and methodological framework for understanding the many interrelated facets of discipline management within the classroom. We will go into detail with those techniques that are most cost-effective for classroom use.

In first reading the book, however, it may appear that it represents basically a collection of techniques. A technique, however, is simply one way among many to do a given job. To regard the procedures set forth in this book as just techniques is to miss the point. To be sure, specific ways of doing things are described—usually several ways for doing any given job complete with a discussion of when and where each technique fails.

But the basic processes underlying the specific modes of application are fundamental and generic—too basic to be replaced by another "fundamental." Limit-setting is not just a way of responding to a disruption, for example, but a careful discussion of the metacommunication of dominance and submission in almost all vertebrate species. "Meaning business" is primarily body language, and we have only one body. We will not reprogram the species by the use of an alternative technique although we may embody "meaning business" within a variety of techniques.

In the same sense, there are not a half-dozen ways to train people to be responsible. Rather, responsibility training embodies a generic three-step process by which all humans and animals learn to govern the rate of consumption of a finite resource in a responsible fashion. Because the mechanics of responsibility training in the classroom may take a variety of forms, responsibility training in a generic sense will ultimately govern not only the way in which we personally use our own time and energy but also the way in which nations consume their human resources, their fossil fuels, and their clean air.

It is not surprising, therefore, that effective teachers often recognize themselves during systematic teacher training or, hopefully, in the pages of this book. The specific skills originally came from effective teachers in many cases. Only after years of work in teacher training, field application, and research did the basic underlying patterns begin to emerge.

A book, however, is a limited medium. It does not provide sights, sound, and experience. It does not provide repeated practice with corrective feedback. It does not provide training. The training program to accompany the book exists, and it is our hope that those who read the book will appreciate that there is a need for much more if teachers are to improve their performance as well as their awareness.

REFERENCES

Dissertations Supervised

Burka, Aden A. Procedures for increasing appropriate verbal participation in special elementary classrooms, March 25, 1977.

Cowen, Richard J. Grandma's rule with group contingencies: A cost-efficient means of classroom management during reading circle, October 28, 1977.

Docteur, Kenneth E. The effects of increasing verbal and non-verbal contingent teacher reinforcement on the level of attentive student behavior, January, 1979.

Weis, Herbert M. Skill training for teachers of problem classrooms at the secondary level, January 20, 1978.

Research Publications

1 Jones, F. H. and Miller, W. H. The effective use of negative attention for reducing group disruption in special elementary school classrooms. *Psychological Record*, 1974, *24*, 435–448.

2 Jones, F. H. and Eimers, R. Role-playing to train elementary teachers to use a classroom management "skill package." *Journal of Applied Behavior Analysis*, 1975, *8*, 421–433.

3 Jones, F. H., Fremouw, W., and Carples, S. Pyramid training of elementary school teachers to use a classroom management "skill package." *Journal of Applied Behavior Analysis*, 1977, *10*, 239–253.

4 Burka, A. A. and Jones F. H. Procedures for increasing appropriate verbal participation in special elementary classrooms. *Behavior Modification*, 1979, *3*, 27–48.

5 Cowen, R. J., Jones, F. H., and Bellack, A. S. Grandma's rule with group contingencies, cost-efficient means of classroom management. *Behavior Modification*, 1979, *3*, 397–418.

KEEP IT CHEAP

Positive Classroom Discipline provides an integrated discipline management system. Rather than a set prescription, it gives the teacher a *repertoire of basic skills* that can be used at the teacher's discretion for dealing with discipline problems in a wide range of management situations. Once teachers have an adequate repertoire of cost-effective management techniques at their disposal, however, they also have the luxury of *choice*. Which technique will be employed for a particular discipline management task?

The *criterion for choosing* between one technique and another in a management situation in which either technique might work is very simple: *Always use the cheapest remedy.* Always use the discipline management technique that takes the least planning, the least effort, the least time and paper work. Always use the cheapest technique for the simple reason that discipline management is not an end in itself. Rather, classroom discipline is only a means to an end—creating a high degree of *time on task* in a pleasant learning environment. Discipline management, therefore, is pure overhead, and it is to the teacher's advantage to reduce that overhead to a bare minimum to free time and energy for instruction.

The issue of cost is tricky, however, since many of the costs of poor discipline management are deferred. A teacher may think that he or she has dealt successfully with a situation by using a few well-chosen words. But, if the situation recurs frequently, the price of management throughout the course of the school year will be extremely high.

To help clarify the nature of the investment that the teacher will make in discipline management, we will need a *criterion of success* to use for judging the effectiveness of any particular discipline technique. This criterion is stringent, but it is the only price that a teacher can afford in the long run. *Any discipline management technique that is working will self-eliminate.* If it does not self-eliminate, no matter how well it seems to work in the stress of the moment, it is a failure.

If discipline management techniques self-eliminate, then it is only a matter of time until the teacher is out of the discipline management business for all practical purposes. That is to say, I could not visit the teacher's classroom 6 to 8 weeks after training and gain comfort from seeing the techniques of positive discipline in prominent use. I would, in fact, be worried and suspect that the teacher was misapplying them. If used properly, they would have for the most part self-eliminated so that I would simply observe a busy classroom with no visible discipline management.

If a technique fails to self-eliminate, it is either the *wrong technique* for the job or it is *actively self-perpetuating.* Poor management techniques are self-perpetuating for the most part because they contain built-in flaws known as "reinforcement errors" which inadvertently feed the problem. We will learn a great deal about reinforcement errors in subsequent chapters.

If a discipline management technique is the wrong technique for the job, then its failure is a clear signal to the teacher to dump that technique and go to another technique better suited to the situation. But, which technique do you go to next? Do you dig deeply into your "bag of tricks" for an alternative under pressure in the heat of the moment? To the contrary, it is at this point that it is most important for the teacher to have a thorough understanding of a sophisticated and highly integrated discipline management *system* which contains a wide range of powerful management options. Understanding a management system includes understanding not only the strengths of each technique but also the weaknesses and trade-offs inherent in each and the logical sequence of choice.

It is important, therefore, to know not only how each management technique works, but also how it fails. The teacher must know when to discontinue one technique and begin another. And the switch must be quick and effortless. Safety comes from knowing what you are doing and always knowing what to do next if you encounter difficulty. For this reason we will study the limitations of the various management techniques as carefully as their strengths, and we will study the transition of each technique to the next. In almost every case the failure of a technique will be signaled by its failure to self-eliminate.

Our objective, to put it simply, therefore, is to get discipline management off your back! The last thing we want to do is to saddle the teacher with a discipline management program that demands the expenditure of a significant amount of time and energy on a daily basis all year long.

But there is no free lunch in the discipline management business. Teachers must pay their dues at some point. The time to pay in any successful management program is sooner rather than later. *Pay your dues up front.* Do it right and do it early so that you do not have to pay over and over again. Fail to pay your dues at the beginning (to implement procedures properly no matter what the initial cost) and you will pay during every class period for the remainder of your career. That is not cheap.

Discipline management, therefore, is definitely a "pay me now or pay me later" proposition. Pay you will. The only questions are when and how much. If you pay early, you will buy prevention. If you pay later, you will buy a perpetual process of remediation. In classroom management, prevention is all that the teacher can really afford.

But where do we direct our efforts? What really pays off in the long run? What are the key issues in discipline management within the classroom? We need to take some time to get oriented. It is very easy to expend a great deal of energy in discipline management going up a blind alley.

THE PRIMARY FOCUS OF DISCIPLINE MANAGEMENT

The most persistent *misconception* about discipline is that the most important problems in discipline management are the biggest problems, the crises. Certainly they are the most memorable. When teachers look back over the year, they will certainly remember the time the fight broke out or the time a student told them to do an unnatural act.

Administrators also share a crisis orientation as a natural by-product of their job. Let's face it, teachers do not send kids to the office because they are having a nice day. Principals do not see discipline problems until there is a crisis in somebody's classroom.

Parents as well share a crisis orientation because crises make news. For the watcher of the 6 o'clock news, violence, vandalism, and dope are the main discipline problems in education today.

Any teacher or administrator with a few years of experience can recall crises that have occurred out of the blue. These crises raise the question: What can you do to prevent a situation like that? Yet, while big problems can occur in isolation, they rarely do. Although they can occur as a result of things that happen outside school, they usually occur as a result of things that happen at school. Big problems usually grow from little problems. Small disruptions usually become big disruptions when they are allowed to escalate or become chronic.

As long as we have our attention focused on big disruptions, we will be resolutely looking right over the most crucial issue in discipline management, which is right under our noses. The most important and costly type of discipline problem in any classroom is the *small disruption*. In a typical classroom, be it secondary or elementary, suburb or inner city, roughly 80 percent of the disruptions are "talking to neighbors." Fifteen percent of the disruptions are "out of seat." That is to say, 95 percent of the disruptions in a typical classroom are simply the two most convenient forms of goofing off and taking a break from work. Most of the remaining 5 percent of disruptions also fall into the "nickel and dime" category. Pencil tapping, note passing, or playing with an object smuggled into class comprise most of the remaining "crimes of the classroom."

You can watch a typical classroom for months without seeing a fight break out. Yet, during an independent work period in an average classroom the students will generate between 0.6 and 0.8 disruptions per student per minute, with 3 being the maximum obtainable on the data system. In a typical classroom, between a quarter and a third of the class engages in goofing off during any given minute of the day.

Many teachers will respond to this point by saying, "That sounds much too high! That sounds like the whole classroom is falling apart. I'm sure I don't have that many disruptions in my class." Indeed, the typical classroom with the average number of disruptions is not loud at all, and it is not out of control. For the most part students are far too shrewd to be loud. Loudness calls the teacher's attention to them, and they get in trouble. Rather, most of the talking to neighbors is surreptitious whispering and fooling around between two or three students who are sitting next to each other. Those who are out of their seats usually have a ready excuse, and the teacher is usually too busy helping some individual to be pulled off task by a low murmur in the background.

The rate of disruptions in the typical classroom increases rapidly as soon as the teacher becomes immobile. Most teachers are well aware of the increase in the level of background noise as soon as they sit down to conduct any type of small group instruction. Disruptions will typically increase by 50 percent within a minute after the teacher's behind hits the chair.

Ironically, therefore, the most important discipline problem in the classroom is the small disruption, not the crisis. It is the small disruption by its very *frequency* that destroys the teacher's patience by degrees and destroys learning by the minute. Big crises, while they have a major impact on the memory, are sufficiently rare so that they have a relatively minor impact on time on task—on the moment-by-moment learning atmosphere of the classroom.

THE COST OF SMALL DISRUPTIONS

What Disruptions Cost the Teacher

Anybody who has ever spent any time in front of a classroom knows that teachers have to be constantly "on their toes." From the beginning of the school day until the room is finally empty, the teacher has to be ready for anything.

But, of course, once the students have gone you can relax. You can sit back, heave a big sigh of relief, and let down. At least you can for the first year or two on the job. After that point your capacity to let down at the end of the school day is for the most part history, and total relaxation is no longer under your voluntary control.

Your body is well designed to deal with stress, or at least the fleeting stresses of survival in nature. The reflex which we and all vertebrates use to deal with physical threat is known to any beginning biology student—"the fight-flight reflex." A fight-flight reflex is the body's rapid mobilization to either hit or run. It includes tensing the muscles, widening the eyes, clenching the teeth, drawing a quick breath, and vascular constriction in the viscera to divert blood flow to the muscles.

Just as crises come and go, so does the fight-flight reflex. The fight-flight reflex, however, although designed to save us, can destroy us under certain circumstances. After teachers have been on their toes for 7 hours a day for several years, the physical mobilization of the fight-flight reflex becomes a chronic condition. It is no longer under our control, and in a perverse twist of nature, every aspect of the fight-flight reflex originally designed to save our lives becomes a symptom of chronic hypertension.

The first price that teachers pay for the typical classroom disruption, therefore, is with their own flesh and blood. Fifty percent of teachers have job-related medical problems, mostly related to stress. The most common problems are high blood pressure (the vasoconstriction of fight-flight), resultant gastrointestinal problems (acid stomach, ulcers), dental problems (teeth grinding), muscular tension (back, neck, and headache), and finally substance abuse to get fast relief. These statistics often omit the most common emotional and physical side-effects: chronic tiredness, depression, short temper, and anxiety.

According to National Education Association (NEA) statistics, teaching is the second most stressful occupation in the United States—second only to air traffic controllers. The average teacher makes approximately 500 management decisions per day. Although the NEA may not be the most unbiased observer, anybody close to education knows that teaching is a tough job. By age 35 most teachers have been on the job for over a decade, and many are beginning to show clear signs of burn-out.

It is the small disruptions that can slowly destroy you. The stress that kills you is the stress that starts at 7 o'clock in the morning and does not let up until 3:30 in the afternoon—that chronic, low-grade stress that we associate with always having to be on our toes. Most teachers spend a considerable portion of their day dealing with students who are talking, who won't get to work, who do sloppy work, who wander around the room, who don't hear the instructions, who are in the wrong place at the wrong time doing the wrong thing day after day. Stress is having to be constantly drained to simply get the ball rolling and keep it rolling. Stress is the energy that goes into just breaking even.

Even though our powers of repression are great, almost all teachers know that their job is stressful even though they may not know the statistics. If you are a teacher, how often do you feel wiped out at the end of the day? How often do you feel like going home and getting horizontal as fast as possible when school is out rather than launching into some new activity? How often do you think, Thank God it's Friday? How many teachers feel by March or April that they will be lucky if they can just hang on until June? How long can you be nurturant in the face of this constant drain? How long can you keep your patience, your sense of humor, your enthusiasm, your caring? You cannot pursue a career for one year after another when it constantly takes more from you than it gives.

Teacher burn-out is getting a great deal of attention these days. According to most descriptions of the phenomenon, burn-out is the exhaustion, loss of caring, and erosion of job performance that affects many teachers after 6 to 10 years on the job.

The signs of burn-out are essentially those of chronic stress. In addition to the physical symptoms already mentioned, it is often the emotional symptoms that are saddest. Typically the first sign that we become aware of is chronic tiredness, the most predictable early symptom of depression. In the end, however, we may finally lose our capacity to care about those we are supposed to care for. The flavor of the feelings vary from person to person and include feeling let down, exasperated, frustrated, not supported, not appreciated, not adequately compensated, and generally resentful. We can begin to feel that our career choice was a colossal mistake.

The main myth about burn-out is that it happens after 6 to 10 years on the job. In fact, it happens every day. Feeling that you want to quit is simply the end of the line, like dying of cancer after you've had it for 6 years. The cancer has been present for 6 years consuming you day by day. Deciding that you don't want to teach anymore is not burn-out. It is simply the final, unavoidable, terminal event. If you feel exhausted and drained at the end of each working day, you are dying professionally by inches.

What Disruptions Cost the Students

Time on Task   The first price that the students pay for classroom disruptions is "time on task." Time on task, like burn-out, has gotten considerable play in recent years as it has emerged as a major variable in teacher effectiveness. At its most basic level time on task means that if students are working on math for 20 minutes, they might learn about 20 minutes worth of math. If, on the other hand, they are working on math for 40 minutes, they might learn about 40 minutes worth of math. The amount of work you get done is related to the amount of time you spend working.

In the time on task literature, the three variables that are shown to affect learning are lumped under time on task. The *first* variable, "allocated time," is the amount of time in a day set aside to teach a given subject. Some teachers allot 20 minutes for reading, and others set aside an hour. The *second* variable, "engaged time," is the amount of allocated time that the students are actually on task. It is this aspect of time on task that is most closely related to positive discipline. The *third* aspect of time on task which relates to learning is the "success rate" of the students while they are working. It is this aspect of time on task that relates most directly to positive instruction.

It comes as a great relief for me that education has turned so much of its attention to time on task. It makes talking about discipline much easier. For years many of my professional colleagues would dispute the importance of the "little disruptions" in the classroom when I would attempt to point out the cost of "talking to neighbors" and "out of seat." They would say, "Some research shows that much learning is accomplished during the informal sharing and give and take of students in the classroom," or "A study shows that students learn more from each other than from the teachers." Although this might be true in certain situations, what I was observing in the classroom could not be classified as peer tutoring. I finally ran across one colleague who referred to the continual, low-level noise of goofing off in the classroom as "the hum of learning." That did it! In every piece of research after that I documented time on task.

If in a typical classroom roughly a third of the students are goofing off at any moment, in a rowdy classroom this figure will easily exceed 50 percent. In an out-of-control classroom the majority of the kids are goofing off. In a recent dissertation which I supervised at the University of Rochester, we documented disruptions and time on task in *nonproblem* math, social studies, and English classes in a suburban junior high school. It fed the high school that turned out more national merit scholars than any other in the county. Monroe County, New York, is a "high-tech" area, and its suburban high schools are aimed at college prep. Nevertheless, the range of time on task for all classrooms studied was from 0.45 to 0.55. And the national merit scholars-to-be were pulling A's in these classes while chitchatting with their neighbors as the teachers moved hurriedly about the classrooms doing their job.

Time off task accumulates over the years, and, although it may only limit the achievement of bright students, for some students this accumulation of wasted time adds up to academic failure. It is a truism in special education that students referred for emotional and behavioral problems almost always have academic problems as well. Failure to master basic skills is a by-product of being off-task year after year. The process of failure, once established, tends to be self-perpetuating. Students, like anyone else, tend to avoid those experiences in which they do not feel adequate and successful. Self-labeling accompanies the process of falling behind and usually precedes teacher labeling by several years. *Self-concept* is ultimately a casualty of time on task.

Nor do behavior and academic inadequacy escape the notice of peers. They know how much of a pain in the neck or how smart or dumb their classmates are with far greater precision than does the teacher. *Peer status* can become an additional casualty of time on task. If you fail to learn quietly, you're simply written off as a classroom cipher. But if you fail to learn noisily, you become known as a jerk. Students, just like adults, do not like to be bugged and do not like to have their time wasted and privileges revoked because of somebody else's misbehavior and irresponsibility. Ironically, while obnoxious students often disrupt to get the peer attention that they may desperately want, they also tend to be low in peer status.

Teachers, particularly frazzled teachers, often fail to appreciate that most students want an orderly classroom. By allowing disruptions, teachers allow the tyranny of the minority. By allowing obnoxious students to ruin school for the more mature students, they unwittingly contribute to the social polarization of the class. When teachers protect themselves with good discipline, they also protect the students.

What Disruptions Cost the District

Learning either occurs or does not occur in a classroom between a student and a teacher. All the costs of buildings and grounds, heat and lights, buses and gasoline, and custodial, clerical, and administrative salaries are nothing more than a support system for the learning that takes place in the classroom. If we are losing 30 to 50 percent of our time on task as a result of small disruptions, it becomes obvious why small disruptions are indeed the most costly type of discipline problem. No other single problem costs you 30 to 50 percent of your entire district budget.

These costs, however, are hidden costs, and it is easy to leave them hidden. Other costs are more direct and obvious. The cost of replacing a broken window is tangible and concrete, but the cost of a student's failure is typically absorbed as a "natural" expense of the district. Yet, the cost of placing a student in a special classroom is usually about double that of a regular classroom. For the more disruptive student it is only a matter of time until their history of management problems and the accumulation of time off task combine to produce a diagnosis of "learning handicapped"—usually accompanied by "emotionally and behaviorally handicapped." Most of these casualties of the educational process are unnecessary. Most could have been prevented by effective classroom management. But until they finally matriculate, each of these students will cost the district double each year while they cannibalize the special education funds that were originally intended for children with nonreversible handicaps.

THE ACTION IMPERATIVE

Something must be done. Steps must be taken in education to turn this problem of discipline around. Everyone needs to become involved, from ineffective administrators to apathetic parents to penny-pinching school boards. Society needs to change in order to deal with social disadvantage and cultural deprivation and declining morals and the dissolution of the family. Everything needs to change, but none of it is going to change fast enough to save your hide.

If anything is going to change soon to give you relief, it is going to have to happen inside your own classroom. And you are going to have to do it yourself.

How To Kill Yourself by Inches

Your efforts to manage a classroom will fail if you don't understand the incredible inherent advantages which students enjoy over teachers when it comes to goofing off. Certain assets of the students are obvious enough. There are more of them, they are younger and stronger, and they send in fresh troops every year. Yet, although youth and numbers account for some of the students' perennial advantage and success, additional factors weigh in their favor. These additional factors include: (1) incredible skill at not getting caught, (2) games students play to get off the hook when caught, and (3) naiveté on the part of teachers concerning the dynamics of the classroom. If discipline is viewed as a struggle to stay on top, your days in the classroom are numbered no matter what your age, commitment, or heroic intent. In a war of attrition in which you must be perpetually on your toes to manage discipline, the students will always win.

The Folklore of Discipline Management   The folklore of discipline management asserts that, for teachers to be successful in classroom management, they must:

Be fair
Be firm
Be consistent
Follow through

Indeed, who could say that this is anything but good advice? It is the "motherhood and apple pie" of the discipline management business. It has been around since my grandma was in school.

If this folklore worked, and it has been around long enough to have had a fair test, then how come we're in the shape we're in? Could it be that this traditional home remedy is flawed and doomed to failure?

Your Life as a Teacher in Four Stages   In their years on the job most teachers pass through four predictable stages in their attempt to "stay on top of things" before they finally throw in the towel. In this section, you will see the career of typical teachers pass before your eyes as they kill themselves by inches doing battle with discipline.

Stage 1, Ignoring it   If teachers are green and inexperienced, when they see two students goofing off together during work time, they may well wait to see if the students spontaneously return to work. Do they? If these teachers have been on the job for very long, they know better.

This miscalculation by the green teacher will have been strengthened by an introductory behavior modification course in college in which he or she was taught that if you ignore disruptive student behavior and systematically reinforce competing appropriate behavior, the appropriate behavior will replace the disruptive behavior which is no longer being rewarded. I have yet to meet a teacher with a year's experience who believes that notion.

Why don't students get back to work if you ignore the disruptive behavior? The reason is simple: *Almost every form of classroom disruption is its own reward.* Being self-reinforcing, disruptions are therefore self-perpetuating. The rewards for a child talking to a neighbor include a respite from work and a pleasant chat with the neighbor. The reward for passing a note is getting a note back with something clever written on it. The reward for strolling around the room to the pencil sharpener for the fifth time (even if it's a mechanical pencil) is to stretch your legs, get away from school work for a few moments, see what's happening on the other side of the room, look out the window, and, perhaps, talk with a friend for a while.

To be technical for a moment, you cannot reduce the rate of deviant behavior by "extinction" unless you control the delivery of the reward for its occurrence and can therefore withdraw the reward at will. Relatively few disruptions in a classroom are inadvertently rewarded by the teacher. Most are rewarded by peers. Therefore, the disruptions continue because they continue to be fun.

When teachers ignore a disruption in the classroom, by their own inactivity they simply declare open season for disrupting. As long as disrupting is free, disruptions will continue to occur and reinforce themselves. If disruptions are allowed to feed themselves, they will grow. Something must be done to put a stop to it.

Stage 2, Ask Them to Stop   Stage 2 requires no great leap of the imagination, but it is a logical enough place to start.

Billy! Susan! Turn around and get back to work!

What do Billy and Susan do? If they have any brains in their heads, they will pull the oldest teacher avoidance ploy in the book. Any child who cannot master this technique by October of his or her first grade year needs special education. You look at the teacher as vapidly as possible and smile. This artful blend of innocence and surprise is known as "smiley face."

If "smiley face" does not get immediate results, the students must then resort to the next avoidance technique—they pick up their pencils. This ploy is known as the "magic pencil" since it convinces so many green teachers that the students are about to resume work.

If the teacher is still looking, the student may even be forced to the next avoidance technique—actually writing something on the paper. Viewing such obvious capitulation, the green teacher smiles triumphantly and returns to help the student who has been waiting. What are Billy and Susan doing 15 seconds later?

Stage 3, Ask Them to Stop Again   The teacher looks up to see Billy and Susan still talking! "Darn them," thinks the teacher. The situation is getting serious fast. There are only four stages and we are at number three already. The ante is rising rapidly. In stage 2 the teacher asked the students to stop. In stage 3 the teacher will have to ask them to stop *again!*

Billy! Susan! This is the *second* time I've had to talk to you!

I have bad news for you. Billy and Susan already know this. In case you didn't know it, every student in your class has a Ph.D. in teacher management! Billy and Susan only have one teacher to keep track of while you have a whole roomful. Who do you think will keep the most accurate books? They had a Ph.D. in parent manipulation before they entered kindergarten, and they have only gotten better since. *We* are the rookies in this league, and the sooner we appreciate that fact, the better.

The next line from the teacher is one of my favorites.

Now listen! I don't want to have to come over there!

Billy and Susan know that too! The last thing in the world you want to do is to quit teaching and walk clear across the room to take care of some typical student chitchat. Knowing that fact, the students will gamble against it. They will give you some more "smiley face" and fondle their pencils until you turn around. Then they will resume their conversation.

Stage 4, Laying Down the Law   Even a patient, loving teacher can take only so much! At some point the students will go too far! You will have to put an end to this once and for all! At some point you are going to have to walk right over to Billy and Susan and *lay down the law.*

This is your big number, so it has to be good. It is time for the trump card. You rise slowly, look the students in the eye while your stomach pumps acid and you grind your teeth. Then you walk over, eyes fixed, shoulders square.

What happens next is highly variable from teacher to teacher, but the general tone tends to be less than sweet.

All right, I've had it! You've done nothing but talk and fool around this whole period. And look! You don't even have your names written at the top of the papers yet! Now, I'm tired of this! I want to see some work done, and I want to see it now! What are you smiling about? You either sit around right now, keep your mouths shut, and get some work done or I'll keep you in this grade until you are old enough to vote! Do you understand!

After this show of force, what have you really accomplished by the time you have come back across the room? By elevating your blood pressure with a show of strength you have, unfortunately, accomplished less than nothing. You have (1) become the biggest disrupter in the classroom, (2) destroyed 3 minutes (3 × 30 kids = 90 minutes) of time on task, (3) upset the disruptive students which therefore guarantees not only their subsequent revenge but also their inability to work effectively for the next half hour, (4) become tired, upset, and more angry, and (5) ended up right back where you started.

How You Can Tell When You're Dead

When you are dying by inches in the classroom the fact that you are finally dead can often slip by almost unnoticed. Teachers often cannot tell when they are burning out until their family or doctor or dentist or therapist tells them. We deny and repress our own stress and burn-out on a day-to-day basis as best we can. It is the only adaptive thing to do in the short run when there is no escape. To dwell on the negative only makes it worse. So, we repress in order to get to work tomorrow and to do our job.

Although you are surviving in the short run, where are you in the long run? The long, slow slide toward burn-out typically passes the following milestones.

1 *Exhaustion.* You are constantly dealing with discipline.
2 *Futility.* It doesn't get any better.
3 *Resentment.* It finally becomes them against me.
4 *Cynicism.* You can't do anything about it anyway.
5 *Rationalization.*
  • It's just the way kids are at this age.
  • I can't teach them if they don't want to learn.
  • The noise doesn't bother me that much.
  • I wouldn't want them to be just little robots.
  • You can't be expected to deal with all the little stuff. You'd never get anything else done.
  • The kids from these neighborhoods have home lives you wouldn't believe. What can you expect?
  • It's all the TV. Their attention span is as long as the time between commercials.
  • Kids learn from talking to each other, don't they?
  • I don't have any "major" problems.
  • It's my job to present the material. It's their job to learn it.

Sensible Trade-offs

How long can you go through the futility of "dying by inches" before you get wise? How long can you run around trying to get every snot-nosed kid to sit up straight and quit goofing off before you begin to realize that you are running your legs off and getting nowhere? You do not have to burn out completely if you know when to quit.

Time To Quit If you are observant of your interactions with your students, you probably realize that it is time to quit hassling with discipline when you realize you are getting nowhere. Your reasoning may sound something like this:

> I can't spend my whole day running around trying to be on top of every little situation that might arise. If I did that, I wouldn't get any teaching done. I studied to be a teacher, not a full-time disciplinarian.

Now, that doesn't mean I'm not going to take care of discipline in my classroom. No! My job includes discipline. I'm not going to let students do as they please or let one student ruin it for all the others. That wouldn't be fair. But I can't be expected to respond every time a student decides to talk to a neighbor. At some point teaching and learning have to come ahead of being a police officer!

A Devil's Bargain   You have just made a trade-off of sorts—a sensible approach to discipline which deals primarily with the major problems instead of running yourself into the ground over trivia. Discretion is, after all, the greater part of valor, especially when you are losing. You do not do yourself or the students any good if you let yourself become tired and frazzled. Discipline isn't everything, you know. Other things come first.

Beware! You have just made a very *expensive* trade-off. You have gotten what you want in the present, but you will have to pay a large price in the future. To understand the real cost of the trade-off you have just made, you must appreciate the fact that students disrupt for only *two* reasons: (1) It's more fun than the assignment. (2) It's free. More fun than the assignment, perhaps. But free? Disrupting in the classroom is free? It may be more fun than the assignment, but how is it free?

Remember, every student in your class has a Ph.D. in teacher management. They know how loud they have to be before you finally do something about it—how silly, how persistent, how "cute"! They know exactly what your limit is by the end of the first week of school and exactly how to plunk your "magic twanger" or how not to. They know when you are going to respond before you know it, and they know whether you are going to follow through or not before you think you have made up your mind. They know exactly where your response threshold is, and they are smart enough to stay right below it all year long. It is the rare student who gets into trouble for being disruptive—the student who was a bit too cocky or careless. Most students most of the time are far too clever ever to have to worry about the teacher intruding into their slack time. It takes even less intelligence to be surreptitious than it does to get off the hook.

How free is disrupting in the classroom? We counted it during one study in third, fourth, and fifth grades, and the picture looked better there than it did in the junior high classrooms I was observing later in the day. The teachers responded to 1 disruption in every 108, usually with a reprimand from a distance which had almost no lasting effect. And these were *not* loud, out-of-control classrooms.

Would you gamble with odds like 107 out of 108? You *did* the whole time you were a student in school, just like these kids. Were they rotten, nasty, heartless—a tough class? Hardly! They were just kids being kids, testing limits and taking whatever the market would bear.

Students are gamblers. They are good gamblers and they know the odds. They will gamble as long as they can get away with it. It is the rare student who "messes up" by going just a little too far and "getting called on it." Most students most of the time are far too shrewd to get the teacher's attention when they don't want it.

THE DISCIPLINE DILEMMA

Damned if You Do, Damned if You Don't

In attempting to deal with classroom disruptions, you are damned if you do and damned if you don't. If you ignore the little disruptions, they feed themselves and grow. If you respond to them, you run yourself to death, and they still don't go away. If you quit, they grow even faster, but who's counting?

You must do something, but what? "Try harder" is not an adequate answer. The folk wisdom of discipline says that you should be fair, be firm, be consistent, and follow through. Stand your ground, get committed, and get tough! The only problem is that you never get done following through until you get too tired to care. The credibility of the folk wisdom of discipline management is dying along with the teachers who tried to do it.

Nor does the answer lie in the realm of administrative fiat. New policies, new codes, and new sanctions will not turn the school around. Effective discipline cannot come from the top down. Only effective support for change can come from the top down. Effective discipline either happens in the classroom or it does not happen at all.

New Alternatives

New alternatives are needed that allow teachers to get almost any student to cooperate when they want them to, with almost no expenditure of time and effort. Teachers need a new technology of classroom management that allows them to succeed at the many complex jobs of classroom management while having the luxury of relaxing, putting discipline behind them, and enjoying the process of teaching, learning, and being with young people. Indeed, one of the most consistent bits of feedback we receive from systematic teacher training is that the trained teachers feel good enough at the end of a teaching day to go out and do something.

But beware! There is no free lunch in the classroom management business. Change can only be purchased at a cost. Investment has to be made in two major areas:

1 *Retraining.* New techniques utilize new skills. New classroom management skills, like all skills, require practice, practice, and more practice with corrective feedback as you learn. The willingness to support training signifies the administration's willingness to support change.

2 *Implementation.* Most of the effort on the part of the teacher that is required to succeed at classroom discipline is paid *up front. First* you work to train your class to live up to your standards, and *then* it becomes easy to maintain those standards. At the beginning, when you are training your class, you invest heavily so that you can reap the dividends for the remainder of the year. Pay you must, but you have a choice. You can pay now or you can pay later—minute by minute for the rest of the year.

CLASSROOM STRUCTURE

CLASSROOM STRUCTURE: RULES, ROUTINES, AND STANDARDS

Structure is organization: setting the stage properly in advance so that instruction and classroom management go as smoothly as possible. It is the objective of structure to make management a matter of routine. Adequate structure is the cheapest form of behavioral management, since once you establish a routine you can produce needed cooperation and rule-following thereafter at relatively little effort. The alternative is the exhaustion that comes from having to establish order afresh every day.

Structure is a broad subject covering topics ranging from how to arrange the furniture in your classroom on the one hand to how to introduce yourself to a parent over the phone on the other hand. In all cases, structure focuses on the predictable—those management tasks that face the teacher continuously throughout the school year.

In a sense, structure deals with the mundane: the nuts and bolts of getting off on the right foot at the beginning of the school year and keeping the ball rolling. But, in another sense, structure is at center stage in classroom management just because it is so basic. Problems of classroom discipline can almost always be traced in part to inadequate structure. Most teachers simply do a quick and sloppy job of it. This and the following chapter will attempt to supply some of the specifics of classroom structure that are so often glossed over or lacking altogether.

THE NATURE OF CLASSROOM RULES

Classroom rules are much more than a list of dos and don'ts. A well-structured class means not only that the students know exactly what is expected of them but also that they have been trained and motivated to do it.

Common Misconceptions

The subject of classroom rules generates ambivalence and misgivings on the part of many teachers and therefore produces its share of funny ideas. The following misconceptions about classroom rules are among the most common.

1 *The students should know how to behave by this time.* The students have known how to behave since first grade, if not earlier. Since then the only relevant question has been: What will the market bear? What do they have to do in your class? How clear, consistent, and committed are you? Is this a work class, or do we get to "kick back?"

2 *I can't take too much time to go over rules because I have so much material to cover.* Teacher effectiveness research[1] indicates that teachers with the greatest time on task and the fewest discipline problems spend most of the *first two weeks of the school year* teaching rules, routines, standards, and expectations. The teachers who gloss over this task, often with the greatest concern and best intentions about "covering the material," spend the rest of the year running after the students.

3 *Rules are general guidelines.* Rules stated as general guidelines announce to the class the teacher's goals and objectives for classroom management, his or her hopes and aspirations for the new school year. General rules, however, must ultimately be expressed as highly *specific* procedures, routines, and standards which spell out the proper way of doing everything that the teacher wants during the day.

4 *Rules are announced.* Rules are *taught!* The announcement of rules, even specific rules, does nothing more than tell the students the name of the lesson that is about to be taught. Exactly how are we going to accomplish *each* specific behavioral objective in this classroom? Until the "exactly how" is taught, the announcement is just noise in the wind. Each routine or procedure or standard represents a *complete structured lesson* which must be taught just as carefully as any lesson that will be taught all year.

5 *If you do a good job teaching your rules at the beginning of the school year, you will not have to deal with them repeatedly throughout the year.* Rules are *retaught!* The only totally predictable outcome of learning is the immediate onset of forgetting. This is nowhere more evident than in the teaching of classroom rules. Rules and expectations must be clarified during each lesson transition, and they must be systematically retaught periodically throughout the school year.

6 *Teaching rules is a matter of being strict.* Teaching rules properly lays the groundwork for *cooperation* based on mutual caring. No amount of schoolmarmish "strictness" can substitute for the goodwill that generates cooperation. You cannot get very far doing discipline like a drill sergeant. Among the most predictable characteristics of good disciplinarians is that they are relaxed, emotionally warm, and free from the daily struggles of establishing order.

7 *Students dislike and resent classroom rules.* Students appreciate and respect a teacher who runs a tight classroom. Most discipline problems represent the tyranny of the few against the many. It is the few extreme disrupters who cause privileges for the whole group to be revoked, who cause enjoyable activities to be terminated, who cause time to be wasted and the stress of the group to be elevated. It is a common experience for teachers who have just been trained in effective classroom management methods to be privately thanked by good students for the change in classroom atmosphere.

Types of Classroom Rules

Classroom rules come in two basic types:

1 *General rules.* As mentioned earlier, general rules announce the teacher's goals and objectives, her or his hopes and aspirations for classroom management during the coming school year. *They do not, however, generate behavior.* At most they set a tone in the class and raise expectations briefly until the students have had time to size up the teacher and judge whether the general rules are for real.

2 *Specific rules.* Specific rules take the form of *procedures, routines, and standards* for carrying out specific, everyday tasks. Specific rules are carefully taught and retaught, and their being taught successfully establishes high behavioral and academic standards in the classroom. General rules are ultimately embodied in a series of procedures, routines, and standards or else they exist only in the teacher's imagination.

General Rules   General classroom rules might be thought of as broad guidelines or expressions of the teacher's values. They typically deal with two topics: (1) good behavior, and (2) good work habits. There is no best and final set of general rules— every teacher must develop his or her own approach. Here are some general rules, however, for making general rules.

1 Do not make any rule that you are not willing to enforce *every time* it is broken. This rule will eliminate many of your other rules. If the behavior in question is not serious enough for you to enforce *every time,* the rule is not worth having. If you fail to enforce one of your classroom rules, you have just taught the entire class that your rules are hot air. Before making rules, sit quietly by yourself for a while and decide what is really important.

2 There should be relatively few general behavior and work rules in the classroom. As a guideline, consider having three to five basic rules governing good behavior and three to five rules governing good work habits. These numbers are not etched in stone anywhere, but I run into relatively few people who can keep more than five of anything straight for very long.

3 Rules must be simple, clear, and shared by all students. There is a point of diminishing returns in making general rules. If the rules are not simple, they will be confusing. If they are not clear, they will become grounds for contention. If they are not shared by everyone, they have not been well taught.

Specific Rules   When training a class to do *what* you want them to do *when* you want them to do it, the unit of consideration is not the general rule but, rather, the procedure, routine, or standard. The most important lessons that effective teachers teach during the first 2 weeks of the school year are "how to do this" and "how to do that." When one totals up the number of procedures that make up a typical school day, it becomes evident why most of the first 2 weeks of the school year are spent in teaching procedures, routines, and standards.

Teachers have no choice about whether or not their specific rules will be taught. They will be taught one way or another, and the students will easily have your number 15 minutes into the school year. Imagine, for example, that you are organizing some handouts on the morning of the first day of school as your first-period junior high students begin drifting into your class. You have just taught your first lesson of the year.

> You may come into my class any way you please.

They will come in quietly and orderly on the morning of the first day because they are walking on eggs. But your failure to establish standards did not go unnoticed.

Imagine that the bell rings, and you say, "Students, I want you to take your seats." You taught your second rule.

> Do not worry about sitting down until the bell rings. Then I will nag you to do it.

They may sit down quickly and quietly on the first day, but, remember, you are on a honeymoon. The honeymoon only lasts for 2 days. Then it will be, "Students, did you hear me? I said take your seats. Will the three of you over by the window *please* sit down!"

Now you will begin to pay for your failure to teach your rules and establish structure. Before the school year was 1 minute old the students in your first period knew that they could "kick back" because you obviously did not know how to "make it happen." In spite of this warning many secondary teachers still think that teaching rules one by one seems terribly elementary. After all, students should know how to behave by the time they get to high school, right?

The effort that you should expend in teaching specific procedures and routines, even at the secondary level, can perhaps be put into perspective by listing the procedures that chemistry teachers have to teach explicitly before they can conduct their first lab. These procedures and routines include:

- How to use the gas and water jets on the lab table.
- How to fill out a lab manual.
- How to check out glassware.
- How to check out elements and consumables.
- How to operate the weights and measures.
- How to operate the microscope (you think they remember this from biology?).
- What to do in case of fire at the lab table.
- What to do in case someone's clothing catches fire.
- What to do in case of cuts from glass.
- What to do in case of contact with acids and bases.
- What to do in case of caustic substances in the eye.
- How to clean a test tube so that it will not contaminate the next class's experiment.
- What to do with the unconsumed elements.
- How to clean up your lab table so it is ready for the next class.

- How to reset your microscope and weights and measures so they are ready to be used by the next class.
  - Who to talk to during lab.
  - How loud to talk during lab.
  - What to do if you need help.
  - What to do if you are done with your experiment before the end of the period.

Imagine now that you have explained to students what to do in case of an emergency—in case they splash acid into their eyes in chemistry class (even if goggles are mandated) or catch their thumb in the paper cutter in art class or run their finger into the band saw in shop. Imagine further that the inevitable has finally happened and you have a hurt student. What is the hurt student doing? You guessed it—probably screaming and panicking. Who will help? Will you always be close by? If you want to get the acid out of the student's eyes before they are irreparably damaged, you had better train the class in first-aid procedures because you might be in the storeroom when it happens. How do you get a panicking teenager's eyes washed out with fresh water when he's yelling and thrashing about? You had better practice—just like practicing procedures in a life-saving class. Do not be surprised if chemistry students leave class on the first day with wet hair and wet shirt and blouse collars.

In addition to setting forth behavioral procedures, specific rules ultimately set forth standards of excellence for classroom assignments. Some students know what a good piece of work looks like, while other students don't. But many do and aren't telling. Exactly how do you expect a paper to look when it is handed in? What do you want for penmanship, for thoroughness, for correctness and completion?

Later sections of this book will deal specifically with methods of training students to produce diligence and excellence. For the time being, let me state the most basic rule of quality control on any job.

> Your standard of excellence on any job is defined by the *sloppiest* piece of work that you will accept.

Your standard of excellence is defined by the sloppiest piece of work that you will accept because it is, by definition, acceptable. The careful teaching of work procedures, routines, and standards is a major component in producing excellence.

Teaching the procedures that comprise your behavioral and academic standards of excellence is never completed. Not only do routines change constantly, but students also forget. Having taught your rules carefully during the first 2 weeks of school, you will now watch student behavior rapidly deteriorate unless the fine points of your procedures are repeated and repeated and repeated.

Task structuring is the repetition of the exact steps of a procedure *immediately preceding* the students' carrying out of that procedure. Task structuring is the art of the *lesson transition*. During the lesson transition, general rules and specific procedures must be quickly reviewed so that the students know *exactly* what is expected of them during the following 2 minutes. A great many discipline problems are generated by inadequate task structure. Soon the students are moving in thirty different directions and the teacher must hustle and yell in order to pick up the slack.

TEACHING CLASSROOM RULES

Beginning the Year with Clarity

You will begin teaching your classroom rules one way or another from the opening minute of the school year. Your choice is not whether rules will be taught but, rather, whether *your* rules will be taught.

Imagine, in contrast to the example of the first day of class presented earlier, that you are the high school advanced mathematics teacher with whom I was recently privileged to work. He structured the simple act of walking into his classroom on the first day of school in the following fashion. When students reached the door to the class the teacher greeted them one by one and introduced himself, shook their hands, asked them their names, handed them a number, instructed them to take the seat corresponding to that number on the seating chart on the chalkboard, and directed them to begin filling out the 3 × 5 card on the desk according to the instructions written on the chalkboard. On the chalkboard was a diagram of his room arrangement which was carefully designed in a manner to be described in the next chapter. On the diagram each desk had a number. On the chalkboard were instructions concerning what to write on the 3 × 5 card: (1) your name, (2) address, (3) home phone number, (4) your parents' names, (5) their place(s) of work, and (6) their work phone number(s). These instructions were accompanied by a diagram showing exactly how the card should look when properly filled out.

This teacher was well into the teaching of a whole series of classroom rules before the bell rang, which included the facts that (1) my enforcement of classroom rules begins at the classroom door, (2) I care who you are and that you know who I am, (3) walk into my class, (4) take your seat immediately, and (5) *begin work* on the assignment on the board before the bell rings. The teacher has also made physical contact signifying mutual respect and caring. The school year is not yet a minute old.

This simple comparison of two modes of beginning the first class of the first day of the school year provides not a prescription for exactly how to begin *your* school year but, rather, a simple contrast in styles that signifies an appreciation for, or a lack of appreciation for, the role of structure in classroom management. Classroom structure of some sort will emerge rapidly. It will be taught one way or the other. Either you will structure the class to achieve your learning goals, or the students will structure the class to achieve their personal and social goals. You will actively initiate the process of structuring the behavior in your class, or you will abdicate that structure.

Teaching a Structured Lesson

I can't imagine spending the first two weeks of the school year teaching rules and routines. I can't think of anything more boring than listening to the same old rules over and over again!

This response to the idea of spending most of the first 2 weeks of school teaching classroom procedures, routines, and standards is common enough to serve as a warning flag. What does it mean to "teach your procedures, routines, and standards as carefully as you would teach any other structured lesson"? What is a structured lesson?

We do not get very deeply into the managing of classroom discipline before we encounter the close interrelatedness of classroom discipline methodology and classroom instructional methodology—a theme that will reappear in greater force later in the book. We cannot even get past the introduction of classroom rules without encountering one of the most basic and most commonly misunderstood processes of instruction—the teaching of a structured lesson. How do you get everyone in the class to be able to perform a given skill *correctly* before the teaching of the lesson draws to a close?

A structured lesson teaches a skill. Skill implies both understanding and performance. Indeed, a skill cannot be said to exist without performance. A structured lesson, therefore, systematically teaches skill performance by transferring in a gradual, step-by-step fashion *performance* from the mind and body of the teacher to the mind and body of the student.

The outline of a structured lesson presented below sets forth the major steps by which skills are gradually transferred from teacher to student. Our understanding of the process of teaching a structured lesson has come from years of training teachers to correctly perform the classroom management skills to be described in later chapters of this book, and that understanding has been greatly enriched by the writing and teaching of Dr. Madeline Hunter of UCLA who has been a pioneer in instructional methodology during the past two decades.[2]

A structured lesson follows a sequence which initially teaches correct performance with a high degree of structure and gradually fades that structure so that skills are mastered by degrees with a high degree of precision within a context of minimal performance anxiety. The outline of a structured lesson presented below, although only one of many possible ways of subdividing the process of teaching a skill, begins with a fundamental division of the lesson into three distinct phases of skill mastery. The terminology made familiar by Madeline Hunter is used wherever possible. The entire process of teaching a structured lesson is discussed in great detail in the companion volume to this book, *Positive Classroom Instruction*.

OUTLINE OF A THREE-PHASE STRUCTURED LESSON

A Setting the stage
  1 *Raising the level of concern.* Why is the mastery of this skill of immediate relevance and importance? (motivation)
  2 *Review and background.* What skills from yesterday and other previous lessons will we be using today? (Perform them as a warm-up.)
  3 *Goals and objectives.* What will we be doing today, and what will we attempt to achieve?
B Acquisition
  1 *Explanation.* What is the exact nature of the skill? Explain the steps of skill performance to provide the verbal/auditory modality of input. Your task analysis provides the *performance sequence.*
  2 *Modeling.* Demonstrate the steps of the performance sequence for the class to provide the visual modality of input. Modeling can be made permanent by pro-

viding graphics or illustrations for each step of the performance sequence. This Illustrated Performance Sequence (IPS) provides a study guide for the students during practice as well as a lesson plan for the teacher.

3 *Structured practice.* Walk the students through the performance of the skill in a highly structured fashion *one step at a time*. The objective of structured practice is to give the students the experience of correct performance—the physical modality of input coupled with the verbal and visual—with maximum safety and precision. The student gets the sequence, cadence, and kinesthetic feedback of performance at almost no risk or error.

C Consolidation

1 *Guided practice.* The student continues to perform the skill semiautonomously with periodic monitoring and corrective feedback from the teacher as needed.

2 *Generalization and discrimination.* Skills must initially be learned in a generic form. But after initial mastery the student must learn the variations of the skill needed for application in varied settings (generalization) as well as the capacity to discern common errors when they occur (discrimination).

3 *Independent practice.* During independent practice students continue to practice entirely on their own; they should be not only capable of discriminating errors as they occur but also capable of correcting them. Independent practice assumes mastery, the thorough internalization of instruction, so that students are in effect their own teachers. Without such thorough mastery a student is incapable of improving with practice since any error will be indiscriminately repeated until "mastered" right along with those portions of the skill that are being performed correctly. Thus, independent practice should only follow a demonstration of skill mastery during guided practice.

Teaching classroom rules as a structured lesson rather than as a series of pronouncements puts the teacher's efforts at establishing consistent rule-following during the first 2 weeks of school into perspective. When the class first lines up, for example, the lesson is: How do we line up? If necessary they will do it over and over again until they get it right. What happens *after* we line up can wait. Or, for example, the first time we use the microscope, the first lesson is: How do you pick up a microscope, walk with it, and set it down? After we gain proper respect for the fragility and expense of a fine piece of laboratory equipment we can move on to: How do you adjust a microscope?

The investment in teaching procedures, routines, and standards is the only cheap way to establish rule-following. Prevention is always cheaper than remediation. Establishing order properly at the beginning of the school year or semester is cheaper than doing it minute by minute, day by day for the remainder of the school year.

Classroom Structure and Personal Competence

In studying the social competence of people in leadership roles, one of the most consistent differences between competence and incompetence is in the preplanning and structuring of management situations. This dimension of competence has been described by the terms "proactive" versus "reactive."

Whether in parenting, teaching, or managing an organization, effective leaders plan, anticipate, structure, and prepare both themselves and the people for whom they are responsible for the upcoming task. Ineffective parents, teachers, and leaders of organizations tend to do a poor job of preplanning, anticipating, and preparing. They launch into a situation and then find themselves in the middle of something that is not going according to plan. They are constantly in a reactive mode, a crisis management mode, a thrashing about to reduce loss rather than to maximize gain.

Structure will be *the major task* of any teacher during the opening weeks of school, and it will be a preoccupation for as long as school is in session. The willingness and capacity of the teacher to prevent discipline problems proactively through structure will determine how many discipline problems will need to be remedied reactively after they have occurred.

METHODS OF DEVELOPING CLASSROOM RULES

Teachers express their individuality in no other area as much as in the building, explaining, and teaching of their rules, routines, standards, and expectations. I have seen a wide range of styles and approaches succeed. The students are not reading your specific content as much as they are reading your savvy and commitment.

One obvious way in which the teacher's commitment to structure is expressed is in how thoroughly the structure is presented and taught in the first place. How much of an investment does the teacher make? It is as though the students were watching and asking themselves, "Is this worth our time?"

The following section describes approaches to presenting structure to a class which give a flavor for the range and variety of methods that have proved effective. These methods are not mutually exclusive by any means. In fact, some of the most effective teachers will use all of them at one time or another. In any case, there is plenty of leeway for a teacher to find a style that is comfortable.

Describing and Demonstrating Rules

In one high school where I was working, one of the most respected English teachers amazed her colleagues when during training she shared a description of the first three days of the semester in her English class. As soon as the students entered the room, they were given a form upon which they were to put their name, address, and phone number. Any students who did not have pencils were given them with a private message that this would be the last pencil that they would ever be given and that they would be expected to bring their own pencil and paper in the future. As this task was nearing completion, with an overhead projector the teacher showed the class a list of basic rules for her class to be copied onto the first page of each student's notebook. While the rules were being copied, the teacher used the information the students had just supplied to fill out her seating chart, grade book, and attendance forms.

After the students had copied the rules, the teacher rearranged the students' seating in alphabetical order, and the students were told that they would be expected to use those same seats in the future. The teacher then discussed the rules, one at a time, for the remainder of the period while answering questions and continually stressing her high standards. On the second day the explanation and demonstration of rules focused on how to do written work acceptable to the teacher. On the third day the explanation focused on the exact nature of the term paper which would be required to receive credit in the course.

Several of this teacher's colleagues expressed surprise at how "rule-oriented" this teacher was, and several volunteered that they had never even considered being so thorough or "tight" about the whole thing. But they did listen, because they knew their colleague was a creative and stimulating English teacher who not only was liked by the students but also had a reputation for having one of the best-behaved classrooms in the building. There seemed to be some discovery in the notion that such a high degree of creativity was compatible with an equally high degree of structure.

Consensus Building

Some teachers are more comfortable with leading a focused and productive group discussion than are other teachers. Consequently, they will exploit discussion to a much greater extent as a means of developing not only classroom rules but also consensus concerning shared values, goals, and objectives. If you are comfortable as a discussion facilitator, it is extremely valuable to involve the students. Time can be spent in clarifying roles, values, and expectations as well as rules of conduct. Some classes even develop a classroom code or constitution. The focus of the discussion is usually as much on general rules as on specific rules, and specific rules will often be proposed by students dealing with issues of mutual consideration and proper conduct. Discussions, which can be augmented by committee work, often deal with topics such as:

- What is a good classroom?
- What are good teachers like?
- What are good students like?
- What obligations and responsibilities serve the common good?
- What kinds of behavior can ruin a class?
- What are some special wishes for classroom rules that the students might have?
- What can our parents do to help?

Teaching the Management System

It is to the teacher's advantage to teach his or her students the classroom management system in detail as well as the discipline policy of the school so that the students will be informed about the incentives and sanctions under which they operate. Such sharing is not only helpful but also shrewd, since it allows the teacher to easily give clear signals concerning the consequences of any student behavior during class. No management system gains anything by being a surprise to the student when implemented.

The manual for teaching your class about discipline, therefore, is contained in the remainder of this book. Use what you will and teach it thoroughly. There are few more effective ways of impressing upon your class your commitment to management than to give them a detailed, inside look at a highly developed management system.

CLASSROOM CHORES

How To Work Hard To Produce an Ingrate

Frazzled Parents, Lazy Children   If you spend a good portion of your life cleaning up after your children, making their beds, preparing their meals, and doing all the other chores required to keep a family going all by yourself, you not only get old and tired before your time, you also produce children who seem to be oblivious to the fact that they should help. Where do children learn that it is important to help out? Certainly children do not learn the value of helping others by being waited on all their lives. Owning a servant, be they a parent or teacher, does not seem to transmit a sense of selfless giving. Quite to the contrary, it trains a child to expect much and give little.

Effective parents train their children to help and to take pride in helping. Ineffective parents either (1) do it all themselves, (2) nag, threaten, and punish to little avail, or (3) kiss it off (lower their standards and make their peace with things not getting done).

Many parents go through life fairly frazzled, producing lazy, ungrateful children, but a classroom teacher cannot afford that luxury. With thirty students, whether they are first or twelfth graders, teachers must train the members of the class to help out or else they will either get *very* frazzled fast or have a lot of things that do not get done.

Value Comes from Being Needed   I have rarely heard of a child thanking a parent or a teacher for making them do chores or for acting responsible when being irresponsible was easier. That thanks will have to come in the future. For the time being we will have to "pay our dues" out of an understanding of what is best for the child. Children are raised from a state of infantile omnipotence and total dependency in their earlier years to a state of maturity by committed parents and teachers with a good deal of kicking and screaming from the kids along the way.

Although children will treat as a servant anyone stupid enough to accept the role, it is the children who most need to learn to help adults in doing adult work. A sense of personal worth comes from being an integral part of a functioning social unit. Personal value comes from being needed. What are you needed for? In what ways are you indispensable? How do you know when you have pulled your weight and have every right to feel proud? To receive a meaningful answer to all these questions, a child at home or at school needs jobs or chores for which they are accountable.

Dozens of routine jobs need to be done in a classroom daily for the class to function. Such jobs, which must be done for the good of all, we will call chores.

In a classroom there are always more tasks crucial to learning than the teacher can possibly perform. Teachers have dozens of students with individual needs, and daily they must prepare and present multiple lessons, grade papers, manage behavior, respond to emotional needs of students, and provide cultural, social, and academic enrichment. There will never be enough teacher to go around!

The implications of the size and complexity of the teacher's job as regards student chores is straightforward. A teacher must train the students to carry some of the burden or else certain jobs will not get done, and everyone will be the poorer. Effective teachers must delegate. They must train their students to carry a portion of the work load so that their time and effort will be freed to carry out higher level professional tasks. The resulting increase in classroom efficiency and the learning of responsibility benefits all.

However, training students to carry out chores is work in the beginning. It takes time and effort invested "up front": a commitment to developing a system for getting things done proactively rather than a passive abdication of structure that leaves jobs undone and students irresponsible. Given the size of the job to be done and the value of the lessons to be learned by students who carry their own weight in the classroom, I would suggest a simple rule for teachers to use as a guideline in assigning chores.

Never do anything for a student that they are capable of doing for themselves.

Getting the Chores Done

Training students to do chores has to be as carefully taught as any of the other structured lessons that go into establishing procedures, routines, and standards. This job will be made considerably easier, however, by responsibility training (to be explained in later chapters).

Before the school year begins, make sure that you have a list of all the things that need to be done in the classroom in the form of chores. You will probably come up with a list long enough to supply every student with a responsibility or chore of her or his own.

Individual Responsibilities   The only liability of assigning chores individually to students is that you also saddle yourself with the relatively high expense of organizing and training each student to get the chore done. This overhead is multiplied if you rotate chores regularly. Imagine thirty students with thirty responsibilities, each one of which you must teach, prompt, and check on. Individualized chores is a wonderful idea if you can afford it. The limiting factor is cost.

Group Responsibilities   The most simple and straightforward way of reducing the complexity and cost of getting chores done is to group the chores into clusters and to group the students into teams that are each responsible for a cluster of chores. Teachers might, for example, divide the room into four teams. They might also divide the chores into four general types. And they might, in addition, have chore rotation so that each group has a particular set of chores for 1 week at a time. At the end of the full rotation (4 weeks), the teacher can either recycle the rotation unchanged or allow the teams to rechoose while keeping the organization of chores the same. Teams can be the same as the teams that you use for learning activities and team games (see Chapter 11).

Below are listed four clusters of chores which may serve as food for thought, particularly in a typical self-contained classroom:

1 Clean up
  • clean up paper and litter in the classroom
  • arrange books and materials on the shelves
  • clean up work areas and take care of equipment
  • clean the chalkboard and erasers
  • clean up a portion of the yard (If all teachers are involved, the yard can be kept in good shape.)
2 Bulletin board and decoration
  • make bulletin boards (Why do teachers spend so much time making bulletin boards themselves when, with a little guidance, the students can do a good job, have fun doing it, and learn in the process?)
  • decorate the classroom
  • plan art projects for the class
  • plan "preferred activities" (see Chapter 11)
3 Enrichment
  • plan enrichment activities
  • plan or help organize learning centers
  • provide suggestions for good TV viewing for the week
  • present a current events show on a daily or weekly basis ("That Was The Week That Was")
4 Grading, passing out papers, and logging
  • correcting papers
  • collecting and passing out papers
  • helping score and record grades under the teacher's supervision (insofar as you are comfortable with it)
  • handling the logging of attendance and the clerical work of dealing with lunch orders, paperback book orders, etc.

This list of chores is only suggestive, of course. Each teacher's needs are different, and the nature of the chores vary greatly from age group to age group and from class to class. In a high school woodworking shop, for example, the chores are much different than they are in a second grade classroom. In home economics the chores are different than they are in chemistry. But there are always chores, and there is always more work than the teacher can do.

Helping the Teacher Teach

Teaching is one of the most fundamental skills in a technological society. Anyone who is responsible for getting anyone else to do anything is a teacher as well as a leader.

Shop foremen must teach the people for whom they are responsible to do their job correctly. The head nurse must train the nurses to do their jobs correctly. The vice president must train the division managers to do their job correctly. The president must train the vice presidents to do their jobs correctly. The teacher must train the students to do their jobs correctly. Everyone in a position of responsibility ends up being a teacher sooner or later, for better or for worse.

Parents are teachers as well, and by learning to teach, students learn to parent. By learning to teach, bright students will learn to help others effectively. By learning to teach, slow students learn the material most effectively—by teaching it.

Later sections in this book describe in detail the fundamental skills of teaching. You, as a teacher, will provide a great service to your students if you teach them how to teach and give them practice in teaching each other. Peer tutoring is necessary in most lessons for optimal instructional efficiency as we shall find out in later chapters, but it is least of all a means of a teacher's avoiding work. It is always more work in the short run to train someone else to do a job than it is to do it yourself.

Techniques are also discussed in later chapters for organizing the room into study groups, "student team learning" and "quality control circles," in which much of the responsibility for skill drill, grading practice exercises, preparing for tests, preparing written assignments, and doing research and committee work will be carried by the students. Experience in the field has strongly confirmed the value of organizing students to carry out as much of their own drill, research, clerical work, and quality control as possible.

Ironically, learning how to teach properly is often easier for students than it is for adults. We have years of bad habits to break, whereas the students do not. Once students have listened to a good teacher teach properly for a month or two, they can mimic the entire routine. I have had elementary teachers that I have trained subsequently train *their* classes to use the advanced instructional techniques in a single day. Once kids know how to teach others effectively and gently, use it! Teaching is, after all, the basic chore being done in the classroom. Everyone needs to help.

OVERVIEW

Throughout our presentation of the skills and procedures that comprise positive classroom discipline we will repeatedly confront the need for teachers to be proactive rather than reactive. If teachers make the investment in training their class to follow their classroom rules early in the school year or as soon as they are trained in the use of classroom management skills, their subsequent investment in rule enforcement will be greatly reduced. If, on the other hand, the structure and expectations of the teacher are not firmly established, the teacher will pay a very high price for his or her naiveté or abdication of responsibility. Lacking well-established patterns of rule-following, the teacher has to scramble daily to establish behavioral boundaries. This endless process ultimately exhausts the teacher.

REFERENCES

1 Carolyn M. Evertson and Linda M. Anderson have functioned as the director and associate director of the Correlates of Effective Teaching Program, Research and Development Center for Teacher Education, The University of Texas at Austin. Their work has focused in particular on the management tasks that confront the teacher at the beginning of the school year and the ways in which effective teachers deal with classroom structure during the first 2 weeks of school. References include:

1 Evertson, C. M. and Anderson, L. M. Beginning school. *Educational Horizons,* 1979, summer, 164–168.

2 Emmer, E. T., Evertson, C. M., and Anderson, L. M. The first weeks of class . . . and the rest of the year. Paper presented in Symposium, *Perspectives on Classroom Management Research,* Annual Meeting of the American Education Research Association, San Francisco, CA, April, 1979.

2 Russell, D. and Hunter, M. Planning for effective instruction. *Instructor,* 1977, September.

CLASSROOM STRUCTURE: ARRANGING THE LEARNING ENVIRONMENT TO YOUR ADVANTAGE

Achieving specific management objectives occurs within a *physical* and *social* context that is structured by the teacher. Teachers must either take responsibility for structuring that environment to support their instructional and management goals or else they will teach at a continuous disadvantage.

Many *physical* characteristics of the classroom may affect learning such as lighting, crowding, chalkboard space, and the availability of various learning aids and equipment. Those aspects of physical arrangement of most immediate relevance to the implementation of limit-setting, however, focus primarily on maximizing the teacher's mobility, physical proximity, and the moment-by-moment accountability of student to teacher. The two most prominent topics in this regard are (1) room arrangement and (2) seating arrangement.

The *social* context of the classroom within which discipline management is carried out often receives even less attention than physical factors. It is not uncommon for high school students in a specific class to be unsure of each other's names after 2 months together, and it is most common for parents to receive no information at all concerning classroom rules and standards and no communication from the teacher until their child is in some form of trouble. Structuring the social context of discipline management will focus on (1) relationship building with students and (2) relationship building with parents.

Finally, we will take a look at the structuring of the first hours and days of the school year to see how the teacher can have all discipline management systems "on line" by the end of the second hour of the school year. Beginning discipline management at the very start of the school year, however, is a topic which will be developed further in later chapters as the nature of specific management procedures are described.

ROOM ARRANGEMENT

If the teacher is 50 feet away from you while you are goofing off in class and if the teacher is separated from you by six rows of desks, it is not too likely that he or she will see you whispering or passing a note, much less do anything about it. If the teacher is standing 5 feet from you and looking at you with no furniture between the two of you to impede movement, chances are that you will be on task. It does not take a genius to figure out the relationship between proximity, mobility, and classroom disruption. Where do all the biggest goof-offs sit on the first day of class? You guessed it—along the chalkboard in the back of the classroom as far away from the teacher as they can get. They already know the two basic principles of room arrangement: *Proximity is accountability. Distance is safety.*

The General Plan of Room Arrangement

The Custodian's Objective and Your Objective   Who arranges the furniture in most classrooms, the teacher or the custodian? The custodian, of course. Custodians know their job, and they will arrange *your* room to help them do *their* job. However, their job has nothing to do with discipline or instruction and neither will their room arrangement. Their job is to run a dry mop or a sweeper between the desks as quickly as possible to clean the building before quitting time. The best possible room arrangement for the custodian is to have desks and chairs in nice straight rows with the teacher's desk in front. This room arrangement is more predictable the older the students. See Figure 4-1.

Unfortunately, the room arrangement that is best for the custodian is an absolute disaster for both discipline and instruction. It makes mobility and physical proximity

FIGURE 4-1
The custodian's room arrangement.

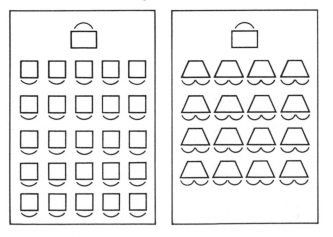

as difficult as possible for the teacher to achieve. Teachers who are individualistic in so many other ways could not possibly achieve such uncanny uniformity in room arrangement if they were to take responsibility for arranging the furniture in their classrooms to achieve *their* objective, which is to maximize learning.

The Logic of Furniture Arrangement   The best possible room arrangement is one which puts the *least distance* and the *fewest barriers* between the teacher and any student in the classroom. Any room arrangement that facilitates the teacher's getting from one student to another quickly and easily is on the right track.

The logic of the physical arrangement of your classroom is the same as the arrangement of work space in a shop or kitchen. In a kitchen, for example, you would attempt to surround yourself with countertops and to arrange sinks and appliances so that you can prepare a meal with the least effort and the fewest steps. In your classroom, the students represent the "work space" to which you will be going, and you will want to get from student to student quickly—with the fewest steps and without winding your way through furniture along the way. In later sections of this book we will see how critically important mobility and proximity are for both discipline and instruction.

The most important aspect of room arrangement, however, is not where the furniture is but where it *isn't*. The teacher must provide *walkways* between tables and desks so he or she can move among the students easily. In order to achieve such mobility the teacher will need walkways that run front to back (longitudinal) and from side to side (lateral). Particular attention should be paid to opening up the middle so the teacher can walk from one corner of the seating arrangement to the opposite corner with as few steps as possible.

Around this walkway the teacher then arranges the students in as *compact* a fashion as possible. There is no best single arrangement of furniture around this walkway, since different teachers have different furniture and different teaching objectives. Leave only 4 or 5 feet between the chalkboard and the nearest students—just enough to allow you to move around easily. Now when you write on the board you are only a step from your nearest students and perhaps six or eight steps from your most distant students. By a combination of proximity and movement you will radically alter the "cost-benefit ratio" of goofing off for students sitting anywhere in your classroom. Remember, proximity and mobility on the part of the teacher produce accountability on the part of the students.

Many teachers imagine, of course, that if the students are placed close to each other, they will disrupt more. This idea is so common that we have systematically studied the subject several times in our research. We have found that when the teacher brings the students close together and moves among them, there is *no* increase in classroom disruptions. Apparently the greater ease of students talking to each other which may be caused by their proximity to each other is offset by their hesitancy to talk to each other since they are closer to the teacher. In any case, there is nothing to be feared by moving the students in close.

If the nature of your instruction precludes optimal room arrangement and physical movement, relax. We have management procedures to compensate for loss of proximity and mobility. For example, in chemistry lab, typing class, home economics class, or shop classes the work stations may be fixed so that furniture rearrangement is impossible. In small group instruction the teacher may be seated so that mobility is equally impossible. To the extent that rearrangement is impossible and movement is inhibited you have a disadvantage that can only be compensated for by a separate management technology which is specifically designed for such situations (see Section 4, Building Patterns of Cooperation).

Where to Place the Teacher's Desk   In most classrooms the teacher's desk is in the front, in the space between the chalkboard and the students. Once again the age-old way of doing things makes the teacher's job difficult. Move the desk out of the middle of the front of the classroom over to the corner or to the side or to the back. *Do not* place the desk between you and the students, and do not place the desk between the students and the chalkboard.

Why remove your desk from the front of the classroom? The reason is simple. The desk in the front of the room is not only a physical barrier to be constantly walked around, but it also inhibits the teacher's physical proximity to the students. When the teacher's desk is in the middle in the front, the first row of students is approximately 10 feet from the chalkboard. This means that, whenever teachers go to the chalkboard, they place an extra 10 feet between themselves and every student in the classroom.

As an experiment, stand 15 feet from a couple of colleagues playing the role of disruptive students. Then have them look at each other and imagine their relative safety in goofing off in your class. Then walk 10 feet toward them and see if they feel the difference.

Any loss of power through loss of physical proximity that you create with your furniture arrangement will be multiplied by the number of students in the classroom times the number of minutes in the day times the number of days in the remainder of the school year. You must ask yourself if placing your desk in the middle of the front of the classroom is worth the stress.

Where to Place Yourself   The arrangement of furniture within the classroom exists to facilitate the teacher's mobility and physical proximity to the students. Consider for the moment the teacher's movement within two contexts: (1) giving corrective feedback to individual students and (2) explaining something to the whole class.

Giving Corrective Feedback   When giving corrective feedback the teacher either goes to the students or the students come to the teacher. If the students come to the teacher, the teacher is out of the action as far as discipline management is concerned. Students will goof off accordingly since the teacher cannot easily see or move. Soon the teacher will be nagging while seated.

Meanwhile, anyone standing in line has a license to either talk to a friend or do nothing while waiting for help. The students who want to stand and talk rather than work have a reason to seek help most often. Thus, the idleness of the teacher in giving corrective feedback from a seated position creates a reward for helplessness and idleness on the part of certain students who become the chronic help seekers.

When giving individualized corrective feedback during seatwork, the teacher's movement from student to student suppresses goofing off in the larger group while greatly increasing opportunities for work check and quality control (see volume two, *Positive Classroom Instruction*). The positioning of the body when giving corrective feedback is critical to keeping students on task. Teachers frequently turn their backs on the class unwittingly while giving help to an individual student, thereby relinquishing the monitoring of behavior. The lateral walkways allow the teacher to step between desks and turn so that she or he can directly monitor the class with peripheral vision while giving help. Such "withitness" replaces a teacher's reliance on "eyes in the back of the head," that is, on auditory cues for monitoring. These cues are not worth much since students can goof off all they wish without making noise.

Explaining Something to the Class   When explaining something to the class, the sitting position is equally disadvantageous. Take it from someone who makes part of his living by addressing large groups; you need only sit down for a minute or two to lose a third of your audience. The first four cardinal rules of public speaking which relate to the attention span of your audience are:

1 Stand up.
2 Move!
3 Create eye contact.
4 Vary the intensity, volume, and emphasis of your speech.

When you address an audience, sameness is death. Movement, variability, and intimacy continually renew the attention of the members of your audience; their minds are not allowed to wander. As in any teaching situation, room arrangement is vital to permit you to move, get close, make eye contact, and draw people back to the presentation from close range. Call it "working the crowd."

Even if you cannot rearrange your class for optimal contact with students during explanations and corrective feedback, you can still gain much of the advantage of proximity through movement. For example, chemistry lab teachers who cannot rearrange their furniture but who are constantly moving from lab table to lab table to monitor the progress of their students will achieve most of the reductions in classroom disruption that might typically be gained by an optimal room arrangement. It is only when teachers absent themselves from the class for several minutes by working with an individual student or by going to the storeroom that discipline markedly deteriorates.

Room Arrangement: Examples

Teachers with whom I have worked have arranged their classrooms effectively in many different ways. They succeeded as long as proximity and mobility were the primary considerations governing furniture arrangement. The room arrangements vary depending on the subject that is being taught, on the type of furniture that the teacher has inherited, on the size and shape of the classroom, on the number of students, and on the presence of immovable work stations such as lab tables, typewriters, stoves, and work benches. The most common and useful of these room arrangements will be presented in the following section.

The Typical Classroom   Classroom furniture typically comes in three sizes: individual desks, small tables for two students, and large tables for four to six students. Some variations will be presented for each of these types of furniture.

Individual Desks   Individual desks are the most flexible type of classroom furniture, permitting easy rearrangement and grouping for differing lesson formats. Three common U-shaped arrangements are pictured in Figure 4-2.

1 *Maximum access.* This first room arrangement has proved adaptable to a wide variety of lesson formats while making it easy for the teacher to move about. Students can see each other and the board easily. And the teacher, by creating an isle from side to side behind the second pair of desks in the middle, can easily move from corner to corner. This "all-purpose" room arrangement allows excellent physical proximity for lectures, group discussions, or corrective feedback during seatwork. Having students in pairs also facilitates team learning without the need to rearrange furniture.

2 *Short horizontal rows around a walkway.* This room arrangement is the most popular arrangement in secondary classrooms, particularly for math. If you take the standard room arrangement provided by the custodian and simply make an isle down the middle and push desks sideways so that they are close to each other, you end up with a version of this room arrangement.

3 *Herringbone.* The herringbone room arrangement is similar to short horizontal rows (above) except that the desks have been turned at a 45° angle. This room arrangement is often preferred by English and social studies teachers at the secondary level because it allows students both to see each other for discussions and to see the board. Open up the middle a bit and have the students angle their desks. This is particularly useful in narrow rooms where there is little space for aisles. Since access to students is via the center walkway, desks on the far right and far left can extend to the walls.

FIGURE 4-2
Typical arrangements of individual desks.

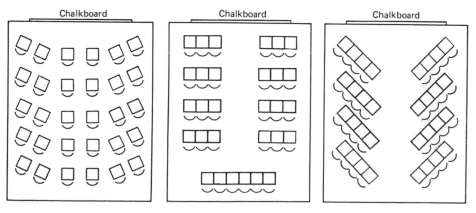

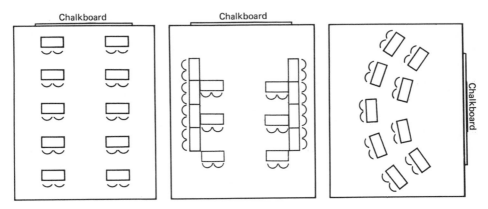

FIGURE 4-3
Typical arrangements of small tables.

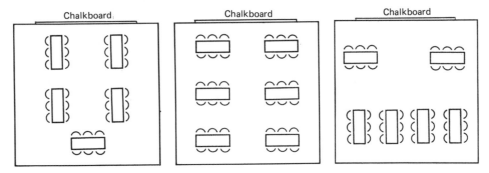

FIGURE 4-4
Typical arrangements of large tables.

Small Tables   Many classrooms are equipped with small tables, often trapezoidal in shape. Those arrangements pictured in Figure 4-3 are most common although variations are required by irregularly shaped classrooms.

1 *Rows.* Rows can be a simple and convenient arrangement, but it can become cumbersome when the class size is large and the number of small tables produce a long walkway.

2 *Double E* (EƎ). The Double E is a remedy for the long walkway that may be produced by rows. By placing some tables at right angles with others, the teacher can increase the seating capacity of a smaller area without sacrificing ease of movement from corner to corner and side to side.

3 *Semicircle.* The semicircular arrangement is particularly useful if the teacher is doing a demonstration in the front of the classroom.

Large Tables   Large tables are probably the worst piece of classroom furniture. They provide the maximum opportunity for students to disrupt by talking to each other

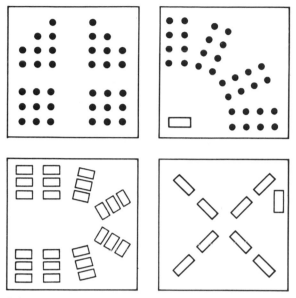

FIGURE 4-5
The "wheel": common departures from the U-shaped room arrangement.

and the minimum of flexibility for room arrangement and student groupings. Some of the more common arrangements with large tables are shown in Figure 4-4, the main objective being to cut your losses as much as possible. Do not, if at all possible, place a student at the end of a large table since that greatly facilitates conversation (unless conversation is your objective).

Miscellaneous Arrangements   Once teachers understand the rationale and objectives of room arrangement, they can ad lib and come up with some very creative and productive variations on the theme. Several are presented in Figure 4-5 as food for thought. As you can see, one of the most commonly preferred alternatives to parallel central aisles or a "U" is a "wheel" in which short rows radiate out from an open central area.

Special Classrooms   In special classrooms where the number of students is small, liberties can be taken with room arrangement that are not possible in a full-sized classroom. With a small group, a teacher can sometimes be stationary. If a teacher has only five students in a small group, for example, she can seat students around her at a table or place individual desks close around her and have the same advantages of physical proximity that could only be achieved by movement in a larger space. Even a primary teacher sitting on the carpet reading to students clustered around him may have a similar advantage of proximity.

With large groups ranging from twelve to fifteen students, a simple semicircle may do for individual work. For students working in teams, pairs, or committees, clustering

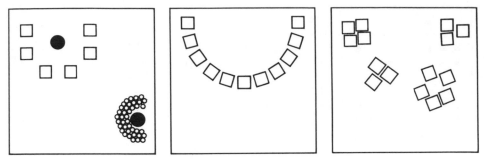

FIGURE 4-6
Typical arrangements for special classrooms and small group instruction.

around a semicircular walkway may provide the teacher with greatest access. Some examples of various small group arrangements are presented in Figure 4-6.

ASSIGNED SEATING

Once the teacher has arranged the physical layout of the classroom to make discipline and instruction as easy as possible, he or she must cope with the next problem of physical arrangement. Unless the teacher takes responsibility for placing the students in such a way as to facilitate discipline and instruction, the students will always do just the opposite.

Students' Choice

When students as a group are given the freedom to sit wherever they want in a classroom, they will always choose the location for themselves that is to the teacher's greatest possible *dis*advantage. As mentioned earlier, on the first day of class, the goof-offs always sit along the chalkboard in the back of the class next to their best friends, with perhaps elbows resting on the chalk tray. They may not have good grades, but they are not dummies when it comes to classroom management. Physical proximity makes them more accountable to the teacher. Consequently, they always place themselves at the greatest possible distance from the teacher where they can fool around and get away with it.

Where do the good students always sit? They sit in the front of the class where they will be noticed and called upon, of course. They are waving their hands in your face because they know the answer. As far as discipline is concerned, you can trust them at the back of the classroom, but they will never choose it of their own free will. Not only will they be called upon less often, but they will be hassled by the goof-offs who have had squatter's rights there since the first grade.

Teacher's Choice

What is the optimal placement of students as far as the teacher is concerned? Place the potentially disruptive students in the front of the classroom and near the walkway where you can easily monitor their activity, and place the students you can trust at the periphery. Proximity is accountability, and accountability is control.

Teachers can *prevent* a considerable number of the disruptions in their classroom simply by arranging the classroom properly, placing the students optimally, getting their own desks out of the middle of the road, and moving so that they are close to the action. In terms of cost-efficiency, these simple preventative steps are extremely shrewd since the cheapest intervention is structure, which eliminates the need for active management.

At the beginning of the year, however, the teacher may not know who the disrupters are nor who the good students are. Consequently, seating students randomly or in alphabetical order may be as good a way to start as any. By chance, some disrupters will be in the back of the classroom, and by chance some disrupters will be sitting next to their friends who are also disrupters. Inform the class that you will be making seating changes in a week or two and that you reserve the right to move students at any time during the year if their behavior warrants. As a result, no one will be surprised when you shift students' seating to your advantage. The first freedom that students lose when they choose to disrupt repeatedly is the option of being close to friends and distant from the teacher.

BUILDING RELATIONSHIP WITH STUDENTS

It takes *time* to build a positive relationship with another person—time in which caring and respect are exchanged. From the giving and receiving of caring, helping, concern, and respect a bond is built between two individuals that can be trusted. This bond is the basis of most cooperation and spontaneous helping.

When adults build a positive relationship with a young person, they place themselves in a position to influence the behavior of that young person. When two people share a positive relationship, pleasing the other person serves as a reward in its own right.

The mutual respect which is a by-product of a positive relationship readily translates for the young person into a respect for the opinions, rules, and values of the adult. That respect ultimately translates into corresponding action. When an adult is in the role of teacher or parent to a young person, a willingness by the young person to please the adult produces both cooperation and mutual appreciation. A reward for cooperation is a further enhancement of the relationship—a cycle by which the younger person is socialized into ways of behaving and believing that are similar to those of the adult teacher.

Relationship is by far the most effective and efficient form of behavioral management. As a by-product of mutual enjoyment the adult receives cooperation for the asking in a wide range of situations. To the extent that a young person can be socialized into appropriate patterns of behavior through relationship, other forms of management will not be needed.

In education positive relationship is referred to simply as *relationship*. To the extent that teachers invest themselves in building *relationship* with the students in their classes, they invest themselves in building a willingness on the part of the students to cooperate with directives and with classroom rules. To the extent that teachers withhold or fail in their attempts to exchange caring and respect with their students, they will have to use other means of discipline management to produce rule following. They are likely to have a very stressful year.

Problems of Anonymity: Or Why Are Junior High School Students So Difficult?

It is hard to care about someone who does not care to know you, and it is hard to feel responsible to an organization in which you are nameless. The basic fabric of social cohesion, caring and mutual respect, begins to deteriorate as soon as people become anonymous in a group.

Almost anyone who has taught or been a school administrator at various age levels will generally agree that junior high school is the most difficult age to manage. At that age students are more squirrelly than elementary students, and by senior high they seem to have mellowed somewhat. But during junior high school, ages 12 through 14, students tend, as a group, to be particularly "off the wall." Why are they so difficult?

The Hormone Hypothesis   The most common theory put forward by exasperated teachers and administrators is the "hormone hypothesis." Students are going through their early adolescence at this age, they have new hormones coursing through their veins, they have hair growing in strange places, parts of their bodies are developing, they are being attracted to each other, they are horny. How can you expect kids to keep their minds on their studies at a time like this? The hormone hypothesis does not say much for good students. It also provides a convenient excuse which diverts us from more basic causes.

Departmentalization and Anonymity   In trying to analyze why junior high students are so squirrelly and generally difficult to manage, most educators overlook the most radical discontinuity that has just taken place in the student's life. They have gone from a self-contained classroom to departmentalization.

In the self-contained classroom of the typical elementary school students have had a single parent surrogate for as many hours of the day as they typically spend with their natural parents. There are plenty of hours in the day for teachers to come to know the students, for students to come to know and trust the teacher, for experiences to be shared and for *relationship* to be built.

The parent-surrogate role of the teacher is particularly important for those children who come from negativistic or disorganized homes. Quite often the classroom teacher provides students with their only stable, positive relationship with an adult—one in which their activities are systematically regulated and behavioral rules are consistently and sensibly enforced.

When students graduate into junior high school, suddenly they are on their own. Departmentalization means that you have your own locker where you keep your own belongings, you are responsible to be at the right place at the right time with the right materials, and you are responsible for getting your work done under your own supervision. In departmentalization, students are treated as if they were mature and grown up.

For the socially mature student, departmentalization can be liberation. They are capable of looking after themselves, and they appreciate the greater latitude in regulating and managing their own affairs. They are free to develop new interests and to invest their time and efforts in ways which more nearly match those interests.

In a typical eighth-grade class, however, the social maturity of the students may easily range from age 5 to 25. Some students are ready for departmentalization and some are not.

The Internal Regulation of Behavior   A child learns responsibility by slowly being made responsible for more and more things within a structure that teaches, prompts, and rewards appropriate behavior. By degrees effective parents train their children not to need continual parental guidance in conducting their affairs. By degrees appropriate patterns of behavior are internalized along with corresponding values. The adult within grows until he or she becomes strong enough to consistently dominate decision making. Freedom and maturity are seen as the capacity to make the appropriate choice without coercion or internal conflict.

In many households, however, the source of behavior control is always *external* to the child. When the parent wants the child to do something, it is nag, threaten, and punish. When the parent wants the child to stop doing something, it is still nag, threaten, and punish.

When a parent habitually takes responsibility for *starting* the child's behavior by nagging, threatening, and punishing, the child learns not to begin until the parent initiates the sequence. Consequently, the child learns to be passive in the face of things that need to be done—a peculiar type of irresponsibility which frustrated parents refer to as "lazy" or "tuned out."

When a parent habitually *stops* a child from doing something by nagging, threatening, and punishing, the child learns to avoid censure and pain. The child learns not to do certain things when the parent is available to nag, threaten, or punish. But control is always an external force, a prohibiting and frustrating force that is resented. Freedom, therefore, is conceptualized in external rather than internal terms. Freedom is the absence of the external authority who is "keeping me from doing what I really want to do." Power is seen as negating the external authority by counterforce or deception so that "I can do what I want to do." Potency, pride, freedom, and self-esteem are positively associated with winning a power struggle against external authority and rule enforcement, and the self-regulation of behavior fails to develop. Moral maturity is arrested at an early childhood level.

When students who have only the capacity for internalized behavior regulation of a young child enter into departmentalization, they are being asked to do something that they have not been prepared to do. They are being asked to govern their own affairs by acting upon a system of internalized controls and values which has never been built. To them, the lid is off! Without any ever-present parent surrogate to act as police, it is time for them to see what they can really do if no authority is there to stop them.

The 50-Minute Parent Surrogate   The odds are stacked against the secondary teacher in building relationship. For the immature student who has just lost their all-day parent surrogate (the teacher from the self-contained classroom of elementary school), the personal respect and caring that can supply motivation for rule following has just been eliminated. A secondary teacher may see over 150 students a day for 50 minutes at a time. That is not much time to pick up the slack that has just been dropped by the transition from a self-contained to a departmentalized situation. Yet, the secondary teacher must pick up the slack or pay a high price by having to put up with misbehavior from many directions.

How can teachers begin to build relationships quickly in the first days and weeks of school? The same basic techniques apply at all grade levels, but the following discussion will focus on the secondary level since secondary teachers have the hardest job to do in relationship building. This discussion of relationship building will be of limited scope due to limitations of space. It will not deal with personality variables and communication skills. Those are topics for an additional book. In this section we will limit the scope of our discussion of management skills to the specific activities that help to structure the teacher's efforts to get off on the right foot within the first few days of the school year. Additional aspects of building patterns of cooperation within the classroom will be the topic of the later chapters on responsibility training.

Beginning To Build Relationship

Getting to Know Each Other

Names and Demographics   On the first day of school, get every student's name, address, and home phone number, parents' names and addresses (if different), and their work addresses and work phone numbers. Have every student put this basic information on a card for your *card file,* and have them put the information on any additional forms you will need for record keeping. *Do not* rely on the office to provide this information for you. They are usually too disorganized and understaffed at the beginning of school to get this information together before Thanksgiving.

The many uses of the card file will be explained in subsequent chapters, but the first use is to help you learn the students' names. One of the most common complaints from high school students is: The teacher doesn't even know my name! Students do not usually put themselves out for a teacher in whose class they are anonymous. You can find out which teachers at a high school are effective in relationship building simply by asking the parents which teachers their children do homework for. Students do homework for teachers who know them and show that they take a personal interest in their students.

Ice-Breaking Activities for the Students   Breaking the ice is one of the important relationship-building objectives for the first day of school. Students need to know each other, they need to feel at home in the classroom, and they need to know that the teacher cares about them. It is a wise investment, indeed, for the teacher to spend time at the beginning of each semester allowing the students to get to know each other, particularly at the secondary level.

Many teachers have learned some ice-breaking or warm-up activities from taking a human relations course at some time, but few teachers use these activities in their own classes. Often, from the best of intentions, teachers will begin the first day of school with their first assignment and leave relationship building and comfort within the learning environment to take care of themselves. Perhaps we need a greater appreciation of the "human relations" dimension of all learning experiences.

Teachers need to feel that they have permission to take the time for warm-up activities, and they need an adequate repertoire so that all the teachers on the faculty are not using the same one or two "chestnuts." The following list will help the faculty begin to build a repertoire of warm-up activities so they may be as varied as possible and so that teachers can feel comfortable with their choices.

A In-depth sharing
  1 *Humana.* Humana is a simulation activity that allows students to get to know each other around issues of values clarification. Humana is part simulation and part discussion. The dilemma that the class faces is the aftermath of a final nuclear war. Each person must imagine that they have been chosen to be placed within a chamber to be sealed off from all contamination for at least a year. Life support will be provided, but in addition each individual can take only ten things. What would they be? Group discussion quickly becomes problem solving and values clarification as students consider everything from hygiene to loneliness.
  2 *Glasser circles.* Glasser circles developed by Dr. William Glasser incorporate a group-discussion and problem-solving format. Topics commonly used for the first day of school might include (1) my biggest fear, (2) my biggest hope and dream, (3) the best thing I did over the summer, etc.
  3 *Life space interviewing*
    a Students pair up and interview their partners. This interview may be structured to a moderate degree by the teacher providing a list of topics to be covered. Interviewers will want to get specifics such as details about family, pets, hobbies, and special interests. Students then go around the room and introduce their respective partners to the class.
    b Teacher interviewing. Teachers can do a lot of relationship building while getting to know their class if, during the first month of school, they simply call students aside and ask them about themselves in a manner analogous to that described above. Simply getting to know the students allows them to feel at home in the classroom and known by the teacher. No sharing with the group

is necessary. This activity might be done in lieu of life space interviewing on the part of the students.

B Graphics

1 Draw a picture that tells about you. Having students begin the year with a brief art project, even at the secondary level, will be both relaxing and welcome. After each student has drawn a picture that tells about him- or herself, he or she tapes it on, walks around the room, and asks the others to explain the pictures.

2 Design a T-shirt that tells who you are. A variation on the activity described above, designing a T-shirt press-on design that shows something about yourself, once again breaks the ice as students ask each other to explain their designs.

3 Photographs. Teachers who take every student's picture on the first day of school have made a wise investment. Photos not only serve as an aid to learning the students' names, but they also serve as an aid for the students getting to know each other. Simply post the photos on the bulletin board. The extent to which the photos stimulate social interaction can be greatly increased by having students bring pictures of themselves as a baby in order to have a contest in which students match current pictures with baby pictures. You can also have humorous contests for baby picture categories such as cutest, meanest, most confused, etc.

C Miscellaneous activities

1 Form groups according to student's place in the family (oldest, middle, youngest). Have the students discuss and list things that they have in common and share advantages and disadvantages of place in the family with the class.

2 "Find the person who . . ."

a Write ten characteristics of yourself. Each person writes ten characteristics of him- or herself in order of importance leaving his or her name off the paper. The teacher reads the first item of each student's list and the rest of the class tries to guess who it is. The process is repeated until the person is identified.

An alternative format is to read all of the "number ones" on the lists in turn going around the room having everybody guess on the basis of first items only. You can have teams. The winner of "round 1" is the team with the highest percentage correct. The process can be repeated with the second, third, and fourth items on the list being added until everyone gets to know their classmates.

b Answering questions in a group. In a simplified version of the Glasser circle, the teacher asks questions for everyone to answer out loud in turn. Begin with some fairly mundane questions and progress to some more revealing questions such as hopes and fears for the year, things that are most important to you, etc.

3 The name game. In the name game students form a circle with their desks and hang 3 × 5 cards on the front of their desks with their first names on it. The first person begins the game by saying his or her first name plus either a rhyme, an adjective, or a nickname. The second person does the same and then repeats what the first person said. The third person does the same and then repeats the second and first persons' names and nicknames. By the time the game has gone around the room, the person has a lot of names and nicknames to remember, but they have the name cards on the front of the desks to aid them, and students are directed to quickly supply missing information if the participating student gets stuck. As simple as it is, this game usually generates a lot of laughing and kidding while it helps students to associate names with faces. Of course, the teacher goes last, and by the end of the class, they probably know most of their students' names.

4 Scavenger hunt. Construct a list of particulars for each person in the classroom either on the basis of life space interviewing or by having students answer a series of easy questions. Collect the lists, shuffle them, and hand them out. Each person's job is to find the person described in her or his list by walking around and asking questions.

5 Introduce yourself. Not to be forgotten, having people take turns standing up and introducing themselves is the oldest one in the book. Yet, when people come from diverse backgrounds, it can be one of the most effective. Having each person address one or two common issues can greatly enhance sharing.

Ice-Breaking Activities for the Teacher   Getting to know each other is a two-way street. Who are you and what are you doing here?

1 Tell about yourself. Allow yourself to be known so that you are a person rather than a figure. Students warm up to you more rapidly when they know who you are. Share some interests and even a few foibles as well as strengths.

2 Share positive goals and aspirations about teaching. Talk about teaching as your own chosen profession from among the same range of career alternatives that will face the students in a few years. Share with them the sources of gratification that you find in teaching. This bit of calculated self-revelation can easily lead into the topic of what makes a good classroom and related topics of mutual consideration, respect, responsibility, and the need to enjoy the process of learning. You are now ready to introduce responsibility training to your class if you wish (see Chapter 9.)

Having Fun Together   As we will learn in later chapters, it is impossible to operate incentive systems in the classroom without learning to have fun as a class. Good classroom management thrives on the enjoyment of learning. Responsibility training, to be described in later chapters, literally requires it.

The times in which a class has fun together as a reward for a job well done are referred to as Preferred Activity Times (PATs). Preferred activity time will become a regular part of classroom life as your management system becomes operative. A by-product of responsibility training and the preferred activity time that accompanies it will be the building of relationship.

Helping Students Do Their Work   As we will find in volume two of this treatment of classroom management, *Positive Classroom Instruction,* the way in which teachers typically help students who are "stuck" with their work produces most of the failure experiences in education. It is during corrective feedback that students learn just how and to what extent they "blew it." In addition, teachers typically get to help only a relative few of the students who need help. There is never enough teacher to go around.

When corrective feedback is done properly, it will *always* be supportive. And, when corrective feedback is given efficiently, it can be given ten to fifteen times more often during a work period while at the same time training the student to work independently. This means, in practical terms, that students who need help will receive help repeatedly during the work period rather than only once, and the help will always be supportive.

One of the major by-products of effective corrective feedback during independent work is the relationship building that comes from frequent and supportive helping. Students who need help and get help repeatedly and supportively from the teacher come to respect and care for that teacher as a result of the frequent contact and personal help. Especially at the secondary level, the quality time that serves to build relationship will always be in short supply unless it is built in as a by-product of correct discipline and instructional methodology.

THE PARENT CONNECTION: RELATIONSHIP BUILDING BEYOND THE CLASSROOM

Needing the Parent

In dealing with parents, a teacher has two alternatives. Parents will be either allies or adversaries. There is little middle ground. For teachers who have prepared the groundwork by extending themselves toward parents effectively, parents can be invaluable allies in dealing with both minor and major problems, discipline as well as motivation problems such as turning in homework. If, however, the first time parents hear from a teacher is at a time of crisis, the teacher has probably created an adversary. It is the parents, after all, who are on the defensive. It is their child who is in trouble. Anxiety is high, defenses are high, and blaming begins.

If you want the parents on your side, be *pro*active rather than *re*active. Build the support in advance so that you have it for the asking when you need it.

Methods of Relationship Building with Parents

Sharing Classroom Rules   Once the class has established their basic rules and standards, put these rules and standards in written form. The form varies greatly from teacher to teacher ranging all the way from a simple list to a classroom constitution. After the rules and standards are in written form, send a copy home to the parents. The parents need to know what rules and standards are governing their child's classroom for the coming year, and they will be appreciative of being informed.

Make Early Personal Contact

Elementary School   During the second and third weeks of the school year, call the parents of every child in your classroom. Make five calls a night so that the job is not burdensome. Do not make lengthy calls; you cannot afford the time. Make it a simple call which accomplishes the followings tasks:

1 Introduce yourself.

2 Share with the parents the kinds of skills that will be learned at your grade level this year.

3 Tell the parents something *positive* or endearing about their child (something the child has done in class, a special talent, a good piece of work, a strong personality trait).

4 Tell the parents that you *need their help*. Talk about your need for their support in conveying to their children the seriousness of the rules and structures in school. Discuss how achievement at school is always a cooperative effort between home and school in which parents and teachers work together to help kids over the rough spots.

5 Mention the written rules that you sent home during the previous week and answer any questions that the parents might have about them.

6 Ask if there is anything special that you should know about their child, such as a medical condition.

Some teachers find it more convenient to schedule a single evening meeting at school for the parents of their class in order to cover essentially the same material that would be covered in the phone call. If half the parents show up, you will have only half as many calls to make.

Secondary Schools   Making personal contact with the parents of your students at the secondary level is more difficult than at the elementary level because a single teacher may see over 150 students a day. That is too many calls to make unless you're bucking for sainthood. The following alternatives may be more practical to a secondary teacher.

1 Phone calls to the parents of the twenty or thirty students who are likely to have the most problems. You cannot call everyone, but you may as well do your best to enlist the help of those parents whose children are most likely to tax your management system.

2 Intermittent calls. Pull the names of two students out of a hat for each class period each week. The parents of the students whose names were drawn will be called over the weekend. In the resulting conversation strengths and assets will be the primary focus, but problems will also be discussed. It is amazing how an on-going, random, spot-check system of feedback to parents can both put students on their toes regarding the following of classroom rules and generate good will from students and their parents. Literally *anything* personal says that you care.

3 A letter home. A form letter home can convey essentially the same information that might be conveyed over the phone. Although less personal than a call, it is a clear attempt to reach out and to communicate, which will be appreciated.

4 The ombudsman system. More and more secondary schools are adopting programs in which each first-year student is assigned a faculty member as an ombudsman. While the nature of the program varies from school to school, in many cases each ombudsman personally visits the homes of a group of students who have been assigned to them. In other cases, the ombudsman makes a phone call similar to that described above for elementary teachers.

As long as the student is at that particular school, their faculty ombudsman will be the person that they or their parents can always contact should a problem arise in which they need access to the administration or to a particular teacher. It is easy for educators to forget that most parents see the school as an unapproachable brick and granite institution and that approaching school with a problem as akin to fighting city hall. Even though the ombudsman system represents an obvious expenditure to all involved, most educators I know who have tried it would never go back to the old way.

Send Work Home Regularly   Sending work home regularly with a provision for parental feedback opens a communication link which will produce greater parent involvement in school and will allow the teacher greater access to parents in solving problems.

The Folder System (Elementary)   At the elementary level the teacher would be advised to send home a folder of the child's work every Thursday. The first writing assignment of the year, in fact, may be the following:

> Dear Mother and Father: This is the folder work that I have done in school this week. It will show you the kinds of assignments that I have been given and the kind of work that I have done. Some of the papers have been graded and some have not been graded. Please look over my work and sign your name in the space at the bottom of the page. If you have any comments, write in the space provided.

The folder system does more than simply send work home so that parents can monitor the quality of their child's performance. It says continually to the parent that the school is looking for their involvement. It also establishes an open communication link so that parents can easily send a message back to the teacher that they might otherwise let slide. Consequently, it is an early warning system to the teacher so that, should the parents perceive a problem with their child, the teacher can get to the parents quickly to deal with it preventatively.

Folders and Projects (Secondary)   Secondary teachers often see the folder system as an elementary school option. Ironically, many secondary classrooms are ideally suited for the folder system, especially in classes in which there is regular written work and homework.

Many secondary teachers, however, prefer to send work home aperiodically—when a project or a unit has been completed and turned in. Whatever the occasion for sending work home, the value for the teacher of regular, structured communication with parents will be no less at the secondary level than at the elementary level.

Preventative Conferences   As mentioned earlier, teachers and parents will either be allies or adversaries when they meet to deal with a student's problem. A conference with a parent while the problem is small can be a relatively relaxed, constructive dialogue. A conference with the parent whose child is in deep trouble is unlikely, in many cases, to be very relaxed, amicable, or even constructive. Deal with problems proactively when they are small by having a brief conference early rather than a horrendous conference later.

Commendations   Students, both old and young, need to be told from time to time in a public and explicit way that they are doing a good job. Students need to hear the news and they need their parents to hear the news as well. Incentive systems within the classroom easily spill over into the home if the teacher simply takes the time to send out the news.

Commendations take many forms. At the elementary level they may be "happy-grams," special awards or just a personal note on a piece of work. At the secondary level, a personal note is most common. The topic of commendations will be dealt with more thoroughly in a later chapter. For the time being simply getting into the habit of writing brief commendations home will be a valuable habit for teachers at all grade levels.

Some teachers expand the notion of sending commendations home and combine it with the folder system to have a weekly evaluation system. A weekly evaluation system can contain (1) samples of the student's work, (2) the child's self-evaluation, (3) the teacher's evaluation, and, (4) room for parent comments. Such a weekly evaluation system is compatible with sending home commendations if the teacher uses positive language in describing the child's strength and the child's needs for improvement.

Home Programs as Needed   The time may come when a special management program is needed which involves the parents directly. The more powerful the classroom management technology of the teacher, the less likely will be the need for home-based management programs. Home-based management programs have many liabilities not the least of which are (1) extensive conferencing, (2) the expense of training parents to do their job properly, and (3) the expense of fixing the programs when the parents drop the ball. Nevertheless, home programs, usually incentive systems for behaving well at school or for completing schoolwork, can be of great value in special circumstances when done properly.

Later sections of the book describe some of these home-based management programs (see Chapter 13). For the time being, however, keep in mind that the cooperation and the conscientiousness of the parents in carrying out any program will probably be a function of the amount of relationship building that you have done in advance.

THE FIRST WEEKS OF SCHOOL

The teacher who is laying the groundwork for a successful, enjoyable, and low-stress teaching year will have invested a great deal in classroom structure by the time the first week has ended. The many suggestions that have been put forth in this chapter are reviewed briefly below as an aid and checklist for the teacher.

Before They Arrive

1 Make lesson plans for teaching rules.
2 Systematically review your management system.
3 Plan your room arrangement.
4 Plan ice-breaking activities and your first *PAT* (see Chapters 9 and 11).

Day One

1 Meet the students at the door with instructions for slowing down and taking a seat immediately. You may wish to hand them numbers which correspond to the number on their desks.

2 Introduce yourself.

3 Have students fill out 3 × 5 information cards (names, address, home phone, parents' place of work, work phone (s)). This structures the first few minutes while you deal with late arrivals.

4 Introduce your general rules and have students copy them into their notebooks. This structures some more time while you make out your seating chart by alphabetizing your information cards.

If you arranged your seats in advance and handed out numbers at the door, placing corresponding numbers on a 3 × 5 card on each desk will greatly facilitate making out your seating chart. Have the students use the opposite side of their 3 × 5 number card which was lying on their desks as their information card. The number card allows students to quickly find their desks, and it also allows you to quickly match students' names to their proper place on your seating chart.

5 Put names on desks. At the elementary level have students letter their names on a large piece of heavy paper or cardboard and tape it on the front of the desk. At the secondary level have everyone print their first name on a 3 × 5 card in big letters and hang it over the front of the desk with a piece of tape.

6 Arrange desks (if they are not already arranged) in the room arrangement of your choosing.

7 Have an ice breaker. One of the easiest and most effective ice breakers is the name game. The name cards displayed prominently makes the game safe by providing a prompt for each person's name, and students spend the whole time associating names with faces.

8 Describe and discuss your classroom rules and procedures and expectations in more general terms. Open up the discussion to characteristics of a good classroom and include the things that both teachers and students do to make a classroom both enjoyable and productive. This exchange brings you to the topic of being responsible and taking *responsibility* for one's own actions.

Secondary teachers will be at the end of their first hour with each of their class periods by now. Continue with the topic of responsible behavior in your second class meeting and introduce responsibility training.

9 Initiate responsibility training with your class during your second hour together (see Chapters 9, 10, and 11). Explain your objectives and procedures carefully. Limit-setting (Chapters 5, 6, and 7) will be in effect from the first moment of school and does not require formal introduction as do other procedures. You may, however, wish to explain limit-setting later in the school year as a lesson in interpersonal effectiveness.

10 Carefully explain your back-up system (Chapters 14, 15, and 16) so that students have a thorough grasp of your classroom management options for dealing with severe disruptions as well as school site rules and policies for following through in dealing with severe or recurrent problems. The more that students know about the discipline system, the more they will respect its coherence and thoroughness and the less likely they will be to gamble foolishly.

The First Week of School

1 Continue rule building.
2 Teach your procedures and routines one by one.
3 Develop a *written* summary of classroom rules.
4 Send the rules home.
5 Assign chores and establish a routine for students doing the chores.
6 Send the first folder of work home on Thursday.

The First Month of School

1 Call the parents and/or establish your ombudsman system.
2 Begin sending home commendations.
3 Have preventative conferences as needed.
4 Continue teaching your rules, procedures, and routines one by one.
5 Review the relevant rules, procedures, and routines with every lesson transition.

OVERVIEW

In structuring the teaching environment as in the teaching of classroom rules, if you want to be successful you must pay your dues up front. You must be proactive in structuring the situation so that the occurrence of problems will be reduced and so that their severity will be minimal should they occur.

Teachers who expend the effort needed to structure their learning environment and their parental support system early in the school year reap the dividends all year long. Teachers who let such structuring slide because it is "too much hassle" or because they have "too many other things to do to get the year started" pay for their folly during every succeeding school day. Being proactive is always cheaper than being reactive. Prevention is always cheaper than remediation. Pay your dues in advance so that you can work your way out of the necessity of establishing order continually throughout the school year.

SECTION **THREE**

LIMIT-SETTING: HOW TO
MEAN BUSINESS

LIMIT-SETTING:
PENNY-ANTE GAMBLING

Rules define limits, but they do not establish limits. Children by their nature will test limits. They must, in fact, test limits in order to define and clarify their reality. They will say to themselves, You said it, but is it really so? To find out whether it is really so—whether the edifice of your classroom structure is solid or just a two-dimensional stage prop—they must push against it to see whether it stands or falls down.

How will we respond to limit testing? How will we enforce our rules when misbehavior occurs? What will be our first line of defense? The answers to these questions have broad practical as well as ethical implications. At a practical level, how can we deal with misbehavior easily—at low stress to both teacher and student? At an ethical level, how can we deal with even oppositional and obnoxious behavior without being backed into punition? It is one thing to want to be kind toward children, but it is quite another to have the skills that permit us to respond both effectively and gently toward a student's provocation. When dealing with limit testing, it is easy to mouth values but hard to deliver.

We have discussed the importance of keeping discipline both positive and cheap. In fact, both these characteristics of effective discipline are not only inseparably linked, but they also apply to the child as well as the adult. The price of punition— the traditional folk wisdom of discipline which ultimately ends in our "laying down the law"—is exorbitantly high for everyone involved. It means upset and burn-out for the adult, but it also means rejection and alienation for the child. The cost of punition is unacceptably high because alienation destroys relationship. It drives a wedge between teacher and student that will ultimately destroy the child's motivation to cooperate. And now with alienation and without cooperation, what price will teacher and student pay for the enforcement of rules?

INTRODUCTION TO LIMIT-SETTING

Meaning Business

Most teachers have known a colleague or two over the years who seemed to have a way with classroom discipline that was almost magic. These "naturals" at classroom discipline almost invariably attribute a large part of their success to the fact that they "mean business." Yet, they never seem to raise their voices, they never seem to get upset, and they never seem to have any difficulty getting students to behave and to follow directions. By the second week of school they can go to the office for a 10-minute emergency parent conference and return to find the class still quietly working.

When something appears magic, colleagues make up magical explanations. The most common magical explanation is the "genetic hypothesis." Some people are just born with it. There are specific genes for classroom discipline. Another magical explanation is the "hypothesis of uncanny selection." Some teachers just manage to get the worst kids year after year. By implication other teachers must somehow be servicing a different student population. Yet another magical explanation is the "silent terror hypothesis." While the teacher who makes it look easy is in all likelihood calm and relaxed around children, colleagues will express their envy and amazement by statements such as, "I don't know what they do, but by the second day of school those kids are so intimidated that they wouldn't dare act up!"

In beginning to learn about limit-setting we will begin to take the magic out of meaning business and replace magic with method. But before meaning business is understood, we will have to explore some of the enduring subtleties of human relationships that are the source of so much misunderstanding about meaning business.

Over the years my colleagues and I have studied and come to understand the process by which certain teachers can train their classes with apparent ease to respect classroom rules and routines, to respect each other, and to respect the person of the teacher. Our attempts to decode the process whereby highly effective teachers convey to their classes that they mean business, however, were initially extremely frustrating. One of the reasons that meaning business was initially so difficult for us to decode was the fact that it is almost entirely *body language*—skills which the effective teachers can neither label nor explain.

Body language is a subtle language which all of us "speak" and instinctively "read" but which few of us can consciously decode. Body language is not only a subtle language, but meaning business with body language runs counter to much of our folklore and most of our instincts concerning classroom discipline. Thus, in order to learn how to mean business in the classroom, we will have to learn a great deal about body language.

Limit-Setting, Body Language, and Interpersonal Power

The body language of meaning business is subtle enough to defy observation and yet powerful enough to train an entire class to respect and comply with an effective teacher's classroom rules within a few hours or a few days. Ironically, the body language of meaning business is also extremely gentle and protective of the student. We call

this subtle, gentle, yet powerful process of enforcing classroom rules "limit-setting."
One might think of limit-setting as *the gentle art of interpersonal power.*

The Unavoidable Issue of Power   Sometimes students follow classroom rules
because they wish to. That is cooperation. Sometimes students follow classroom rules
because they feel that, under the circumstances, it would be the wisest course of action.
That is control.

Control by a teacher can be either heavy-handed or gentle. Yet, control will always
have its part to play in the drama of classroom discipline simply because goofing off
is a constantly available and pleasurable alternative to the rigors of learning. Limit-
setting is gentle control, and it soon trains the class to follow classroom rules out of
habit and out of a genuine desire to cooperate.

The enforcement of classroom rules, however, is ultimately an issue of interpersonal power to a considerable degree. The questions at stake for the student are: Will
I follow the classroom rules and do what I am expected to do now, or will I do something else of my own choosing? Will I do it the teacher's way, or will I do it my way?
Who is controlling whom? In interpersonal relations *control is power, and power is
control.*

Power as a Part of Life   Interpersonal power comes with you when you are born.
You transmit it to those around you in one form or another at all times whether you
want to or not. Power is exchanged between people whenever they meet as they communicate self-assurance by their bearing and eye contact even before words have been
spoken. The irony of limit-setting is that the issue of power and control can be resolved
so gently. Yet it should not really be so surprising that power and gentleness can be
highly compatible in the relations between adult and child. How else could gentle,
loving parents raise gentle, loving children who know right from wrong and who respect both the rules of fairness and the parents who enforce them?

When someone is highly skilled at conveying interpersonal power, they are typically described as diplomatic, confident, self-assured: they mean business. The fact
that a mild-mannered gray-haired lady who never raises her voice can be powerful
enough to get consistent rule-following from a roomful of students all year at no apparent effort while being described as kind and supportive would suggest that we have
a lot to learn about interpersonal power and control. It would also suggest that perhaps
many of our stereotypes about interpersonal power are inaccurate and misleading.

Overpowering   The most traditional and misleading stereotype about the personality capable of wielding interpersonal power depicts one who acts and talks tough.
This kind of people have power by virtue of being overpowering. They lay down the
law and tell you how it's going to be. They get discipline by demanding it. Leadership
of this stripe kicks ass and takes names. It seems to be modeled after drill sergeants in
the movies. The basic notion seems to be that students will finally shape up when they
see that you are about to get angry. Call it "management by adrenaline."

Underpowered   In sharp contrast to the notion of gaining interpersonal power by
exuding hypertension is the vain hope that if we are simply loving and patient and
lucky, we won't have to deal with the issue of power at all. Many adults feel uneasy
and even squeamish at the notion of consciously exercising power over children in

order to control their behavior. The idea of wielding power and control in relation to a child often conjures up a vision of power which is overpowering, harsh, and arbitrary—an image, perhaps from one's own past, that is frightening and distasteful.

A great many adults are, therefore, highly ambivalent about being assertive with children. This ambivalence will be conveyed immediately with their body language as hesitancy and vulnerability. In the classroom such vulnerability will, unfortunately, give rise to a vicious cycle in which fear of power produces a greater abuse of rules by the students owing to the teacher's not meaning business. Yet, given enough bad experiences with coercion during their own childhood, capitulation may seem the lesser of two evils to many adults.

Limit-setting is in a class by itself among methods of rule enforcement in its capacity to skillfully navigate the shades of gray that separate coercion and capitulation. It is only in this area that adults can exercise power sufficient to carry out their proper role as enforcer of appropriate rules and definer of limits without distasteful power struggles that are as stressful as they are destructive of relationship. Before we become capable of such finesse, however, we must learn exactly how power is most effectively communicated by our bodies.

The Power in Limit-Setting

Calm Is Strength   The basic irony of meaning business—of exercising interpersonal power to gain rule compliance at seemingly little effort—can be summarized in two statements: *Calm is strength. Upset is weakness.* When you are calm, who is in control of your mind and body? You are, obviously. When you are upset, who is in control of your mind and body? The person who is upsetting you, of course.

Control is power, and power is control. The question of power is, simply, *who is controlling whom*? Any person who is upsetting you has power over you because at that moment he is controlling you. Signalling that you are about to lose control of yourself by getting upset, therefore, is the antithesis of interpersonal power. *Do not imagine that you will be able to control anyone else, particularly a classroom full of young students, until you are in control of yourself.*

During the time in which I was coming to understand the power politics of the classroom, and in particular the power of calmness in my teachers who were "naturals" at discipline, my eye was drawn to a sign on the wall of a roadside restaurant. It was a timely bit of folk wisdom: "My life is in the hands of any fool who makes me lose my temper." The power of calmness and the control of interpersonal situations which is mediated by self-control has, I am sure, been observed and commented on by folk philosophers and saints alike over the ages. Yet the strength of serenity has a natural enemy in biology. As long as our bodies are programmed for the fight-flight reflex under conditions of threat and provocation, we will have to spend part of each new day coming to grips with the ever-present destructiveness of our natural tendency to become upset in response to an unruly child.

Perhaps the most enduring misconception of most people concerning the exercise of interpersonal power, therefore, is the equating of power with force. Indeed, most people, I imagine, would look at you most skeptically if you were to assert that the two were unrelated. Overpowering a child with threat or coercion can, as anyone knows, put a speedy end to an unacceptable behavior. Is that not power, or is that only the illusion of power? Ask, will your use of such power *self-eliminate*? Will children learn to follow rules when you are *not* there to enforce them? Will they resent the enforcement and thereby have an incentive to break rules in your absence? Most people would find it strange if you were to assert that power and force were unrelated, and more yet would find it strange if you were to assert, as we will, that within the context of enduring human relations power and force are not only unrelated but *negatively* related.

Relaxation Training and the Body Language of Power   Body language is the language of emotions. It is by our body that we telegraph feelings and intent, usually before we are consciously aware of them ourselves. When teachers respond to a classroom disruption, their intent, their confidence, and their commitment to carrying out that intent are immediately apparent to all. Even an 18-month-old reads body language, as do your dog and cat, and students only get better as they get older. Your level of arousal is only the first cue among many that your students will read in order to learn whether or not you are one of those few teachers who know how to mean business.

Relaxation and Willpower   It is difficult to relax in the face of provocation. Yet, relax you must if you are to be in control of your own mind and body. Teacher training in the area of limit-setting, consequently, includes a considerable amount of relaxation training.

Perhaps the hardest lesson to learn about relaxation is that relaxation is *not* an act of the will. Rather, relaxation is a skill, and, like any other skill, it is learned by practice, practice, practice. Teachers cannot simply decide to be relaxed so that their students will not get to them anymore. Rather, teachers must be trained to systematically relax themselves in situations of provocation in which all their natural reflexes are designed for emotional mobilization. Considerable practice is required to create a new set of reflexes that is strong enough to override the natural mobilization reflexes of the body.

Relaxation Skills   One of the most useful cues for self-relaxation is a *relaxing breath*. The use of a simple breathing exercise to induce relaxation is a common self-relaxation cue used in many forms of relaxation therapy, stress management, and prepared childbirth training. A relaxing breath is an ordinary breath—a slow, shallow breath that fills one-third to one-half of your lungs. You do not inhale suddenly or fully since to do so is part of the fight-flight reflex and is therefore incompatible with relaxing. Rather, a relaxing breath is the kind of breath that you might take if you were bored or about to doze off. Whereas a relaxing breath is quite unremarkable when you are calm, it is quite an accomplishment when you are being provoked.

The relaxing breath does two jobs: (1) it calms your mind and body, and (2) it slows you down and paces you so that your movements are unhurried. It signals your mind and body to unwind and wait before proceeding. With training it triggers a learned "let down" reflex which counters the mobilization of fight-flight.

Without extensive training most teachers will tend to do the steps of limit-setting far too rapidly while remaining upset. They will thereby squander most of the potential effectiveness of self-control and interpersonal power that might have been conveyed by limit-setting. Relaxing breaths, therefore, are central to implementing the notion that calm is strength and upset is weakness.

The Objective of Limit-Setting

Your objective in limit-setting is to *calm the students and get them back on task.* Your emotions when you are attempting to get the student back on task are, however, contagious. If you are calm, you will calm the student. If you allow yourself to become upset, you will upset the student, and for that upset you will pay.

If you allow yourself to become upset, you will immediately affect the student in two ways, both of which are highly counterproductive. *First,* you will generate resentment, and it is for this resentment, compounded with public humiliation, that you will pay most dearly. *Second,* your upset will trigger a shot of adrenaline into the student's bloodstream just as it did into your own bloodstream. That adrenaline will not be out of either of your bloodstreams for approximately 28 minutes, and during that time the student will be hyperreactive to external stimuli and will have a shortened attention span. When a teacher yells at a student, the student does not do much schoolwork for the remainder of the period. The reasons for this loss of learning time are both psychological and physiological.

Real interpersonal power is the power of calm in which room is left for both parties to retain their dignity and sense of volition—the door is constantly left open for affirmation and, if necessary, reconciliation.

The Limit-Setting Sequence

Limit-setting is the most cost-effective method of dealing with the typical forms of classroom disruption: talking to neighbors, out of seat, and general fooling around. When used properly, limit-setting will eliminate from 70 to 90 percent of the disruptions in a typical classroom. It is basic to all other methods of classroom management as well because all techniques of management rely to a greater or lesser extent on the students' perception of the teacher as meaning business. Limit-setting is also basic in another sense because the body language of limit-setting will appear in every subsequent method of dealing with classroom disruptions.

In this chapter and the next I will describe limit-setting as a predictable series of transactions between student and teacher—a sequence which proceeds by degrees from "penny-ante gambling" through "high rolling." Being able to understand the gamesmanship of goofing off in the classroom will forearm the teacher against becoming rattled by the unexpected and "blowing it." Knowing what to do next, no matter what happens, gives teachers peace of mind—especially when they finally realize that meaning business is really the *art of doing almost nothing* from a series of eight predetermined locations.

Breaking limit-setting down into its parts, however, misrepresents it since it usually occurs during the fluid, unobtrusive movements of the teacher about the classroom.

Effective teachers make discipline invisible, and they will almost never stop what they are doing to perform an eight-step routine right in the middle of class unless severely provoked. Unobtrusive limit-setting is "working the crowd"—the pattern of continuous mobility during seatwork, lectures, and group discussion that either prevents goofing off or nips it in the bud.

Working the crowd, better known as limit-setting on the wing, is described in detail at the beginning of Chapter 7. Working the crowd during seatwork, however, is the subject of the first two sections of *Positive Classroom Instruction,* the companion volume to this book. Until both volumes are read and understood, it is impossible to fully understand limit-setting within the context of instructional methodology and classroom management as a whole.

Think of the limit-setting sequence, therefore, as "body practice"—a series of drills that is used during systematic teacher training to help teachers gain control of their bodies under conditions of provocation which might typically produce upset. Think of it also as a kind of game plan: a decoding of the moves the other person is most likely to make so that yours may be poised rather than off-balance. Only with practice and experience will the moves of limit-setting become wedded with the moves of effective instruction so that they become invisible.

The limit-setting sequence is a set of reflexes that become increasingly second nature with practice. Each step represents a decision point for teachers as they respond to a student's behavior at that moment. At any step the progress of the limit-setting sequence may be terminated by the teacher if the students return to work. There are three major blocks of behavior in the limit-setting process: (1) moving in, (2) dealing with back talk (when necessary), and (3) moving out.

In our analysis and description of the limit-setting sequence we will use the most common disruption in the classroom as a vehicle for describing the unfolding sequence: two neighbors talking to each other rather than working. At each step in the sequence, we will imagine both the students returning to work and the students escalating their misbehavior. In this fashion we can follow the teacher's thoughts as she decides to move in (escalate) or move out (deescalate). The point at which the students return to work marks the end of the teacher's "moving in" and the beginning of the "moving-out" sequence.

As we examine the process of limit-setting, we will walk through a series of vignettes or scenarios in which students disrupt with increasing intensity. In this chapter we will deal with the low-intensity "fooling around" of typical classroom disrupters. In the next chapter we will deal with more provocative and outrageous behavior—the "high rolling" of the discipline game. In Chapter 7 we will look at both common variations as well as realistic limitations of limit-setting in the classroom.

LIMIT-SETTING SCENARIO 1: "JUST TESTING THE WATER"

Moving In

Limit-setting always progresses according to the same series of steps. The only variable is the number of steps that the teacher will use before the students return to work.

Through body language both the teacher and the students carry on a *dialogue of interpersonal power.* It will be the teacher's objective to resolve the issue of power and control effectively: by having the students return to work without the use of any form of punition.

Step 1: Eyes in the Back of Your Head   The first skill of limit-setting is to know what is going on in the rest of the room. You cannot respond to a disruption if you are unaware of its occurrence. This capacity for teachers to monitor or "track" what is going on in the *entire room,* behind them as well as in front of them, is sometimes referred to as "withitness."

Monitoring the entire classroom is made easier by *standing so that you can survey as many students as possible with your peripheral vision* or with a quick glance. Especially when helping a student who is working at her or his desk, place yourself so that little will ever be going on *behind* you. If you cannot monitor the class with your eyes, however, you will have to monitor it with your ears. Practice listening to what is going on around you and behind you—the scoot of the chair, the giggle, the rustle of paper. Then check it out with a glance. If nothing is happening, a look has cost you little.

The constant monitoring of the classroom, if it is not a habit now, can become one if you make it a preoccupation for a period of time. Some teachers either overfocus on the student they are helping or have learned to cope with disruptions by not paying attention to them. Such habits, although perhaps difficult to break, are an invitation to disaster. Students always gamble against the odds of getting away with disruptions, and failing to monitor students provides them with an invitation to gamble. See Figure 5-1.

Step 2: Terminate Instruction   Imagine that you glance up to see a pair of students talking to each other and fooling around across the classroom, and you catch the eye of one of them. The dialogue of body language has just begun. There is no turning back now without paying a very high price. You have both just lost your innocence.

What if you do turn back around and ignore the disruption for the moment while you complete your instruction with the student you are helping? What lesson did you just teach? You just taught your disrupting students that you do not wish to deal with a typical classroom disruption contrary to your stated rules. This is not a lesson that you can afford to teach. The two students already have your number as does anyone else who cared to observe.

Imagine, instead, that the dialogue of body language begins differently as you give signs of meaning business. As soon as you see that the students are disrupting, no matter how small (80 percent of disruptions will be simply whispering to neighbors), *immediately terminate instruction.* Break your sentence in midstream, abort your thought, make a hand gesture to the student you are helping to show that you are stopping with him. Quickly excuse yourself with a few words such as:

- Excuse me, Philip.
- Just a second, Sandy. I'll be right back.

FIGURE 5-1
Eyes in the back of your head.

The act of excusing yourself after seeing the disruption will occur within a time span of milliseconds. It is not a judgment call—something that you briefly weigh or debate within yourself. It is a reflex.

For any student who happens to be watching your body language, you have just telegraphed your most basic behavioral priority within the classroom (and it is always the disrupters who will be watching you most carefully). Your priority for dealing with discipline is simple: *Discipline always comes before instruction!* Why does discipline always come before instruction? The reason is not a matter of theory or philosophy but, rather, a practical matter. It is impossible to read, write, or do arithmetic while goofing off with your neighbor. First, take care of discipline to create *time on task.* Until you do that, your instruction is wasted. See Figure 5-2.

Step 3: Turn, Look, and Say the Students' Names   As soon as you have excused yourself from the student you have been helping, stand, turn all the way around, relax, and wait to see what they do. This movement sounds simple enough, but remember that body language is a subtle language. There are at least a half-dozen ways to do this simple movement wrong, each one of which will greatly reduce your effectiveness. A lot can happen very quickly in body language, so let's slow it down and look at the pieces one at a time.

The Mechanics

TURN AROUND   Turn around *completely* and face the students *squarely.* For the time being the disruptive students are the most important students in the classroom,

FIGURE 5-2
Terminate instruction.

and they will receive the teacher's *full* attention. The sooner the students can read the signal, the sooner they will respond to the inevitable.

Many teachers will turn around only partially. A failure to face the disrupting students squarely by as little as 10 to 20 degrees signals to the students that you have not made a full commitment to dealing with them. You have just said in body language, "Hey, give me a break. I'm trying to teach over here." Do not expect the disrupters to give you a break. Such a partial gesture will have almost no effect.

LOOK THEM IN THE EYE   Make eye contact with one of the disruptive students, preferably the biggest disrupter. Eye contact is one of the most sensitive barometers of emotional calm or upset on your body. *Unwavering eye contact* on the part of the teacher signifies calmness, which is interpreted as self-confidence.

Have you ever talked to someone who would not look you in the eye? You probably concluded that they were anxious, uptight, or not sure of themselves. Poor or furtive eye contact is universal body language that even your dog or cat can read. To quickly reduce your power in the interaction, you need only look around a bit or glance away from the student once or twice.

To put it technically, the easiest way to reduce anxiety is to look away from the fear-producing stimulus. At any moment the vast majority of sensory input is usually visual. Eliminating visual input reduces the intensity of the frightening experience. That is why people often instinctively wince and close their eyes during a scary or gory part in a movie. It is a self-protective, comfort-producing reflex. Looking at a potentially fear-producing stimulus, in contrast, indicates that you are not particularly afraid.

When your eyes dart around so that you break eye contact, you signal to the students that you are uncomfortable and anxious. Seeing the body language of stress, they rightly conclude that you do not want to stay in this situation, much less follow through. They are obviously more comfortable in the situation than you are. Do not expect them to give up what they are doing even though you might get an innocent smile.

Yet, although eye contact is nice, it is not necessary for successful limit-setting should it not be forthcoming from the students. In some subcultures, especially oriental, hispanic, and native American, children will not make eye contact in a disciplining situation since to do so is a sign of impudence and disrespect. In anglo and black subcultures, in contrast, eye contact is typically expected as a sign of paying attention, and looking away is typically interpreted as disrespect. Parents in these subcultures may say, "Look at me when I'm talking to you!" Take it as it comes, and move on. The student will know that you mean business soon enough through a variety of other signals.

FACIAL EXPRESSION   The next critical piece of body language is facial expression, or, to be more specific, *smiling*. Without repeated training in total relaxation (which leaves your face expressionless) many teachers will have a pleasant curl at the corners of their mouths as they say the students' names. Far from being an innocuous pleasantry, this piece of body language is crucial. To appreciate its importance one needs to first understand that in primates "smiling" (baring the teeth) and in the extreme case "grinning" widely and "laughing" (a shrill staccato in monkeys) is *submission behavior.* Baring the teeth and "laughing" stops fights and, in particular, the competition of mating fights between male monkeys.

In humans smiling or laughing in a stressful situation also constitutes "submission behavior"—the desire to terminate the competition. A common but fairly intense everyday example of submission behavior in humans is "nervous laughter." It says, "I'll be your friend if you'll be my friend, OK?" If two people are meeting for the first time, reciprocal submission through smiling is a ritual which allows everyone to relax with the understanding that the situation is noncompetitive. Everyone wants to be everyone else's friend.

In limit-setting even a slight smile says, "Ah, come on. I sure would appreciate it if you guys would quit fooling around and get back to work. Let's not take this any further, OK?" Do not be surprised if you get no results.

If, in contrast, you are *relaxed,* your face will be *expressionless* as you maintain perfect eye contact with the biggest troublemaker. Wait. Do not be surprised if they smile. You have their submission. They very much want you to smile back—to say, in effect, "Aw, it's all right." Instead, *relax* and wait. Think of yourself as Queen Victoria who, in responding to a bad joke, said, "We are not amused." As you wait you too are not amused, nor are you upset. You are simply waiting as the student decides what to do next.

When I ask teachers during training to describe the effect this bland facial expression (actually a lack of expression) in conjunction with proper body orientation and eye contact has on them, they often say things like: "I want to find a place to hide!", "I give up," or "Yes, you mean business. Now please stop!" They attribute great power to a facial expression that is, in fact, no expression at all. You have to tense muscles to make a facial expression. They are responding, rather, to the sum total of body language which consistently communicates across all channels the message, I know what I am doing, and I am both thoroughly comfortable with it and committed to doing it.

ADDITIONAL BODY CUES Every part of the body speaks, and contradictory messages of calm and upset are usually interpreted as upset. It is impossible to fake relaxation and self-control. Even if you slow down and try to take the edge off your voice, students can still tell exactly how upset you are by whether your jaw is set or how wide open your eyes are. They can read these subtle cues from across the room, and they will behave accordingly.

While we are standing and facing students, we convey calmness by relaxed posture. When we speak, the higher in the air our hands are, the more animated or upset we are. Let your arms hang comfortably. Even arms folded or on your hips often conveys impatience, a form of upset. You may place your hands in your pockets or at your side if you prefer, but I suggest placing them behind your back at the beginning since it hides nervous mannerisms with your fingers.

SAY THEIR NAMES Say the students' first names only, say them once only, and say them loud enough to be heard. Say the names with a bland or flat feeling tone in a matter-of-fact fashion. Be neither sweet nor sour. Sweetness says, "I'll be your friend if you'll be mine" and sour says, "Do you want a fight?" Since your emotions are contagious, you will get exactly what you give. Blandness on the other hand conveys calm which conveys self-control just as in facial expression. See Figure 5-3.

The Emotional Part Step 3 of the "moving-in" sequence is something of a sleeper. It looks simple at first blush, yet it contains the most difficult skill in the limit-

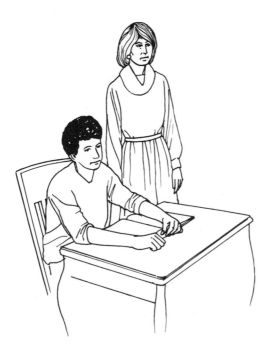

FIGURE 5-3
Turn, look, and say the student's name.

setting sequence—*total relaxation*. Self-relaxation in response to provocation is the real beginning of limit-setting, in fact, since it is the most crucial, most frequently used, most difficult to master, and most easily forgotten skill of the entire limit-setting process.

We are used to turning and swinging into action when provoked. It is part of the fight-flight reflex which constantly seeks to undo us. Our mouths are open and our nerves are on edge before we have even had time to think.

> All right, the two of you. Turn around and get to work! I'm tired of looking over there and seeing you fooling around!

One of the hardest parts of step 3 of limit-setting is learning to turn, physically commit ourselves, and then "swing" into *inaction*.

As was mentioned previously, one of the most effective self-relaxation cues is a "relaxing breath." It is slow, gradual, and shallow. Relaxing breaths are taken in minimal doses of two at a time. If you are ever in doubt as to what to do next, take two more relaxing breaths and wait. Once you have made a move, it is up to the student to decide what to do next, so be patient. Two relaxing breaths take about 15 seconds. Relaxing breaths are taken at the following times during step 3:

* Turn around fully and face the disruptive students.
* Make good eye contact with the most disruptive student (or look directly at him or her if she or he fails to look at you.)
* *Relax* (two relaxing breaths).
* Say the students' first names loud enough to be heard.
* *Relax* (two relaxing breaths).

The Decision to Stop or Continue   As you stand waiting after having said the students' names while taking two relaxing breaths, you must make a decision to continue moving in with limit-setting or to stop moving in and begin moving out. If the students are back to work, the teacher stops. Remember, the objective of limit-setting is simply to calm the students and get them back on task. Many times a teacher can terminate a disruption simply by turning fully, looking at the students, and waiting. Consequently, the rule of thumb is: *Do not go any further with the limit-setting sequence than is required to produce the desired result.*

But, beware lest skillful students fake you out! They may be giving you "smiley face." How can you tell if they are really going to get back to work or whether they are going to start talking as soon as you turn around? In order to answer this question you must be able to predict the future. How can you predict the future? It is now time for you to read *their* body language if you want to know what to do next.

The Transition to Moving-in Step 4

Reading the Student's Body Language   While you are looking one of the students in the eye, check *underneath* the table with your peripheral vision. That part of the student's body that is *above* the tabletop will tell you *nothing* about the student's intention since it will be part of the "smiley face" routine. The real story is told by students' *knees and feet*. Until students' knees and feet are turned all the way around underneath their desks so that their bodies are facing directly forward and they are working, you have accomplished nothing! They have not made a thorough physical commitment to returning to task. A student with a knee pointing toward a neighbor will usually continue talking to that neighbor as soon as you let her or him alone.

Beware of pseudo compliance! Students who turn halfway around have not committed themselves to getting back to work. Partial compliance is designed to throw you off the scent. In fact, the school of hard knocks has taught us that, if students are turned four-fifths of the way around in their desks yet are not fully around facing their work, in their minds they do not have to comply. Consequently, you will get nothing for your efforts. So, be a stickler! Students are reading your commitment as you are reading theirs.

If a student looks at you as though to comply while leaving the lower portion of the body partially turned toward a neighbor, she or he has just taken limit-setting one step further. Continue to step 4 of the "moving-in" sequence.

The Discipline Poker Game Students are game players with the issue of compliance to classroom rules. In watching the exchange of teacher and student moves in the dialogue of body language over the years, I have thought most of the following analogy. Limit-setting is a poker game—a continuous body-language poker game that begins during the first minute of the school year and runs until school is out. Those students who have an eye toward fooling around a bit rather than getting to work know the odds of success at any moment. With limit-setting the teacher responds to rule-breaking with calm, clear signals of meaning business. Students read the odds and gamble accordingly.

Poker is an infinitely subtle yet basically simple game. You look at your cards and you either ante up or fold. You either pay to stay in, or you cut your losses and get out. It all depends on your cards and your nerve. If you think you can take the hand, you either match the bet on the table or you raise the bet. When the price of playing poker exceeds the strength of your hand, you turn your cards over and fold. Good gamblers do not throw good money after bad.

If you have a distaste for gambling, put it aside for the moment. Simply regard limit-setting as a poker game of body language in which student and teacher raise each other until somebody folds. The poker-game analogy just might help you get "inside" the dialogue of interpersonal power spoken in body language.

Teachers who mean business must train their students early in the school year that disrupting is a gamble that they cannot win. If the teacher has the cards, which she will if she knows how to do limit-setting, then she need only play her cards one at a time and continuously raise the ante until the high rollers in the class fold. Then everybody knows the odds, and for most of the class the gambling is over.

Limit-setting self-eliminates as soon as the class becomes convinced that the teacher always holds the winning hand and can take the pot at will with no upset. When the teacher knows how to play the game, the students' shrewdness at gambling becomes an advantage to the teacher since good gamblers never throw good money after bad. Play your hand out early in the year with those most eager to bet against you until you have made your point. Then you will have trained the rest of the players to fold early.

The poker game goes fast, however, and the hapless teacher who does not know the game that is being dealt does not stand much chance of winning. Imagine, for example, that the teacher simply looks at a student who is goofing off on the first day of school and then continues individual instruction with the student that the teacher was previously helping. The game is already over, and the class knows the odds. The teacher is the dealer, and the students have just opened the betting at a nickel. The teacher looks at the bet and turns away from the disrupting students to continue instruction. Turning away is the body language of folding. The students just beat the dealer and took the pot on a nickel bet. Not much of a management system.

Imagine, instead, that the teacher "sees" the nickel bet (eyes in the back of the head), terminates instruction (step 2 of limit-setting), turns completely, looks squarely at the disrupting students, relaxes, says their names loud enough to be heard, relaxes again, and waits (step 3). The teacher has just seen the nickel bet and raised it to a dime.

Now the students must look at their cards and rethink the situation. If they want to go to 15 cents, the students need only sit facing toward each other while giving the teacher "smiley face." They are waiting the teacher out, but the teacher can relax for the time being since it is the students' move. After a moment the students just might turn around and start working. They know what is expected of them, and they have just acknowledged your savvy and commitment by their folding at 15 cents. If the students have not turned around and resumed work after the required number of relaxing breaths, the teacher must either raise the bet to 20 cents by proceeding to step 4 of limit-setting or fold and get out of the game.

Pheasant Posturing   At this point in the betting it is helpful to become acquainted with the term "pheasant posturing." Male pheasants are noted for putting on quite a show for the sake of spectators during the mating season. A pair of male pheasants spread their feathers and fly at each other squawking and clawing ferociously in a battle that, to a first-time observer, would clearly appear to be a fight to the death. To a seasoned observer it's just the same old squawk and dance. For all the noise and fury, male pheasants never hurt each other—not even a scratch.

Pheasant posturing has therefore become a term in anthropology that is used to describe people's behavior when they are trying to make a lot of squawking and flapping look as though they are really going to do something when, in fact, they are not. It may look like the end of the world, but in the language of the poker game it is all bluff.

Teachers often make an art form out of pheasant posturing as they fold in the poker game of limit-setting. They turn, and, rather than taking relaxing breaths, make the cardinal error of opening their mouths with a timely reprimand which might sound something like this:

> All right, you two! I want to see you turn around and get to work! I'm tired of looking over there and seeing you fooling around. Now, this material is going to be on the test. Do you understand? When I get over there, I want to see some of it done!

In response to some looks of contrition, the teacher then *turns back around* to continue instruction. What does their body language say? The teacher just folded. She turned around and left without getting compliance of any kind from the students (look at their feet and knees)! She folded with her body in conjunction with some clap-trap nagging that passes for discipline only to someone who is unable to discern pheasant posturing from meaning business. If you don't think students can spot pheasant posturing a mile away, you had better think again.

Step 4: Walk to the Edge of the Student's Desk

The Mechanics   If the students simply look at you after having heard their names but do not turn their bodies completely around and get to work, walk in a relaxed and fairly slow fashion to the edge of the more disruptive student's desk and stand upright for *two relaxing breaths*. Walk at an unhurried pace similar to that which you might use while walking across your own living room to pick up a magazine. Do not hesitate or stop in midcourse under any circumstances, and do not stop until your legs are touching the edge of the student's desk. Stand calmly, stand up straight, and shut up as you look at the student and take your two relaxing breaths. Do not repeat the students' names (they know their names), and do not repeat classroom rules (they know them too). This is not the time to speak.

Why do you take two relaxing breaths and wait at the edge of the student's desk? *First,* you need to calm yourself down. *Second,* you need to give the student time to calm down. And, *third,* you need to give the student time to think and make a decision. Cooperation is, after all, a voluntary behavior under the control of the other person. Far better that the students decide to get back to work than that you push them. Besides, this poker game is rigged so that you always play the same hand in the same way with the odds stacked in your favor, so give the student a minute to calculate and conclude that cooperation is a shrewd move under the circumstances. See Figure 5-4.

Decision to Stop or Continue   If the student in front of you suddenly decides that it would be a good idea to turn all the way around in his or her seat and get back to work, wait until he or she has been working for a while and then begin the steps of "moving out." If, however, the student has not turned *all the way* around and thoroughly invested him- or herself in getting back to work, proceed to step 5 of the "moving-in" sequence. If in doubt, take two more relaxing breaths and then decide. In this scenario we will imagine the student getting back to work, which signals the beginning of "moving out." In the next scenario we will take limit-setting further.

Moving Out

As mentioned earlier, getting a student back on task is only the first part of limit-setting. This is accomplished by "moving in." Keeping the student on task is accomplished by the steps of "moving out." Even though a student's staying on task can never be guaranteed, its likelihood can certainly be maximized if moving out is given as much care and consideration as moving in. If done sloppily, moving out can pull the rug right out from under moving in.

FIGURE 5-4
Walk to the edge of the student's desk.

Step 1: Thank Them, Wait, and Relax

Thank the First Student   When the student in front of you returns to work, watch her work for at least two relaxing breaths (15 seconds)—long enough to see that she is well into the task. Then lean over and gently and sincerely thank the student using her first name. "Thank you, Jennifer." The "thank you' is genuine and warm. This is no time to be sarcastic or cute. You have a lot to be grateful for.

Wait, Relax, and Kill Time   Next, stand in front of the first of the two students and watch her work some more. She may look up at you to see if you are still there. When she sees you waiting and watching, she will have learned a lesson. You are *serious* about her getting back to work. It is literally worth your time. By investing time in this fashion you have signaled commitment with your body. Killing time at the right time is an extremely important facet of body language. If students look up and find you gone, you may expect their conversations to continue.

Move to the Second Student and Wait   As a point of strategy, always go to the bigger troublemaker first. If you do not, the students will perceive that you have signaled a reticence to do so. If you go to the "accomplice" first and he or she folds, the instigator may feel obliged to up the ante as a matter of pride and principle. If, on the other hand, you go to the bigger troublemaker first and he or she folds by getting back to work, the second student will almost always be on task by the time you get there.

Nevertheless, if the second student is already on task, go to him and give him *equal time*. If you do not, you have picked on one student while letting the other one off the hook. Stand in front of his desk for at least two relaxing breaths and watch him work.

Thank the Second Student and Wait After watching him work for two relaxing breaths, lean over, thank the second student exactly as you did the first student, and watch him work for at least two more relaxing breaths. Remember, time spent watching students work at this point is interpreted by the students as commitment and follow through. It is as though they were saying to themselves, "Gee, this person must really be serious about this whole thing!" Indeed, your commitment to the student's returning to work was powerfully transmitted by your body as you simply waited, watched, relaxed, and killed time.

Step 2

Return to the Student You Were Instructing After thanking the students and watching them work for a while from the edge of their desks, turn and walk back to the student you were originally helping before limit-setting began. Imagine for now that there is no further disturbance or "parting shot" from the students.

Walk away slowly. Quick movement says in quite unmistakable body language, I want out of here. As a general rule in limit-setting, *speed kills*. Moving in fast means you are upset, and moving out fast says you are uncomfortable. You can never go wrong by slowing down and taking your time.

Turn and Wait Before you do any instructing, turn and look at the disruptive students for at least two more relaxing breaths. They will probably glance up at you, and when they see you still monitoring their behavior, they will in all likelihood resume work. They have been taught once again that it is *worth your time* to ensure that they return to task. You are serious enough and committed enough to take the time to follow through. You mean business.

LIMIT-SETTING SCENARIO 2: "PUSHING A LITTLE HARDER"

Let's imagine a new scene which begins like the last one but which ends a bit differently. When you walk across the room and stand in front of the students' desks, they just look up at you as if to say "big deal." What do you do next?

Moving In

Remember that the sequence and nature of the steps of moving in never change. We simply add some new steps.

Step 1: Eyes in the back of your head
Step 2: Terminate instruction
Step 3: Turn, look, and say the students' names
Step 4: Walk to the edge of the students' desks

Step 5: Prompt We are now in new territory. You have walked to the edge of the more disruptive student's desk and you have taken two relaxing breaths while watching and waiting, and the student has not budged. In the body-language poker game, the student just saw you and raised you again. Now it is back to you.

The Mechanics   Lean over at the waist while resting your weight on one palm and give the reluctant student a prompt—a message that tells him or her *exactly* what to do next. The prompt will often have both a physical and a verbal component. The *physical* component of the prompt may consist of moving the student's work around in front of him and away from a partner, handing the student a pencil, opening his book, and/or taking some diversion away such as a paper airplane, a piece of paper with a tic-tac-toe game on it, or an object that the disrupters have been playing with. The physical prompt is a gentle way of redirecting the student's attention back to the task at hand. You may also motion in the air with your hand for the student to turn around in her or his seat but *do not touch the body.* Body pushing is an act of provocation that is especially resented by teenagers.

The *verbal* part of the prompt is equally straightforward: one or two simple, declarative sentences that tell the student exactly what to do next. Tell the student to turn around (all the way) and begin work on a specific task. Keep it short and keep it simple. Do not engage in repetition of the student's name, repetition of rules, or blaming of any kind. Typical verbal prompts might be:

- Turn around in your seat. Let's begin copying the next problem.
- Put your feet under your desk—all the way around. That's good. Now, let's finish this paragraph.
- Jimmy, you have two more problems until you are done. Let's finish them up.

After having given the prompt, *stay down,* look at the student, and take two relaxing breaths. This gives the student time to realize that you are not leaving until she or he complies and the student gambles accordingly. It also gives you time to judge whether the student is going to comply. Students who have been "playing dumb" up to this point usually fold since to fail to do so is overt disobedience, which raises the stakes. Having one hand on the desk also gives you close physical proximity and improved eye contact which can be highly persuasive. See why we call this moving in? See Figure 5-5.

Decision to Stop or Continue   If the student gets back to work, watch him or her work for two relaxing breaths, thank the student, and *stay down.* Take two more relaxing breaths as you watch the student work, and then move sideways (no need to stand up) to the second student's desk to repeat the process. If either student fails to turn around and get back to work or if either student begins to talk to you, continue to step 6.

Do not engage in formal instruction at this time. Do not respond to the student's apparent need for help by reexplaining something. The reasons for this will be discussed more fully in the next chapter, which deals explicitly with the topic of back talk. For the time being, simply realize that any formal instruction at this point in meaning business signals to the student that you can be sidetracked by a little helplessness. The proper way of getting instructional help as part of your classroom structure should be thoroughly understood by all, and we will assume for now that talking to your neighbor is not it. For now, the only relevant question is one of compliance;

FIGURE 5-5
Prompt.

will the students return to work and do the best they can without your help or will they escalate the betting by their failure to turn around and get to work?

Step 6: Palms   If the prompt has not produced a student who is back on task, lean slowly across the desk and place both your palms *flat* on the *far side* of the student's desk on either side of his or her work. Rest your weight on your palms with elbows locked and take two or more relaxing breaths while continuing eye contact. This movement brings your upper body and face almost a foot closer to the student's face than step 5—eyeball to eyeball, so to speak.

Sometimes a student may not pay much attention to your moving in until he sees your hands on his desk. This is particularly likely if last year's teacher let him talk all he wanted. If the student has not looked at you before this point, he will look at you now. The body language of "palms" indicates that you are there to stay. You have planted yourself. Look at the student, take two relaxing breaths, shut up, and wait. Do not repeat the student's name, do not repeat classroom rules, and do not get sucked into an instructional interaction. See Figure 5-6.

As you move across the student's desk from the semistanding position of prompting to "palms," move slowly. Do not "swoop in" since it is upsetting rather than calming to the student. One teacher whom I trained described the speed of this movement most vividly as "oozing in." It is impossible to imagine oozing in suddenly or rapidly.

Moving Out

The vast majority of students will find within themselves a good reason to be on task by this time. It is a fool's choice to continue disrupting with a teacher at such close

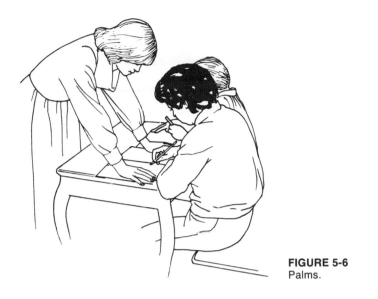

FIGURE 5-6
Palms.

range, especially one who seems calm and confident and especially one who seems to have all day to give to such matters.

If the student does not yet know you well enough to realize that you mean business, he or she may foolishly continue to look at a neighbor or attempt to avoid the confrontation by some delaying or diversionary tactic such as back talk or excuse making. Take two relaxing breaths. We will deal with such tactics in the next chapter.

If in contrast the student has quieted down and gotten back on task, watch him work for two relaxing breaths, thank him, and *stay down* for two more relaxing breaths while you watch him work. Then move to the second student and repeat the entire process including the "thank you" and the relaxing breaths. Stand in front of the students' desks for two more relaxing breaths as you watch both of them work and then continue "moving out" exactly as before.

Please realize, however, that only rarely does a teacher get beyond step 6, even with a difficult class. The effective use of relaxation, slowness, and physical proximity is incredibly powerful, and most students are smart enough to realize that the best bet at this point is to fold and get back to work. Most teachers report after training that they have never had the opportunity to go beyond palms although they would like to do so just to try out the rest of the limit-setting sequence. In fact, few report ever having gotten to palms.

OVERVIEW

So far we have examined the anatomy of limit-setting up to the point where normally squirrelly students in regular classrooms usually leave off. If a student opens her mouth to make excuses or give you back talk, she is high rolling—the subject of the next chapter. For now simply focus on the fine points of body language and remember that if you do it right and pay your dues up front by taking enough time with disruptions early on, you will rarely have to repeat the process. The cost effectiveness of limit-setting or any other successful discipline technique does not come from its being cheap the first time out but, rather, from the fact that, when done properly, it self-eliminates over time.

Throughout limit-setting the teacher is constantly communicating with the student in a dialogue of body language along three primary channels. These channels and the messages communicated by each are:

1 Confidence: calm
2 Commitment: time
3 Intensity: proximity

Once one understands the main channels of communication and the messages being sent, the irony of communicating interpersonal power with body language becomes more apparent. Any time you want to increase your power, (1) shut up, (2) slow down, (3) relax, (4) get close, and (5) kill time. Get upset and you immediately begin pheasant posturing.

Limit-setting, then, is little more than calmly *killing time from a series of predetermined positions.* As the students bet, you move in. When they fold, you stop, prompt them back to task if necessary, thank them politely, and slowly move out. The students can bet as much as they want, but if you know how to play the game, you cannot lose. Power is control, and control begins with self-control. Stay in control of yourself long enough and you will eventually control the situation. Yet, in a sense, the students are in control because they can get rid of you any time they want—by getting back to work.

LIMIT-SETTING: HIGH ROLLING

High rolling begins when back talk begins. When a student opens his or her mouth, the stakes in the limit-setting poker game gain the potential for rapid escalation. Yet, although it is the student who decides to create the problem, it is the teacher's response to such verbal provocation that will determine whether the problem gets better or worse. It is the teacher's job to have enough sense to relax and keep his or her mouth shut so that the teacher can play *his or her* game instead of the student's game. It is the teacher's job to keep the stakes as *low* as possible for everyone.

Back talk is an artistic medium in which students display stunning creativity. Back talk comes in every conceivable form from a compliment to vile profanity. Dealing successfully with all the imaginable varieties of back talk would be a hopelessly complex task if teachers were to fight fire with fire in an attempt to talk their way out of the situation. Any student worth his or her salt will always have the last word.

By attempting verbal countermeasures the teacher inadvertently structures a game of "Can You Top This"—that thrill-a-minute contest of wit and mental agility in which student tries to outwit teacher. Each verbalization by the teacher produces the next verbalization by the student as the student attacks, defends her- or himself, or plays "wronged and righteous" in an attempt to gain ultimate victory. By not knowing when to shut up, the teacher institutes an incentive system that rewards bigger and better back talk.

THE OBJECTIVE OF BACK TALK

For the teacher ever to experience a sense of invincibility in the face of such a broad and dazzling array of verbal flim-flammery, the teacher has to grasp one simple, central, relief-producing truth: All back talk is the same.

All back talk is the same insofar as it all has the same objective. The objective of back talk is *control,* of course—the central issue of power politics in the classroom. Consequently, back talk is a power play regardless of the specific form it takes. The goal of the "lippy" student is to control the situation with talk, throw the teacher off-balance, change the subject, derail the teacher, and ultimately get *off the hook.* Whether sweet or accusing, whiney or nasty, back talk is an attempt to turn the tables on a teacher who is attempting to mean business—a predictable tactic when the ante has been raised and the student experiences some heat.

In coming to appreciate the gamesmanship of back talk, it is helpful to be reminded of one of the basic rules of controlling a public meeting. Who controls a public meeting even before it begins? The person who controls the *agenda,* of course. If you want to bring up some important issue at the meeting that others do not wish to deal with, you can be thwarted by simply being told that there is no room left on the agenda to deal with your concern. Sorry—maybe next week. Your important issue has, in fact, already been dealt with.

Back talk is a public meeting of sorts which conforms to the same rules of power, namely, who controls the agenda controls the meeting. Your agenda as a teacher is simple: will you get back to work or do I continue moving in with limit-setting? Any other topic which the student brings up is an attempt to change the agenda and abort the objective of limit-setting.

All forms of back talk, therefore, attempt to get the teacher to *sucker for some side issue other than the student getting back on task.* The changes in agenda typically proposed by students are fairly predictable. Not all of them are overtly nasty, however. In fact, some of the most consistently effective are cleverly camouflaged so as not to sound the least bit unpleasant. Knowledge of the terrain will forearm teachers lest they fall for some of the oldest "sucker plays" in the book.

The following section will describe the standard types of classroom back talk in order of ascending nastiness. Remember, however, that all forms of back talk are variations of the same control game, just varieties of bologna. Do not let the *content* disarm you into foolish responding. If you listen to the content and take it too seriously, you may just get upset and sucker for the bait.

TYPES OF BACK TALK

The Seven Basic Varieties

There are seven major types of back talk in the classroom, and they have probably remained unchanged since the days of the Greeks and the Romans. Each generation of students seems to reinvent the same old tactics. Some forms of back talk are *non-confrontational* and have as their objective simply tricking the teacher into pursuing an important-sounding side issue rather than the central issue: Will you or will you not get back to work? Other types of back talk are *confrontational,* a more naked use of provocation or nastiness to gain control over the interaction. Whether nasty or nice, blunt or sly, all back talk is cut from essentially the same cloth. Once you know them, they all appear as fairly blatant attempts to get off the hook. The basic types are:

Type 1: Helplessness   When using helplessness, the student attempts to sidetrack the issue of discipline into an issue of instruction. Make a pained request for help with the assignment and see if the teacher bites. A request for help usually comes when the teacher prompts the student to get back to work or at the moment the teacher moves in to palms. Who can turn down a student who seeks only to understand? Some examples:

- But I don't understand how to do this.
- I will if you'll just show me how.
- I keep getting the wrong answers. Can you help me figure out where I'm making my mistake?
- I feel like quitting. I'm so frustrated! I just don't understand this assignment.

Beware! Helplessness is the "sucker play" of all sucker plays. Most of the teachers who get hopelessly sidetracked while first learning to do limit-setting get wiped out on the helplessness gambit. Most teachers, in fact, do not even perceive helplessness as a form of back talk (until informed otherwise) because it is not overtly nasty or obnoxious. Unaware of the change of agenda that is about to take place, they perceive it as an expression of genuine need independent of the discipline agenda.

But the student knows the score, even if the teacher does not. If you are drawn into a helping interaction in the middle of limit-setting, the issue of discipline is put on the shelf. The agenda of "will you or will you not get back to work?" has been replaced with "how do you do this?" The student is off the hook. You fell for it!

The consummate skill of students in diverting teachers from meaning business by a show of helplessness has produced our next rule of limit-setting: *Never mix discipline and instruction!*

Why never mix discipline and instruction? Because if you do, you have just rewarded the disruption! You have taught a lesson to the class.

> If you disrupt in my class, you may get away with it. If you do not, I may come over to your desk to set limits. If at that point you play helpless, you will get the same tender, loving, one-to-one, individual help with your schoolwork that all the other students in the class want but are not smart enough to get.

Don't just raise your hand and wait, dummy. First disrupt in order to draw the teacher near to you, and *then* tell him or her about your problems. You get to goof off and still get extra help. You just can't beat a deal like that!

Consequently, if the interaction *begins* as discipline, it must *end* as discipline. When the student professes helplessness, you will not provide help *at that time!* You will look at the student from close range with that expression of total relaxation that conveys control, sometimes referred to as "withering boredom," and you will *wait.* Saying nothing is usually the best response.

If you feel that you must eventually say something after the student has fallen silent, make sure it is a brief prompt, nothing more, and only say it once. For example, you might reprompt them with the word "try." Or, if you wish to be a bit more personal, you might say something like, "Do what you can. I'll be back to help you later." Turn a deaf ear to any further protestations that usually begin with words "Yes, but . . . ."

The simple exhortation to try might be considered a temporary holding pattern for the student. In *Positive Classroom Instruction,* you will learn how to tell the student exactly how to proceed correctly with his or her work by pointing your finger and uttering a four-word sentence. Such a sophisticated and efficient prompt is sufficiently brief that it can be instructionally rich without "feeding" the disruption with teacher attention. For right now, however, the less you say the better. Take two relaxing breaths and wait.

Type 2: Denial   A profession of innocence does not require genius on the part of the student.

- I didn't do it.
- I was just sittin' here. What are you pickin' on me for?!

This is no time to engage in self-justification by explaining *why* you are "picking on them."

Because, you were disrupting.
No I wasn't. I was only . . . .

Self-justification by the teacher inadvertently acknowledges that the appropriateness of your action is debatable. The student will respond with more self-justification since the tactic seems to be working. Talk by the teacher at this moment is like throwing gasoline on a fire. Therefore, do not debate. Relax, shut up, look at them, and wait.

Type 3: Blaming   Blaming, often referred to as "ratting on your neighbor," also does not require a stroke of genius on the part of the student and is often paired with denial. It is, however, a tried and true way of playing the game of divide and conquer. If both students blame each other, who is the teacher to believe? If you are foolish enough, you may attempt to answer the timeless question: Who *really* started it?

- She was bugging me. I didn't start it!
- He didn't know how to do this problem. He was just asking me for help.
- Would you get him to leave me alone!

The lameness of blaming as a justification for talking to your neighbor when you are supposed to be doing your own work can be seen more clearly if we simply paraphrase the student's statement.

Gee, teach! The only reason we was talking back here is on account of we're trying to further our education through peer tutoring.

Type 4: Accusing the Teacher of Professional Incompetence   A great many teachers will back off when it is explained to them by the student that his or her learning difficulty is, after all, the teacher's fault.

- Well, you didn't explain it at the board! How are we supposed to understand?
- I got all mixed up when you went through it so fast.
- When you explain stuff it's all confusing.

Once again, the absurdity of this ruse can be seen if we simply paraphrase the student's excuse:

> Gee, teach, the only reason we was talking back here is to further our education by peer tutoring in order to compensate for your methodological shortcomings in the area of instruction.

In fact, you may or may not have explained the work clearly at the board. But whether you did or did not, you will never get a valid readout from a student who is trying to get off the hook. For the time being the only relevant question is: If you are stuck, how do you get help in my classroom? Chances are, it is not by gabbing with your neighbor.

Type 5: Excusing the Teacher to Leave   The person who controls an interaction is the person who tells the other person what to do. Telling the teacher where to get off is no more evident than when the student excuses you to leave. The following might be considered variations on a theme.

- OK, I'll get back to work. (short form)
- OK, I'll get back to work if you'll just leave me alone. (long form)
- OK. Quit buggin' me! Just get out of my face! I'll do it! (bratty adolescent)
- Geez! Come on! What are you, a fag or something? Don't get so close! I'll do it! I'll do it! Just bug off! Shit! (emotionally handicapped junior high)

Type 6: Insult   Insults define the lower boundary of real high-stakes gambling for the class "high rollers." To use insults the student has to be pretty cocky, upset, or stupid. In any case insults almost always pertain to one of three topics: (1) your grooming, (2) your hygiene, or (3) your clothing. Would any of the following remarks throw you off-balance?

- Hey, where did you get that suit? At a garage sale?
- Who buys your ties, Bozo the clown?
- Hey, where did you get that dress, at the Salvation Army?
- Your eyelash is falling off.
- Hey, you have dark roots, did you know that?
- You have a zit on the end of your nose.
- Hey, don't get so close, man! You've got *bad breath!*

Before getting any further into the topic of insults, any teacher must make peace with a painful topic—*bad breath.* Throughout our lives we have been sensitized by ads to be concerned about bad breath. If you should ever go to "palms" in limit-setting, you will be close enough for the student to smell your breath. Thus, in order to succeed in limit-setting, any teacher must appreciate two basic facts about bad breath. In the *first* place, you never know whether or not you have it. Let's face it, if the kid accuses you of having bad breath, the kid just might be right! In the *second* place, however, remember that in limit-setting bad breath is no disadvantage! Relax, shut up, hang in there, and do nothing until the student runs out of hot air. If you can control your emotions long enough to avoid pheasant posturing, you will ultimately control the situation.

Type 7: Profanity Profanity may be used by high rollers when push comes to shove. Profanity comes in two sizes: (1) small or garden variety, and (2) large. Garden variety profanity is limited, for the most part, to everyday vulgarities such as "hell," "shit," and "damn."

Large profanity carries two different titles. At the elementary level large profanity is usually the "F word" or its first cousin, the "S word."

> Would you believe that Randy said the "F word" right out loud in class?

Among adults only teachers refer to the "F word." If you were not conversing with another teacher, the other person could not possibly know what in the devil you were talking about.

At the secondary level, however, teachers tend to refer to the F word by its natural name. Students there say "fuck" so often that you hear it four times before you can get from your classroom to the teacher's lounge. After a while many teachers get used to it and even start using it themselves. As distasteful as the topic may be, we need to talk about the word "fuck."

Is fuck a sexual reference in the classroom? "Fuck you!" "Fuck off!" "Fuck this stupid assignment!" Does it have to do with reproduction or genitalia? Of course, it has nothing to do with either. It is, when used toward a teacher, a power play, pure and simple. It is the student's last ditch effort to rattle your cage, upset you, call the shot, and control the situation. Say "fuck" and watch the teacher blow.

If you are a classroom teacher and the word fuck still rings your bell, you are in an extremely vulnerable position. At the uttering of a four-letter monosyllable, the student instantly gains control of your mind and body. It is like dropping a coin in an old-time movie machine. They push your "fuck" button and watch you pheasant posture: "Nobody talks that way in my classroom!"

That response proves that you were not listening. In fact not only was it said in your classroom, but it was also reinforced by your becoming upset. You are a sucker, my friend—a puppet on a string. If the word fuck gets you in the gut, no face-saving bravado or show of strength will undo the fact that you are being controlled by a mouthy student with almost no effort.

Such language is obviously obnoxious and distasteful, and that is the whole point! It is designed to cause us to respond to the *content* of the verbalization rather than to the *context*. The context is the most important part of the interaction—a student who is fooling around and wondering whether you can be "had" or whether you need to be taken seriously. Keep in mind the objectives of discipline—to get students *back on task!* If you can be upset and diverted from your objective as you deal with the content of particular language, your objective has been derailed. Imagine, for instance, that you make a show of strength in response to the content of the student's back talk by saying:

> All right, that's it. I don't put up with that kind of talk! Get out of here now! Go down to the office! I don't want to see you the rest of the day! I will not tolerate that kind of language in my presence!

Your bravado is covering your weakness. Who has decided when they will leave the classroom? Who has decided under what conditions? Who has called the shot and pulled the string? It's certainly not the teacher. Who flips you the bird as they go? And, who is going to be back in 10 minutes? Do you call that control? Can they do anything in the office to prevent the student from getting your goat the next time he or she wants to? Will the use of the word fuck self-eliminate in your classroom?

Does all this mean that you are going to put up with profanity in your classroom? Are you kidding? Of course you will not put up with profanity! It is absolutely unacceptable. But the more pertinent question is: How do you respond so that profanity goes away? The critical question is a tactical question, not a moral or a philosophical question. Rather than responding like a bull in a china shop, how do you respond so that the problem self-eliminates?

For the time being think of your response to profanity in terms of a short-term strategy and a long-term strategy. The *short-term* strategy is very short—just long enough to get past your fight-flight reflex in order to avoid pheasant posturing. Relax, shut up, hang in there, and wait. The student has just taken his or her best shot, and if it does not blow you away, what is there left for her or him to say?

Remember, as you remain calm, that this poker game is rigged so that the student has to take all the chances while you do nothing. In the short term you want to checkmate his or her provocations with calmness and ultimately control the situation by getting the student back on task. If the profanity fails to upset you, it is useless.

The *long-term* strategy is quite another matter. In the long term you can do whatever you think is necessary. Any additional sanction can be added, and the fact that it is being added can be signaled to the class by saying as the students file out of class, "Jennifer, I would like to speak with you." Someone may say, "Oh, oh, Jennifer," but no one will go home and tell their parents that you allow profanity in your classroom. That issue was resolved definitively when the profanity took place and Jennifer ended up back on task. Students are too shrewd at gambling to miss that play.

At the break in private you can have any conversation with Jennifer that you want. If you judge that some additional sanction is called for, this is the time to deliver it. Whatever you say or do, however, will be more successful in private than in the heat of the moment with an audience of peers watching. But remember, if the student folded in the face of your silence, self-control, and proximity, you have already delivered a consequence for back talk that has succeeded, and the issue of control has been resolved. You have nothing that you need to prove, so consider some listening and perhaps even some reconciliation. You might find that the student is hurting about something quite unrelated to you, or you might just get an apology.

Variations on Back Talk

Most of the diversionary tactics that a teacher encounters are standard and predictable, but some strategies exhibit more guile. Some of the more common variants will be listed below so that you may be prepared to spot an effort to get off the hook that is something other than the seven basic varieties. Remember, however, that the objective of these behaviors is identical to the standard types of back talk already described, namely, *control*. They are designed to throw teachers off balance, confuse them, derail them, change the topic, and gain the upper hand.

Variant 1: Crying   If all else fails, make like a whale and blubber. Breaking into tears as the teacher "oozes in" to "palms" is most often encountered in the primary grades with girls, but it has been observed several times in junior high and once or twice in high school.

Take a few relaxing breaths, shut up, and stay where you are. The blubbering will fade to a few silent sobs and then disappear as the student realizes that it isn't working. There is no sympathy, no apology, no getting off the hook—just a teacher who is waiting. Soon it will occur to the student to try the only thing left, getting back to work. Watch her work for several relaxing breaths before the "thank you."

Variant 2: Compliments   Compliments, like crying, are also more common among the younger set.

- Oh, Mrs. Jones, your perfume smells so pretty!
- That is the most lovely pin you are wearing.

Stifle a yawn and hang in there. This too shall pass.

Variant 3: Tangential Statements   Sometimes students, modeling the incompetencies of their parents, simply change the topic whenever they are faced with owning up to their shortcomings. The result may be a tangential question or remark that has nothing to do with the situation at hand.

- When's recess?
- Are we going to have art after lunch?
- I forgot to give you my lunch money.

Hang in there and overwhelm them with inactivity. You should know just what to do by now.

Variant 4: Pushing You Aside   Physically pushing your hand or arm aside as a form of overt impudence is most common at the secondary level. While touching the flesh may seem like a big provocation, make the *least* of it with a limp or noncommittal bodily response, then return your limb to its original position. When students find themselves right back where they started, they typically give up on that stratagem and fold.

If a student is upset to the point of being potentially assaultive, stop at the edge of the desk or as soon as you pick up the cues, and abort limit-setting. Limit-setting is not designed for such extreme situations (see next chapter).

Variant 5: Romance   I trained a female junior high teacher who had a male student with no small amount of self-confidence who leaned up and kissed her on the nose when she was at "palms." She remembered the *golden rule* of dealing with back talk: *When in doubt, do nothing*. She did nothing, and with each passing second as she held her ground and waited impassively without so much as a hint of embarrassment, Prince Charming wilted and was slowly transformed into a frog.

LIMIT-SETTING SCENARIO 3: "WHINEY BACK TALK"

Orientation and Review

Back talk is self-limiting. It will starve unless you feed it. If you have the good sense to shut up and wait, the student will eventually run out of hot air.

To put it somewhat differently, the objective of back talk is to get a response from the teacher, a response other than the enforcement of the classroom rule that the teacher has set out to enforce. Anything that the teacher does other than what he or she sets out to do abdicates control of the situation. The student has succeeded in changing the agenda by throwing the teacher off-balance and off-course.

To put it somewhat differently, when the ball is in the teacher's court, you must do something effective or lose the point. To make life easy on yourself, always keep the ball in the student's court. Make the student the person who always has to respond and do something. By your passivity the student is forced to take all the chances and experience all the anxiety. As long as you don't lose, you win.

So, exactly what do you do when you move in on a student to, say, "palms," and he starts to give you a ration of bologna? The specifics are spelled out below, but remember the golden rule of limit-setting: When in doubt, do nothing. If you can keep this principle in mind, you will not only succeed in dealing with back talk, but you may rise to a position of great leadership.

Moving In

Let us imagine that we are setting limits in the usual way and have moved in as far as palms.

Step 1: Eyes in the back of your head
Step 2: Terminate instruction
Step 3: Turn, look, and say the students' names
Step 4: Walk to the edge of the students' desks
Step 5: Prompt
Step 6: Palms

You are resting your weight on your palms at close range while relaxing and waiting. Suddenly in an attempt to get off the hook, the student begins to speak. Imagine for now that it is not too nasty—just the "whiney" back talk of blaming and excuse making. What follows is a slow but predetermined response that bears no relationship whatsoever to the content of what is being said. Your next position is known as "camping out in front."

Step 7: Camping Out in Front

The Mechanics Imagine that there is an invisible trip cord that runs from the student's mouth to your elbow. As the student begins to speak, slowly bend the elbow of the arm that is *between* the two disruptive students and ooze down so that your weight is on your elbow. Take two relaxing breaths, look at the student with indifference, shut up, and wait.

Camping out in front greatly increases the proximity of the teacher to the student and improves eye contact. Leaning on your elbow with your full weight also signals to the student that you are both calm (not afraid to move in) and committed (there to stay). If the student seems to be running out of "hot air," stay where you are and *wait.* When he sees that his tactics are having no effect, his back talk will probably peter out.

If the student has stopped fooling around and is looking at you, take two relaxing breaths and break the tension of the unstructured situation by repeating your prompt for him to turn around (all the way around) and get back to work. In addition to structuring the situation, the repetition of the prompt indicates that you were not listening to a word he said. Shut up, look at him, and wait. See Figure 6-1.

Decision to Stop or Continue The prompt will almost always induce the student to get back to work. Once he is back on task, wait for two relaxing breaths, thank him, stay down, take two more relaxing breaths before doing anything else, and then slowly move over to the second student and repeat the same procedure. After you have thanked the second student and watched him work for a while, stand and take two more relaxing breaths before continuing with moving out.

If however, the disruption escalates, you will be forced to proceed to the next step of limit-setting (step 8). You will be forced to continue in almost all cases *not* by the student who has your direct attention, but by the talk of his *partner.* Typically the partner's participation will be solicited by the student you are dealing with as he attempts to get off the hook.

- Hey, man, can you believe this?
- Neither one of us can figure it out. He didn't explain it, did he?
- Hey, tell this lady to buzz off, huh? She's so close I can smell her armpits.

FIGURE 6-1
Camping out in front.

If the second student comes to the first student's rescue, he has just made an error of judgment. It is the *intrusion of the partner* in the form of direct back talk to you or continued conversation with the first student that forces the next step.

When the two students interact while you are "camping out in front" with one of them, they are ganging up on you—going two against one. In any sport your chances of scoring are great when you are "two on one." With limit-setting you can only do one job at a time with one student at a time, or you end up fragmented and derailed. Consequently, your next objective is to divide the two students so that you can continue limit-setting one on one.

The next step of the limit-setting sequence is "camping out from behind." Camping out from behind serves as a means of separating the students so that you can deal with the *first* student free of the intrusion of the second student.

Step 8: Camping Out from Behind

The Mechanics   If during camping out in front the students speak more than a sentence or two to each other in spite of your presence, stand slowly and walk around the desks until you are standing directly between the students. Slowly oozing in between the two students, lean on the table with your elbow just as you did during camping out in front while again facing the *first* student. Leaning down on your elbow brings your face back into close proximity with the first student, and turning your body sideways blocks out the second student. You are one on one again. Reestablish eye contact from close range with the first student, take two relaxing breaths, and wait. *Do not* change students. See Figure 6-2.

Decision to Stop or Continue   Imagine that camping out from behind puts an end to the back talk. Whiney back talk, consisting of blaming and excuse making, rarely continues for very long once you have (1) cut the student's partner out of the action

FIGURE 6-2
Camping out from behind.

and (2) increased proximity to the point where your face is less than 12 inches from the student's. In all likelihood the talkative student will discover the value of doing the assignment at this point.

Moving Out

The Objective   Moving out is the body language of *follow through*. It says that the students' *remaining* on task is a matter of utmost immediate concern to you—as important, if not more important, as their getting back on task in the first place. Remember, the students are judging not only confidence but also commitment from your actions. Commitment is primarily conveyed by the expenditure of *time*.

The Mechanics   Moving out begins as soon as the first student returns to task. Let us imagine that you have received whiney back talk from the first student while camping out from behind. You coped with it beautifully by doing next to nothing. Finally, the blaming and excuse making have died down. You have perhaps repeated your prompt, and the student has picked up a pencil and is now back on task.

Moving out begins with a "thank you" to the first of the two students. The following steps take you from this point back to helping a student on the opposite side of the room where you began.

Step 1   Thank the first student as he returns to work.

Step 2   Relax. Take two relaxing breaths as you watch the student work. *Stay down,* stay close, and wait. Experience has shown us that when the teacher moves out rapidly after saying "thank you," the student often falls off task with equal rapidity. Wait long enough for the student to make a meaningful physical commitment to working on the assignment.

If the student says anything else to you, just stay where you are and wait longer. Sooner or later the student will do what you want just to get rid of you. With just a little experience he will realize that he can minimize the duration of your close physical proximity only if he gets to work and does not try to get cute with his mouth.

Step 3   Turn to the other student. Without standing up, simply shift your weight to the opposite elbow and face the student who has thus far been cut out of the limit-setting interaction. Establish eye contact.

Step 4   Relax. Take two relaxing breaths. Students rarely give back talk after seeing their partners fold, but they may be sitting there doing nothing.

Step 5   Prompt. The prompt to second students of disruptive pairs will not be necessary if they are already back on task. They are usually working because they would like to see you leave. If they are *not* back on task, break inertia with a simple prompt.

Whether second students of pairs are back on task or not, they should receive equivalent treatment. If they do not require a prompt, they should get *equal time*. Just stay close while watching them work and do nothing for two relaxing breaths. Then thank them. Remember, if you do not give second students equal time, they will think that they got away with something, and the first student will feel unfairly picked on. The giving of equal time to each of the two disrupting students applies at any point in the moving-out sequence.

If, however, you *do* receive back talk from the second of the two students while camping out from behind, respond as usual. Relax, shut up, hang in there, and wait for the student to dry up. Then wait some more before prompting.

Step 6   Thank the student as he or she returns to work.

Step 7   Relax. Stay down on your elbow and take two relaxing breaths after thanking the student and wait as you watch her or him work for a while. Then, continue moving out.

Step 8   Stand and relax. Stand slowly but do not walk. Take two relaxing breaths. When the students glance at each other and find that you are still there, they will usually return to work knowing that you are really taking this whole thing seriously. Your calmness conveys confidence, and your investment of *time* conveys commitment.

Step 9   Walk to the front of the students' desks, turn, and relax. After camping out from behind, walk around slowly to the front of the desk, stand facing the students for a while longer, and take two more relaxing breaths. If you were only camping out from in front, simply stand and take two relaxing breaths. Maintain good eye contact and kill some more time if the students are showing signs of acting squirrelly.

Step 10   Walk back across the room, turn, and look at the disrupters again while taking two relaxing breaths. If you have been interrupted in the midst of helping a student, you will probably return to that student. But *before* you continue instruction, turn again and look at the disrupting students one last time from across the room as you relax. When they glance back at you, which they may well do if they are attempting to understand your behavior, they will see that you are still committed to dealing with them. A quick glance at you, and they return to task.

Step 11   Turn so that the disrupters remain in your peripheral vision and continue instructing. The limit-setting sequence is over for the time being. Continue tracking the behavior of the disrupters, however, lest they repeat the disruption.

We should take pains, when we are initially training our students to follow our classroom rules with limit-setting, to be extremely tight with the limit-setting sequence and, especially, to relax, slow down, and follow through thoroughly. The most difficult part of the sequence and the part most commonly slighted is the taking of two relaxing breaths between each move. When relaxing breaths are omitted or taken rapidly (two relaxing breaths take about 15 seconds), we tend to lose both our composure and our timing. The pace of limit-setting is much slower than most of us are accustomed to moving in the classroom.

LIMIT-SETTING SCENARIO 4: "NASTY BACK TALK"

Orientation

Let us imagine this time that the students are more lippy and obnoxious than the students in the preceding scenario. Rather than simple blaming and excuse making, they are high-rolling gamblers who go for insults and profanity. How does our response change under these circumstances? We will focus on our response to nasty back talk which occurs during camping out from behind, and we will imagine as well that the student throws in a "cheap shot" as we walk away.

Dealing with Nasty Back Talk

Limit-setting has proceeded through the eight steps of moving in much as it did in the preceding scenario:

Step 1:	Eyes in the back of your head
Step 2:	Terminate instruction
Step 3:	Turn, look, and say the students' names
Step 4:	Walk to the edge of the students' desks
Step 5:	Prompt
Step 6:	Palms
Step 7:	Camping out in front
Step 8:	Camping out from behind

It is during camping out from behind that the first student of the pair gets nasty. We first examine the mechanics of responding. Then in the following section we examine the transactions and hidden meanings that are conveyed by limit-setting with nasty back talk.

The Mechanics   As you ooze down onto your elbow to separate the two disrupting students with camping out from behind, imagine that the student with whom you are dealing lets fly with some choice words.

> Fuck off, man! Get out of my face! You're always coming over here and buggin' us. We weren't doin' anything—except this stupid-ass assignment you gave us (laugh). Hey, come on! Don't get so close. You got rhinoceros breath! Shit! . . . You're ugly, too.

Let us slow down the interaction and walk through it step by step.

Step 1   Relax. Calmness is strength. React instinctively to provocation by taking relaxing breaths coupled with inactivity.

Step 2   Move slightly closer. Moving slightly closer as you relax signals confidence, and moving away signals fear. Do not startle, pull back, or stand up. Think of your body as a ratchet that only moves in one direction until the student is on task.

Step 3   Wait. Wait passively while the back talk continues until the student runs out of hot air. Maintain a relaxed, mildly bored facial expression as well as eye contact with the student. If he "mocks you out" with a counterstare, simply look down at his work. This leaves the student looking in your ear which is rather dull, and soon he will look down at his work too.

The most difficult part of waiting is in stifling your need to *do something*. Shut up, wait, and suppress any impulse to reiterate classroom rules, to preach, to attack, or engage in sarcasm. If you are foolish enough to speak, the student will either try oneupmanship, or he will engage in excuse making, self-justification, and blaming. Relax and let the student do all the work.

Step 4 Clear your mind. While leaning down and relaxing on your elbow, waiting for the storm to blow over, you may find yourself listening to what the student is saying. This is a poor tactical move because the content of what he is saying may upset you. The antidote, of course, is not to listen. Many teachers, however, find it difficult not to listen. For this reason, we will supply you with a formal procedure to keep you from getting "sucked in."

PROCEDURE FOR DOING NOTHING   As you lean down on your elbow, looking at the student as vapidly as possible, repeat the word "boring" over and over to yourself silently within your head. As the student rattles on about your inadequate teaching and your silly-looking clothes and your bad breath and your family lineage, remember your breathing exercise and continue repeating to yourself the word "boring." Back talk is, after all, rather boring—a predictable and trite series of manipulative remarks that are pure bologna. It is not worth getting upset over. As you gain experience, however, you may find yourself capable of looking students in the eyes as they attempt to wheedle you to death while thinking to yourself, "Let's see, on the way home tonight I need to pick up a loaf of bread and a quart of milk and stop by the cleaners."

Step 5 Prompt. Wait passively until students run out of hot air. When they have petered out, wait for two relaxing breaths to let them unwind. Then prompt them back to work. Your prompt will be identical to the prompt you gave earlier from in front. As mentioned before, this prompt not only structures the situation for students (which may come as a relief to them by this time), but it also conveys to them that you were not listening to a word they said.

Sometimes students will immediately engage in a resurgence of back talk after you prompt, and you may feel that you have made the wrong move. Indeed, any talk on the part of the teacher may raise the hope of the wily student that you have forgotten your purpose and suckered for a side issue. However, this second effort on the part of the student will be short-lived as you once again fall silent and wait. When students run out of hot air the second time, simply do nothing for a while until they pick up their pencils and start.

Step 6 Thank students as they return to work. After students are back on task for several seconds, thank them graciously, using their first name. Your thank you is warm and genuine. This is no place for sarcasm. The student has, after all, complied with your wishes and has cooperated. Courteousness is most appropriate at this point in order to (1) signal to the student that the interaction is over, (2) hold out an olive branch, and (3) model courteousness and good manners.

Up to this point your emotion has been neutral—the by-product of total relaxation. During the thank you, however, it is appropriate to smile or to touch if you think it is appropriate, while going from emotionally neutral to emotionally warm. The only time you touch the student is during the thank you. Then relax again and go back to emotionally neutral as you take two relaxing breaths.

Step 7 The "last hurrah." Occasionally the thank you from the teacher will produce one last face-saving gesture on the part of the student. In response to your thank you he or she might say something like:

• For what?
• I don't *believe* this.

- You're *welcome!*
- This assignment is *so dumb!*

Students are experts at making an adult feel like a total jerk for being strict or tight. These skills are used at home too, and any teenager has been practicing them for over a decade. To get a feel for it, practice standing in front of a mirror; roll your eyes back and with a smirky smile and tone of exasperation say softly, "I don't *believe* this!"

Relax as you hear the "last hurrah," stay down, and wait for the student to get on task. Remember the golden rule of limit-setting: When in doubt do nothing. Kill time and watch the student for a while as you take two relaxing breaths.

Moving Out

The Standard Routine   Moving out will continue as it did in the preceding scenario. If the first student fails to "get your goat" with nasty back talk, the second student will almost never have the nerve to try. Shift elbows and turn to the second student to give her *equal time*. If nasty back talk occurs, repeat the steps outlined in the preceding section. If no back talk occurs, proceed with moving out by (1) watching the second student work for two relaxing breaths, (2) thanking her, (3) watching her work for two more relaxing breaths, and then (4) standing between the two students for two relaxing breaths. Watch them work for a while before walking back around to the front of their desks for two more relaxing breaths.

Only after you have seen a meaningful physical commitment to staying on task from both students will you walk back across the room. Then turn as before and watch for two more relaxing breaths to make sure work is continuing before resuming instruction. Slow and patient follow through keeps the students separated and on task while signaling your commitment to see them return to work.

The "Cheap Shot"   There is one additional type of back talk that was not described earlier in the chapter—having the last word *after* you have set limits. As you walk away from the students, imagine that you hear one of them say audibly but under his breath "big deal" or "so what."

Will you ignore such a cheap shot? Are you kidding? Having the last word is, like any other form of back talk, a power play which allows students to imagine that they have controlled the interaction. What do you do?

Turn around, take two relaxing breaths, and *recycle*. Go through the limit-setting sequence again complete with relaxing breaths, moving in as far as necessary to get the student(s) back on task. In most cases go as far as palms and wait for a few extra relaxing breaths as the student resumes work just for emphasis.

Once the students are on task, repeat the moving-out sequence from where you stand, beginning with a thank you. Your emotion is no different (relaxed); your timing, your behavior, and your objective are no different. You simply give the student a second dose. With a second dose, you have trained the student that cheap shots are not cheap. They represent a foolish and expensive gamble which will probably *not* be repeated.

HIDDEN DIMENSIONS OF LIMIT-SETTING: THE PROTECTION AND BUILDING OF RELATIONSHIP

In your response to back talk, in addition to quelling the disruption and getting the students back on task, you have taught many lessons "between the lines." The students have been *unkind* toward you, and you have been *kind* toward them. Yet you have prevailed. By your proficiency at meaning business, you have said to the students: There is nothing that you can do that will destroy our relationship. Even though you get out of line to the point of acting nastily, there is nothing you can do that will make me angry at you or dislike you. I am too good in my job for me to let things go that far.

The learning environment must be, above all else, safe. It must be safe to make errors in learning and it must be safe to make errors in behaving. For the process of growing up to be relaxed and enjoyable rather than traumatic, it must be safe to engage in trial and error. Limit-setting deals definitively with students' errors of judgment while preventing the alienation so common to classroom discipline that is destructive of both relationship and future cooperation.

Nasty back talk is the ultimate testing ground for limit-setting. Nasty back talk is the hardball of power politics in the classroom which reveals both teacher and technique for what they really are. If the teacher is in control of himself, he will be able to resolve a seemingly harsh provocation with apparent ease. But, if he has been faking "niceness" while only hoping for the best, nasty back talk will ultimately force him into an adversary relationship with the student and into the use of harsh countermeasures much to everyone's disadvantage.

The following section examines some of the subtleties and hidden dimensions of limit-setting so that we may better appreciate the richness of this complex transaction. In becoming familiar with the strengths of limit-setting, we will also come to understand the potential of an interaction in which adult disciplines child for conveying an entire constellation of positive meanings and values.

Transactions of Gambling

Why do students almost always shape up when you respond to back talk with calm and patience? To get rid of you, of course!

By your calmness you force students to take all the chances. They walk further and further out on a limb, and you are smart enough not to go out there with them. You have avoided being sucked into their melodrama—of being set up to play the role of bad and unreasonable parent. Sooner or later students realize that they are out on a limb all by themselves. Their gambit is not working. By *not* grabbing the bait, you have retained control of the situation.

When students realize the vulnerability of their position, the tone of their voices will begin to lose its conviction: They are petering out. You may be daydreaming by this time, but don't worry. You will not be called on to do anything fancy. Just wait until the talk has died out, take two relaxing breaths, and then reprompt.

If dealing successfully with back talk required that we outsmart or one-up students, we would be dead. No teacher can be that clever all day every day. And, besides, almost anything you say, no matter how clever, feeds the back talk.

If mouthy students cannot get rid of you by outsmarting you, they will have to get rid of you with the only way left: by getting back to work. It takes very little training time by a skillful teacher to teach the entire class how to get rid of you once limit-setting has begun.

When students are back on task, the "thank you" signals to them that it is all over. They can relax now. It is not an experience that they may wish to repeat, but it has not left your relationship with them scarred. Quite to the contrary, in most cases the students will feel indebted to you whether they can admit it or not. They are smart enough to know the chances they have taken and the ease and kindness with which you extracted them from their own foolishness. It is impressive how often, after a student has gone through some little tantrum only to return to work at the teacher's prompting, the student will spontaneously say, "I'm sorry." That is not only her or his apology, it is a prompt to the teacher for a little more reassurance before the teacher leaves. A touch is often enough.

Protecting the student, however, like relaxing, is not a natural act for most people nor is it an act of the will. Promises to ourselves to do better next time usually break down under pressure. Rather, it is a result of caring coupled with technical proficiency. Such technical proficiency will come in only one way—practice, practice, practice.

By far the hardest part of limit-setting is relaxation. And by far the most indispensable part of limit-setting is relaxation. By our capacity to relax we not only preserve ourselves but we also preserve the student. With practice we learn that discipline problems are not something to be afraid of.

Taking Responsibility for One's Actions

The calmness and quietness of the teacher not only saves students from getting into serious trouble, but it also helps them to acknowledge and accept responsibility for their own inappropriate behavior. Admitting that you were wrong does not come easily, especially to children, and it is learned only if skillfully taught by adults.

In the midst of their provocation and back talk students want very much for the entire predicament to be the teacher's fault. They will *externalize responsibility* for their predicament if given half a chance. They know they are taking chances, and they want to be able to say "It's *your* fault" with conviction.

If teachers lose their composure and open their mouths to engage in any arguing, blaming, or self-justification, they have just undermined any likelihood that the student will ever take any responsibility for his or her provocation. They have provided the nail upon which the student will hang all excuses and rationalizations. Indeed, the teacher has joined the student in his or her foolishness, and the teacher has clearly become part of the problem. If you open your mouth for anything but a simple prompt or a thank you, it will all be your fault in the student's mind.

Externalization of responsibility produces an instant release of tension. Righteous attack or defense is cognitively simple compared with owning up to one's own shortcomings.

To be calm and quiet denies the pretext for externalization of responsibility and forces students to stew in their own juices until it becomes painfully obvious who is making all the noise, who is being snotty and unkind, who is the cause of the problem. Only at that point is there any chance of the students' ownership of responsibility for their misbehavior. Such ownership is a precondition for true reconciliation. The spontaneous "I'm sorry" signals the need for a final affirmation that the matter is history and all is forgiven.

Limit-setting is a very special kind of sanction for misbehavior—an encounter with a teacher that forces students to an encounter with themselves. In the strength of his or her calmness, the teacher provides limits along with acceptance of the student which leaves the door open for the student's self-acceptance, acceptance of responsibility, and reaffirmation of relationship. Limit-setting in its strength and calmness is therefore actively supportive of students. It helps them through their mistakes and helps them to grow up gracefully with a minimum of scars. It creates the occasion for an internalized decision to cooperate rather than a decision to capitulate to force temporarily under protest.

Modeling Maturity and Competence

What is the alternative to the calm strength of limit-setting in dealing with classroom disruption, particularly when considered within the demanding context of nasty back talk? Unfortunately the typical alternative is upset, angry, and unnecessarily harsh negative sanctions.

One of the most pervasive and tenacious misconceptions concerning the disciplining of children is that the *size* of the adult's upset equals the *power* of the response: "If you keep doing that, I'm going to really get upset!" If power is seen as counterforce, then the degree of upset signals the nearness of the use of force. Power seen within this framework is necessarily punitive. Discipline then becomes a series of variations on the theme of nag, threaten, and punish. Whether you do a slow burn or engage in criticism, sarcasm, threats, yelling, or hitting, the outcome is always the same: two people resentful of each other. Reconciliation is remote.

In addition, when rule enforcement is based on punition, obedience is a matter of immediate necessity rather than a choice to cooperate. Behaving properly because you have to, not because you want to, is not very conducive to the student's accepting responsibility for her or his own misbehavior. It is easy to externalize responsibility to the unreasonable SOB who is always on your back trying to cram a bunch of stupid rules down your throat. Thus, a reliance on punition blocks social maturation as it precludes reconciliation.

We have already examined the price that teachers must pay in stress if they attempt to manage a classroom full of students with "nag, threaten, and punish." The price of "management by adrenaline" and "laying down the law" is too high, and the students know it. Exhaustion and burn-out are the teacher's only long-term prospect. To cut their losses teachers finally nag and threaten from where they stand in the room. Rule enforcement has become pheasant posturing—a parody of rule enforcement.

Throughout this often-repeated farce of classroom management, students are having presented to them a model of adult problem solving that is primitive and infantile. How are the students to learn the customs of civilization if not from the adults around them? How can children understand that power and gentleness go together unless they experience it directly? How are they to raise their children unless they learn the subtleties of child rearing from us?

Patience and Common Courtesy

Patience for a great many parents and teachers is synonymous with forbearance— putting up with something unpleasant as an act of kindness toward the person who is out of line. Such patience is not kindness but rather cowardice or naiveté. In limit-setting teachers, in contrast, respond immediately rather than waiting and hoping. Their patience is expressed in their calmness and slowness as they deliver immediate and meaningful consequences for unacceptable behavior from close range. Patience is the gentleness with which the teacher responds in the present. Such patience allows students to wrestle with their feelings and finally accept responsibility for their own actions within an atmosphere of both strict standards and interpersonal affirmation. Patience is waiting without censure and allowing students to come to terms with their behavioral trial and error in lieu of overpowering counterforce.

Yet, it is one thing to be patient with children while they are struggling with their own feelings, and it is quite another to let them off the hook. To be relaxed and patient with children in a single situation while they are struggling with their feelings, even while they are giving you back talk, does not fly in the face of providing realistic consequences for children's behavior. It is possible to be patient and strong simultaneously. To let them off the hook, on the other hand, and to eliminate the sanctions that they have earned by their misbehavior in the name of niceness or patience is to abort discipline and render rules useless.

Similarly courtesy, which is all too uncommon, is also essential to the appropriate use of power by adults in limit-setting. It is a new experience for most children to be confronted by the strength inherent in the calmness and patience of limit-setting. And it is a new experience for most children to have their compliance, even after the unkindness of back talk, met with a thank you.

Thank you is a formality, but it is far more than a hollow formality. It is a genuine expression of gratitude for cooperation which is also rich in metacommunications such as:

- *That* is what I wanted.
- Moving in has stopped.
- I am grateful.
- You can relax now.
- We will do it my way, won't we?

Thank you is a common courtesy which models and teaches courtesy and good manners. Manners are both habits and meaningful communications—formalities full of meaning. Courtesy demonstrates an overriding message about power as used by adults toward children for the good of the child. It is possible to use power and at the

same time honor and affirm the other person, free of demeaning and free of the resentment and alienation that quickly follows. Power can be protective, gentle, and
generous. Indeed a teacher can only afford such protectiveness and gentleness and
generosity from the position of safety and security that comes from the effective use
of interpersonal power. How many children, or adults for that matter, can even con-
ceive of power and control as anything but aversive? How can you if you have never
lived with it? And how then can common courtesy make any sense as anything but an
empty formality?

OVERVIEW

Students are gamblers: shrewd and precise gamblers. The question being answered
during limit-setting is: "Do I have to?" Students will fold when they judge that you
have the stronger hand and are committed to playing it out.

In spite of the outrageous behavior that students are capable of within a classroom,
the vast majority of students are penny-ante gamblers. They are used to gambling with
stacked odds. As mentioned earlier, the vast majority of disruptions in the classroom
are absolutely free. Students win most of their brave gambles with nickel and dime
antes because of our own ineptness. Students are accustomed to being experts in
teacher management in a situation in which the teacher is an amateur in student management. As soon as a teacher effectively and consistently puts a price on disruption,
the students will learn quickly to gamble accordingly and fold early. Nothing seems to
impress students more dramatically than seeing a teacher deal with back talk from one
of the high rollers and prevail with seeming nonchalance.

Yet, while limit-setting is predictable, it is a complex and subtle set of interpersonal
transactions that must be performed correctly to get the hoped-for result. In no way
can a teacher remember all the steps of limit-setting under pressure while simultaneously relaxing, without *practice*. Practice is the price of correct performance. Under
pressure in the classroom ideas won't help you—only reflexes will.

LIMIT-SETTING: VARIATIONS AND LIMITATIONS

The skills of limit-setting described in such careful detail in the two preceding chapters are more than a single classroom management technique. Body language is *generic*—it is "spoken" and interpreted at any time that two human beings can see each other. Every aspect of limit-setting described thus far operates, for example, between parent and child within the home or between colleagues at work. Our analysis of limit-setting simply provides a "fine grain" analysis of some of the more basic aspects of meaning business within the context of the classroom.

Yet in order to study limit-setting carefully we have by necessity reduced the scope of our description to a single although common classroom disruption—two neighbors talking to each other when they should be doing their own work. While this limitation of focus is necessary to produce a clear and consistent picture of the limit-setting sequence, it also produces an overrigidification of our understanding of limit-setting. What liberties can you take with the limit-setting sequence to successfully adapt it to varied situations? What liberties, if taken, cause limit-setting to fail or lose much of its effectiveness?

In this chapter we expand our examination of limit-setting in order to reach a deeper understanding of how it can *succeed* and a clearer understanding of how it can *fail*. We will break out of the narrow mold of responding to "talking to neighbors" to acquire more generalization in our understanding of the appropriate uses of limit-setting as well as greater discrimination concerning misapplications and realistic limitations of limit-setting.

The first section of this chapter, "Variations of Limit-Setting," covers not only common situations in which modifications must be made in the limit-setting sequence but also changes which occur during the self-elimination of limit-setting over time. The second section, "Limitations of Limit-Setting," will deal with (1) when limit-setting fails, (2) paradoxical reactions to limit-setting, and (3) inappropriate applications of limit-setting.

Keep in mind throughout, however, that limit-setting is only one discipline management technique among many, a basic technique certainly, but not a panacea. It is the teacher's preferred response to *common* disruptions rather than to crises, and it works best when the teacher is mobile and dealing with the group as a whole during seatwork and group discussions. The further the application of limit-setting diverges from this range of "best fit," the more difficult, costly, and problematic will be its use. Learning the limitations of limit-setting, therefore, is as important as learning its strengths, for when the cost of using limit-setting gets too high, it is time to *dump it* and go on to another management technique better suited to the situation.

VARIATIONS OF LIMIT-SETTING

Common Variants

In this section I will describe some of the more common variations of the limit-setting sequence. In describing a specific response to a specific situation my purpose is to shine light on additional facets of limit-setting, not to offer management prescriptions. As I emphasized at the beginning of the book, the management milieu of the classroom is far too complex for pat remedies to have much chance of consistent success. Rather, to cope with the infinite variety of management settings and student personalities, teachers must have a thorough mastery of a repertoire of fundamental management skills—mastery which allows teachers to "customize" their response to fit the situation without undermining the effectiveness of the management technique. Think of the following examples, therefore, only as possibilities which broaden our understanding of limit-setting rather than as definitive answers to "what if" questions.

Limit-Setting on the Wing Although it is extremely important to understand and be able to perform the limit-setting sequence as described in the two preceding chapters, it is rare that the teacher will actually do it, at least in that form. Rather, the form in which limit-setting is usually employed is far more subtle—a continuous pattern of mobility which we refer to as "limit-setting on the wing" or "working the crowd." Moving among the students and using body language effectively at all times prevents most disruptions which might otherwise call for the beginning of the formal limit-setting sequence. Instructional skills described in the volume *Positive Classroom Instruction* further prevent the onset of disruptions. Indeed, the full limit-setting sequence may be done never at all or only a few times before it self-eliminates if done within the proper context of "limit-setting on the wing." But, hang on to your limit-setting skills. You will need them when we get to the back-up responses contained in our back-up system (Chapters 15 and 16).

Moving in Unobtrusively In Chapter 4 we discussed four fundamental skills of public speaking which teachers use constantly while speaking to their class in order to keep the students' attention focused on the material being presented. These four skills direct teachers to: (1) stand up, (2) move, (3) make direct eye contact with each member of the group as they move, and (4) vary the timing and intensity of their speaking. These skills may be referred to collectively as "working the crowd."

These skills of public speaking incorporate elements of the body language of limit-setting which can be used whenever the teacher is explaining something to the class. If you have the room arranged properly so that you are constantly moving within your walkways, you will be within a few steps of any student at all times while intermittently making direct eye contact. Such movement, proximity, and eye contact produce sufficient accountability to prevent a great many student disruptions not only during explanations, lectures, and the giving of directions but also during the corrective feedback of seatwork.

Furthermore, if two students begin to talk while you are explaining something to the class, you may simply *continue your explanation* while walking slowly toward the students and establishing eye contact with them. As soon as either of the students realizes that he or she is the sole recipient of your eye contact, the student will probably stop fooling around and attend to you. The student will most certainly be attending to you by the time you are standing over his or her desk looking directly at him or her as you speak.

Once you have their full attention, you may simply turn toward the rest of the class and continue your explanation, staying near the disruptive students momentarily before moving. Attend to the students frequently as you move about so that they are aware that you are constantly tracking their behavior. The teacher has systematically used those elements of the limit-setting sequence that get the job done in this situation, namely: (1) relaxation, (2) proper body orientation, (3) increased physical proximity, (4) eye contact, and (5) waiting at the edge of the student's desk.

Such a partial use of "limit-setting on the wing" meets the teacher's needs while being far less intrusive than the whole limit-setting routine described earlier (complete with stopping your presentation, turning, taking two relaxing breaths, saying the students' names, etc.). The teacher has terminated a disruption almost invisibly while simply "working the crowd." In fact, the entire limit-setting routine may be viewed as overkill or even as disruptive in a situation in which you are trying to keep the class focused on your explanation.

Breaking Your Train of Thought to Get Attention   Sometimes students may be talking to a neighbor as you are explaining something, and they are so absorbed in their side conversation that you fail to get their eye contact from where you stand even when you turn toward them. An age-old ploy is to simply stop talking abruptly in midsentence as you look at the offending students. They usually look up to see why you stopped. You now have their eye contact. Pick up your sentence where you left off and walk toward them as you continue working the crowd just as in the previous example. The relaxation, body orientation, eye contact, slowness of movement, proximity, and waiting until you have full compliance (with a prompt if necessary) are all elements of limit-setting on the wing.

A Physical Prompt as You Move   Another variant of limit-setting on the wing is to deal unobtrusively with pencil tapping or some analogous form of noise making from a student as you speak. As you walk past the student, simply place your hand gently on top of the "nervous habit" to bring it to the student's attention without bringing it to the group's attention. A little extra eye contact can be added for emphasis. This is obviously a minor transaction when you are mobile. But if you are sitting on your behind or leaning against the chalkboard, what would you do? Would you nag and reprimand from a distance, or would you just learn to live with it?

Taking Objects   Imagine that, as you glance over your shoulder, you see a paper airplane or a tic-tac-toe game that is quickly crumpled up, or imagine that you see a paper wad about to be thrown. As you excuse yourself and turn around to take two relaxing breaths, the paper wad disappears into an innocent-looking student's lap. If you do not get the wad, you know that it may soon go sailing. What do you do?

Remember, you do limit-setting with your body, not with your mouth. Go through the limit-setting sequence as slowly as ever, taking two relaxing breaths at each step along the way until you get to camping out in front. Then, once you are leaning on your elbow eyeball to eyeball, turn the palm of your hand up to make a cup in which the student can place the wad. Relax, breathe slowly, maintain eye contact, keep quiet, and kill time as you wait for the wad to be handed over. Sooner or later that student will do almost anything you want for one simple reason—to get rid of you. Don't forget the thank you and stay down until they are fully on task.

Reverse Order   Imagine that you are toward the rear of the classroom, and you look up to see a student turned all the way around in her seat talking to the person behind her. Excuse yourself immediately, stand, look, relax, say their names, and relax again as usual. Imagine that you get nothing but smiley face as the student in front remains turned around in her seat—a classic case of upping the ante.

Walk toward the two students, but rather than going in front of the desk of the student who is turned around (which would follow the limit-setting sequence perfectly but which would be rather stupid since it would leave you staring at the back of the student who is turned), camp out from behind, that is, *between* the two disrupters, to separate them and get the student who was turned around to face forward. Follow that student around as she turns forward in her seat, which will leave you camping out in front. Go to palms and then give her a prompt to get her back to work. From this point continue the limit-setting sequence until you have thanked her and are standing in front of her watching her work. Then go to the second student who is sitting behind the first student and give him equal time, complete with prompt if needed, thank you, and plenty of relaxing breaths.

You have just performed the limit-setting sequence in reverse order beginning with camping out from behind; rather backwards according to the formal protocol, but rather sensible considering the physical placement of the students. The moral of the story: take the terrain into account and proceed in the most economical fashion. You will be fine with an altered sequence as long as it makes sense and as long as the individual steps of the sequence are performed calmly and slowly.

Dealing With Humor   Imagine that you are camping out from behind with a high school student, and he makes a remark that is hilarious. You crack up as does the rest of the class. Such an eventuality becomes more likely the older the students become.

When young students try to be cute or funny in such a situation they are usually just silly by adult standards. But, secondary students can be really funny.

As you are laughing, you wonder, "What do I do now? Have I irretrievably blown it?" Relax and have a laugh. Your job is not to be the original stoneface. Time is on your side, so just "hang in there." After the laughter has died down, resume your camping out as before. Nothing has changed, the student is not off the hook. You must still be dealt with from close range, and sooner or later the student will probably return to task for the usual reason—to get rid of you. Relax and keep the ball in his court. As long as you don't lose, you win. How many great one-liners can he come up with?

The topic of humor in discipline, incidentally, runs in both directions—from teacher to student as well as from student to teacher. Sometimes a bit of humor from teachers can do wonders in diffusing a tense situation or in disarming a bit of foolishness. Indeed, sometimes humor is the best management technique of all, and if you can use it to your advantage, use it for all it is worth. I will not spend much time on it, however, because I have not yet figured out how to teach anyone to be funny. If it is not part of your natural way of being, it tends to look rather awkward and artificial under stress, and it can easily turn into sarcasm. But some teachers can do magic with a bit of kidding, self-effacement, or exaggeration.

Heckling from Behind   Imagine that you are at palms with one of two disruptive students and from behind you comes some "lip" as a classmate attempts to pull you off course.

> Hey, what are you pickin' on them for? They weren't doing anything. Besides, this lesson is stupid anyway.

The situations may seem outrageous, but it is really a variation on a theme—the disruptive student's partner joining in the back talk to fragment you by teaming up two against one. In this case the partner is simply behind you rather than sitting next to the student you are dealing with.

Remember, you can only do one job at a time. Stay with the student you started with and follow the limit-setting sequence through to its conclusion with *no alteration whatsoever.* If there are two disrupters sitting next to each other, deal with each of them in turn as you normally would until you are standing in front of both of them watching them work. Only after you have completed the limit-setting sequence with the students you started with do you respond to the heckler in any way.

If you have done your job properly and have ignored the heckler completely up to this point, he usually will have fallen silent. His objective was to cause you to abort limit-setting in midstream, and when he fails, he usually folds. Whether he is silent or still babbling, turn, relax, look at him, relax again, and wait. If he is still talking and you wait long enough, he will usually dry up and return to task. If not, continue with the limit-setting sequence as always by walking to the edge of his desk, etc. Rarely will you have to walk if you stand, relax, and wait long enough.

If at this point the class falls silent, you wipe the slate clean and start fresh. There are no old debts to settle. Most of the noise behind your back, if there is any, is typically a giggle or a few whispers—symptoms of mild nervousness on the part of the spectators. If they are silent when you turn around, they are indicating that they have learned the lesson that you were teaching.

Beware of your "worst possible case scenarios." A typical "what if" question at this point is: What if you are being heckled from several different directions and the class is coming apart? Many teachers, after first being introduced to the limit-setting sequence and seeing how slow and thorough it is, imagine that the rest of the classroom will be going bananas behind their backs by the time they are finished. While you have many techniques at your disposal to deal with such a "worst possible case scenario" by the end of training, those techniques are rarely needed in this situation. In nearly all cases, when you first employ limit-setting, those students who notice its occurrence watch quietly with full attention. You are teaching a lesson to the entire class—a lesson that the most disruptive students have the highest motivation to learn. Exactly what is the teacher doing? How will it turn out? What are the real rules in this classroom? How must I behave? Typically you can hear a pin drop no matter how long you take.

Open-Field Situations   Imagine that you are on yard duty or that you are an athletic coach in the gym or on the practice field as some student is misbehaving nearby. Can you use limit-setting outside a classroom in an open-field setting?

The answer to that question, as always, is a matter of cost. The cost of your response is determined by at least these three factors:

1 How far away is the student?
2 How mobile are you?
3 Will the student stand still or walk away as you move?

If the student is a reasonable distance away and is not likely to move, you can use limit-setting as you would anywhere else. Physical proximity is the same whether it is between two standing individuals or between one standing and one sitting. Gaining proximity to a squirrelly student on the other side of a large shop class, a gymnasium, or an athletic field may seem exorbitant, however, simply because of the distance to be covered, the time involved, or the intrusion into another important teaching activity. When the cost is too high, dump limit-setting and rely on (1) incentive systems (usually responsibility training) to build patterns of cooperation, (2) your back-up system to put the lid on, or (3) both.

The Self-Elimination of Limit-Setting

The most predictable variants on the limit-setting sequence are the partial uses of limit-setting that result from its self-elimination. Although effective teachers will "pay their dues up front" by carrying through the limit-setting sequence as far as needed to gain compliance while they are training their class, the span of hours or days during which they must pay a high price to remediate a single disruption will be brief. The students are not stupid when it comes to gauging teacher confidence and commitment, and limit testing will become rare once limits have been clearly established. Thus, you only pay a high price to deal with a single disruption early in the training of your class as an *investment in the future.* Once the students become convinced that you mean business, you will rarely have to remind them that you still know how.

From Physical to Verbal to Nonverbal   Once students have become convinced that you both know how to handle disruptions and are thoroughly committed to doing so, limit-setting will begin to wither away. The limit-setting sequence will self-eliminate in a very predictable progression: from *physical* to *verbal* to *nonverbal*—in reverse order.

Although you may need to walk over to disrupting students the first time, the second time you may only have to turn, look at them, and say their names. They have become older and wiser now, and they know exactly what you will do if they continue their fooling around. They return to work because they have learned to fold early in a game they cannot win. Limit-setting has just evolved from a *physical* interaction (walking across the room, etc.) to a *verbal* interaction (saying the students' names). Later you may simply turn, relax, and look at the disrupters with the same result. They look at you, decide that continuing the disruption would be a bad gamble, and get back to work. Limit-setting has just gone from a *verbal* interaction (their names) to a *nonverbal* interaction (turning and looking).

Limit-setting is what is known as a "behavioral chain"—a predictable sequence of events with a predictable outcome. In a chain, because of its predictability, each event in the sequence becomes a cue or discriminative stimulus (Sd) for the onset of the next event in the sequence. As students become familiar with limit-setting, they become better able to predict all the events that will follow once the sequence has begun. If each step becomes more uncomfortable for the disrupter with the ultimate outcome foreordained, the student will avoid as much of the sequence as possible. Consequently, students learn to fold as soon as they are able to discriminate that the sequence has begun. Finally you may quell a budding disruption just by glancing up and catching the student's eye without even standing or turning. Such control is the mark of a well-trained class, but you cannot *begin* training with such a small gesture and expect it to convey potency.

Generalization   After your class has been trained, limit-setting is always in effect in every situation. Once students have learned that you mean business, that perception will generalize to any situation in which you are present. Thus, even if you are *seated* in small group instruction such as a reading circle or committee work, a setting not well-suited for limit-setting because of your lack of mobility, you may get the effective results with just a look and a student's name. This spreading of the effectiveness of a management technique from the training situation to other related situations is called generalization of learning. All effective management techniques will generalize to one degree or another. Consequently, to the extent that limit-setting colors the students' perception of the teacher, it is in effect at all times.

Eventually, as students come to trust your effectiveness and commitment in setting limits, your mere physical presence becomes a discriminative stimulus signaling to the class that particular rules are in effect and being enforced and that everyone is to be on task. Thus, as limit-setting self-eliminates, behavior control rapidly becomes cheaper and easier. Behavioral control eventually becomes nonverbal and highly generalized—your mere presence in the classroom. The investment in limit-setting has paid off. Early intervention has self-eliminated to the point of being prevention.

Thus, limit-setting as a full-blown routine is rarely observed in the classroom of a teacher who is using limit-setting. Most teachers who have been trained report never having gone past palms, and even saying students' names soon becomes a thing of the past. If an observer were to visit the class a few weeks after training and count the number of times the limit-setting sequence was employed as a criterion of implementation, he or she would conclude that limit-setting was not in use. But he or she would have missed a chance to count limit-setting because the training of the class would have been long past. Now the potency of the limit-setting sequence is embodied in the *person* of the teacher and the continuing *perception* of the students that he or she means business.

LIMITATIONS OF LIMIT-SETTING

Although limit-setting is basic to discipline management and although it is generic as a means of communicating interpersonal power and commitment, limit-setting is not fail-safe nor is it a panacea. As mentioned earlier, it has a range of effectiveness beyond which its use becomes more costly and problematic. In addition, it can be ruined by misapplication and sloppy execution.

Knowing when limit-setting can fail is as important as knowing when and how it succeeds. Positive classroom discipline will supply the teacher with an array of management techniques designed to pick up where limit-setting leaves off. One of the more important aspects of mastering limit-setting, therefore, is to learn its limitations so that you know when to *dump it* and go on to some other management option. With adequate mastery you can make the transition from one technique to another smoothly and effortlessly in anticipation of new management demands rather than experiencing failure as you hang onto limit-setting for too long and run it into the ground.

When Limit-Setting May Fail

Limit-setting may fail owing to characteristics of either the teacher or the students. Some of these characteristics have been described in conjunction with the initial description of limit-setting and are only mentioned briefly, whereas others are discussed more fully.

Teacher Characteristics

Anger and Upset   Limit-setting typically fails when the teacher is angry or upset. Indeed the motions of limit-setting when the teacher is upset are not limit-setting at all. Limit-setting fails worst when the teacher is upset and the students are emotionally or behaviorally handicapped. These particular kinds of students will not only mirror but will amplify the alienation that the teacher broadcasts with her or his anger. Limit-setting done by an angry teacher is an invitation to do battle. Nothing could be more counterproductive to classroom discipline.

Limit-setting is a confrontation of sorts, but it is a very special kind of confrontation. It is the relaxation, the slowness, the gentleness, and the predictability of limit-setting that produces most of its power and safety. Power when used effectively does not produce what one usually thinks of as a confrontation or intimidation. It merely produces a situation in which the student, within a context of calm and safety, judges that cooperation is the more expedient course of action. A *power struggle,* in contrast, is usually a sign that the teacher has squandered his or her power by becoming upset and has thereby put the issue of power up for grabs.

Poor Relationship   Limit-setting, like any other management technique, relies to a considerable degree for its effectiveness on the students liking the teacher enough to be willing to go along with him or her. If the students dislike the teacher or are angry at the teacher, they will exact a high price from the teacher for the teacher's lack of caring or lack of self-control. There is no management technique that can carry a teacher who becomes easily upset or who does not particularly care about or personally like the students.

Limit-setting, ironically, is an important ingredient in the building of positive relationship just as positive relationship is a precondition to successful limit-setting. Nagging, threatening, and punishing destroy positive relationship, and they can destroy relationship even faster than it is being built in the classroom of a caring but inept teacher. Limit-setting, in contrast, reduces the "bad time" of teacher-student interactions so that the good time that is shared can serve to build relationship without being continually undermined.

Fast and Sloppy   Limit-setting can fail when done rapidly since rapidity signals the absence of relaxing breaths and since moving in on students quickly may threaten and upset them. Most teachers without coaching will do limit-setting two to three times as fast as they should. The first time teachers walk through limit-setting with coaching they almost always report that it seems incredibly slow. The whole sequences seems as if it takes 5 minutes although it rarely takes much more than a minute and a half. Nevertheless, our natural pace in the classroom is typically more rapid than is limit-setting as we attempt to get from one student to another to help as many students as possible.

Although our natural pace in the classroom might be too fast for limit-setting, which will typically result in some difficulty in our slowing down, our natural fast pace amounts to a hidden advantage. When you do slow down, turn around, look at the students, and take two relaxing breaths, the students will pick up simply by your change of pace that you are setting limits. Your change of pace, therefore, can be the discriminative stimulus that students learn to respond to even before you have said their names.

Fast and sloppy tend to go together. Without adequate training, it is easy to look at a disruption, turn around, say the students' names, start walking, get to their desks, and go to palms feeling that you have done all the steps of limit-setting correctly when, in fact, each one of them has been done *wrong*. The more sloppy a teacher becomes, particularly if she or he goes too fast, the more likely it is that limit-setting will degenerate into a confrontation and a power struggle. There is no such thing as skill proficiency "in general"—there is only mediocrity or the skill proficiency that comes from *practice*.

Immobility As mentioned earlier, it is nearly impossible for you to teach effectively and manage an entire classroom full of students while you are sitting. If you want to teach the class from your chair, with the exception of small group instruction, you have already retired on the job. Any effectiveness of limit-setting that you get from the sitting position will represent generalization from the standing position. Such generalization can allow some effectiveness while you are seated if you are on your feet setting limits intermittently when possible. Should you begin sitting too much, however, you will find the generalization short-lived. You most certainly cannot train a class that you mean business unless you are on your feet.

Inappropriate Structure Limit-setting cannot compensate for inappropriate classroom structure. One of the most common examples of inappropriate structure is having students sit for too long. No amount of limit-setting can compensate for a teacher's unawareness of the physiological limitations of children. If, for example, a primary teacher asks his students to sit quietly and work for an hour and a half, he is running counter to biology.

Secondary teachers may imagine that sitting still is only a problem for little children. Yet students of all ages require intermittent kinetic activity or their attention will begin to fade and they will become restless. Reflect for a moment on the fact that the basic rule of discipline in high school might be paraphrased as follows: "We expect you all to sit in your seats for the next 4 years, pay attention, take notes, and remember everything that is said because it might be on the test." Is it any mystery that fifth and sixth periods are traditionally difficult and exasperating for teachers because of considerations of structure?

"Withitness" If you don't know what is going on around you or if you don't care, there is little reason to expect management of any kind to occur. A lack of "withitness" comes in many varieties. They represent naiveté, apathy, or social incompetence. Although teachers with these characteristics are relatively rare, they are known, resented, and avoided by active and knowing parents, and they disproportionately color the public's stereotype of the teaching profession.

1 Repressors and Rationalizers. Occasionally I will train teachers to do limit-setting only to watch one of them fail to use it at all in the classroom. I asked one such teacher why and she said, "Oh, the noise doesn't really bother me that much." I ran across one elementary teacher who taught his reading circle with his back to the rest of the class. When I asked him why, he said, "They distract me when I'm trying to teach." Amazing! From my experience I would judge that dealing with the confusion around you by pretending it is not there represents a coping style of longstanding that is quite resistant to change.

2 Depressed Teachers. One of the first symptoms of depression is loss of energy, and the first things lost in the classroom seem to be mobility and a willingness to cope with minor disruptions. The result, of course, is that the minor disruptions turn into major disruptions. Life crisis, personality disorders, or career "burn-out" can all produce the appearance of apathy or giving up. Burn-out with a touch of racism is a particularly nasty combination. When a teacher was asked why he was not implementing the management skills learned in training, he gave the classic reply, "Oh, it won't work. You can't teach these children anything."

3 Disorganized Teachers. Disorganization and personality fragmentation can range from moderate to severe and crippling. One common characteristic of disorganized teachers is an apparent inability to anticipate problems and eliminate stress by responding to problem situations *proactively.* Rather, they appear chronically off-balance, overstressed, and on a reactive footing. Fragmentation and disorganization are double jeopardy, therefore, since the lack of preventative action causes the natural stress of the job to be amplified.

Timidity No management technique can cover up the fact that a particular teacher is afraid of the students. A teacher who is afraid of students, particularly at the secondary level, is like a piece of meat in a pool of sharks. Experience in training teachers to perform limit-setting seems to indicate that you cannot put backbone into a teacher who is a certified "wimp."

If you are being hassled mercilessly by your students and you find that you cannot do limit-setting, consider seeking some formal training in either classroom management or an alternative profession. While meditating, keep in mind that vulnerability does not stimulate compassion in the heart of a child.

Student Characteristics

Repeat Disruptions No discipline technique comes with a guarantee. No matter how well you perform limit-setting, you cannot preempt the possibility of the disrupters starting to disrupt again soon after you have returned to instruction. Some few students are quite sly, in fact, in folding early only to resume the disruption quickly. There is no point in repeating limit-setting frequently. If you give a student six warnings, you only define the first five as hot air.

When a disruption is repeated you must make a choice. If the students are not typically disruptive, repeat limit-setting once more, upping the ante to at least palms. If the students are frequently disruptive, go to a more stringent management technique (described in subsequent chapters).

Multiple Disruptions If the class is laughing about something that was funny, you can often prevent a game of "Can You Top This?" between students from developing by simply talking over the background noise. Expound on some intelligent-sounding topic as the class settles down. Your noise keeps them from focusing on each other's oneupmanship. As you move about, make what eye contact you can and attempt limit-setting on the wing.

In a less benign situation—the class is coming unglued and disruptions are coming from many directions—dump limit-setting and go to another technique. Limit-setting can only do one job at a time.

Agitated Student The teacher may not wish to use limit-setting if a student demonstrates that he or she has a big "chip on his or her shoulder." If you are walking toward a student, perhaps early in the year before you know each other very well, and you see the student draw a fist or become agitated, stop at the edge of the desk, take several relaxing breaths, and abort limit-setting. Do not go any further because nobody pays you enough money to stick your face down close to some kid's fist. Discretion is, after all, the greater part of valor. Besides, limit-setting is only one technique among the many that you will need to succeed at discipline.

Limit-setting may particularly upset students whose home life contains a lot of corporal punishment or child abuse. These students are more common in special classes, but they can certainly be part of regular classrooms. If at home an adult walking toward the child signals that she or he is about to get slapped or hit, it is not too surprising that the student might get upset at the approach of the teacher. The tension and drawn fist are often part of a learned physical defense response.

Remember, the objective of limit-setting is to *calm* students and get them back to work. If you are not having a calming affect, the technique is counterproductive. Dump limit-setting and go to another technique.

Bolting Out of Chair   If the student suddenly and unexpectedly bolts out of her chair as you lean over to go to palms or camping out, remember the *cardinal rule* of limit-setting: When in doubt, do nothing. Stand, relax, look at her, and wait. After she calms down, she will probably feel increasingly awkward as she stands there. She will usually sit down of her own accord eventually. If not, a gentle hand gesture toward the chair will suffice as a prompt.

Physical Threat   A teacher must make a judgment if she is physically threatened. The judgment is very simple. Is the student bluffing or might he really hurt me? If the student is bluffing, stand your ground, relax, and then follow through. If he is not bluffing, excuse yourself politely and get help.

Paradoxical Reactions

Starved for Touch   Students who are starved for touch and adult attention become indiscriminate in their interpretation of adult proximity. They will typically want you to attend to them and to come close to them no matter what the circumstances.

I am finding increasing numbers of regular primary-age students exhibiting this syndrome of social deprivation, whereas in previous years it was more rare and typically confined to special classrooms. A kindergarten or first grade teacher may have five or six such students for whom moving in produces smiling and even hugging of the forearms. More socially developed students are highly discriminating of the meaning of physical proximity within the context of limit-setting, whereas the socially deprived student may read none of the subtlety.

Loving teachers will often want to give more to the needy child, but they must do so skillfully. They must, in fact, structure the needy child's access to their proximity and touch much more than normal so that appropriate rather than deviant behavior produces proximity and intense adult attention. This may force teachers to often act in ways that feel far more strict than teachers in their hearts would like to be.

The Explosion Syndrome   Some students have been trained at home that nothing will happen as far as discipline is concerned until the parent blows up and starts yelling. Such children learn to ignore nagging and threats and to shape up quickly only when the parent shows signs of "blowing." This interaction pattern transfers to the classroom and provides ample confirmation for upset-prone teachers that only getting angry gets results. Unfortunately, the good behavior which follows teacher upset is usually short-lived, and, consequently, upset as a means of behavior control never self-eliminates.

Limit-setting may be slow to take hold with such students since they do not read subtle communications as "meaning business." Relax, hang in there, and pay the price of *retraining* the student to read body language. The alternative is to play his or her game and to do discipline in the same primitive way as their parents with equally short-lived results. With time and persistence you can retrain the child to respond to the customs of civilization.

Praise Makes Worse   Some children predictably act out soon after they have been praised. Thus, the praise of limit-setting may seem to have a paradoxical effect. This paradox is commonly observed in clinical work with emotionally and behaviorally disturbed children who have an extremely negative self-concept. Praise for such a child produces cognitive dissonance between his or her self-concept and the positive feedback that she or he has just received. The quickest way to reduce dissonance is to quickly earn negative feedback which is consonant with the poor self-concept.

Self-concept is largely a by-product of the feedback that the world gives us for our actions. We learn about who and what we are by the effects that we produce. When children are raised with constant criticism and censure, the only logical self-attribution is that they are bad. Be patient and keep trying, for children can only learn to accept themselves by being accepted by you.

Inappropriate Applications

They Won't Start Working   What if the student says, "I'm not going to do this assignment!" Do you go to camping out or what?

One type of potential back talk that was explicitly *not* dealt with under the topic of back talk in the previous chapter was the student who refuses to work. It certainly sounds like provocative back talk when a student says, "I'm not going to do this dumb assignment. You can stand there looking at me all day long, but I'm still not going to do this stupid work!"

The first reflex in the gut of the teacher may be to say, "Oh, yes you will, or else. . . ." Take two relaxing breaths and collect yourself. This not the time to get upset, and it is certainly *not* the time to do limit-setting.

In all behavioral management there are only two fundamental objectives: (1) to *start* a behavior you want and (2) to *stop* a behavior that you do not want. If you are effective at starting the behavior that you want and stopping the behavior that you do not want, you are a behavior management whiz. However, management techniques such as limit-setting that are effective for stopping behavior are typically not effective for starting behavior.

Limit-setting is a management technique designed explicitly to stop an unwanted behavior. This is *rule enforcement*. It is not designed to start a behavior such as doing an assignment. That is *motivation*. If the student picks up her pencil and begins to do her work as a consequence of limit-setting, it is because she was already motivated to do the work in the first place and therefore returned to task when alternative forms of entertainment were blocked. If a student says, "I'm not going to do this dumb assignment," you are dealing with a *motivation* problem in addition to a discipline problem, and you need a motivation technique to get her started.

Motivation will be dealt with in the volume *Positive Classroom Instruction.* For the time being, simply realize that limit-setting is not the answer to the student who folds her arms and says, "I won't do it."

Now that we have established the general parameters of limit-setting, however, it is important to explore the gray area between stopping a behavior and starting a behavior, for it is here that limit-setting may produce some "funny" results. It is here that you may *finesse* with limit-setting to get a student on task who claims that she will not do the assignment, and it is also here that the teacher may be seduced into thinking that limit-setting can do more for starting behavior than it really can.

Imagine that you are setting limits with a fairly testy individual who has been disrupting with her neighbor and imagine that you have proceeded in the limit-setting sequence as far as palms. She says, "I'm not going to do this dumb assignment! You can't make me!" This talk on the part of the student immediately draws the teacher closer to the student—from palms to camping out in front. The teacher takes two relaxing breaths, looks at the student, and waits—the standard reaction to a student "mouthing off." The student continues to protest about the stupid assignment—how boring it is and how you've been on the same assignment for 3 weeks. Take two more relaxing breaths, and as the child drones on, think to yourself, "Boring." In most cases, the student will run out of hot air as in any other form of back talk, give a sign of exasperation, and get back to work with perhaps the help of a prompt. If the student gets back to work, you have every right to feel smug inside, because you "finessed" the situation.

The student usually gets back to work as a result of limit-setting for the usual reason—to get rid of you! By waiting her out you have gotten the student to *start* a behavior—a result which runs thoroughly counter to the basic nature of limit-setting. Please realize that you have skillfully exploited preexisting motivation. And, please realize that you have just gone as far as you can possibly go with limit-setting in inducing a student to start to do a task that she might not otherwise want to do.

If, however, the student folds her arms, digs in her heels, and persists in saying that she will not do the work, remember the *cardinal rule:* When in doubt, do nothing. Do nothing for a good long time—you have nothing to lose. If you feel about ready to quit because nothing is happening, stay a little bit longer. Experience has shown that the student is having much the same experience. If you are ready to quit, hang in there a little longer, and more often than not, the student will fold at just about the time you were ready to give up.

If, however, you finally conclude that the student is not going to get back to work under any circumstances, bail out, and cut your losses. Say to the student:

> Carol, if you are not going to do this assignment, that is your choice. I will talk to you about it at the break. For right now, the least I will expect from you is that you leave your neighbors alone so that they can do their work.

Take two relaxing breaths before making any movement whatsoever, stand slowly, take two more relaxing breaths, and proceed with the moving out sequence. You have terminated the limit-setting sequence at the point of diminishing returns—the point at which the technique reached its natural limitation. It cannot induce a student to begin working who has made a serious commitment not to work. But it can prevent her from bothering her neighbor since that constitutes stopping an unwanted behavior rather than starting a behavior. Have a heart-to-heart talk with the student at the break and spend part of that evening giving some serious thought to motivational techniques and, in particular, incentives for diligence and excellence (see *Positive Classroom Instruction*).

Property Disputes   When discussing limit-setting, we explicitly did not bring up a situation in which two students were having a property dispute such as fighting over a pencil. Limit-setting is usually the wrong technique at the wrong time to settle a property dispute.

When you begin the limit-setting sequence and arrive at the students' desks only to be met with "She took my pencil. She won't give it back!", take two relaxing breaths and consider an alternative technique. In the first place, you do not even know who the pencil belongs to, and in the second place, you do not have time to find out. Consequently, use a technique specifically designed to deal with property disputes such as one of the following stratagems:

1 Use responsibility training (described in the following chapters).

2 Tell the students that you will discuss whose pencil is whose during the next break (or recess) if the problem is not immediately resolved. It is amazing how rapidly such problems can go away when the alternative is to lose break time.

3 Tell the students to settle it themselves. If the students are having a genuine difference of opinion and are not just engaging in low-level hassling of each other, many teachers have found it effective simply to excuse the students for a brief period in order to settle their differences. Obviously, this is a judgment call that hinges on the sincerity and social maturity of the students.

4 Exhortation. Tell the students to return the pencils to their rightful owners from palms or camping out in front. Then *wait*. It's cheap, and sometimes it even works.

5 Take the pencils and issue crayons for writing until the end of the period for persistent offenders (bizarre, perhaps, but effective for young students).

Dealing with a property dispute is another example of *starting* a behavior, in this case returning a pencil. As in the preceding example, you have to know when to cut your losses. You do not want to debate the issue in the middle of class, so put it back on students. Make them responsible for solving the problem if at all possible and make it expensive to dilly-dally around.

Overexposure   What if the students are junior high-school or high-school-aged girls, and leaning over them might put a male teacher in a compromising situation?

Clothing is an issue that must be seriously considered by secondary teachers, both clothing worn by female students and the clothing worn by female teachers. We deal with the two issues separately.

If the female *students* have low-cut blouses so that camping out would place a male teacher in an embarrassing or compromising situation, do not camp out. You can always walk to the edge of the desk, look at the student, wait, and give a prompt. If at this point you do not get the result you desire and do not want to proceed with limit-setting, abort limit-setting and use responsibility training (discussed later). Remember, there are many ways to get the students to quit fooling around and to get back to work.

What if a female *teacher* is wearing a low-cut blouse so that her leaning over to camp out with male students might make them feel uncomfortable? If a piece of clothing were to keep me from using one of the most effective management techniques in existence, I would consider not wearing that piece of clothing. Easy advice for a male to give. In fact, however, this advice will place almost no practical limitation on the wardrobe of the female teacher. During the first week or two of school while you are training your class that you mean business, don't wear low-cut blouses. After the students know that you mean business, you will probably never have to camp out. For the rest of the year, you can wear whatever you want. If some difficult situation should develop at some point later in the year, and if you are wearing a low-cut blouse, use another technique.

OVERVIEW OF LIMIT SETTING

In learning to perform limit-setting we learn about ourselves. In practicing the skills of relaxation and self-control under pressure we learn how difficult it is to be calm, how easy it is to "pheasant posture" and reprimand while losing the student's respect, how quickly events can turn sour. We learn to accept power as part of our role, but we learn to use our power to protect rather than to threaten. We also learn that caring for and looking after young people is not just a matter of love but also a matter of skill.

More than anything, perhaps, we have seen that "disciplining students" is not only compatible with nurturance, but also a necessary precondition. It is impossible for us to be consistently kind and supportive of young people while we are being repeatedly stressed, hassled, and frustrated. To grit your teeth and be "nice" in the face of provocations and disrespect is counterfeit patience and counterfeit nurturance. For nurturance to be congruent or valid, it must be an exchange of good things between people who are mutually considerate of each other. It must be reciprocal.

This exchange of good things between teacher and student, however, must be structured by teachers as a result of both their caring and skillful use of power. As teachers we must disallow the ruining of positive relationship by the tendencies toward goofing off and fooling around that are endemic to childhood.

Yet the terms "power" and "rule enforcement" have diverse meanings in the public mind—most of them negative. To most people discipline means punition, and "disciplining a child" is synonymous with punishing the child when he or she has done something wrong. Within the classroom of an effective teacher, many students will gain a new understanding of the relationship between adult and child. Children who are reprimanded, criticized, or yelled at by parents at home may learn that there is another, more effective way of responding to provocation that has a healing rather than a destructive effect.

In limit-setting there is a calmness that conveys acceptance of the student without implying acceptance of the misbehavior. Silence, calmness, and genuine rather than counterfeit patience from close range allows students to confront *themselves* rather than the teacher and to finally accept responsibility for their own misbehavior. Patience, however, is not waiting and hoping for the best—the deferral of the setting of limits. Rather, patience is part of that relaxed demeanor with which you confront the problem while you wait for the child to make emotional peace with himself so that he can return to task voluntarily. Even the thrashing about of nasty back talk finally ceases in the face of the composure of real adult power.

In limit-setting there is always an olive branch proffered at the end of the interaction, a reestablishment of relationship and a reconciliation between teacher and student. At no time is the interaction allowed to heat up so as to emotionally polarize teacher and student. Consequently, the reestablishment of relationship between the teacher and student can be a relatively simple and unobtrusive act of affirmation—a simple thank you. In this low-key, emotionally uncharged interaction in which people have not publicly made large commitments to winning or losing, the teacher can be genuinely gentle and patient. Within this context students can come to understand that the teacher is always there for them and cannot be alienated, driven away, or emotionally lost as a result of their own misbehavior and foolishness. It is this steadfast quality of the teacher while firmly setting limits without punition that produces genuine respect on the part of the child.

BUILDING PATTERNS OF COOPERATION

COOPERATION, RELATIONSHIP, AND INCENTIVES

A careful analysis of when limit-setting might fail raises the obvious question: What do you do next? Do you then rely on negative sanctions such as a warning, a name written on the board, the loss of a privilege, detention after school, or being sent to the principal's office? These are the traditional remedies, but they share one liability. They are punitive.

Perhaps the central meaning of limit-setting is that it is possible to suppress unacceptable behavior without the alienation which characterizes punition. It is possible to deal with not only the most common types of disruption in the classroom but also extreme disruptions such as nasty back talk while being both kind to yourself and kind to the student. Limit-setting can even appear to produce cooperation since most of the students are cooperative most of the time when not actively engaged in the joys of goofing off.

Yet, limit-setting has its limits. It does not, in fact, produce cooperation. It only eliminates the goofing off that competes with cooperation. Nor is limit-setting particularly effective from a great distance, or when the teacher is in a seated position, or when students disrupt repetitively in spite of effective limit-setting. Limit-setting is basic, but it is not a cure-all.

If our classroom discipline technology leaves us with only negative sanctions at the point where limit-setting leaves off, then teachers will be left by default to rely on punition repetitively in the course of their daily work. Such a technology would have to be judged as primitive—not yet complete.

This chapter will begin laying the groundwork for our second major method of discipline management, "responsibility training." Responsibility training will pick up where limit-setting leaves off and will succeed in most situations in which limit-setting is not well suited. Responsibility training, therefore, will give the teacher management

143

alternatives in situations in which she might otherwise be tempted to nag, threaten, or punish. Our ultimate objective is to produce cooperation within a positive classroom atmosphere in which the need for the use of punition is extremely remote.

COOPERATION, VOLITION, AND INCENTIVES

Cooperation and Control

The control of unacceptable behavior is typically thought to be the major issue in the management of classroom discipline. However, in the management of discipline within the classroom control is not the most pressing issue. The most pressing issue is the ability of the teacher to produce not only control but also *cooperation*.

Cooperation is a central issue in the management of classroom discipline if for no other reason than frequency. Imagine that a secondary teacher has five class periods a day with thirty-five students in each, and imagine that before the bell for first period rings the teacher wants the students to (1) show up on time, (2) bring pencils and paper, (3) bring books and lab manuals, (4) walk as they enter the room, (5) take their seats, and (6) start working on the assignment on the board. The teacher has made six requests for cooperation from each of his thirty-five students—210 requests for cooperation before the first bell has even rung! Before the day is over, the teacher will make thousands of requests for cooperation from all the students in all their various class periods. Issues of control will arise from time to time, but they will arise seldom compared to the frequency of the teacher's need for cooperation.

Whereas control deals with the issue of *stopping* unwanted behavior, cooperation deals with the issue of *starting* appropriate behavior. Cooperation means that the students take it upon themselves to do what they are supposed to do. They act appropriately and voluntarily, without being forced. The issue of cooperation, therefore, is synonymous with the issue of responsibility. How do you train an entire class to take responsibility for doing all the things that you need them to do during a school day in order to make the job of teaching pleasant and the classroom atmosphere positive?

Who Is Responsible?   Anytime students do not take responsibility for doing what they are supposed to do, the *teacher* ends up responsible by default. If, for example, a student dawdles and comes into class late, who ends up being interrupted and who ends up having to do the paper work to deal with the tardy? The teacher, of course. And, if a half-dozen students come to English composition class without their pencils, who ends up in the "pencil management business"? The teacher, of course. The teacher must deal with the problem one way or another. If the teacher exempts the students from writing because they do not have pencils, no one will come with a pencil the next day. So what do teachers do about pencils? Do they give pencils? Do they loan pencils? Do you really want to get into that?

Thus, anytime that students abdicate responsibility for being in the right place at the right time with the right equipment doing the right thing, the teacher inherits a management dilemma. How do you train an entire class to be responsible at almost no effort to yourself? How do you pick up the slack in classroom management where limit-setting leaves off so that you will not be forced into the position of having to nag, threaten, and punish?

Cooperation and Volition   How do you get one person to cooperate consistently, much less an entire class? Getting young people to cooperate and take responsibility for their own affairs is enough to try the souls of both teachers and parents.

Eliciting cooperation provides any teacher or parent with a quick lesson in impotence. Any parent or teacher can be frustrated, often to the point of rage, by a 2-year-old who simply folds his or her arms, sits down, and says no! The problem with generating cooperation in other people which makes the issue of responsibility so difficult to manage is that:

1 Cooperation is always voluntary.
2 Cooperation is always under the complete control of the other person.

You cannot *make* someone cooperate. To attempt to force a person to cooperate is the opposite of cooperation—coercion. Cooperation is *voluntary*. It is a gift. Someone either gives you cooperation because they want to give it, or you do not get cooperation at all.

So, how do you get students to volunteer to be responsible—especially considering that half your students are not too cooperative to start with? How do you get the thousands of things done in the classroom that need to be done in a typical day without a high level of frustration, without working too hard, and without the need to rely on punition?

The Incentive Imperative

Volition and Incentives   Voluntary behavior is under the control of incentives. Incentives answer one simple question: *Why should I?* People need a reason to volunteer to do something, and that reason is known technically as a reinforcer. A reinforcer, most simply, is anything that anyone will work for. If it does not generate work on the part of your students, it is not a reinforcer even though it may appear desirable to you.

An incentive system is a coherent program for generating work based on the systematic delivery of reinforcers. For purposes of explanation, I will use the terms "reinforcer" and "reward" interchangeably since teachers typically use the terms interchangeably. Please remember, however, that for a reward to be a reinforcer, it must be a reward in the eyes of the recipient—a reward that is meaningful and potent enough to generate work.

In a classroom, therefore, the voluntary behavior that the teacher needs will ultimately be generated by incentive systems. While some students will cooperate out of habit, the cooperation of other students will have to be arranged systematically by the teacher. Teachers have to become expert at the management of incentive systems or else they will not be able to enjoy the degree of cooperation that they would like. To set the teacher free in classroom management, we will need an incentive system that gets everybody to do what they are supposed to do, when they are supposed to do it, to the teacher's standards as a result of simply having been asked.

Built-In Resistance   The notion of managing formal incentive systems for the entire class all day every day in order to generate a consistently high level of cooperation on the part of students does not sit well with many teachers. Most teachers are not accustomed to operating formal incentive systems and know little about them. What little they know typically puts teachers off, especially secondary school teachers. Formal incentive systems in the classroom tend to be equated with "behavior modification," and behavior modification is associated with special education and the primary grades. To tell high school teachers that they will want to operate formal incentives at all times within their class will typically be met with the response, "Oh, no I won't!"

Before the lesson on responsibility training gets off the ground, therefore, we have a rather hard job of "raising the level of concern." The suggestion of extensive incentive management within the classroom will be met with responses ranging from inquisitiveness to disdain to raw anxiety.

- But I can't afford to go to all that trouble.
- Rewards! What are you going to use for rewards for high school kids? They would laugh in your face if you gave them that B-Mod stuff like stars and points and rubber spiders.
- Why should you have to reward students for cooperating? They are supposed to cooperate! They should want to cooperate, and I don't think I should have to pay them to do it.

Whether it is because it looks like a lot of work, or because it looks inappropriate, or because it runs counter to our values, many teachers will repeatedly say, "No, not me. I'd like to do it some other way. I'm getting along just fine without it, thanks." But, in fact, no one gets along all that well without the systematic management of cooperation. And, if cooperation is not systematically managed, what will a teacher substitute for incentives when her or his level of frustration reaches its peak?

The Three Management Options   Limit-setting is unique in its capacity to eliminate unacceptable behavior gently and compassionately. But beyond limit-setting, how many options are left? We will find that the more we learn about incentive systems, the more we come to realize how few our management options really are. Beyond limit-setting we have only three options:

1 Teach well and reward well.
2 Nag, threaten, and punish.
3 Lower our standards and make our peace with the fact that cooperation will not be forthcoming.

Excuses as to why incentive systems might not be your cup of tea will ultimately do you a disservice. Without the systematic use of incentives you will get cooperation only from those students who feel like giving it to you, and you will get nothing from the rest. Without full cooperation you will either become punitive or lower your standards.

Thus, the question of incentives in the classroom is ultimately a question of values. When blocked and frustrated by a lack of cooperation from the same minority of students time after time, how then will you be the kind of person with children that you want to be? Without sophistication in the management of classroom incentives, what answer will you find for the question "Why should I"?

In the following sections we will deal with the technology of formal incentive systems. But, we will come at incentive systems from a new direction: one that will allow us to see how incentive systems operate all around us at all times. Until we understand incentives, the reasons for people doing or failing to do "what they are supposed to" will always seem confusing and mysterious. Thus, we must come to understand how normal, decent, cooperative behavior is generated by the incentive systems of everyday life. Once we understand how incentives operate in our lives at all times, it may be easier to make our peace with operating incentives in our classrooms at all times.

FORMAL AND INFORMAL INCENTIVE SYSTEMS

The type of discipline that we ultimately attempt to instill in our students and in our own children is self-discipline. In addition, we want self-discipline to be internalized in the form of values. We are not typically paid for doing what is right, and we do not want our children growing up expecting to be paid for acts of common decency. Self-discipline is ultimately inseparable from cooperation, the volition to follow appropriate rules and to work for appropriate goals. But how do you create self-discipline?

Incentive systems can be described in many different ways according to many different systems of categorization. For purposes of training children to be responsible and cooperative, it might be best for us to first understand incentive systems as either formal or informal. *Informal* incentive systems are the incentives that govern almost all our responsible, appropriate, adult behavior. Very few of the things that we do in life are governed by *formal* incentives. Your paycheck is perhaps the most prominent example of a formal incentive system—an explicit, negotiated, agreed-upon reward for a piece of work. If the paycheck were removed, the rate of our showing up to work would probably decrease to say the least. But formal incentives are the exception in life rather than the rule. All day long we do all kinds of things as a result of informal incentives—simply because they are the right things to do. How did we learn to act this way, and why do we continue to act this way?

Informal Incentive Systems

Relationship   The rewards in an informal incentive system are emotional rewards of affirmation—love, caring, respect. In education we have an umbrella term for informal incentive systems, "relationship." How is relationship an incentive system?

It is hard to imagine having a relationship with someone without spending time with that person. Time is the sharing of life space, and to imagine a relationship without that sharing of life space is to imagine a pseudo relationship such as the adulation of a fan for a movie star. Yet, a relationship takes more than just time. Many of the adolescents we teach will have been with their parents for a decade and a half, and both parent and child will be quite happy when the kid finally leaves. Similarly in a marriage, years together can produce nothing more than divorce. For time to produce a positive relationship it must be good time.

We have all learned about the importance of "quality time" in building relationship. But there is still more to relationship than quality time. One of the most persistent *myths* about the building of relationship is that bad time somehow does not count. We think of the arguments, the hassles, the nagging, and the bickering as experiences that pass—that blow away like the smoke from a chimney on a windy day. Quite to the contrary, *bad time kills good time*. If a parent and a child spend 45 minutes during a day playing together and 45 minutes during a day arguing and bickering, they end the day even. No relationship has been built at all. If you want a good 25-cent definition of relationship, it is *good time minus bad time*.

We can now begin to see how limit-setting is part of the process of building relationship. By dealing constructively with unacceptable behavior, limit-setting builds trust while minimizing bad time. By cutting our loses, therefore, limit-setting preserves the good time that we give to children at home and at school.

A Developmental Perspective   Where does cooperation come from in children? It would be helpful for us to know because we are going to have to generate a ton of it during the school year. Let's imagine for purposes of illustration that you are the parent of a newborn. What is your first, most immediate, most pressing job in *child discipline*?

Most people draw a blank when thinking of discipline in terms of a newborn. Feed it? No, that is just life support. Change it? No, that is just hygiene. Don't spoil it? No, you cannot spoil a newborn. Give it whatever it needs.

What, then, is the first thing that you do with a newborn to begin the management of child discipline? The answer is pick it up, hold it, rock it, snuggle it, love it, bounce it, nurse it, play with it, snuggle, hug, hold, play, play, play. "Well, I would have done that anyway," you say. Good, that is the only reason the human race has made it as far as it has. You play with your baby because you love it and because it feels good to you. But, things are happening on many different levels from parent-child bonding to neurological development to aiding digestion. One of those levels is discipline.

As far as discipline is concerned, the time you spend playing with your child is *money in the bank*. Playing and holding and nurturing is the good time which is the universal currency of relationship. *Pay your dues in advance*. Play with the baby as much as you can as early as you can. The day will come only too soon when you will have to draw upon the deposits that you have made. If you have not paid your dues in advance, when that time comes you will be broke.

Imagine that your child is now 2 years old and has learned that first word: No! The child has a will, and as a result, the question of cooperation is most relevant.

Let's imagine further that your home is a lucky home for the child—the dues have been paid. Now let's take a situation in which your 2-year-old is cooperative. Let's imagine, for example, that you forgot to "childproof" the house after some guests left last night, and there is a valuable glass object on the coffee table. You turn around to see your 2-year-old picking up the glass object and you say instinctively, "Oh, please put that down!"

The child looks at you, and he *calculates*. You see, a 2-year-old is not yet what we would think of as a "moral being." That will come later. Rather, a 2-year-old is simply a pragmatist, a shrewd, Machiavellian gambler. The child is old enough to know the odds *and* the first lesson of the birds and the bees: A smart bird does not do-do in its own nest. He looks at you, he hesitantly puts the object down, and he looks at you again tentatively with a smile. You pick him up, unaware of the economics of building cooperation, and you give him hugs and kisses and say, "Oh, thank you. You are a dear!"

It worked again! Do anything that halfway pleases mommy and daddy, and you get hugs and kisses—a good gamble for someone who has been well-taught. Cooperate and you get loved immediately. Two-year-olds, shrewd gamblers that they are, simply bet on the best odds for receiving pleasure calculated on the basis of their past experience with us. What behavior has the best odds of paying off? With our giving of good time in the past we have taught them to bet on cooperation in the present.

But the lessons of cooperation are far richer than simple compliance. Through the love that we have given, the time that we have given, and the dues that we have paid, we have taught the child that *if you give good things, you get good things*. We have taught a concept that does not take up much space in a typical psychology textbook— trust. You can trust the people around you to provide love and nurturance to you if you are considerate of them. We have also taught the child to delay gratification—to *trust* that small pleasures relinquished in the present will produce greater pleasures in the future. We have taught the child that she or he can trust the future to bring happiness if she or he works for it.

And values? What about the internalization of values that will form the basis of both self-discipline and moral behavior? You might say that morality is a habit most of the time and a conscious choice only occasionally. Patterns of appropriate behavior and the consideration of others that accompanies it become part of our self-concept over time. We internalize the entire transaction of acting cooperatively—both the behavior itself and the affirmation that follows. As we grow older we simply do what is right and feel good about it. Doing what is right is the pattern of behavior that has been internalized, and feeling good about it is the love and respect that has been internalized. Through the love given by others we have been taught to love ourselves. Some of our self-love, our positive self-concept, is noncontingent just as is the love of a parent. And some of our self-love is contingent just as is the approval of a parent when we act cooperatively and responsibly. In adulthood, therefore, when nobody is around to reward us explicitly for doing what is right, we will feel good about what we have done anyway. The informal incentive system is now part of us. Behavioral scientists tend to be self-conscious when talking about morality and values, so they refer to adult moral behavior as "contingent self-reinforcement."

But now, let us imagine a different child—one less lucky. Imagine an uncooperative child. Imagine a child for whom the dues in "good time" were not paid. And, frankly, it makes no difference to the child why the dues were not paid. Perhaps you didn't have time to play because you were working too hard, you were in graduate school, you were starting a business, you had a business going bankrupt, the pregnancy was unwanted, you don't like children anyway, or you are just an obsessive-compulsive personality who would rather do repairs around the house or run a vacuum cleaner. You may as well file the excuses, because all the kid knows is that the dues weren't paid.

Now, you see the child holding the glass object and you say, "Oh, dear, put that down!" Just like the cooperative child, this one looks at you, and calculates. The child asks the timeless questions of incentive systems, "Why should I? What's in it for me?" The answer is nothing! So, like a good gambler, the child bets on the sure thing. In this case, however, the sure thing happens to be this fascinating, glittering glass object.

"I *said*, put that down! Did you hear me? If you don't put that down, I'll . . . Damn! That kid won't do a thing I say!" Now, since you have not paid your dues in good time, you will pay dues in bad time. There is no "money in the bank," no reserves of trust and goodwill that produce a confidence in impending reward for cooperation. The parent is broke. With little trust that cooperation will produce a greater good than the one the child holds in hand, the child bets on the only option with decent odds: immediate gratification.

It is now too late to get cooperation for the asking. See how fast a fragile relationship can turn sour? See how easy it is to generate bad time in lieu of good time? In these two homes the ratio of good time to bad time over the years will probably be as different as day and night. Are you now left with only coercion?

You are up against that timeless economic reality of discipline management: "pay me now or pay me later." Discipline will be managed one way or another—either proactively or reactively. In the long run it is cheaper to pay in advance. Only by paying your dues in advance do you ever get compliance for the asking. Paying in advance is also more pleasant than paying later, but pay you will. Cooperation is never free. The only difference between a cooperative child and a noncooperative child is the odds, not the nature of the gambler. Gamblers are quite predictable; they will always bet on the best odds. You the parent and you the teacher create the odds.

Relationship is an incentive system just as clearly as any incentive system that was ever consciously and purposefully designed. The child works for a reason. The reason is supplied by a history of love, caring, and respect. But the question "Why should I?" must be answered. Only two characteristics make relationship in any way unique among incentive systems. In the first place, the cooperation is bought with good time characterized by love, caring, and respect. And, in the second place, you pay for the cooperation *in advance*. Fail to build relationship, and you will have to get compliance in some other way. Will it be coercion, or will you pay for cooperation using some other, more costly incentive system?

The Mythology of Relationship   The most persistent myth concerning the building of cooperation through relationship is that relationship is enough. If you simply care about children enough and are good-hearted enough and love enough and give enough, then you will get the cooperation you need in return. The myth of relationship is that it is not only *necessary* but also *sufficient*.

Necessary relationship most certainly is, but sufficient it most certainly is not. As mentioned earlier in regards to limit-setting, one of the child's most basic jobs in life is to test limits in order to test reality. One reason that children will not cooperate at times is simply to see what will happen if they do not. Can your love be trusted, or does it turn to nastiness with a little provocation?

If you have children of your own, think whether you get all the cooperation from them that you would want during any given day. Do they always do what they are supposed to just because you ask them once? Do they always make their beds, pick up their toys, put their clothes in the hamper, hang up the towels after they bathe, hurry when you need them to hurry just because, God knows, you have given them the best years of your life? If you were the perfect parent, do you think you could get 100 percent cooperation? If you do, you obviously have the joys of parenthood to look forward to. And, what if you have two children? It gets more difficult when they can fuss and fight with each other. What if you have three children? Now they outnumber the parents.

Now that we examined the likelihood of perfect cooperation at home, look at the classroom. There are thirty-five students, none of whom you have raised, none of whom owe you anything before the first day of school, and half of whom have been blatantly mismanaged since the day they were born. Now ask yourself, are you going to get all the cooperation you need from all those students all year long just because you love them and care for them and are willing to go the extra mile? Will relationship alone be enough? Are you kidding?

What will you do, however, when the cooperation is not spontaneously forthcoming? How will you pick up the slack? Will you nag, threaten, punish? Now that we know where cooperation comes from, we are free of the illusion that perhaps we can pay enough dues in a school year with our charm and good looks to get all the cooperation we need from thirty-five kids who didn't even know us before September. *Formal* incentives must pick up the slack where "relationship" leaves off.

Indeed, caring is not enough. When I observe the classroom of a young green teacher who cares, I typically see someone who is struggling through the day with a giving heart, a stiff upper lip, and a massive expenditure of energy. They survive by their determined effort to learn the ropes without going under. They do their best to succeed with thirty-five squirmy bodies each going his or her own direction when half the time they really don't know what to do.

Burned-out teachers are usually not uncaring people although they may now seem that way. Most of them cared once. Most people have enough native intelligence not to choose a profession that places you in a roomful of children all day for the rest of your life if you really don't like kids. Even though some teachers cared more than others, most cared enough to succeed had they been equipped with adequate skills. Most could have grown to like their job more rather than less if they had been able to feel a high degree of success at an affordable price. They needn't have burned out, but they did because, given their entry level skills and the lack of adequate ongoing professional development and support, they never had a chance.

If limit-setting, relationship, and *formal incentive systems* are not used early, skillfully, and deliberately under conditions structured by the teacher, the teacher will have to manage as best they can later under the worst of conditions. I have seen teachers become predictably punitive in only one context—when the students have become so unruly and disruptive that the teacher has his or her back against the wall. In that case the teacher must bring some kind of order out of chaos or be a complete joke within his classroom. Under such pressure teachers usually do what they feel they have to do, and the ax falls where it must. Off balance and under stress, patience, humor, nurturance, and support are luxuries that the teacher cannot afford. Students are yelled at, demeaned, threatened, scolded, and punished.

There are no easy alternatives to a teacher's acquiring the technical expertise to implement formal incentive systems. Discipline is either done early and effectively, or it is attempted when it is too late. Only formal incentive systems in conjunction with relationship and limit-setting will have the power and flexibility to consistently generate cooperation and harmony from a roomful of students who come from all kinds of homes and backgrounds.

If you have ever been taught that humanistic and behavioral psychology are different animals, you have been mistaught. They are not only identical at their core, but they also need each other to produce consistently successful results in the field. Indeed, the only real differences between formal and informal incentive systems are the explicitness and the timing of the payment. See Table 8-1.

Do not imagine for a moment that formal incentive systems are an option. Do not imagine for a moment that, even though you are a teacher of supposedly grown-up high school students, you can afford *not* to operate formal incentives sophisticated enough to generate genuine cooperation when relationship proves inadequate. Cooperation you must have, and cooperation you must buy. Whatever you cannot buy with informal incentive systems, you must buy with formal incentive systems.

In the final section of this chapter we will take a look at the fundamental principles

TABLE 8-1
SIMILARITIES BETWEEN INFORMAL INCENTIVES (RELATIONSHIP) AND FORMAL INCENTIVE SYSTEMS

Informal incentives	Formal incentives
Pay in advance.	Pay as you go.
The currency is "good time" with you.	The *best* currency is "good time" with you.
The result is cooperation.	The result is cooperation.
By-products include: • love • caring • respect • trust • enjoyment	By-products include: • love • caring • respect • trust • enjoyment
Rewards are given spontaneously in most cases and are implicit.	Rewards are formally planned and are explicit.
Adequate compensation is assumed on the basis of past experience.	The price is agreed upon in advance.

that underlie the design and implementation of formal incentive systems. As we become more familiar with the basic principles governing incentives, we will lose some more illusions about the use of formal incentives as we learn how few our choices really are in regards to design and implementation.

SIMPLE AND COMPLEX INCENTIVE SYSTEMS

Having resigned ourselves to the necessity of operating formal incentive systems in the classroom, it is time to become familiar with some of their characteristics. We will find, after we get past a few of the technical basics, that when properly implemented in a classroom, formal incentive systems produce enjoyment and build relationship as a by-product. We will not buy cooperation with money, or stars on a chart, or points, or rubber spiders. We will buy cooperation with learning, and we will have fun doing it.

At this point in our discussion it would be most useful to divide formal incentive systems into two basic types: *simple* and *complex* incentive systems. Simple incentive systems will be used quite extensively in the classroom to create diligence and excellence. Learning about simple incentive systems will teach us many of the basic principles of incentive systems that we need to know. But complex incentive systems are far more useful for discipline management.

Simple Incentive Systems

Grandma's Rule Formal incentive systems, whether simple or complex, are based on one simple principle known as "grandma's rule." Although grandma's rule sounds deceptively simple, within it are incorporated some of the most demanding characteristics of incentive management. *Grandma's rule: You have to finish your dinner before you get your dessert.*

Grandma's rule is simple, but it is also strict, and therein lies the rub. You do not get *any* dessert until *all* the dinner is completed. Tucked away in grandma's rule is a simple standard of excellence which has characterized the teaching profession at its best for centuries: We are simply going to keep doing it until we get it right!

A simple incentive system has three basic parts (see Table 8-2). The first is dinner—the task. The second is dessert—the reward or reinforcer for doing the task. But, it is the third part of a simple incentive system, only implied in grandma's rule, that is by far the most expensive. The third part of a simple incentive system is *accountability.*

TABLE 8-2
PARTS OF A SIMPLE INCENTIVE SYSTEM

Dinner	the task
Dessert	the reward or reinforcer
Accountability	strict monitoring of the quality and quantity of work as it is being done

Grandma, of course, would be rather dotty if she simply handed out dessert without checking to see how much dinner anyone had eaten. So it is with all incentive systems: the quality and quantity of work must be strictly checked before any reward is issued. It is safe to say that the major cost of implementing any incentive system is accountability—the main component of any quality control system.

Group Management and Cost Containment   The ultimate limitation for the use of any incentive system in the classroom is cost. How many incentive systems can you operate at any one time without going bananas? Are you going to have a separate one for every student? Are you going to have a separate one for good behavior and another one for good work? Are you going to keep individualized records and pay for rewards out of pocket? How can you go to that much effort and expense for each member of the class?

The answer, of course, is that you cannot. Individualized management programs are out the window. Classroom management is, as the name implies, management of the *class*. Consequently, our incentive systems will have to be *group* incentive systems rather than a collection of individual incentive systems. The cost of a single group incentive system will be greatly reduced since you need only one reward and one system of accountability for the entire class. It is a classic example of "all for one and one for all." Yet, while group rewards are affordable, they have some important side effects for group dynamics. One unavoidable result is peer pressure which must be managed so that it is benign rather than nasty. Another unavoidable result is extremely high standards of compliance. Any group incentive system requires that the *entire* group cooperate for *anyone* in the group to get *any* reward.

Simple group incentives, therefore, are perpetually vulnerable to failure because any one student in the class can ruin it for everyone else at any time. It only takes one person to "blow it" and the reward cannot be given. If this happens very often, the class loses faith in the management system and they quit working for the reinforcer. At that point the system folds up and dies.

Because of the stringent standards that accompany simple incentive systems when applied to a group, they are almost useless in the management of classroom discipline. They usually fail because they have no teeth—no way of suppressing abuse by one or two students long enough to allow the teacher to reward the entire group for cooperating. For this reason, simple incentive systems are used primarily to reward excellence and diligence in the completion of assignments, a topic that will be covered in detail in *Positive Classroom Instruction*. For our present purpose, it is enough to know that some additional elements will have to be added to our simple incentive system for it to function as a powerful and economical tool for producing cooperation.

Complex Incentive Systems

Additional Elements   Complex incentive systems are complex because they have more parts than simple incentive systems. The two additional parts complex incentive systems have are (1) bonus and (2) penalty. Complex incentive systems will be more useful for managing classroom discipline because they have teeth. It is the job of the penalty to suppress goofing off and noncooperation by the few long enough to permit the teacher to reward the many. Thus, even though complex incentive systems may have a penalty clause, they are still overwhelmingly reward-based. The penalty, in fact, strengthens the use of reward insofar as it allows us to give reward more often to everyone.

Group Rewards   The type of group rewards most commonly used in the classroom are activities. A teacher can have activities with their group quite economically, whereas any form of tangible reward would be both expensive and difficult to distribute. Yet, to serve as a reinforcer, an activity reward must be highly desired or preferred by the students. Thus, activity rewards tend to be referred to as "preferred activities." The activity must be preferred over what the students are currently doing at least to the extent that the students will work for access to the preferred activity.

Preferred activities, of course, take time. The time that a teacher sets aside for preferred activities, therefore, will be referred to as Preferred Activity Time (PAT). Preferred activity time is obviously a time of enjoyment and stimulation—something that students not only look forward to but also work for during the day or during the week. Preferred activities, of course, can be anything from a party to recess, but they can also be *learning-related activities*. If the preferred activity is "fun and games," we lose the preferred activity time for learning. For the sake of efficiency, therefore, we will learn to have fun with learning so that PAT represents no loss of time on task.

With preferred activity time we are back to basics in building cooperation through "good time." Our complex incentive systems within the classroom will ultimately be based on good time with learning just as relationship is based on good time with nurturance and play. We will, in fact, be able to make test review and skill drill the preferred activity which will generate an entire day's or week's cooperation from an entire class. Thus, the students will have more fun with learning, and the teacher will have more fun with her or his students at a greatly reduced level of stress and without having to nag to get compliance. When an incentive system is properly designed, everybody wins.

Complex Time Incentives   We refer to a time incentive as any incentive in which the reward is measured in time, such as preferred activity time. In a time incentive (Table 8-3), time is used as the medium of exchange. Teachers are literally buying cooperation with good time just as we do in relationship. Indeed, when properly designed, formal time incentives build relationship as a by-product of PAT since they create good time between teacher and student.

TABLE 8-3
TIME INCENTIVES

Reward	good time (PAT)
Bonus	more time
Penalty	less time

Once time is used as the universal medium of exchange in a group incentive system, complex incentives become simple and easy to administer for the class. Bonuses and penalties are measured in time just as is the reward which they augment. Thus, bonus becomes *more* time and penalty becomes *less* time.

The shape of the formal complex incentive system most useful for discipline management in the classroom is now becoming apparent. The only incentive system that you can afford is a group incentive system, and group rewards are activity rewards. The time that is required to give the group an activity reward is called preferred activity time, and preferred activity time can be lengthened for extra cooperation (a bonus) or shortened for lack of cooperation such as dawdling (a penalty). Indeed, a teacher can buy any behavior they want with *time*. Time is our universal medium of exchange, and by learning to use time effectively in the classroom, we will be able to train the entire class to be responsible at all times so that everyone can have a maximum of preferred activity time.

OVERVIEW

The principles of formal incentive systems are rather simple, as we have found. The difficulty of operating incentive systems in the classroom, therefore, is obviously not the theory but, rather, the mechanics and the logistics. A poorly designed incentive system can cause the teacher a tremendous amount of work while being extremely failure-prone. A well-designed incentive system can be extremely economical, relatively failsafe, and fun. Responsibility training is such a system. In fact, the "good time" of responsibility training can be fun with learning so that the reward for the behavioral incentive system becomes part of the teacher's instructional program.

Any block to the widespread use of formal incentives in the classroom to buy cooperation from students in lieu of punition, therefore, no longer lies in the mechanics, logistics, or cost of formal incentive systems but, rather, it lies in our heads. Many teachers are afraid to use formal incentive systems because all they know of incentive systems are the expensive, custom-built programs of behavior modification that are primarily used for young or handicapped students. Many high school teachers don't want to be bothered with any programs that they imagine their students might ridicule, and some secondary teachers don't every feel that the management of cooperation is their responsibility.

We have discussed relationship at some length in this chapter so that we might understand better how incentives operate all around us and so that we might understand not only what relationship can do for us but also what it cannot do for us. Only when we have dealt with the issue of cooperation to the point where we have been disabused of our illusion that "relationship is enough" will we be in the market for formal incentive systems. And, only when formal incentive systems are truly economical can teachers afford to be bothered with them. In the following chapter we will see how to manage cooperation and build responsibility systematically at a price that any teacher can afford.

RESPONSIBILITY TRAINING

The ultimate goal of discipline is to train young people to be responsible for their own actions. Responsible behavior is appropriate behavior freely chosen. Responsible behavior is cooperation that has become a habit. Being responsible for one's own actions means that patterns of appropriate behavior have been internalized so that a person is self-directing. Individuals not only choose a socially constructive course of action, but they also see that the habitual choice of that action as well as its consequences belongs to themselves.

PRODUCING RESPONSIBLE BEHAVIOR

For people to take responsibility for a choice, they must have choices and they must have the freedom to exercise choice. More specifically, for anyone to ever learn to be responsible, the following three conditions must be met:

1 They have something for which to be responsible (a resource of finite quantity).
2 They have control over the consumption of that resource.
3 They must live with the consequences of their decisions concerning the consumption of that resource. In particular, they must live with the consequences of their own foolishness.

Something For Which to Be Responsible

Imagine that you are attempting to train your child to be responsible with money. If the child never had any money, it would be difficult to learn to spend money responsibly. Before children can learn to spend money wisely, they must have some experience. They must have some money to spend.

Yet, while the child must have a resource, it must be a finite resource. How can a parent train an adolescent to save and spend wisely if the child has immediate access to a 5 million dollar trust fund? Even if the parent wants to train the child to watch nickels and dimes, the parent will have a hard time answering the question "Why should I?" to the child's satisfaction.

Control over Consumption

If the child has some money to spend but the parent dictates what it will be spent for, how will the child learn to spend wisely? They never get to decide how to spend it. Although good advice from one's elders certainly has its place, at some point the child must be free to choose. The parent must relinquish the last vestige of control—veto power.

Living with the Consequences

One's first attempts at governing one's own affairs are not always successful. Imagine, for example, that the child was given a week's money to spend on lunch at school and miscellaneous needs. Imagine that the kid ate at the local fast-food hangout and blasted money away on computer games so that he was broke by Wednesday.

If the child says, "Hey dad, can I have a couple of bucks to see me through the week?" and gets it, will he ever learn to be responsible with money? No. You have violated the first condition of learning to be responsible by granting the child a resource that is not clearly finite. If the cash flow is not finite, then you have created an incentive system to produce a wheedler who will try to find out how close to infinity he can get. Being savvy about the incentive systems of everyday life, you hold the line.

Sorry, son. That's it for the week. I don't lend money.

But, dad. I'll starve! I'm out of lunch money.

Well, don't worry, son. There will be plenty of good food on the table at breakfast and dinner. Nobody ever starved to death between breakfast and dinner.

Aw, dad! You're tight! Besides, I don't have any date money.

That's OK, son. You're welcome to bring your date home and watch TV if you're broke.

Are you kidding? . . .

Brace yourself for the onslaught. All teenagers with an ounce of creativity can make any inexperienced adult feel like an absolute jerk for having any standards whatsoever. The first part of their routine is to roll their eyes back, raise their arms in a sign of exasperation, and then badger you with excuses:

You're so tight!

Yea, but you don't understand.

I don't believe this!

You're kidding, aren't you?

You never give me anything when I need it!

This place is like a penitentiary!

Are you for real?

Now, however, the child must live with the consequences of his foolishness and squandering. And based on his experience and his continued control over a finite resource, the child must now choose how to spend *next* week's allowance. Last week's experience informs next week's choices.

Until there is control over the choices which govern the consumption of a finite resource and no way to sidestep the consequences of those choices, there is ownership of neither the choice itself nor the long-term consequences of the choice. There is no reason to plan. Of all the things that I want, what do I want most? Do I want something badly enough to save for it? Now the child is beginning to think responsibly.

PRODUCING RESPONSIBLE BEHAVIOR IN THE CLASSROOM

The conditions that produce responsible behavior in general provide a clear-cut guide for producing responsible behavior in the classroom. The students must have something to be responsible for, but it most certainly will not be money or tokens or trinkets or candy or rubber spiders. The students must also have control over the consumption of their resources, but the teacher must also be in control of the class at the same time. And the students must live with the consequences of their choosing but without the risk of their becoming resentful or angry at each other.

At this point we must go back to where we left off at the end of the preceding chapter. How is it that you can get almost any student to do almost anything that you want her to do when you want it done to *your* standards as a result of having asked her only *once?* That is cooperation. How do you arrange the students' reality for them to freely and habitually choose what is best for them so that those choices become internalized values over time? That is responsibility. What resource will you use to buy the cooperation and responsible behavior that is not forthcoming on the basis of relationship?

As we learned earlier, relationship is not enough, especially with a classroom full of kids from all kinds of home situations. To generate consistently good behavior from all class members, we will have to use a *complex, formal* incentive system that utilizes (1) bonus and (2) penalty. To be affordable, it must be a group incentive system that utilizes (1) group rewards (preferred activity time) and (2) group accountability (one for all and all for one). Preferred Activity Time (PAT) is the reinforcer—"good time" just as in relationship. Bonus and penalty become simply *more* PAT and *less* PAT. A management program which uses time as a universal medium of exchange will be referred to as a time incentive.

There is a resource at the teacher's disposal that the students always want, which the teacher controls, and which is absolutely free. That resource is *time.* Time can be used as the universal medium of exchange in the classroom. Teachers can, if they know how, buy cooperation at will with the skillful manipulation of not just time but time on task. Time is the resource that teachers will give away just so they can hold the class responsible for the way in which it is consumed. We are now ready to turn a corner to encounter a classroom management system of almost embarrassing simplicity. It is called "responsibility training."

RESPONSIBILITY TRAINING

Responsibility training is an advanced type of time incentive that gets almost any student to do almost anything you want her or him to do when you want it done to your standards as a result of having asked only once. Responsibility training, of course, has three basic components:

1 Something for which to be responsible (a resource of finite quantity). The class is given a fixed amount of preferred activity time *in advance* of any cooperation or good behavior on the part of the students. It does not have to be earned and is not a reward for performance of any kind on the part of the students. It is a gift.

2 Control over the consumption of that resource. Any student can consume any amount of PAT at any time in any way. Thus, teachers *give* and students *consume*. PAT is consumed when any student decides to have a PAT. Of course, the class could have the PAT all together, but individuals can have a PAT whenever they decide to take a mini-vacation in the form of fooling around, dawdling, or disrupting when they should be on task.

3 Living with the consequences of decisions made concerning the consumption of the resource. When the PAT is consumed, it's gone! There ain't no more.

Giving PAT

Responsibility training is a management system oriented toward *giving* by the teacher and toward *enjoyment* by students within the bounds of responsible behavior. Before the system is a month old it may have self-eliminated to the point where its only remnant is PAT. PAT is what you are left with, and PAT is where you begin. The core of responsibility training is the enjoyment of learning. In fact, in sophisticated incentive systems enjoyment is a classroom imperative. Teachers will always err in the direction of generosity, and they will make not one gift but *three*.

1 *PAT.* The teacher will give to the class a quantity of PAT which is regularly scheduled and added to the class's daily or weekly routine. PAT should not be some normal activity of the class which has been glorified and given a new name (such as time to finish your assignments at the secondary level or recess at the elementary level). Normal parts of the school routine are not perceived by students as a gift but, rather, as a birthright. PAT is a new addition to class life which has the enjoyment of learning as its main purpose.

2 *More PAT.* The teacher will give bonuses to the class whenever they do an excellent job of cooperating and being responsible. We will be generous. We will use the giving of bonuses to generate more responsible behavior than you can imagine.

3 *Structure of PAT.* The PAT will be planned by the teacher with the help of the

students to ensure that PAT is truly something to look forward to. PAT is *not* free time to "kick back" because such an abdication of structure by the teacher usually produces boredom and the negation of PAT. Since most students can "kick back" for the remainder of the day as soon as school is out, there is usually a glut of free time on the market. With the teacher's leadership the class will have to give some serious thought to the problem of having fun with learning at school.

Do not worry about frittering away valuable work time in mindless fun and games. PAT, when properly planned, will permit you to use skill drill, enrichment, and even test review as a PAT capable of producing good behavior in a secondary classroom for an entire week.

Responsibility training is incentive management turned upside down, and consequently it takes some getting used to. Its most heretical feature is its first component— the gift of PAT to the class *before* it is earned. We must violate grandma's rule—a difficult mental hurdle for someone trained in incentive management. We shall give the class its reward for being responsible before they have done anything to earn it. Grandma would be appalled! We've giving out dessert before dinner. How do you expect anyone to work for a reward if they already have it? There is no incentive!

Quite to the contrary, we will be generous to a fault with our incentives, and the students will work for them. But training a class to be responsible approaches the subject of reward from a different angle than straightforward reward for a job well done. We must change our approach, or we will be stuck with 1970s vintage behavior modification forever. We will give the reward away first because, until the class has a *resource* for which to be responsible, you can't hold them responsible.

The Teacher's Role   In responsibility training, the teacher's role has two prominent aspects: (1) giver and (2) timekeeper or accountant. The teacher's mood ranges from warm and generous when dealing with giving to benign and neutral when dealing with noncooperation. The benign role of the teacher in the management of responsibility training eliminates a reliance on forms of punition such as nagging, for which everyone can be grateful.

The Teacher as Giver   As a giver, the teacher begins responsibility training by making three gifts: (1) time (PAT), (2) more time (bonus PAT), and (3) structuring PAT for the sake of enjoyment. The teacher gives within a context of warmth, praise, and generosity. First, teachers can arrange bonuses for almost anything they want done so that almost any decent effort on the part of the students can produce some bonus time. Second, teachers show warmth and approval as they praise the students for earning bonus PAT. In addition, they make a public display of that approval by going to the blackboard to publicly record each bonus.

The Teacher as Timekeeper or Accountant   To operate responsibility training teachers pair their gifts with strict and accurate accountability. They must keep an accurate record of time given and time consumed. They must keep track of bonus and penalty with sufficient accuracy so that no one ever has reason to argue with the final tabulation of PAT. Above all else, teachers need credibility.

Remember, in any incentive system strict and accurate accountability is usually the greatest expense. So how do you keep dead accurate records of the behavior of an entire classroom for an entire day or week at almost no effort? This question has a simple answer only with a group management system when the universal medium of exchange is time. All records can be kept by a single record of time gained (bonus) and time consumed (penalty).

Keeping a public record of the time a group earns or consumes can be done for a given class period or for an entire day or week very simply. Table 9-1 displays the class's planned PAT of 15 minutes plus several bonuses. Keep a separate record somewhere else to discourage anyone from tampering with the numbers on the blackboard.

Whereas bonuses can be recorded publicly on the blackboard within the context of praise, time loss (the squandering of PAT) will be recorded within a context of respectful silence. The recording of PAT that is squandered must be accurate lest the students wheedle and argue, and it must be free of reprimand lest the teacher undermine the positive tone of their incentive system with nagging. Silence and time allow the students to choose and to own their choice.

Teachers can keep a running account of the consumption of preferred activity time in a number of ways. When a student is fooling around, they can simply turn toward the student, say the student's name, and wait until the student is back on task. They can then make a notation of the amount of time that it took the student to get back to task on the board, on a 3 × 5 card, or in their head. The student just took a mini-PAT. He consumed whatever amount of time it took him to get back on task after the teacher started monitoring.

To keep track of the time, a teacher can look at her watch or the sweep second hand on the classroom clock, or she can estimate time in her head. She can even count the seconds out loud—anything that will give the teacher a reasonably accurate running account of time consumed with a respectable degree of accuracy and minimal expense. In years of experience with responsibility training, however, one method of keeping track of the consumption of preferred activity time stands out from all the rest. Use a stopwatch.

When you see a student goofing off (assuming that it is not possible to use limit-setting in this situation), excuse yourself from the student you are helping, turn to the student, say her name, take two relaxing breaths and then, if necessary, pull out your stopwatch and hold it up in plain view. Any student who does not understand what is

TABLE 9-1
PAT RECORD WITH FOUR
BONUSES RECORDED

+	−
PAT 15:—	
1:05	
:36	
:18	
1:—	

about to happen after having it explained is in bad shape. If the student wants to return to work, she does so at no cost to preferred activity time. If she wishes to continue goofing off, however, the teacher simply presses the button on the stopwatch (buy one with a loud click) and waits. Take some more relaxing breaths and look at the student with the expressionless, mildly bored look of relaxation. It is not your time that is being wasted, after all, it is the *students'* time. You give the preferred activity time; they decide how to use it.

Once time is gone, it can never be brought back. There is no more concrete proof of time flying than to hear a clock tick. Students typically realize that there is no possible benefit from prolonging the interaction since they are wasting the group's preferred activity time. They cannot even engage you in back talk as a last ditch effort to get off the hook unless they do it on their own time. Students, for the most part, do not have a leg to stand on. Like any smart gambler who does not hold the cards, they fold.

Consuming PAT

Whereas anyone can consume any amount of PAT they wish at any time they wish, they cannot do so without becoming responsible for their action. The resource that the student may decide to consume belongs to the whole class. Remember, this is a group incentive system with a single PAT—one for all and all for one. Thus, while students may be free to choose, they must do so as part of a larger group in which they will be held accountable for the appropriateness of that choice. They must live with the consequences.

The Student's Choice   Students, beware! It is easy to fritter away your PAT. When deciding how to consume your PAT, you have two choices:

1 *Be selfish and squander.* Any student who is so inclined can consume a small amount of PAT whenever he feels like it. Two students may carry on a conversation for a minute, or a single student may wander around the room for a minute, or several students may dawdle a few minutes after the work period has begun. Each student can take a little break, a mini-PAT. If many students decide to take the liberty of having many small PATs by themselves or with a friend, they could conceivably squander much of the reward. When the PAT is consumed a little at a time, no one gets very much of anything. That is squandering, and it is also selfish on the part of the students who do it.

While explaining responsibility training to the class, you want to present selfishness and squandering as a real possibility that can consume a considerable amount of the PAT. Such a discussion is more a part of values clarification than anything else. In fact, no such selfishness and squandering will be possible when responsibility training is properly implemented. There are many safeguards to prevent PAT from being consumed irresponsibly because, as soon as the PAT is gone, so is your management system.

2 *Save and share.* The second alternative for consuming preferred activity time is for the class as a whole to save the entire PAT. If no one fritters away any of the PAT during the week by squandering or being selfish, everyone can share in the maximum possible amount of PAT. That is smart. And it would be smarter yet to add to the PAT through bonuses.

Although the class is obviously better off as a whole if they save and share their preferred activity time, the choice to do so belongs to the members of the class. It is not the teacher's role to get upset or nag. The teacher makes the gift of PAT, and the class members decide how the PAT will be consumed. If members of the class decide to squander the preferred activity or to be selfish with it, that is a decision that the class must live with.

Peer Pressure   As time passes, the disruptive student must consider the peer group. What about the peer group? Wouldn't they love to kill the student who has just wasted some of their preferred activity time?

As mentioned earlier, any group management system unavoidably creates peer pressure. Since group management is the only thing that we can afford as a means of generating cooperation from all our students in the many situations typical of a classroom, peer pressure comes with the territory. The question is not whether we will or will not have peer pressure. The only question is, can we render it benign.

To begin with, peer pressure in responsibility training is typically far more benign than we might imagine in our "worst possible case scenarios." Typically, peer pressure toward one or two students who are squandering PAT takes the form of a few urgent whispers.

Hey you guys. You're wasting time!

Quit talking, will you?

Hey, will you guys sit down. We're losing PAT.

As you can see, the class has begun to take responsibility for enforcing your (their) classroom rules. Usually a whisper or two is enough. Peer approval and disapproval are typically far more powerful than yours. By taking yourself out of the enforcer role, you have robbed power struggles of their meaning.

But what if, God forbid, some lippy, snippy kid is actually cruel to a classmate who has requested that he shape up? Such encounters occur mainly in your dreams, apart from special education, but they deserve to be dealt with here. If some student should be nasty to another student with a remark such as "Hey, sit down, you jerk!", the teacher can very quickly train the class not to engage in such behavior. The teacher turns toward the student who has made the rude remark, takes two relaxing breaths, and walks over to that student as in limit-setting while letting the watch run. The teacher then stands in front of the student for two relaxing breaths, slowly leans over, and privately says to the student: "Trisha, we do not speak to each other unkindly like that in my classroom. Do you understand?"

The student, realizing that her rudeness is causing more time to be wasted than the other student's misbehavior, will typically fold with an apology. Thank the child, stand, take two relaxing breaths, turn to the other student, who is probably back on task at this point, and thank them. Click the watch off.

The use of a stopwatch as part of responsibility training seems to be more powerful than any of the other methods of accountability because it is a concrete auditory and visual reminder that preferred activity time is, in fact, being consumed. Students do not argue or wheedle with the watch, and if they do, they do it on their time. Nor do they blame the teacher for the fact that time is passing. It is abundantly clear who is responsible for PAT being consumed. Nor do they say that it is not fair. It is incredibly fair—accurate to a tenth of a second. For these reasons, the physical mechanism of the stopwatch effectively conveys to the students both that time is passing and that they are responsible.

In the final analysis, however, the stopwatch is just one particularly effective method among many to provide the teacher with accurate and easy accountability for the behavior of an entire class for almost any length of time. If you do not want to use a stopwatch, you certainly do not need to use one for responsibility training to succeed. But if you decide to use a stopwatch, buy a two-button stopwatch so that you can record continuous elapsed time (rather than continuously resetting it to zero with a single control button), or consider buying a new wrist watch with a stopwatch function.

With the recording of time the cost problems of providing accurate accountability for the behavior of many students for almost any length of time have been licked. Having overcome problems of cost-effectiveness in the use of a group incentive system, we are now free to use a highly powerful time incentive all week with everyone in the class at almost no effort. At this point, however, many teachers might drag forth their "worst possible case scenarios" as a means of coping with the unfamiliar.

Do I have to carry a stopwatch around all year?

What if everybody in the building is using it?

Who is going to buy me my stopwatch?

What if some kid tells you that they don't care if the watch is running?

Won't the students think it is strange?

Take two relaxing breaths and do not become overly concerned with the mechanics and "what ifs" of responsibility training. They will be dealt with in the next chapter.

Bonuses

Responsibility training, being a complex incentive system, has both bonus and penalty. Students control penalty by their decisions to cooperate or not cooperate. The teacher is merely an accountant. The teacher does have direct control of bonus, however, and she will give generously for the benefit of all. The use of bonus by the teacher to reward cooperation is limited only by need and by the teacher's imagination.

There are two major types of bonuses, (1) hurry-up bonuses and (2) automatic bonuses. The rule on which all bonuses are based, which is often repeated by the teacher, is: *If you save me time to use for instruction, I will always give it right back to you.*

Hurry-Up Bonuses   How do you get students to hustle rather than dawdle? You can nag your life away to no avail, or you can make them an offer they cannot refuse. The following example is from a high school chemistry class.

> Class, let me have your attention. I want you to return your microscopes to the shelf, clean your glassware thoroughly, return any unused substances to the storeroom, sponge off the tops of your lab tables, and take your seats. You have 5 minutes to get that done, but if you hustle, you can get it done in half that much time. Remember, any time you save by hustling I will immediately add to your PAT. Let's go, because I have some things I want to cover before the end of the period.

Give the students plenty of time so that any decent effort will produce some bonus. You have just answered the question "Why should I" to everyone's benefit.

Automatic Bonuses   Sometimes students hustle or do what they are supposed to do, but the amount of time they actually save is indeterminate. How much time, for example, did the class save for instruction by being in their seats when the bell rang? You will never know. It all depended on how late some kid might have been. So, when you do not know how much time was actually saved, put a price on the cooperation and give the bonus automatically. In high school everyone being in their seat ready to work when the bell rings is usually worth about a minute.

Bonus with Penalty

While the use of bonus alone is effective in getting the entire class to act responsibly, bonus with penalty is *more* effective. For maximum power we will need to juxtapose time gain and time loss to provide a crystal clear demonstration of the advantages of cooperation. If, for example, even a few students "just don't care," they can keep the rest of the class from receiving a bonus. Penalty or time loss puts enough teeth into the management system to suppress abuse by the few, so reward may be given to all. The role of penalty in a complex incentive system produces our next incentive system guideline: *Bonuses are usually more powerful when used in conjunction with penalties than when used alone.*

Yes, it's the carrot and the stick—as old as time and inescapably basic. Bonus and penalty, however, become simple, powerful, and gentle when the medium of exchange is *time*. Remember, in a complex time incentive:

$$\text{Reward} = \text{PAT}$$
$$\text{Bonus} = \text{more PAT}$$
$$\text{Penalty} = \text{less PAT}$$

One of the most simple, useful, and clear-cut combinations of bonus and penalty is used in getting students to hustle instead of dawdle. The hurry-up bonus of responsibility training, therefore, will often have both bonus for hustling and penalty for dawdling.

Hurry-Up Bonuses with Penalty Perhaps the best illustration of the need for a penalty clause in conjunction with a hurry-up bonus is the lesson transition. The lesson transition at any grade level is typically 5 minutes of wasted time on task as well as pure stress for the teacher.

> Students, you've had enough time to sharpen those pencils. Now let's take our seats! Ralph, get away from the window and sit down. Let's not take all day!

Getting kids to hustle is no mean feat of management when one considers the natural incentive operating to reward dawdling at all times: social interaction in place of work. For this reason alone the lesson transition at any grade level will require at least the potential for time loss.

The logic of a complex hurry-up bonus is simple. If the students hustle, they get whatever time they save as a bonus. But, if they dawdle past the amount of time allotted for the activity, the amount of time wasted is subtracted from PAT. The students, in effect, decided to take a little PAT now rather than later. The students are neither prohibited from dawdling nor nagged for not hustling. They are simply allowed to dawdle on their time rather than on school time if they so choose.

PAT Contests The juxtaposition of bonus and penalty is not limited to hurry-up bonuses. You can even use bonuses to reduce penalties by setting up a PAT contest.

PAT contests are used most commonly at the secondary level because of departmentalization. Secondary teachers within a departmentalized setting must record bonus and penalty at the end of each class period. To keep records straight and to keep students informed, many teachers keep a tally of PAT bonus and penalty time on the board (and at their desk). Penalty time is kept in one column, bonus seconds are kept in a second column (mainly for hurry-up bonuses), and bonus minutes are kept in a third column (mainly for automatic bonuses). A typical PAT record may look like Table 9-2 early in the use of responsibility training before the recording of time loss has self-eliminated.

Early in the use of responsibility training we found that when the teacher publicly posted penalty time, the amount of time loss was almost halved. Apparently the class periods were trying to outdo each other. This chance finding gave us an idea for increasing the incentive for cooperation with a formal contest.

As a bonus, and to make a game out of the whole thing, we awarded bonus minutes at the end of the week on the basis of a given class period's "league standing" in terms of *least time lost*. Table 9-3 shows the PAT contest bonuses for the "PAT for the Week" tally in Table 9-2. The teacher, however, can use almost any criterion for choosing a winner including (1) least penalty, (2) most bonus, or (3) most total PAT (bonus minus penalty). In addition, the teacher can award an automatic bonus to any class that stays below a certain cutoff point in time loss. In a cutoff point contest, for example, any class could get a PAT bonus if they lost less than 1 minute all week.

TABLE 9-2
PAT FOR THE WEEK

Class period	Penalty	Bonus	
		Seconds	Minutes
1	1:16	:41	ʬ I
2	:35	1:18	III
3	2:30	1:05	II
4	:22	2:20	ʬ
5	4:10	1:47	III

TABLE 9-3
PAT CONTEST BONUSES

1st place (4 minutes)	4th period
2d place (3 minutes)	2nd period
3d place (2 minutes)	1st period
4th place (1 minute)	3rd period
5th place (0 minutes)	5th period

The "Rule of Penalties"   The use of penalties within the classroom is a worrisome subject which deserves careful attention lest a teacher come to rely heavily on penalties. If a complex incentive system is poorly implemented so that the penalty component of the system becomes at all sizable relative to the reward, the system is on the verge of failure due to the abuse of penalty.

While bonuses can be used by themselves, penalties should not be used by themselves. One of the easiest ways to produce a complex incentive system that self-destructs is to have penalty within the context of inadequate offsetting bonus. For this reason, the designing and implementation of any complex incentive system will be governed by the "rule of penalties": *Every penalty implies a corresponding bonus.*

When a complex incentive system is properly implemented, there will always be bonus opportunities that are constructed to *more than offset* opportunities for penalty. The proper administration of complex incentive systems will all but guarantee that the amount of bonus equals or exceeds the amount of penalty under most normal operating conditions.

Without the rule of penalties, many teachers will mistake responsibility training for the far more primitive and punitive time incentive which most of us experienced in our youth. In the past time has most typically been used as a weapon to punish misbehavior (in violation of the rule of penalties). We can all remember the teacher standing angrily in front of the classroom saying: "Group, I am counting! The longer it takes you to get in your seats and quiet down, the longer it will be before we go out for recess!"

Recess was the preferred activity, and the teacher was docking time as a penalty for the students' fooling around. A penalty clause in an incentive system used by itself in anger will be highly counterproductive because it represents management by punition. In this case, the teacher's docking time produced:

• Resentment
• Undermining of relationship
• Rebellion by some
• Negative peer pressure

Any teacher standing in front of a classroom using such a system can feel the tension, and most teachers are sensible enough to realize, as a result, that they cannot use this form of time incentive very often. It was used as a weapon that was pulled out only when the teacher was at the end of her or his rope.

The violation of the rule of penalties is obvious enough. Yet simply offering bonuses to offset such time loss during the school day is not enough. Such a use of penalty as retribution is primitive and destructive, and no amount of bonus will eliminate its negative effect on relationship. Bad time is never erased, it is simply offset. We must learn to use complex incentive systems to manipulate time without generating bad time. We must learn to operate responsibility training in a relaxed, low-key fashion. When students are clearly and efficiently made responsible for their behavior, there is no need to nag.

Penalties Alone

Penalties alone? I thought the rule of penalties said you couldn't have penalties alone. Remember, for every penalty there must be a corresponding bonus. The rule keeps burned-out teachers from zapping the kids all the time, right?

Well, yes and no. In the pristine logic of my mind, the rule of penalties is forever inviolate. But in the real world, rules are made to be broken. If a teacher actually tried to pair bonus and penalty so that each was at all times perfectly offsetting the other, the teacher would soon go stark raving nuts.

Before we confront the dark subject of penalties alone, however, let us first recall our purpose. In a complex incentive system such as responsibility training, bonuses may be used alone but penalties are never used alone. The most predictable violation of the rule of penalties while operating responsibility training would be to record time loss with no opportunity for offsetting time gain. However, in our earlier, more naïve days, we operated responsibility training in exactly that fashion, and it worked beautifully in the hands of most teachers. But occasionally I would run across a teacher who would abuse the system to death—sometimes going so far as to dock the class recess or lunch time or even to keep the class after school without ever having given a PAT of any kind. Some few teachers do indeed have a talent for turning almost any conceivable management system into a weapon, and these few teachers caused me to worry.

The use of penalty is always a double-edged sword. As discussed earlier, an incentive system without penalty is about as effective in dealing with your prize disrupters as an old dog's gums are in chewing a bone. Yet, the use of penalty creates the possibility of overpenalization and abuse. You are faced with a weak system on the one hand or risk on the other—the inherent price of harnessing the power of complex incentive systems.

To help reduce the risk, we explored and expanded our use of bonuses to "sweeten" the system and to remind teachers to notice and praise cooperation. We also invented the rule of penalties. This explicit emphasis on bonus did a lot to civilize responsibility training and to reduce the likelihood of abuse.

But the rule of penalties is not applicable on a moment-by-moment basis with the exception of hurry-up bonuses and a few other situations. Sometimes a student acts irresponsibly outside the context of a convenient time frame, and the teacher must respond without the luxury of devising a perfectly corresponding or offsetting bonus on the spot. Rather, teachers record time loss as it occurs and rely on good judgment, generosity, and proper use of the system to ensure that, on the whole, bonus exceeds penalty.

Having given this preachment on the virtue of kindness and generosity, I must admit that the use of penalty alone is often a delight to behold. It is strict accountability with tongue firmly placed in check. It allows the teacher to combat the countless scams and flim-flams which students devise with a calm that can only come from having discovered the perfect antidote.

The scams devised by students in their years of enforced idleness are indeed outrageous and hilarious in many cases—or at least they would be if they did not destroy so many teachers and so much learning. To gain insight into both the typical scam and its antidote, we will use as an example one of our most basic needs—going to the toilet, and one of education's most enduring bits of foolishness—the hall pass. What book about children would be complete without a section on toilet training?

Going to the Toilet   To appreciate fully the absurdity of the hall pass, which for some strange reason seems to be used more often the older the students (it is epidemic in the typical high school), we need only reflect on one simple biological fact. *The average 3-year-old can sleep through the night dry!* At 3 years of age average children are not only capable of going 8 hours at a stretch without wetting themselves, but they can do it while *unconscious*. In an average high school, there are seven opportunities during a six-period school day for a student to go to the toilet should nature call. But no! Tens of thousands of teenagers from all parts of the country on any given school day demonstrate by asking for a hall pass that they are incapable of sitting through a 50-minute class period without having to urinate. Either they are suffering from an epidemic urinary infection, or we are being flim-flammed!

To understand the behavioral economics of the situation, imagine that you are working in a factory, and imagine that this factory has a humane rule concerning the answering of nature's call—"when you gotta go, you gotta go." This rule constitutes the factory's toilet training policy. It assumes responsible behavior on the part of all employees. No one would abuse the freedom which this rule grants by pretending to go when they really don't gotta go, would they?

Such a rule may be practicable with a uniformly dedicated work force, but it flies in the face of both the imperfection of human nature and the built-in incentives for bowel and bladder problems which it contains. Even if going to the john brought no physical relief whatsoever, there would still be the rewards of getting away from work and having some time to yourself. You could sit on the throne and while away many a peaceful moment. You may read a magazine, daydream, plan how to get rich and famous, or simply hallucinate. When you return to your work station, you say to your friends, "Gee, sorry fellas, you know my problem."

For lack of explicit management for going to the toilet the company has left the natural rewards available for deviant behavior to assert themselves unfettered. Not everybody hides out in the john, of course. But, as long as you can go to the john on company time, there will always be a built-in incentive to go to the john on company time.

Now imagine that the company has a different rule—If you gotta go, do it on your break. Instead of going on *company* time, you now have to go on *your* time. At this point, you are faced with a decision. Is that the way I want to spend my break? It's your choice, but at least the conditions exist for it to be a responsible choice. Remember: (1) a finite resource, (2) control over its consumption, and (3) living with the consequences.

Now, let us transport ourselves back to the typical classroom to look at the built-in rewards for taking the hall pass in the middle of fifth period English. First and most obviously, you get out of English class. And do students zip to the toilet and zip back in record time? Are you kidding? The students are free, and while they are free they just might stop by the lost and found to talk with their loved one or stop by the book-store to chat with a friend. In most cases a student who has purportedly been called from class by nature will not be back for at least 10 minutes if at all during the rest of the period. Indeed, it is amazing how many students zip through the door to lay the hall pass on the teacher's desk just as the bell for the end of the period is ringing. Do you think they were waiting outside?

Now, let us suppose that you are the teacher of the class with the teenagers who have become accustomed to the use of the hall pass, and you wish to do away with this foolishness. Let us imagine further that you have instituted responsibility training in your class.

"The End of the Hall Pass"

Scene: Typical classroom

Bill: Teacher.
Teacher: Yes, Bill.
Bill: May I please have a hall pass?
Teacher: Sure. (Pull out stopwatch. When student stands to get the hall pass, start the stopwatch. Click.)

Class: Cool it, Bill. Hey, Bill! Geeze! (urgent whispers)
Bill: Oh! Well, I guess I can wait.
Teacher: Thank you, Bill. (Click. Stop the stopwatch.)

Funny how responsible students can become when they are goofing off on *their* time rather than company time. Students can always go to the bathroom if they want to, but they will have to pay for it. Is it worth the price?

At this point I typically encounter a question from someone in a group of teachers that demonstrates how gullible we have become over the years. But what if students wet their pants? I have come to the conclusion that all teachers, even high school teachers, have a primordial fear of the "yellow puddle." And, I have also concluded that we have been so thoroughly bamboozled by students' pseudo helplessness over the years that many of our colleagues now find it hard to believe that children of school age can actually learn to govern their own bladders.

Let me ask you, how many teenagers do you know who are willing to wet themselves in school—who would rather wet themselves than take a hall pass that is readily available albeit at a price? It is hard to find a second grader who cannot learn to "go" during the break when the price is right much less a high school student. Sometimes I almost feel as though certain teachers want the institution of the hall pass as much as the students because it reduces their class by one goof-off during every period of the day.

The hall pass has been used to illustrate a simple point. Students begin to act responsibly fast when all their goofing off is done on their time rather than company time. By simply timing them as they goof off, you hold them strictly accountable for their actions without having to say anything more than "of course" and "thank you." You are out of the nagging business for good.

While timing the duration of a flim-flam, however, the teacher is using *penalty alone.* There is no immediate offsetting bonus although there could be a delayed bonus offered if the class could go a full day or week without engaging in this particular type of foolishness. But such bonuses are usually not necessary. Nor is the timing of such foolishness necessary for very long. Once the class has made a habit of acting responsibly, you can quit training them. Like any successful classroom management technique, it is self-eliminating.

Showing Up without a Pencil   It is a downright tragedy that in thousands of secondary classes across the nation students show up every day without a pencil. This habit on the part of "select" students seems intractable in a great many cases. Some students manage to forget every day for the entire semester in spite of the fact that the teacher keeps reminding them. The tragedy of the whole situation is that, for lack of a pencil, the poor child is unable to do any work!

> Geeze, teach, I can't write the English theme that you assigned today on account of insufficient equipment.

In addition to nagging and threatening, teachers, driven to desperation, go to great lengths to make sure that no child is disqualified from learning "on account of insufficient equipment." Some teachers give pencils to students who forget to bring them, but this can get very expensive very quickly. Other teachers loan pencils only to see their pencils walk out the door at the end of the period. Other teachers in desperation require that the student give them collateral when they loan a pencil to make sure that the pencil is returned. All this ludicrous horseplay flies in the face of the fact that the student is always rewarded for not bringing a pencil. Once again, deviant behavior always seems to concoct a reward for itself. What to do.

In your classroom, there will no longer be the loaning of any pencils. In fact, you will not worry very much about pencils at all. When a student raises his hand and says, "I don't have a pencil," you say, "Does anyone have a pencil that Billy can use today?" If a pencil is not quickly forthcoming, pull out your stopwatch, take two relaxing breaths, and, if Billy still does not have a pencil, start the watch. If Billy does not have a pencil yet, he will have one soon. Someone will give him a pencil. Someone may toss him a pencil from across the room. But no matter how it is delivered, Billy will have a pencil!

Now it is the "forgetful" student's problem to show up with a pencil, not your problem. It is some other student's problem to get her pencil returned after class. You are free to teach. Soon students will learn to show up with pencils because if they fail to do so they have to answer to each other whether it be in time loss or begging for pencils.

Sharpening Pencils   Sharpening pencils also drives teachers nuts from the first grade through the twelfth grade and beyond. Students are always getting out of their seats and wandering back to the pencil sharpener, often while the teacher is still explaining the assignment. To the student intent on goofing off, pencil sharpening is an iron-clad gimmick which is superior in many regards to the hall pass. Any time a student wishes to quit working and take a stroll, all she has to do is lean on the pencil a little bit until *snap*. "Oh, darn! I guess I'll have to sharpen my pencil."

Yet, the teacher is over a barrel. What are you going to do with a student who just broke her only pencil? If you let her go, she takes a brief vacation from your assignment while distracting half the class. But, if you don't let her go, she can't do the work! Caught between the devil and the deep blue sea, what is a teacher to do?

Having initiated responsibility training, we will now eliminate pencil sharpening in five steps with our *"pencil-sharpening routine."*

Pencil-Sharpening Routine

1 Introduce a rule to your class that there will be no pencil sharpening during work time.
2 Have a canister of sharpened pencils on your desk. A frozen orange juice can works fine as a canister.
3 Fill your canister with fairly short and fairly grungy pencils. Do not place nice, long, new pencils in your canister, or you have just constructed an incentive system

that rewards the student's breaking the lead of their old pencil so that they can steal your new pencil. On the contrary, if you have nice, new, long pencils, break them in half and sharpen *both* ends. Or, next time you are on yard duty, look under the bushes for those chewed-up little pencils without erasers. Of, if you play golf, save your score pencils and put them in the canister.

4 Do not sharpen the pencils yourself. Make it a privilege and some kid will sharpen them at the break.

5 Announce your pencil-sharpening routine to the class, which is as follows:

  a If you break the lead of your pencil, hold your pencil in the air.

  b When I see you holding your pencil in the air, I will nod to you. That is your sign that you may go *exchange* your pencil.

  c I will start the stopwatch.

  d Go to my desk, place your pencil on the desk, take a sharp pencil from the canister, and return to your seat.

  e When you are back in your seat and *on task,* I will smile and nod and stop the stopwatch.

  f Exchange pencils to get yours back *after* the bell if you care to. (If they keep yours instead, who cares? It was a grungy pencil to start with.)

In a few days at the most you will have trained the entire class to do what no amount of nagging could ever have done—to take responsibility for sharpening *several* pencils before class.

OVERVIEW

These few examples of the use of responsibility training have attempted to convey the flavor of a classroom management program based on both reward and penalty, which is an extremely cost-effective way of generating cooperation to say nothing of generating enjoyment at school by the scheduling of PATs. Because of its power, simplicity, economy, and flexibility, responsibility training will be our *basic* or *foundation* classroom incentive system. It will not only serve as our main classroom management labor-saving device, but it will also serve as the vehicle upon which we can attach a myriad of other individualized and specialized time incentive programs at almost no additional cost (see Chapter 12).

Responsibility training epitomizes the characteristics that one looks for in a sophisticated incentive system. It is cheap, it has simple mechanics as well as strict accountability and generous rewards, it builds relationship as a by-product, and it is relatively fail-safe. The students get more of what they want (enjoyment and a productive learning environment), and teachers get more of what they want (learning at lower stress with more enjoyment). When an incentive system is properly designed, everybody wins.

CHAPTER 10

FIELD APPLICATIONS OF RESPONSIBILITY TRAINING

A management program cannot consistently succeed in the ever-changing environment of the classroom unless a teacher is wise enough to adapt the program when necessary without destroying its intent. In nearly a decade of systematic development and trial and error, we have gained an understanding of both the adaptations that are commonly needed and the liberties that can legitimately be taken with responsibility training.

This chapter will extend the reader's understanding of responsibility training (RT) by adding some of the lessons of the school of hard knocks. We will look at (1) various program adaptations to get a notion of the flexibility of RT, (2) methods of presenting RT to the class, (3) typical uses and modifications of RT, and (4) the most common ways of making RT fail.

ADAPTATIONS OF RESPONSIBILITY TRAINING IN THE FIELD

War Stories

The "Trouble Bubble" A staff psychologist from a regional special education center in New York state who spent 1 day a week consulting at a small neighborhood elementary school nearby was asked to help with some extremely disruptive students. It just so happened, by the luck of the draw, that there were five boys in the fifth grade who were not only best friends but also the worst cutups ever seen in that part of the country. By the fifth grade they had already accounted for the resignation of two teachers. Every day on their way to school they would hold a meeting to plan what they would do to the teacher that day. Their present teacher was threatening to resign, and the principal approached the psychologist to set up "some kind of program."

The psychologist, Melonie, first tried the traditional group therapy approach in which everyone talks about their feelings, but the group process turned into a riot. The children were fighting, changing their names every time they were called on, and laughing at everything Melonie said. Sending two out of the group only produced a series of skirmishes and foot races. On the way out of the meeting the children proudly announced to Melonie that their group had an official name. They called themselves the "Trouble Bubble." Melonie wondered whether they had a blood oath as well.

We put our heads together and decided on responsibility training even though it was then untried in a zoo. Melonie demonstrated that, under pressure, the entire system could be explained in less than 15 seconds. She had a bean bag game that she knew the kids were dying to play. She met them at the door, showed them the stopwatch, told them that if they were disruptive she would start the watch and they would not get to play the bean bag game. The students, looking a bit confused, took their seats with the help of physical proximity.

Melonie had two language lessons that were high-interest activities, and she told the group that she expected 20 minutes of good work in exchange for 10 minutes with the bean bag game. However, it was not long before the leader of the group started testing the limits. That was, after all, his job as leader. The leader did a tap dance with the four legs of his metal desk while simultaneously working on the assignment. Melonie called his name, held up the watch, and waited for two relaxing breaths. When nothing happened as a result, she started the watch, looked passively at the leader, and waited as he protested his innocence and claimed unfairness in a style worthy of his rank. After a while, however, one of his accomplices whispered, "Hey Robbie, the watch is still running!" Robbie finally folded after 37 seconds, a duration of time loss for a single disruption which was at that time the world's record. During the remainder of the period each member of the Trouble Bubble did their number so that, by the end of the 20-minute work period, they had lost 1 minute and 23 seconds, causing the work period to be extended by the same length of time.

During the half-hour period, however, all the Trouble Bubble members worked for 20 minutes, completed the assignment and had 8 minutes and 37 seconds of preferred activity time. Melonie said later, "As I sat there with the watch running while doing nothing, I realized how much control over the situation I really had. I had nothing to lose and they had everything to lose."

I saw Melonie about a month later, and I asked her how the program was working.

She said, "Oh, that? I haven't used it in couple of weeks."

"Why?" I asked crestfallen.

"Well," she said, "they learned that I intended for the rules to be followed, and they realized that they were only hurting themselves when they gave me a hard time. So, they quit giving me a hard time. They kind of got into a routine of doing what was expected of them, I guess. Also, having PATs together helped us get to know each other and like each other. After a few weeks I found that they would do things because I asked them without my even getting out the stopwatch. Once or twice in the last 2 weeks they have started to get a bit rowdy or have dawdled when I asked them to do something, but when I said, 'Look, do you want me to get out the watch?' they said no. Now they are almost totally responsive to a simple verbal request."

It was fascinating to see in this and in many subsequent situations how responsibility training trained the group to follow rules with only infrequent, intermittent enforcement. The self-elimination of RT followed the same progression from physical control to verbal control to nonverbal control that we had come to expect from limit-setting. In this case physical control was in the form of a stopwatch indicating time loss rather than in the form of body language and physical proximity. In both cases, however, the students learned the same lessons: the rules were for real, the teacher meant business, and trying to upset the apple cart was a bad gamble.

Retarded, Aggressive, and Big   The most severe behavioral problem in a special classroom of thirteen multiply handicapped retarded children with mental ages in the preschool range was a large, 13-year-old girl named Bernine who was physically aggressive and frequently threw tantrums. She would throw one or two major tantrums a day that were triggered either by the teacher asking Bernine to do something that she did not want to do or by the teacher intervening when Bernine hit a smaller classmate. In either case, Bernine would become garrulous, yell and swear regardless of what anyone did, throw objects and turn over desks, and sooner or later would end up throwing a full-fledged screaming tantrum on the floor. Bernine would continue her tantrum until she was carried, usually kicking, spitting, and biting, down to the principal's or counselor's office. There she would calm down, often with some counseling, before returning to the classroom 15 or 20 minutes later. This pattern of behavior had been relatively constant since Bernine had entered the special education center at the age of 5, and the problem was approaching a crisis as the girl grew larger. Nobody in the building would volunteer any longer to carry her down the hall. Even the gym teachers quit helping after being bitten.

I explained responsibility training to an openly skeptical teacher and aide during a training session, and they agreed to at least give it a try. They used the sweep second hand on their wall clock, however, rather than investing in a stopwatch owing to their lack of optimism. I saw the teacher a week later and asked how the system was working. She gave me a scolding look and said, "I'm glad you weren't here Tuesday or I would have told you what you could do with your clock system." I knew I was in trouble. "The first time she had a tantrum, I ran off 6 minutes of our 15-minute preferred activity time!" (The worst I had ever seen up to that time was 1 minute and 23 seconds with the Trouble Bubble.)

"That's not the end of it," the teacher said. "I had the children put their heads on their desks for 6 minutes at the *beginning* of the preferred activity time (the usual tactic for children who cannot yet tell time), and Bernine would *not* put her head on her desk. She ended up throwing another tantrum, and this one lasted 5 minutes!"

"Eleven minutes! That's awful! That's a new world's record!" I said. "Well, give me the rest of the bad news. Did you dump the system?"

Finally the teacher cracked a small smile. "Well, the kids only got 4 minutes of their preferred activity time, and I thought the whole system had just bombed out," she said. "At the end of the day my aide and I discussed what had happened, and my aide reminded me that we had not taken Bernine to the office that day. That didn't mean too much to me, frankly, because that had happened a few times before, but we agreed to try it one more day. To make a long story short, she threw a tantrum once on the second day for a total of 4 minutes, the entire class lost only a minute and a half on the third day, and on the fourth day, the group lost only 40 seconds. At one point during the fourth day a different student started to disrupt, and Bernine said, 'Hey, you better sit down if you know what's good for you!'"

Bernine's last major tantrum for the year occurred on the third day of the program after 8 years of being out of control. Furthermore, this chronic and severe behavior problem which would usually upset the classroom and several staff members on a daily basis was handled as a part of a single *group* management system. Individualized behavior management programs are very rarely needed with responsibility training even in a special education setting because the system is so powerful. For this reason we never set up relatively expensive individualized management programs for students until the group management program is in place. Bernine's tantrums on the first day which cost 11 minutes of preferred activity time still represent the world's record of time loss in the classroom of a trained teacher.

Uncanny Precision

Goody Two Shoes   In almost every reading group there is a "Goody Two Shoes." Such kids are always good readers, and they rarely pass up an opportunity to prove just how smart they are. One of the easiest ways to show off while being "helpful" in a reading group is to feed the correct word to a child who is blocking. This immediately makes the teacher want to strangle little Goody Two Shoes for having aborted the other student's attempt to sound out the word. But it is too late for the teacher to do very much. Reprimands have little effect since such nagging by the teacher does not negate little Goody's self-delivered reward of having proved to the group that he or she is smarter than anyone else. And, the child who was stuck is off the hook and reading again.

Enter responsibility training. Now, when Goody interrupts, the teacher simply looks at Goody, clicks the stopwatch, and waits for two relaxing breaths. The teacher may say (while the clock runs), "Goody, remember, we only speak when it is our turn." Take two more relaxing breaths just to run off a little more time if you think the message needs some added emphasis.

This simple use of penalty self-eliminates rapidly since the cost of being Goody Two Shoes now clearly outweighs the benefit. RT is quick and precise enough in this situation to give the teacher effective control over an obnoxious but momentary situation that would otherwise be here and gone. A bonus for no interrupting is usually only worth the effort if several children have recurring difficulty in quietly paying attention.

The Short Attention Span   In a special education elementary classroom we worked with a boy who had a 5-second attention span. The child was being tutored in reading one-to-one, but the child's eyes would blink and wander regardless of the teacher's prompting and rewarding.

We told the child that he would get to play for the remainder of a 10-minute period as soon as he had completed 3 solid minutes of work. We would start the watch as he started working, and we would stop the watch as soon as he began to lose his concentration. The teacher watched the child's eyes and eyelids and clicked the watch as soon as any wandering or fluttering of the eyelids was observed. The click gave the child a precise auditory cue as to the onset of attention loss. The child would quickly look back at the work motivated by the reward that was decreasing the longer he was off task. We shaped a consistent 10-minute attention span within 3 weeks.

Enforcing a Decibel Level How do you keep the class from getting too rowdy during PAT? Or, how do you keep the group from getting too loud during committee work or any other lesson format such as art or shop or a laboratory in which students are free to move and talk?

Responsibility training has the unique ability to enforce a decibel level as a classroom rule—to deal quickly and effectively with a rising level of noise. Limit-setting could never do this for you, and nagging is the most common alternative. Instead, simply hold the stopwatch over your head (or point to the wall clock) and say: "Class, we are beginning to get too loud. Let's hold it down."

The word will quickly go around to cool it while you wait. Rarely will you need to start timing. Add a bonus for particularly good cooperation, and you have satisfied the rule of penalties.

More Common Uses

Small Group Instruction The need for a management system such as responsibility training first became apparent in the early 1970s as a result of a chance finding. In taking data on the use of limit-setting to reduce disruptions during group discussions in elementary classrooms, my data takers and I would often arrive at the classroom a bit ahead of schedule. As we waited for the lesson transition which would begin the group discussion (I was doublescoring to establish interscorer reliability), we would usually take a few minutes of data on whatever was going on just to warm up. Often the preceding lesson format was some sort of small group instruction—usually reading circle. We would record disruptions and time on task for those students who were *outside* the reading circle and at their desks working independently.

Scoring the independent work habits of the majority of the class while the teacher's attention was consumed by a small group proved to be a revelation. The rate of disruption was approximately double the normal rate, and the percent of time on task was about half. Yet in spite of the high rate of goofing off in the class, disruption was surreptitious—a constant murmur short of the provocative loudness that would arouse the teacher to put the lid on.

I realized that I was witnessing an educational disaster that was probably being replayed in most classrooms in the country on any given day. Small group instruction is common at all grade levels, but it is the typical way of spending a large portion of any day teaching reading and math in any self-contained classroom. And, the same pattern of mass goofing off could be observed whenever a teacher sat down to tutor an individual child. As soon as teachers sat down, they were out of the action, and the students gambled accordingly.

Seeing this hemorrhage of time on task during small group instruction and seeing the absolute uselessness of limit-setting or reprimands (the ineffectual substitute for limit-setting used by untrained teachers), I set about devising a whole new method of management that would permit rule enforcement from a sitting position without any reliance on mobility or physical proximity. Responsibility training began with the reading circle.

A primitive version of responsibility training was first experimentally tested during reading circles in five primary classrooms, grades one through three in an elementary school serving a lower-class, racially mixed neighborhood of Rochester, New York.[1] There was no appreciation at that time of the use of either bonuses or the rule of penalties. Rather, the students were simply promised a 15-minute preferred activity time at the end of reading, and if anyone in the class disrupted while the teacher was busy in the reading circle, the teacher would (1) call the student's name(s), (2) hold up the stopwatch, and (3) wait. If the student(s) got back on task, nothing further would happen. But, if they failed to get back on task, the teacher would click the watch and wait until the students were back on task. Any time wasted during reading period as recorded on the stopwatch would be subtracted from the PAT.

In spite of only brief instructions to the teachers regarding preferred activities and the finer points of incentive systems, responsibility training reduced disruptions by an average of 63 percent during the first 2 weeks and by an average of 85 percent during the final 2 weeks of the study some 5 to 8 weeks later. Time *off* task was reduced by an average of 43 percent during the first 2 weeks and by an average of 62 percent by the final 2 weeks of study. During the first week of the study the students earned an average of 95 percent of their preferred activity time, and from the second week until the end of the study the students earned an average of 97.3 percent of their preferred activity time. This last piece of data was perhaps the most important because, if the students had lost a sizable portion of the preferred activity time, we would have gone back to the drawing board. Indeed, the primary purpose of this initial experiment was to test (1) the responsiveness of the class to so simple a means of accountability as a *single* recording of time loss for the group (the stopwatch) and (2) the vulnerability of the system to generating excessive time loss.

Additional data on teacher performance indicated that, before the intervention, teachers noticed and commented on 1 disruption out of 108, whereas, using the stopwatch, they noticed and commented on one disruption out of eight. From a student's point of view, getting caught once in every 108 disruptions and having to pay for it by listening to a little "yakkity yak" from across the room was not a bad gamble. When, however, that same disruption produced one in eight odds of costing the group some PAT, the cost/benefit ratio of disrupting was radically altered. According to the data, the cost of disrupting was different enough to eliminate over 95 percent of the disruptions in two of the classrooms. Even in one classroom where the teacher used the stopwatch very inconsistently, disruptions decreased by 60 percent and time on task increased by 42 percent by the final 2 weeks of the study.

These improvements in the classroom learning atmosphere were achieved at a very slight inconvenience to the teachers. The only procedures they had to utilize during class apart from pushing the button of a stopwatch were (1) to sit facing the room so they could perceive disturbances out of their peripheral vision and (2) to look up from the reading group occasionally. Believe it or not, one teacher (the one who used the stopwatch inconsistently) sat with his back to the classroom during reading circle before we began the experiment so that he would not be "distracted."

How About Emotionally Handicapped Junior High?   Before the school year was over we had the opportunity to repeat our reading circle experiment in our special junior high classrooms of emotionally, behaviorally, and learning-handicapped students. The system produced a 54 percent decrease in disruptions and a 35 percent increase in time on task within the first week, and these gains remained stable in the weeks following. The incentive system was explained to the teachers in a half-hour prep session as before, and little time was spent in explaining structural fine points of implementation (many of which were not yet appreciated). Consequently, much of the difference in the effectiveness of RT between this experiment and the previous study can be accounted for not only by the difficulty of the class, which was admittedly the "all star game" of disrupters, but also by the fact that we had not yet learned the kinds of activities that the students genuinely preferred. It was in this setting, for example, that we learned *not* to use unstructured free time as a preferred activity.

This experiment also gave us an opportunity to test the interrelationship between incentive systems and limit-setting. Subsequent to the initiation of responsibility training, the teachers were given performance training in the skills of limit-setting. Limit-setting in conjunction with responsibility training produced a 62 percent reduction in disruptions and a 50 percent increase in time on task. This would indicate, as one might expect, that the two systems put together are more powerful than either one used separately.

Open-Field Settings

Gym Class   Gym class can present extremely difficult management problems because, whether indoors or outdoors, it is usually in an open-field setting. Students can easily leave the area where you are instructing to fool around in the bleachers or on the far side of the field. Yelling, reprimanding, and docking grades have a long tradition of failure in this setting, and limit-setting is hardly suited to a situation in which the students are 25 yards away (although it can work when they are standing nearby). Responsibility training, however, is readily applicable and has been used repeatedly with success in gym class. One teacher in Minnesota explained the system to his class as follows:

> Today I am going to be showing you some skills in gymnastics down at the far end of the gym, and I want you to stay close and pay attention. You will each have your turn to use the equipment. The first half-hour of class will be *my* time, and during my time, I expect you to pay attention, participate in the activities, and refrain from goofing off. The last 10 minutes of the period will be *your* time. During that time, you may play ball or use the equipment.

You all know the rules, and if any of you are fooling around, I will simply say your name, hold up this stopwatch as a signal to you and wait a second or two. If you are not yet back with the group within that time, I will start the watch. I will let the watch run until you join the group and pay attention. Then I'll stop the watch. Any time that is on the watch at the end of the half-hour represents time that you have taken from me during my instructional time. You will have to give it back during your play time.

On the first day the students collectively lost 1 minute and 12 seconds. At the end of the 30-minute instructional period the gym teacher had the students line up and stand at attention as gym classes traditionally do. Then the teacher said:

Now group, you did good work during the first part of the period. For the most part you paid attention very well, and you all worked hard learning new skills. During that time I ran the stopwatch when kids were goofing off. We have a total of 1 minute and 12 seconds on the watch. That represents the amount of time that you took from me when I was trying to teach you, and that is the amount of time that you will give back now from your play time. So, we will just stand here for 1 minute and 12 seconds.

Try standing at attention for 1 minute and 12 seconds some time. It is a "psychologically significant" interval. When the time was up, the instructor said: "Well, group, the time is up. We're even. Let's play!"

No one was singled out for criticism, the teacher was spared the typical stress of reprimanding or nagging the students to cooperate, and the class received a PAT for the first time. In addition, the group spent less time in free play than they usually spent in goofing off during class. Most of the students did gymnastics during preferred activity time anyway so that "play time" did not have the "do nothing" flavor that free time typically has in a classroom. Thereafter, the amount of time lost was usually below 20 seconds until the system self-eliminated after 2 weeks. The PAT remained, of course, and the coach got better at structuring the PAT to incorporate bonuses and to achieve learning goals. Even at the beginning, however, when the program still had a few rough edges, paying attention and cooperating with rules quickly became a habit.

Passing Through the Halls and Sitting in Assemblies   Another open-field situation in which discipline is particularly difficult is when a class passes through the halls and sits in an assembly. Running, hassling each other, getting rowdy in the halls, and making noise in the assembly are part of everyday school life. How do you get students to walk quietly through the halls, and how do you keep students from making noise when they are at the far end of a row in the auditorium?

By now, you have probably guessed that you use responsibility training as part of the answer. Carefully review your rules for going to and sitting in an assembly and plan a preferred activity which will be available to the students on their return. Put the rowdy students at the *back* of the line and walk with them so you can see everyone while staying close to the potential troublemakers. This bit of structure also places the troublemakers sitting near you in the assembly. If a student starts running in the hall, say her or his name, hold up the watch, press the button if necessary and keep walking.

The student will almost always slow down and rejoin the group thanks to reminders from peers. In the assembly should the disruptive student be seated at the far end of the row, even if the orchestra is playing the 1812 Overture with cannons going off, when you lean forward and click your watch, the disrupter will hear the click. The rest happens automatically as the squirrelly student notices all the other people in the row looking at him or her.

Shop, Chemistry, Typing, and Home Economics   Many classroom settings, especially at the secondary level, do not permit an optimal furniture arrangement, and many of them do not permit any rearrangement at all. For example, shop, chemistry lab, typing, and home economics are typically held in large rooms with fixed work stations which make limit-setting more difficult.

Teachers get the best results, however, when they move among the students constantly to monitor work and to use limit-setting as needed rather than staying in one place for a long time. Responsibility training is used to pick up the slack. RT allows the teacher to have discipline from a distance just as in reading circle, and it allows the teacher to conveniently enforce a reasonable noise level.

INTRODUCING RESPONSIBILITY TRAINING TO THE CLASS

Every teacher finds his or her own words for explaining responsibility training to a class. I have supplied more background and rationale for responsibility training in the preceding chapters than you would ever need in explaining it to your class. As long as the class understands that PAT is a gift and that they, as a group, are responsible for the way in which it is consumed, you are in fairly good shape.

During the first year of its use in the classroom following training, most teachers treat the system gingerly lest they ask too much of it and cause it to fail. If training occurs just before the beginning of school, most teachers will wait until October when "things are under control" to initiate their classes to the mysteries of RT.

With experience the teachers learn how flexible and robust the system is—as long as you are having a good time with it. By the second year these same teachers say to themselves, "Why did I wait until October and put up with all that hassle? I think I'll start out with it right from the first day!" Indeed, that is the easiest way.

The Beginning of School

The procedures for getting started on the first day of school were outlined in Chapter 4 as one of the basic aspects of classroom structure that lays the groundwork for good relationships and good discipline. After breaking the ice and arranging your room, describe and discuss your classroom rules and procedures and expectations to your students in a more general sense. Open up the discussion of what makes a good classroom to include the things that both teachers and students do to make a classroom enjoyable and productive. This brings you to the topic of being *responsible* and taking responsibility for your own actions. Secondary teachers will be at the end of their first hour with each of their class periods by now, and they will continue from here tomorrow.

Introduce responsibility training. One of the easiest entry points to the explanation of RT is to describe the three prerequisites of learning to be responsible: (1) something to be responsible for, (2) control over its consumption, and (3) living with the consequences. The resource you have to give is time. In fact, you have *three* gifts to give. For a review of this presentation, check the preceding chapter.

Getting Off on the Right Foot

Brainstorm PATs   Explain the basic objectives and mechanics of responsibility training crisply and finish in 5 to 10 minutes. Before getting into answering too many "what if" questions, say:

> Before we go any further, let's spend some time brainstorming the kinds of things that we might do during preferred activity time. We'll make a list. There are only two ground rules that govern whether we can add some activity to our PAT list:
>
> 1 It has to be something that you genuinely want.
> 2 It has to be something that I can live with.
>
> A PAT has to be something we all want, so we both have veto power with no big need to self-justify. Now, let's take the business of enjoying ourselves with learning on a regular basis seriously and come up with some ideas for PATs.

The main business of this 10- to 20-minute brainstorming session is *not* to come up with PAT ideas. They already exist. The main objective of brainstorming is to allow the class to test you—to find out whether you are trying to put something over on them or whether you really are willing to accept their suggestions. They may need to suggest things like playing chess or Boggle or checkers or to see a movie and experience it being accepted by you before they actually realize that it is *their* PAT. Some of the class members, if they are teenagers, will assume that the whole thing is a scam— some stratagem for making them do more work—until they get to test the nature of PAT. By the end of brainstorming almost all the class will be saying to themselves, "I'll be darned. We really can do things we like to do. Maybe this is worth a try."

Give the First PAT Free   The next half hour will be spent in your giving the class their first PAT, just so they can get the feeling of it. Make it a good one, a high interest academic enrichment activity. By now the notion of enjoying your class as a regular, planned, premeditated activity with you playing the role of giver and protector of the PAT will probably be taking hold in even the most standoffish classes.

Vote on Responsibility Training   Voting on RT at the elementary level is rarely necessary, but it can be a wise move at the secondary level. Say to the class:

> Now you know what responsibility training is, and you know some of the kinds of things that we might do during preferred activity time. The next thing we're going to do is decide

whether or not we want to try it. You know as well as I do that if *you* don't want it, it won't work anyway.

In addition, rather than signing our lives away, let's just agree to try it for a while, say a month. Then we'll know if we want to keep it, and a simple majority will say whether we do or we don't.

Almost always the class agrees to give it a try—an overt confirmation and commitment which is more meaningful the older the students. In fact, usually classes just blurt out "sure" or "let's do it." Why shouldn't they? Who would be foolish enough to turn down such an offer?

Well, actually, sometimes a class is foolish enough—usually a class led by a clique of hypermature big mouths who would vote down anything suggested by the teacher. So, it's voted down. Big deal. You didn't have RT last week; you'll survive without it this week. But rarely will you have to survive without it for very long. The student grapevine will take care of that for you. The conversation goes something like this:

Student A: Hey, what are you guys doing for PAT in Mr. Jones' room?
Student B: Oh, we don't have PAT.
Student A: You don't? How come? He let our class have it.
Student B: Oh, we voted it down.
Student A: You mean you voted down PAT?
Student B: Yep.
Student A: Gee, that's dumb. What did you do that for?

Sooner or later the class will realize that they cut off their own noses to spite their faces, and they will come to you and ask to vote again. It takes about a month for them to wise up. Naturally, you will say yes.

Exploiting the Honeymoon   During the first few days of school students are wary and righteous. Nobody is going to stick their neck out too far until they "scope out the situation." This is the honeymoon. You are lucky if it lasts for two full days.

As the honeymoon comes to an end, the bravest and most squirrelly students begin to test the limits, and soon everybody is trying to get in on the act. Perhaps by mid-October, with considerable stress and energy having been expended, you finally have things pretty much under control. The class looks good—it is only you who is dying by inches.

The trick of discipline at the beginning of school is to start so fast with a management system that is so tight and positive that you never get out of the honeymoon. Routine is most easily established if the class never learns that there is any other way to do things.

Traditionally "tight" discipline means "uptight," or "don't smile until Christmas." Teachers who are concerned with relationship building often hold back on rule enforcement to their own detriment lest it poison the atmosphere. To me, however, "tight" simply means a boat that does not leak. If done properly, tight means preferred activity time with strict accountability, plenty of bonuses, and the occasional use of limit-setting—a relaxed classroom atmosphere in which learning is the objective and discipline is in the background.

With PAT, relationship building is an integral part of tight discipline. Preferred activity time is, in fact, an icebreaker and a relationship-building activity in its own right. It sets aside time for enjoyment which you actively protect, and it gives you a chance to loosen up. Begin tight the first day with your entire management system operational, and the honeymoon may never end.

USES AND MODIFICATIONS OF RESPONSIBILITY TRAINING

Typical Uses

Responsibility training has two primary uses in a classroom. They are, in order of importance, (1) elimination of nagging (i.e., getting students to hustle and be conscientious) and (2) discipline from a distance.

1 *Elimination of nagging.* All teachers, particularly at the secondary level, will use responsibility training to get students to be at the right place at the right time with the right materials doing the right thing without having to nag in order to get them there. Typical applications include training students to:
   - have quick lesson transitions
   - be in their seats ready to work when the bell rings
   - show up with proper books, pencils, and other materials
   - eliminate hall passes
   - eliminate pencil sharpening
   - facilitate room cleanup
   - rearrange furniture quickly
   - line up quickly
2 *Discipline from a distance.* Responsibility training is useful when limit-setting is useless. It can be used either in a situation in which limit-setting is totally impractical because the teacher is sitting down or too far away *or* when limit-setting is too slow and cumbersome. Typical examples include:
   - reading circle and small group instruction
   - open-field situations such as gym, shop, home economics, and science lab
   - enforcing a noise level rule for the entire group during a lesson format in which movement and talking are permitted
   - dealing with an obnoxious behavior of short duration for which limit-setting is too slow (Goody Two Shoes or a nasty remark)
   - for the student who becomes upset with physical proximity but who cares about his or her status in the peer group

Responsibility Training as a Back-up for Limit-Setting

While the primary uses of responsibility training are (1) to eliminate nagging and (2) to enforce classroom rules from a distance, there is a third use for RT, which is more rare and more worrisome. Responsibility training can be used as a back-up response for limit-setting in certain situations in which limit-setting is running into problems. The benefit of RT as a back-up response is that it can easily resolve a difficult problem on occasion. The liability is that teachers may become seduced into substituting RT for limit-setting frequently since it is quick and easy. You can do it while sitting down. The result may be overuse and abuse of penalty which may create resentment toward RT and ultimately destroy it. The real issue from a practical point of view is that without adequate training many teachers will use time loss punitively as a back-up response in lieu of more subtle and positive management techniques, so we had better talk about it.

At any time in the limit-setting sequence a teacher can *substitute time for distance*. Both limit-setting and responsibility training use the same or similar body language: calmness and relaxing breaths, turning toward the student, calling their name(s), and waiting up to the point where the teacher either (1) walks to the edge of the student's desk (step 4 of "moving in") or (2) presses the button on the stopwatch. Both "moving in" and time loss represent mild negative sanctions to suppress an unacceptable behavior. They are functionally equivalent, and for that reason they are to an extent interchangeable. Rather than walking across the room to deal with the disruption personally from close range, a teacher can stand where he or she is and press a button on a stopwatch to time the disruption while the peer group takes care of enforcement. The teacher can even govern the intensity of peer pressure at almost no effort by training the class that anything in excess of urgent whispers will produce both physical proximity and added time loss as described in the preceding chapter.

There are times when using time instead of physical proximity may be to the teacher's advantage. Examples include:

1 *Disruptions from behind you during limit-setting.* Imagine that, as you are at "palms" with one disruptive student, another student behind you begins to heckle you or give you "heat." Many teachers imagine early in training that this might happen frequently, but in practice it almost never happens. You could in any case ignore the heckling for the time being as you follow through with limit-setting (see Chapter 6) and then turn to face the heckler when you are done. You could also, however, casually pull out your stopwatch and hold it behind your back where the rest of the class can see it. Click the stopwatch on and continue with limit-setting unperturbed. The class will most likely fall silent. Continue with limit-setting until the student is on task and you are standing in front of her or him relaxing. Then turn to the class and wait for two more relaxing breaths to make sure there is silence and that students are working. Thank the group and click the watch off.

You have just dealt with two types of disruptions from two different directions using two different discipline methodologies simultaneously—one with limit-setting which emphasizes physical proximity and the other with responsibility training which emphasizes time. Such a blending or doubling up of limit-setting and RT can be particularly helpful when the whole group is getting noisy while you are trying to set limits.

2 *Back talk and "hair-trigger" confronting.* Just as limit-setting and responsibility training can be operated simultaneously, so also can one be exchanged for the other on the spur of the moment. Imagine, for example, that you are setting limits on two disruptive students, and their continuing disruption has caused you to go as far in "moving in" as step 4: Walking to the edge of the students' desks. As you walk toward the more disruptive of the two students, he or she shows signs of upset or belligerence.

You continue to the edge of the desk, stand taking two relaxing breaths and remember the *cardinal rule: When in doubt, do nothing*.

If the student is looking for a confrontation with an adult authority figure, he or she may give you back talk before you move any closer. You have several options: (1) wait (good for starters), (2) move in farther (if you feel physically safe), (3) use your back-up system (see Chapters 14 and 15), or (4) switch to RT. The choice is a *judgment call* on the part of the teacher.

If you decide to switch to responsibility training, pull out your stopwatch, wait for two relaxing breaths, and prompt the student to get back on task from a standing position. Wait, since the next move is up to the student. If he stonewalls you by doing nothing or if he back talks, click the stopwatch to start timing and wait (take more relaxing breaths) as the student talks. He is now using up PAT to give you "heat," and the peer group may supply some heat of their own as the group informs the big mouth that they do not think he is being too cool.

By switching techniques you have taken yourself out of the "enforcer" role of the adult authority figure and you have made the student answerable to peers instead. If the student likes to flaunt adult authority, this represents a very shrewd tactical move, especially if the student values peer status.

3 *Repeat disruptions.* You may deal with a disruption using limit-setting only to have the problem recur. No discipline technique, after all, comes with a guarantee. At that point you may conclude that, knowing the students, more limit-setting is a waste of time. Rather than escalating to your back-up system and the use of the negative sanctions contained therein, you may opt instead to use RT and simply time the disruption rather than "moving in" again with limit-setting. You can always substitute time for distance.

The first two examples show how a teacher can turn a potentially nasty situation around by coordinating the use of limit-setting and responsibility training; the third example brings us to the brink of abuse. While substituting RT for limit-setting may represent a shrewd tactic, it may also represent impatience and/or laziness. A teacher may use the stopwatch just because it is easier than walking. Teachers are particularly prone to overusing RT in lieu of limit-setting if they are either poorly trained, burned-out, or highly uncomfortable with the assertiveness of meaning business. The result can be repeated violation of the rule of penalties and excessive time loss. The teacher is on the verge of using responsibility training as a weapon. The result can be student resentment and the end of cooperation.

Simplified Versions of Responsibility Training

Although the mechanics of responsibility training have been spelled out in detail, please remember that RT is a general approach to incentive management in the classroom that can be embodied in a variety of procedural forms. The heart of responsibility training is the accountability of students to each other that takes the teacher out of the enforcer or nagging parent role. Those "nuts and bolts" presented thus far are simply the most commonly used and, in general, the most cost-effective and fail-safe. Other procedures can be substituted successfully if done skillfully. But most variations are accompanied by a heightened vulnerability of responsibility training to abuse in the hands of a less-sensitive or less-experienced teacher. Some example of liberties that have been taken successfully may help to expand your conceptualization of responsibility training.

No PAT   Rather than giving the class any PAT as a gift, one junior high teacher gave it only as earned. The class earned PAT rewards of fixed amounts for carrying out classroom routines correctly and promptly. The class could earn a minute for such things as (1) being in their seats when the bell rang, (2) being on task when the bell rang, (3) having all necessary books, manuals, pencils, and equipment, (4) handing in homework (everyone must do it, of course), etc. The class could supplement this liberal use of automatic bonuses with hurry-up bonuses as well, and time was taken from the PAT that had been earned as students dawdled and fooled around.

The teacher who chose to operate responsibility training in this fashion had good rapport with his students and had no trouble being generous with them. He gave so much more PAT than he took that he would end up the week with as much PAT as his colleagues who had begun the week by giving 30 minutes as a gift.

PAT can be "earned as you go," but not all teachers are generous enough to come out so far to the good. Starting with a gift makes the system more resistant to abuse which might come from (1) overpenalizing and (2) inadequate giving of bonuses. A gift of PAT is not a necessity, but it makes RT far more fail-safe, particularly in the hands of a beginner.

No Stopwatch or Time Exchange   Although the use of time as a medium of exchange within the classroom gives the teacher amazing precision and flexibility of incentive management at low cost, some teachers simply cannot warm up to the idea of using a stopwatch or even to the idea of timing students at all. While infrequent, this perception usually occurs in male high school teachers who are afraid that the whole notion will be rejected by the students as uncool. In fact the giving of PAT produces quite the opposite perception on the part of almost all students, but if you have never tried it, how are you to know?

As a fallback position a teacher can use "points" instead of time. One teacher simply put the numbers one through ten on the board and crossed the numbers out in reverse order (10, 9, 8 . . .) as students dawdled or disrupted. The first five points were free (no PAT time loss), but each number after that cost 2 minutes of PAT.

The system worked for this teacher, but I would expect it to fail in the hands of many teachers. PAT can disappear very rapidly 2 minutes at a time, and what do you do if the disruption continues? Without excellent rapport with the students you could soon end up nagging or taking excessive PAT or both. By substituting points for time the teacher must penalize with minutes rather than with seconds. They have, in effect, made a blunt instrument out of a precision one and all for the fear of using a timer. (For a more thorough discussion of point systems see Chapter 13.)

Substituting Academic Privileges for PAT   A few teachers have substituted, instead of PAT, rewards that relate to grades and deadlines for work with good results. One teacher, as in the previous example, put the numbers 1 to 10 on the board and crossed out a number for each instance of blatant dawdling or disruption. If the students ended the week with one number left that was not crossed out, the week counted toward the earning of an academic privilege. At the end of the grading period if two-thirds of the weeks had ended with a number left on the board (4 out of 6 weeks in this case), each student could choose one of the following privileges.

1 A half-grade bonus on the midterm or semester exam (C+ = B, B = B+) or a 5 percent bonus if grades were computed as percentiles.

2 A postponement of the due date on the term paper for 3 days.

3 Being told in advance the poem or short story upon which the test would be based. (Obviously this was an English class, but similar bonuses can always be found for any subject.)

4 Being able to make up two-thirds of a test grade by retaking a test over the same material. (Students made up a pool of questions and posted them in advance.)

While academic privileges may work with academically oriented students, they may bomb in another population as may the use of points. And, carrying a reward across several weeks delays gratification and thins the schedule of reinforcement, both of which might be expected to weaken an incentive system. But knowing that it has at least been attempted with success may help you be more flexible with the implementation of responsibility training should some "customizing" be to your advantage.

The license that teachers have taken successfully with responsibility training helps us to see RT as a generic type of group incentive rather than as a rigid and narrow set of procedures. Yet keep in mind that the procedures in the previous chapter are the result of years of trial and error. They are the most cost-effective and the most fail-safe. Keep in mind as well that most teachers do not have extensive experience with incentives so that most of their attempts at improvising cause additional problems.

Hybrid Programs

Most classroom management situations are inherently complex. Classroom routines are at best well-worked-out strategies for doing several different management jobs at once using several methods simultaneously. Getting the class started after the bell rings is one of those predictable parts of the day that requires a routine which is a hybrid of several management techniques. Examining this management dilemma may give us a feel for combining several management methods to create a single well-oiled routine.

The Problem of Getting Class Started How do you get everyone in their seats working when the bell rings? The first 5 minutes of almost any class period are spent in just milling around and getting started. Just about the time you have everyone seated you have your attention diverted by an announcement over the intercom or by recording the roll or by dealing with some student who came late with an excuse. Apart from being a chronic five-period-a-day hassle, this problem consumes 25 minutes of time on task per day per student.

One solution, of course, is responsibility training—a solution that has proved consistently successful. A *second* solution is a back-up system at the school site which provides clear and guaranteed negative consequences *every* time a student is tardy or cuts class. A *third* solution—structured review—greatly enhances the other two.

The Hybrid Solution   Most class periods would do well to begin with a brief structured review of the salient concepts from the day before. Place three to five fairly easy but basic review questions on the board 1 minute *before* the bell rings that must be answered by everyone. This routine provides an incentive for showing up a bit early. Any student will be able to answer the review questions who was among the living the day before. Collect the papers 3 minutes or so *after* the bell rings. If students arrive late, they miss the opportunity to take the review test.

Tell your students that these daily review quizzes will be used to determine the grade of anyone who is on the borderline between one grade and another. Scan the papers rapidly as they come in and make a mark in your grade book for any paper that looks credible.

Structured review not only provides review while giving students an added reason to get to class early, but it also provides structure for the first few minutes of class which keeps the students busy while you deal with roll, late students, and students with written excuses, etc. Without some form of structured activity you frequently get sidetracked momentarily by clerical details and then have to struggle belatedly to impose order. Learning games can also function as "bell work."

The teacher, therefore, has three separate methods of getting students to be in their seats working when the bell rings: responsibility training, negative sanctions (school policy) for being tardy, and structured review. Each of the three methods of getting students to class on time can succeed on its own under fairly favorable circumstances. Of the three, responsibility training is probably the most powerful, flexible, and fail-safe. But together all three constitute a simple, well-choreographed routine that is extremely powerful and academically beneficial.

HOW TO MAKE RESPONSIBILITY TRAINING FAIL

There are many ways to make responsibility training fail. Most of them have to do with misapplication by the teacher, particularly in the use of penalty, although a few of them have to do with the characteristics of the class. A careful review of these lessons from the school of hard knocks might help us avoid making the same errors. Please understand, however, that the batting average of a trained teacher is excellent, whereas the batting average of someone who has only heard about responsibility training secondhand is anything that you can imagine.

Teacher Characteristics

Poor Relationship versus Positive Relationship   If the students like you, they will go along with almost anything, especially something that is as positive as responsibility training with its preferred activity time. If, however, the students think you are a jerk, little that you suggest will be acceptable. If you have few opportunities and little time to interact personally with your students, preferred activity time will help you get to know them.

Poor Limit-Setting versus Good Limit-Setting   Limit-setting is the first line of defense against typical disruptions in the classroom. Responsibility training is no substitute. With a well-trained teacher, limit-setting will usually eliminate 80 percent of the disruptions in the classroom, and responsibility training will pick up most of the slack by training the students to hustle and by providing discipline from a distance. If teachers were to attempt to use responsibility training for everything pertaining to discipline in the classroom, you might well imagine them clicking the stopwatch constantly.

People will ask, What if everyone in the school is using responsibility training? The fantasy is that if you were to walk down the hall, the watch clicking would make it sound like a tap dance academy. Such a fantasy is plausible only with a faculty of punitive teachers who know nothing of limit-setting. In fact, well-trained teachers rarely click their stopwatches for anybody. Their mere physical presence is a reminder of the ever-present possibility of limit-setting which prevents most of the problems. Simply showing the stopwatch to a student while relaxing and giving a prompt takes care of most of the rest. Students almost never gamble against a sure thing. The penalty part of responsibility training, therefore, is rarely used and is the first thing to self-eliminate.

Good discipline is a *system* which requires many specific techniques to be used properly *together* in order to achieve optimum results. Successful responsibility training presumes successful limit-setting along with the careful teacher training required to produce successful limit-setting. You cannot just buy a stopwatch and click your blues away.

Angry, Upset Versus Relaxed, Calm   A teacher who is angry and upset is very likely to use responsibility training as a weapon and dock the student's time in anger. Such a use of any management system is a breach of positive relationship. For any act of bad faith in caring between people teachers reap what they sow. For this reason responsibility training *follows* limit-setting in a systematic teacher training program because in limit-setting teachers learn to relax, gain control of themselves, and minimize the base rate of disruption. Until you have control of yourself, you will not have thorough control of your classroom no matter what technique you are attempting to use.

Poor Structure Versus Clear Structure   In Chapter 3 we stressed that teachers do a rather quick and dirty job of structuring their expectations for students' behavior during most times of the day. Clear structure will reduce the need for discipline, but it will also render discipline justified when it is given. Students often feel that the teacher has been unfair when the teacher has suddenly confronted the student over an expectation that was poorly spelled out. This general principle applies to responsibility training no less than to any other form of discipline. To lose PAT over a rule that was not stated or not clearly spelled out produces the resentment that one might expect.

Few Bonuses and Many Penalties Versus Many Bonuses Without thorough training many teachers will violate the rule of penalties. Most people equate discipline with "punishing the offense," and consequently it is easier for many teachers to understand taking time than it is for them to understand *giving* time. In fact, with effective limit-setting and the proper use of responsibility training, time is rarely docked. Bonuses, on the other hand, are always available and constantly given.

Waiting Too Long Versus Proper Time Frame The selection of a proper time frame for RT (to be discussed in the following chapter) is an important element of program design which is usually lost on a teacher who has not been carefully introduced to the fine points of responsibility training. To put it briefly, the length of time that students are asked to wait for their PAT must be related to their social maturity. I received a call from a teacher who heard me give a brief introductory presentation, and she said that responsibility training was not working in her classroom because the students were losing all their time. I asked how often she had preferred activity time. She said once a week on Friday according to one of the examples that I had given in my talk. I asked her to describe the class. She said it was an emotionally handicapped third grade. She might as well have asked such young and immature students to wait until the beginning of the next school year for their reward. I have learned, by the school of hard knocks, not to talk about responsibility training during brief introductions.

Boring PATs Versus Good PATs The mechanics of responsibility training once mastered will become second nature very quickly. That aspect of responsibility training which becomes a permanent facet of classroom life is preferred activity time—regularly scheduled enjoyment with learning which is protected and enhanced by the teacher. Yet, the preferred activities must be genuinely preferred—something worth looking forward to. There is no way to operate a sophisticated incentive system for an entire classroom without learning how to have a good time. Having fun with learning represents the key area of continuing growth for most teachers who are using responsibility training.

Student Characteristics

Relatively few characteristics of a class make it difficult to administer responsibility training. Even in special classrooms for emotionally and behaviorally handicapped students, the opportunity to enjoy school is not taken lightly. Yet, on rare occasions there can be some "glitches," and the following are the most common.

When an Individual Student Professes Not to Care about Peer Pressure and Is Willing to Run Out All the PAT during a Confrontation with the Teacher In about one out of three special classrooms and rarely in a regular classroom you will run across a student who says, "I don't care if I use up all the time. You can't make me!"

Of course, we will never give a student the power to destroy a system that is as

effective as responsibility training, nor will we immediately revert to the use of negative sanctions to bring them into line. We will simply respond to this particular dilemma by using a specialized incentive system known as "omission training." Omission training will be discussed in Chapter 12 when we look at management programs
for students with special needs.

**When a Clique in the Class Reinforces Their Own Deviant Behavior So That
They Are Immune to Peer Pressure**   On one occasion a teacher had a group of four
hot-shot students bedecked in letter sweaters who caused most of the trouble in the
classroom. When the teacher used the stopwatch and one of the peers said, "Hey, you
guys, sit down," super jock turned and said, "Shut up, dog face! I'll sit down when
I feel like it!" Super jock was immediately rewarded for his bravado when his three
pals started laughing. Super jock and his friends were a peer group within a peer group
which short-circuited peer pressure by its capacity to exert counterpressure.

There is no pat remedy for this rare dilemma. In this case the teacher talked to the
clique of students after class and threatened a negative sanction that was particularly
clever and effective:

> I'll give you a choice. You like to sit together, right? As long as you cool it in my class, you
> sit together. If I have any other instances like today when you band together to ruin preferred
> activity time for the rest of the group, the first thing I'm going to do is split you up and sit
> you in opposite corners of the room. Do you understand?

Another teacher had a group of students, a large group, who fooled around and
wasted most of the preferred activity time in third period even though most of the class
was generally cooperative. This teacher scheduled preferred activity time for 10 minutes at the end of each class period—a scheduling option that is common in departmentalized settings. The problem with third period was that it was followed by lunch.
The 10-minute preferred activity time of third period was followed by the 45-minute
preferred activity time of lunch which produced a glut of preferred activity time for
third period. PAT is a commodity, and responsibility training was failing due to an
oversupply of PAT on the market which lowered its value. To put it in a nutshell, half
the class really didn't "sweat it" because 5 minutes more or less on a 50-minute
preferred activity period was not that big a deal.

The teacher got mildly irate and said to the class (without asking me first):

> Class, for the last 2 weeks I have given you 10 minutes of preferred activity time at the end
> of each period, and you have managed to waste over half of it in most cases. You have
> indicated to me that preferred activity time is of no great value to you.
>
> My objective in giving you preferred activity time was to provide you with an incentive
> to cooperate. That is obviously not working. Preferred activity time was a gift from me, and
> I will remind you that "the Lord giveth and the Lord taketh away." From now on, any time
> that you consume on the stopwatch will be taken off of your lunch period, and you will sit
> here after the bell rings until we are even.

Being late to lunch was a terrible penalty for the class to pay since they not only had
to wait at the end of the lunch line, but they also didn't get to sit with their friends
since the tables were already full. The teacher did not bother to explain to the students

that she was breaking a state law at the time. The stopwatch worked powerfully during the following week. At the end of the week, the teacher said to the students:

> Students, I want to talk to you about responsibility training. You have seen me use the stopwatch two different ways. In the beginning I used it as part of responsibility training. I gave you preferred activity time and bonuses as a gift if you wanted them. You did not. Since then I have not used responsibility training, and I have simply docked you the amount of time you wasted as punishment. I can do it either way, either pleasantly or unpleasantly. Now, let's talk about the way you would like to have it in the future.

After some values clarification and a brief discussion, the class agreed that "the Lord giveth" was far better than "the Lord taketh away." From that time on responsibility training worked like a charm.

When There Is No Peer Cohesion In one or two instances I have observed a class in which the cohesion between peers was so low that peer pressure did not exist to any appreciable degree. These were in all cases classrooms for emotionally and behaviorally handicapped students. It is therefore conceivable, although most unlikely in regular classrooms, that there might be no peer pressure. When that is the case, use another management system.

When There Are No Preferred Activities Classes of culturally deprived students often draw a blank when it comes to having a good time. The only things they are often able to suggest are (1) listening to music and (2) kicking back. There seems to be, in fact, a kind of cultural hierarchy of PATs with the most outstanding students wanting a chance to do their homework (because of the press of extracurricular activities) or an independent studies project, most students thriving on fun with learning, and culturally deprived students relating only to childlike play—often without an idea in their heads as to what they would really like to do.

With culturally deprived students, PAT takes on an added significance. PAT is the teacher's opportunity to give to the students some of the joy of childhood that they have missed by teaching them how to play. The more culturally deprived the students, the more PAT doubles as a remedial socialization experience. In this one situation fun and games may be preferable to learning-related activities.

OVERVIEW

Responsibility training is both a simple notion and a complex set of procedures. The core of responsibility training is a simple notion—that students can learn mature patterns of responsible behavior more rapidly and thoroughly by being responsible to each other than by being responsible to an adult authority figure.

Indeed, a progression from adult enforcement of norms and standards to peer enforcement parallels in many ways the normal developmental progression of socialization as children pass from the parent-dominated world of the preschool years to the peer-dominated world of middle childhood and beyond. In the classroom as in almost any healthy peer culture of childhood, adults have a major input into the norms and standards that the peer group encorporates. Yet, in a peer-enforced culture decisions by young people to conform to peer values tend to be more volitional than they are within the context of adult enforcement alone. The peer group, therefore, plays its role in the socialization process as an intermediate stage between the external control of behavior typical of early childhood and the internal control of behavior typical of mature adulthood.

Translating this conceptualization of learning responsibility into a flexible, cost-effective, and relatively fail-safe classroom management program represents approximately a decade of trial and error and experimentation in the field. This blending of theory and practical experience has produced a program with both a solid conceptual base and a wealth of "nuts and bolts"—examples of success and prescriptions for failure that put flesh on the theoretical skeleton. We have taken the time and space to share some of these experiences in the hope that these lessons learned in real classrooms might help you to succeed.

Our feeling after years of work in studying classroom discipline is that there are relative few basic processes that must be thoroughly understood and mastered in order to produce consistent success in teaching. Our objective is to present those fundamentals thoroughly at both the theoretical and applied levels rather than trying to dazzle you with the plethora of programs and findings that constitute the experimental literature.

In the life of the classroom the proper objective of field research is to develop a program that solves multiple problems at minimal cost. All too often classroom management procedures described in the experimental literature are more a result of the testing of an independent variable in order to produce a dissertation than a programmatic attempt to fix a problem. When the practical problems are put first and the wisdom and experience of the teaching profession and the behavioral sciences are pooled, rapid progress in applied technology can be made and practical, affordable solutions can be found.

REFERENCES

1 Cowen, R. J., Jones, F. H., and Bellack, A. S. Grandma's rule with group contingencies—a cost-efficient means of classroom management. *Behavior Modification*, vol. 3, July 1979, 297–418.

INITIATING PREFERRED ACTIVITY TIME

Once responsibility training has been implemented, it simply becomes part of the teacher's normal daily routine. While the giving of bonuses continues, the use of penalty and the need to record it typically self-eliminates as one would expect of any successful discipline management procedure. What does not self-eliminate is Preferred Activity Time (PAT). Indeed the enjoyment of PAT and the relationship building that accompanies it are the aspects of responsibility training that become a permanent part of classroom life.

Preferred activity time by being the main permanent feature of responsibility training, however, also becomes the main cost consideration in the long run. How much time must be given over to PAT during the year, and how much planning is required? If time away from learning and the time and effort spent in planning are great, the cost of responsibility training may be judged excessive regardless of its promised benefits.

This chapter examines both cost considerations and the procedures for initiating preferred activity time in the classroom so that implementation may be smooth and cheap. Topics covered in this chapter include (1) the cost of PAT, (2) mechanics of implementing PAT, and (3) a PAT starter set.

THE COST OF PREFERRED ACTIVITY TIME

The cost of implementing any incentive system, as mentioned earlier, is contained primarily in (1) accountability and (2) reward, with accountability usually being by far the greater expense. By the use of a group time incentive with the recording of time loss kept cumulatively on a stopwatch, responsibility training all but eliminates the cost of behavioral accountability—the main barrier to the comprehensive use of incentives for good behavior on a classroomwide basis. Yet, even though cost problems of accountability have been overcome, is the price of reward too high?

The cost of PAT can be calculated primarily in terms of (1) time away from learning in class and (2) planning time. If either is exorbitant, we may be back to the drawing board.

Time Away from Learning

Time away from learning is the first cost consideration that typically worries teachers after the basic concepts of responsibility training have been explained. A secondary teacher may say, "Do you mean I have to give up a half hour a week for PAT? I don't have a half hour to give up for anything! I have 6 days worth of material to teach and only 5 days in which to teach it."

In order to understand that PAT is really the classroom management equivalent of a "free lunch," you need to appreciate savings as well as expenditures. Savings will come in the form of (1) increased time on task and (2) using PAT for learning.

Increased Time on Task   Let us begin with a consideration of the real cost of preferred activity time: time spent for reward minus time saved by reduced fooling around. Research at the elementary level during reading circle for those students working independently at their seats revealed an *increase* in time on task as a result of responsibility training from a baseline of approximately 40 percent to 75 percent following intervention. In the classes studied, roughly twenty students would be working independently at their seats and ten students would be in the reading group (three reading groups per class) so that the 35 percent increase in time on task would apply to approximately 40 minutes of independent work for each student. Thirty-five percent of 40 minutes is 14 minutes—1 minute less than the cost of the PAT, which was 15 minutes. Thus, for all practical purposes the PAT was *free*—a potential loss of time on task offset by gains in time on task due to improved classroom discipline.

At the secondary level gains in time on task to offset PAT can be far more dramatic. If the teacher saves only 5 minutes per class period by having students on task when the bell rings and by reducing dawdling during lesson transitions, they have recouped almost all the time typically set aside for PAT in an entire week. Additional savings of time on task per class period across the entire week due to improved discipline are usually well in excess of an hour, although these data include the effects of limit-setting as well as responsibility training.

In summary, the notion that the teacher is giving up time for PAT is an illusion. PAT is an investment that pays quick and handsome dividends in time on task which offset or more than offset the time set aside for reward.

Using PAT for Learning   Since responsibility training produces increases in time on task which offset the investment in PAT, no *net* expenditure of classroom time is required to operate the system. Increasing student cooperation while reducing teacher stress at no net cost in learning time is a shrewd investment.

But, if you can turn PAT into a *learning activity,* you not only recoup your invest-ment in time required to reward your class for cooperation, you also come out ahead by the additional margin of the duration of your PAT. Thus, if you are clever enough to convert PAT into an enrichment activity or skill drill of some kind, responsibility training not only produces increased cooperation, but it also produces increased aca-demic learning time *and* increased time on task.

Planning Time

The methods of making PAT academically rich and useful is the subject of the final part of this chapter. This "PAT starter set" is intended not only to help upgrade PAT from "fun and games" to learning, but to save teachers planning time as well. Students go through fewer PAT ideas than you may imagine during the year since they like to repeat their favorites. Consequently, this starter set may keep you going for quite some time.

As regards planning time, however, a problem needs to be addressed. There is a great difference between the ease with which elementary and secondary teachers take to the planning of PAT. Elementary teachers are surrounded by PAT options and are accustomed to using them as a normal part of their class although usually not as part of an incentive system. Thus, for example, primary teachers typically punctuate their day with kinetic activities such as art, music, recess, story time, skill-drill games, and nature hikes. They routinely plan diverse activities because their students' attention spans are relatively short.

When these primary teachers are introduced to the notion of time incentives and PAT, they often say, "Great, now I can work in some of the projects and enrichment activities that I haven't had time for!" For them a PAT is usually something they would have done anyway, time permitting. They just bless some of their enrichment activities and call them PATs.

Middle school teachers may have less diversity of activity during a school day than primary teachers, but they still rarely have difficulty coming up with plenty of PATs. Even their junior high colleagues who have had elementary experience usually take to PAT like a duck to water with little concern over the difficulty of planning PATs.

At the secondary level, however, we begin to encounter problems. Diversity of activity becomes less and less as students progress through the grades and teachers become more specialized. For a junior high or high school teacher who teaches five periods of math, social studies, science, or English per day, making the learning of their subject consistently "fun" may seem like a tall order.

During systematic teacher training we practice PATs which can double as skill drill or review for next week's test so that having fun with learning is a comfortable and familiar process rather than an imposing, formless imperative. In addition, immedi-ately following training, teachers form into "continuation groups"—support groups in which the entire training process is repeated over a 3-month period and in which PAT ideas are shared and practiced. With adequate support for continuation groups from the principal, colleagues can help each other grow both in their understanding of the uses of PAT and in the breadth of their PAT repertoire. With a little help from your friends, planning PATs can be an opportunity to build teaching skills while building colleagueship.

MECHANICS OF IMPLEMENTING PREFERRED ACTIVITY TIME

Scheduling PATs

How often do you have a PAT? How long do the students have to wait to receive their reward? This varies, of course, with the age of the students, but it is primarily a function of their social maturity. With greater social maturity students can delay gratification longer and, consequently, they can wait longer between PATs without losing sight of the reward. Yet estimating your class's social maturity takes some informed judgment. A remedial ninth grade class may be less mature than a regular fourth grade class.

The *time frame* of responsibility training is the amount of time from the beginning of one PAT until the beginning of the next PAT. The time frame tells how frequently you punctuate your work schedule with PAT. The time frame of PATs can vary from once every hour or less for preschoolers to once a week for junior high and high school students. The following guidelines (see Table 11-1) will help you judge the frequency of PAT for your class. When in doubt, be conservative and give PAT *more often* to start with until you get the feel of it.

Collecting PATs

You the teacher will need to come up with most of the new preferred activity ideas including learning activities, enrichment activities, and fun and games. These ideas will come from past experience, from training, and from the sharing among colleagues during "continuation meetings." Do not assume that all the students in your class know how to have fun. Most games that you assume everyone knows will never have been played by at least half the class. If you are unsure of whether a new PAT will go over, teach it to the class on your time for free rather than for PAT.

TABLE 11-1
GUIDELINES FOR CHOOSING A PAT TIME FRAME

Kindergarten.   A PAT approximately every hour.

First and second grades.   A PAT at mid-morning, end of morning, and end of afternoon. A mature class may go to twice a day (end of morning and end of afternoon) after the school year is under way (November).

Third and fourth grades.   A PAT at the end of morning and at the end of the afternoon. A mature class may go to once a day.

Fifth through seventh grades (intermediate).   A PAT at the end of each day.

Junior high and senior high school (secondary, departmentalized).   A PAT once a week. It will often be convenient and useful, however, to have a PAT at the end of each period, especially when the teacher utilizes PATs which review that day's instructional input.

Learning how to enjoy learning in class is an activity that the class must pursue throughout the school year. The PATs that are collected during class brainstorming sessions may well be as good as any you find. Some of these may be "fun and games" ideas, but many will be enrichment activities learned from previous teachers. Impress upon the students that when they have a new preferred activity idea, they are to share it with you.

Establish a storage area in your classroom where students can leave games and equipment for PAT. The idea of a "game cabinet" is just as useful at the secondary level as it is at the elementary. Give students permission to bring game activities such as checkers, chess, Chinese checkers, Boggle, Scrabble, Rubik's cube, etc. Even though fun and games will not be the mainstay of your preferred activity time, nevertheless the ready availability of these activities can serve as a safety valve when you have a group PAT planned. Remember, everyone gets the same amount of PAT, but they do *not* have to do the same thing. For example, if you have some enrichment activity planned for the group and a students says "Do I have to?", you say:

> Of course you do not *have to*. You can do your own thing as long as you do not interfere with the rest of the group. Would you like to get something from the game cabinet?

In most cases, the student will join the group for the group activity. She just wanted to know if she "had to."

Choosing PATs

Some teachers go to a lot of effort in choosing the preferred activity for PAT, sometimes going so far as to take a vote. There are easier ways to get the job done while still giving the students a sense of control over their preferred activity time.

Individual Activities   You can have students engaged in a wide variety of individualized activities. Everyone may be "doing their own thing" as long as it is structured. Only the most mature of high school classes can structure their own time successfully. For all other groups, it will be vital that the teacher provide structured activity for preferred activity time.

The school of hard knocks has taught us that free time in which everyone "kicks back" is an invitation to disaster. Children, even teenage and college-age children, have an amazing capacity to bore themselves to death! Given nothing in particular to do, they will do nothing in particular. After a few preferred activity periods of doing nothing, they will lose interest in the whole thing. "Rapping" they can do any time. You have to give them a better reason than that to cooperate.

When you are having individual activities, the game cabinet comes in particularly handy. It will provide you the materials to allow students a wide range of choice. Some of your best students at the secondary level may simply do their homework, since they have so many extracurricular activities, but most students will need more input from the teacher. For young students, individualized preferred activities may be planned on a weekly or biweekly basis by the teacher to help simplify getting students started at the beginning of PAT. For example, a teacher may have students bring a shoe box from home and put their names on their boxes as a place to store materials such as art supplies that may be needed for their individualized PAT. When it is preferred activity time or when students have completed their work early, simply excuse them to get their box off the shelf and start to work.

Smorgasbord   An alternative way to structure preferred activity time is to set up four to six PAT centers around the classroom. Many of these learning centers may already be part of your classroom and require no setup at all. Learning centers are common at the elementary level, but they can be developed for most high school classes as well. Developing them may not be too much effort if you let the students do most of the work.

One of the advantages of a smorgasbord is that it allows for variety and self-determination in the selection of preferred activities by students. Of course, if some student should find nothing to his or her taste, you always have your game cabinet to fall back on.

Group Activities   Most of your preferred activities will probably be group activities because they are simple to plan and organize. If the activity is desirable, it is rare that you will have to provide alternatives for anyone. Most of the time you simply announce what the preferred activity will be, and you start.

Sometimes, however, you may wish to give the students a choice between several PAT ideas. However, you do not want to get yourself into a full-blown class election from a long menu of preferred activities. At most, choose three preferred activities that you are willing to deliver on a given day and ask the class for a quick show of hands for the one they would most like to do. After students have gotten used to the notion that preferred activity time is for genuine enjoyment, the necessity for student input on the choice will fade.

PREFERRED ACTIVITY TIME: A STARTER SET

Responsibility training can die for want of preferred activity ideas. Consequently, teacher training provides trainees not only with a manual of preferred activities which are practiced, but also with training in developing preferred activity ideas. Within the present context we will have to settle for a brief introduction to the development of preferred activities which will serve as a starter set for you.

Preferred activity ideas are presented under six headings: (1) team competition: games with lineups, (2) team competition: games without lineups, (3) team competition with complex work, (4) path games, (5) enrichment activities, and (6) fun and games. As you can see, team competition represents a preferred means of converting learning activities into preferred activities.

Team Competition: Games with Lineups

Team competition is perhaps the most reliable motivational "hook" for preferred activity time. It allows you to turn skill drill and even test review for almost any subject into a preferred activity. Team competition must be benign, of course, so that playing is fun and losing is either painless, nonthreatening, or nonexistent.

In the following section I describe some generic team games which are particularly flexible in converting lessons into preferred activities. You will find that there are not really that many games in the world. Once you have learned a basic few, you can generate many others. I will begin with a game which has one of the most complicated sets of rules: *Baseball with a Lineup*. Baseball with a Lineup is chosen to start because it incorporates many "tricks of the trade" which I have collected over the years. These subtleties produce maximum safety and maximum time on task. I will then progress to simple variations that will help in generalizing the ideas contained in Baseball with a Lineup. Once you have learned Baseball with a Lineup, you will be halfway home.

Baseball with a Lineup   Before you can play baseball, you have to have teams. I suggest four to six teams in your classroom since competition is more interesting when there is a league or a tournament. You can always combine teams to make only two if you want. These may be the same teams that you form for classroom chores and peer tutoring, and they may represent rows in your seating arrangement.

Choosing Teams   How do you get equal teams? Remember, never do something for students that they are thoroughly capable of doing for themselves. Pick four (or six) students from the class of roughly equal scholastic ability to be captains. They do not need to be fast students. In fact this is a good chance to honor some of your slower students. Give them your class list and say:

> I want the four of you to take this class list and go to that table in the back of the room. Make four equal teams for me. Horse-trade until they are equal because you will have to live with them.

The students will balance the teams better than you can, and they will never complain to you that the teams are not equal. If you wish, to add a further guarantee of fair play, say to the students:

> It is your job to choose and trade until the teams are equal. After you have four equal teams, you will draw lots to see which team you will be captain of. You will probably not be able to keep the team that you choose.

This is a variation on the old gambit that parents use to get two children to divide a candy bar equally. One child gets to divide the candy bar in half, and the other child gets to take first pick.

Protecting the Players   Baseball with a Lineup means that the captain arranges the players in a lineup (with cleanup hitters, etc.), and each batter knows when his or her turn is coming up. How do you protect students so that they do not get asked questions that are too difficult for them? One way is to have questions of different levels of difficulty—singles, doubles, triples, and home runs—from which the students can choose. But how do you get all those singles, doubles, triples, and home runs without going to a lot of extra work? Are you going to go home and write out those questions in preparation for preferred activity time? Are you crazy?

Have a review period for an upcoming test which will cover the same material that will be reviewed during preferred activity time. This review period can occur a few days before PAT, and it will be presented as a generous gift on the part of the teacher to give students an extra opportunity to prepare for an upcoming test. Say to them:

> I want each of you to take out four separate sheets of paper. Today we will be reviewing the material for next Monday's test: Chapter 5, pages 73 to 89. As you are reviewing this material during today's study period, I want you to take those four separate sheets of paper and write a review question at the top of each one. I want you to write a single, double, triple, and home run question. Make your single question fairly easy but not a cinch since it might be asked to the other team. And, don't make your home run question a killer because you might get it. Play it straight and give me four questions of increasing difficulty, one on each piece of paper.
>
> Next, after you have written the questions, I want you to write the answers to the questions on the same piece of paper in the space below the question. Write the answer in the form of a paragraph of at least six sentences with a topic sentence, four sentences developing the topic sentence, and a summary sentence. I'll be coming around to help you with your paragraph development, and I expect good grammar and good handwriting.
>
> Finally, at the bottom of the page write the page reference for your question so that we can look the answer up in case of any controversy. In the next half hour, therefore, you'll write four questions and four answers with the page reference. Any questions?

At the end of your "review," collect all the single, double, triple, and home run questions separately, and you will have all the questions you need to play *Baseball with a Lineup.* You may, in addition, have students who finish assignments early write additional questions for PAT. Bright students frequently enjoy this learning activity and do not tend to regard it as added work.

Pitching, Batting, and Fielding Imagine that preferred activity time has finally come, and you have announced to the class that today they get to play baseball. You may be the pitcher by asking the questions yourself, or you may have a few trusted students be the pitchers while you do something else. In most cases it is to your advantage to join in the fun.

Let us imagine for the moment that you are the pitcher. You turn to the first batter on team 1 and say, "What will you have, a single, double, triple, or home run?" The student picks one, and you read the first question off the appropriate stack.

Imagine that the student asks for a double and answers the question correctly. How do you keep track of who is on first and what is on second? Do you remember it or write it on the board? You are going to too much effort! Have the student stand up and go to second base. Make a diamond on your classroom floor, and give students a chance to stretch their legs and strut their stuff a bit. When the student is on base, you turn to the next batter and say, "What will you have, a single, double, triple, or home run?"

Let's imagine that the second batter picks a double in an attempt to drive the runner in. If she or he were to get a double, she or he would advance two bases and the runner on base would also advance two bases. But what if the batter gets the question *wrong?* Is she or he out? Not yet! We are now going to bring team 2 into the action.

One of the problems with any team competition game is that the team on defense goes to sleep while they are waiting for their turn. Being clever game players we will not allow anyone to fall asleep. A sophisticated set of PAT game rules will maximize time on task. When the second batter gives the wrong answer to the question (they have 10 seconds to begin giving the answer), you turn to team 2 and say, "Fly ball."

What is a fly ball? A fly ball means that someone on the defensive team (team 2 in this case) has to catch the fly ball to put the batter out. To catch the fly ball he or she has to answer the question correctly. If he or she does not answer the question correctly, the batter is on first base with an error and all runners advance one base.

But who do you call on to answer the question on team 2? To begin with you do not call on anyone. *Wait for 5 seconds* before calling on a player from team 2. That forces everyone to think of the answer. If you simply called on someone without waiting, only one person would think while everyone else slipped back into a coma. Now, call on someone, and if she gives the right answer, the batter is out. If she does not give the right answer, the batter is on first base with an error.

What if someone on *defense* blurts out the answer before he is called on? That's an error, and the batter is on base with everyone advancing. What if someone on the *offensive* team blurts out the answer to the batter or whispers to her surreptitiously? That's an out! We thereby have incentive systems built into this game to keep people from giving away the answers.

Next, is it better to play Baseball with a Lineup "open book" or "closed book"? The answer, of course, is open book! If you play the game open book, team 2 (the defense) starts looking up the answer as soon as you give the question to team 1. After all, at any second that question could become a fly ball with anyone being called on to answer it. The batter on team 1 can also look up the answer. If he knows the material well enough, he just might be able to find it in time. You will find that most of the other players on team 1 are looking up the answer as well.

How do you keep the fielder on *team 2* (the defense) who was called on to catch the fly ball from being wiped out by a hard question? If you are the pitcher, use your judgment. If you are not the pitcher, teach your student pitchers how to pitch. Give them the following advice.

> When there's a fly ball, wait 5 seconds before you call on anyone. Then be sure you call on someone for whom the question is neither too hard nor too easy. Here is how you can tell. If you do not know whether a particular person will give you the right or wrong answer, ask them. If you know the student will give the right answer, the question is too easy. If you know the student will give the wrong answer, the question is too hard. If you don't know, it is all right.

How do you speed up the game *and* keep one team from being at bat for most of the PAT? Have *two baseball diamonds* and *alternate questions between teams*! It is like having two parallel games going simultaneously. Of course, this makes innings irrelevant, so compute the final score for each team as *runs minus outs*. You can even do away with the lineup. Simply read a question to the team at bat and wait while everyone digs for the answer before calling on someone just as you would with a "fly ball."

What have you accomplished for your half hour preferred activity time on Friday afternoon in high school social studies class? You have, in fact, had a concentrated open book test review session! It was a preferred activity simply because we were smart enough to make it fun.

Football   Did you know that baseball and football have almost the same rules? They do during preferred activity time. In fact, we will find that there are only a handful of basic team games in the world, and as soon as you learn the generic rules, you can play almost anything you feel like playing on the spur of the moment.

For Football, divide into teams and generate your questions in exactly the same fashion as with Baseball. There is only one major difference between Baseball and Football. Instead of singles, doubles, triples, and home runs, we have 10-, 20-, 30-, and 40-yard questions. A 10-yard question is a running play. If a student on team 1 cannot answer the question correctly, turn to team 2 (defense) and say, "Sack!" Wait 5 seconds and then call on a defensive player. If he answers the questions correctly, he throws team 1 for a 10-yard loss.

If the player on team 1 chooses a 20-, 30-, or 40-yard question, it is a pass play. When a team passes, they can be intercepted. If a student picks a 20-yard question and cannot begin to give the correct answer within 10 seconds, turn to team 2 (defense) and say, "Interception!" Wait 5 seconds while everyone tries to look up the answer, and then call on a defensive player. If she answers the question correctly, her team has intercepted and they get possession of the ball *at the line of scrimmage*. If they cannot answer the question correctly, team 1 loses the down but retains possession of the ball.

One other difference between baseball and football, of course, is that football is played on a gridiron. Draw a gridiron on the chalkboard and if you have a theatrical bent, begin with the flip of the coin. Team 1 begins on the 50-yard line. They have three downs in which to score. A remedial class or a special class may be given four downs to score if you like. With your chalk, simply draw the position of the football on the gridiron and follow its progress up and down the field as the teams move the ball, lose the ball on downs, or get intercepted. Always return interceptions to the line of scrimmage to keep the offensive team from throwing a "bomb" on their last down for the sake of field position.

Any Game with a Lineup   Have you ever thought of football as simply a path game? It is when you play it on the chalkboard in the classroom. Once you recognize football as a path game, you can use the rules for Baseball with a Lineup to play any sport in which players move a ball from one end of a court or field to the other end by degrees. You could, for example, play Basketball with a lineup with each question either moving the ball down the court or being a shot. Draw two (easy) or three (difficult) concentric half circles around each basket, and the court looks something like a gridiron. Start by bringing the ball in bounds under the opponent's goal, and move the ball exactly as in football. Intercepting or "stealing the ball" is even the same as in football. If the team can move the ball close to the basket on their first two questions, they can get a layup (single) for the basket. If you are not close in, the last player must take a longer shot. You can, in fact, play for court position alone and let the recipient of the final question earn the opportunity to actually shoot a paper wad at a wastebasket from close in or far out. You can even play Soccer with a Lineup the same way you play Basketball using questions for either field position or a chance to score.

As you have guessed by this time, many games can be played with a lineup in basically the same way. You can play Hangman and ask the first participant if he wants one, two, three, or four body parts. You can also play Jeopardy. Organizing your questions into subject categories is particularly effective for review. Imagination is the only limitation.

I was training a high school chemistry teacher who, halfway through responsibility training, said:

> Listen, if you think I have a half hour a week to blow on fun and games for preferred activities, you can forget it. I have both lectures and labs to teach each week and only five days to teach them. I don't have any time to waste on PAT!

I said, "Relax. Try it and you'll like it."

When we finally got to team competition the lights went on. This teacher used teams for the remainder of the year to review each week's chemistry on Friday afternoon. He didn't ask anybody for a vote either. He just told them what the game for the day would be, and they started to play. They played football during football season; they had a superbowl; they had basketball during basketball season; they had their own NCAA playoff, and they went on to baseball. He added an additional twist, however, in the form of some questions of his own. He said:

> Class, we're going to play football during our preferred activity time this afternoon to finish off the week. I want to remind you of one thing before we get started. As you know, we always have a test on Monday covering this week's material. During preferred activity time every one of Monday's test questions will be asked at some point.

After a month or two of preferred activity time, the students in his fourth period class came to him with a proposition. Fourth period class followed lunch, and the students asked, "If we get back early from lunch and save time, can we have extra preferred activity on Friday?"

The teacher, being something of a curmudgeon, replied, "Only if you are all back." Fourth period averaged between 2 and 5 bonus minutes a week during the remainder of the year for getting back early from lunch—all of them! And for what? Reviewing chemistry!

Team Competition: Games *without* Lineups

Baseball without a Lineup   Baseball *without* a Lineup is the quick and simple version of baseball that a teacher can play on the spur of the moment. You need teams, of course, but the questions can come off the top of your head or right out of the book or lab manual. They are quick questions, and the game goes fast. Once you know Baseball with a Lineup, the rules for Baseball without a Lineup are easy. You play both offense and defense exactly as you played defense when there was a lineup.

To play Baseball without a Lineup you simply turn to team 1, ask the question, and wait 5 seconds. After everyone has had adequate time to scramble, call on someone. They either know the answer or they don't. If they know the answer, it's one run. If they don't know the answer, it is a fly ball, and you turn to team 2 (defense) to repeat the procedure. Ask the question again and wait the same amount of time before calling on someone. If the defensive team answers the question correctly, it is an out, and if they don't answer it correctly, the question counts for nothing (a foul ball). Go to the next question and call on a different player on team 1. It is, therefore, the same routine for both teams. The offensive team must answer correctly to make a run. The defensive team must answer correctly to make an out. Three outs and you change sides.

Volleyball   The only difference between Volleyball and Baseball without a Lineup is that a volleyball team can score continuously as long as they keep giving correct answers. Thus, team 1 can answer 15 questions in a row and win the game 15–0. If team 1 misses a question, the service goes to team 2 and they can keep the service as long as they can run out a string of points. Thus, team 1 could make five points and lose the service to team 2 who might then go on to win 15–5 without the ball again changing teams. Yet, the ball usually changes hands rapidly and can change at any time, so everyone has to stay awake. Ask a question, wait 5 seconds, and call on someone. For an incorrect answer, the same question immediately comes to the other team as you say, "Change of service!" If the second team cannot answer the question, they lose their service and the next question comes back to team 1.

College Bowl   College Bowl is another variation on Baseball without a Lineup with one adaptation of the rules. You ask one question to team 1 *as a group,* and if they get it, they receive a point. You could have, of course, 10-, 20-, 30-, and 40-point questions if you want to get cute about it. If team 1 does not answer the question correctly, the question goes immediately to team 2 who can then score. The second question begins with team 2 so that the teams alternate at getting first crack at a question. The third question in the series is a toss-up question. The toss-up question is a speed question or race, and the first person with his hand in the air gets to answer for his team. Giving that person a chance to confer with teammates is optional. If you want to make all the questions speed questions, you end up with Family Feud.

By way of review, we have looked at two major types of team games so far: games with and without lineups. The rule variations between games both with and without lineups are minor.

Team Competition with Complex Work

We are beginning to see how skill drill and test review can be made into a preferred activity. Games with lineups permit brief essay-type answers whereas games without lineups only permit short answers. But how do you turn complex work into a preferred activity? How do you make a PAT learning game out of computing quadratic equations or doing long division or supplying the capitalization and punctuation for a paragraph or translating a paragraph from English into French? If you play baseball and ask a batter to compute a quadratic equation, the whole stadium will be asleep before he or she finishes.

We will give you a few ideas as food for thought in this section. But, as usual, we can do no more than scratch the surface.

Math Teams   How do you make a PAT game out of complex work such as math problems? One way is to have members of separate teams sit next to each other during preferred activity time. Thus, each row of students is a separate team with six rows being a league of six teams. You may wish to base your room arrangement around seating your students in pairs anyway for reasons that will be discussed in the volume *Positive Classroom Instruction*. Begin the competition by saying:

> Let me have your attention, class! For the first problem of the tournament you will have 2 minutes. [Write the problem on the board.]
>
> OK, go! You have two minutes from right now.

Give the class a warning when they have a half minute to go and when they have 10 seconds to go so that everyone will know when they are running out of time. When time is up, go through the following routine, which will take 20 seconds at the most.

- OK, everybody. Exchange papers. [Each student exchanges his paper with the person sitting next to him in the row.]
  - The answer is . . . [Show the class the right answer.]
  - Grade the papers, then return them to their owners.
  - How many got the answer right on team 1?—on team 2?—on team 3?, [etc].
  - Good. The next problem is a 3-minute problem. Get ready. Here it is!

The paper-grading routine is quick and accurate for the following reasons. When you told the class to exchange papers, each student gave his or her paper to a neighbor who was on another team. After you give the answer, no one will cheat for their neighbor because the neighbor is on another team. Return the papers, and then ask team 1 how many got it correct. They will report honestly because their neighbors, who are on other teams, graded their papers. If someone tries to get cute, the neighbor will say, "Hey! Put your hand down. You didn't get it right."

The motivation to work diligently to get the right answer is high because everyone is working for their team. The motivation level of being on a team is incredible— especially for those students who usually do little work. Kids who lapse into a coma during a typical assignment will usually be hustling during preferred activity time because they do not want to let their team down. (Remember, kids will do things for their peer group that they will never do for you or their parents or their own future well-being.)

You can spend an entire period doing a whole series of problems with a final tab- ulation of team performance for the sake of league standings. Yet, it was a concentrated work period that (1) was a preferred activity which incorporated complex work, (2) had a high motivation level, and (3) graded all the papers by the end of the period. You could have put the same problems on a ditto and killed the assignment by making it schoolwork.

Cut Throat   Cut Throat is an excellent game for English grammar (supply all capitals and punctuation) or foreign language translation although many other uses can be found. Have every team "number off," and send two members from each team to the board saying something like: "OK, numbers 3 and 5 go to the board." The third and fifth person from each team will then go to the board to represent their team in Cut Throat.

After the two team members have taken their places at the blackboard or at a work table, we will give them their task. Let's imagine a paragraph in English which you will ask each team to translate into French. Give them the paragraph (having it written on chart paper in advance will help) and say, "Go."

The team at the board must produce a perfect translation of the paragraph. However, *they can consult with other members of their team at any time.* This produces an immediate huddling of the rest of the team as they work on their translation of the paragraph as a check against the students at the board. Either of the students at the board can check with their team at any time if they have a question. The natural division of labor is for one student at the board to be the writer and the other to be the runner who goes to check with the team as needed. This simple mechanism produces (1) peer tutoring, (2) total participation, and (3) a feeling of security for the two people at the board since they are not on their own.

Cut Throat is a speed game and the first team finished signals that they are done by putting their chalk in the chalk tray or by raising their hands. If there are four teams participating, the first team done gets 1000 points, the second team gets 800, the third team gets 600 points, and the fourth team gets 500.

Now, we play Cut Throat! Imagine that team 3 was the first team done. The teacher goes to their work on the board, turns to the class, and says, "Now we play Cut Throat. Can anybody see anything here that needs to be corrected?" The teacher assigns a value to various types of errors depending on how well the students should know the material. Of course, the teacher is the ultimate authority as to what anything is worth. One student finds a spelling error and it's worth 50 points. Another student finds a verb in the wrong tense. That is a type of verb that we have been studying all week, so it is worth 200 points. Whenever an error is found the teacher subtracts the points from the team's total and *briefly reviews the skill.*

This particular round of Cut Throat is finished when all four paragraphs from all four teams have been critiqued. Subtract the penalty Cut Throat points from the number of points each team originally earned for speed and you have their final totals which go on the scoreboard. The next round of Cut Throat has new players and a new paragraph.

Cut Throat will go fairly rapidly because most of the potential errors will have been taken care of by the process of peer tutoring. The only errors that remain will be errors that genuinely need to be reviewed by the teacher because an entire team did not see them. Ironically, Cut Throat is one of the safest of all team games since no one is ever participating all by themselves, and it is one of the best ways for a teacher to find and review those skills which have not been thoroughly learned.

Path Games

As mentioned earlier, football on the chalkboard is just a path game—one of those games in which the players advance along a path square by square with the first team that reaches the end being the winner. Although path games are infinitely variable because of bonus and penalty squares that can be sprinkled along the path, the ones most useful in the classroom tend to be the simplest. To provide some food for thought, let's look at examples from a few different subject areas.

Spelling   How do you make rote learning motivating? Spelling words, like multiplication tables, just have to be learned, and it can be very difficult indeed to infuse some students with a sense of urgency. In one fourth grade class the teacher asked for help because only a third of her students were making perfect marks on their weekly spelling tests, and many students were hardly trying.

We divided the class into four teams with the idea of structuring some kind of team competition to increase motivation. While brainstorming to come up with a team game, we noticed that the teacher had cut-outs of the planets of the solar system above the chalkboard across the front of the room. The cut-outs showed their relative sizes and their relative distances from the sun. The teacher got the idea to make a path game across the front of the room called Race in Space in which teams would race from the sun to Pluto. We decided, since there were seven students on each team, to require the students to accumulate seven perfect scores on spelling tests collectively in order to advance one square. Rocket ships were cut out of colored paper for each team with the team members' names written on each rocket ship. We were gambling that the students would work harder for the sake of the peer status gained by contributing to their team score than they were presently working for the sake of literacy.

Within 2 weeks 80 percent of the class were making perfect scores. Then we got greedy and announced the following rule.

> You can make a perfect score any time before the end of school on the Tuesday following the spelling test on Friday. So, if you miss a few words, study them and retake the test so you can add to your team score.

We had kids staying in from recess on Monday to retake the spelling test, often with the urging of teammates. The teacher could even "farm out" the giving of the make-up tests during recess, class period, or after school by letting someone from a different team administer the test. No cheating at all!

Race in Space was a straight motivational incentive system rather than a discipline management system like responsibility training, which has bonus and penalty. But we fused the two by adding an automatic bonus to PAT every time a team advanced three squares. Then we practiced spelling words during PAT by playing a variation on Volleyball. The first team to serve was given a spelling word, and each team member in turn had to supply the next letter of the word. If the wrong letter was given, the word went over to the other team, and they continued spelling it. The team that finished the word got the point and the next word.

Typing   A typing teacher was having trouble motivating a group of "jocks" to work on their typing skills. To make progress public the teacher put a race track (path) around the room above the chalkboard and had each student cut out a Formula 1 race car with his or her name on it. Students picked up speed, so to speak, as winning or losing the race became a spectator sport. What jock, after all, wants to be lapped by a "nerd"? Once again the motivational program was fused with PAT as automatic bonuses were awarded whenever a car finished the race course.

Bingo   Bingo is stretching the concept of path games somewhat (a lot of short paths?), but it is easy and a perennial favorite. Just put twenty answers on the chalkboard—answers to any kind of question. Have everyone make their own bingo card—a piece of paper divided by four vertical and four horizontal lines making twenty-five squares. Place the numbers 1 to 20 randomly on the card and repeat four of them while labeling the center square "free." Read the questions and have students mark the number of the corresponding answer on the chalkboard on their bingo cards.

Enrichment Activities

Among the most common types of learning-oriented preferred activities are enrichment activities. Almost anything that you may use for enrichment can also be used during PAT—interest centers in an elementary classroom, computer terminals in high school math, creative activities of any kind, a film that you have already seen once. The sky is the limit.

Often I will be asked by art or band teachers in high school, "What do you use as a preferred activity in an elective class which is already a preferred activity?" The simplest answer to this question is that if the class is an elective, students must obviously want to do what the class offers. So give them more of the same, but at a more advanced level.

Art in high school provides an example. Freshman art is defined as any artistic activity that uses cheap materials such as pencil, paper, charcoal, straightedge. For a preferred activity you need only give the class access to a medium or specialized instruction that they are usually denied. Give them an opportunity to use a more advanced medium such as pastels, acrylics, or clay or give a special enrichment lesson with what they have.

Another example is provided by high school band. Band is usually an extension of the athletic program. Some kid likes to play clarinet, and what does he or she get?—John Phillip Sousa and instruction on how to march at halftime of a football game. How many teenagers do you know who use their spare money to buy John Phillip Sousa albums? What would the kid like to play on his or her clarinet during PAT? Just let *them* have the choice, and they will work for a chance to practice it on Friday.

Another enrichment activity that often escapes the class is exposure to some area of particular talent or interest on the part of the teacher. If you have a special talent or interest, share it with the students! Share it during preferred activity time. After all, this is the students' only chance to get this special gift of yours. Do not make excuses to yourself for taking up valuable class time with your avocation.

Fun and Games

Finally, we get to fun and games, the category of preferred activities which you may find yourself relying on the *least*. As explained earlier, fun and games from the "game cabinet" always provide an escape route for a student who does not want to participate in a group activity or in the smorgasbord that has been laid out by the teacher. Yet while we have learned to make learning the preferred activity, do not feel constrained to always make learning the preferred activity. Parties are fun, and with responsibility training to control the noise level, you can even keep it from getting rowdy. Give the students a chance to eat food, and they will love you forever. Have them bring it from home, or you provide it. Even seniors in high school love popcorn parties.

The one overriding misconception concerning fun and games, particularly at the secondary level, is the notion that you have to come up with some super fantastic game that will somehow manage to thrill thirty-five jaded and worldly teenagers. Nothing could be further from the truth. Anything that students have ever enjoyed during their lives, they *still enjoy.* When assessing the level of activities that your students might enjoy, do not be fooled by their grownup bodies and pseudo mature manners. When thinking of preferred activities, such as fun and games, think of your students not as 15 going on 25, but rather as 15 coming from 7. If it was ever fun, it is probably still fun.

Following training, a high school English teacher who had been working on poetry with her class for the preceding month brought paper and crayons to her PAT along with several other enrichment opportunities as part of a smorgasbord. She said:

> Class, I have several activities set out around the room on the tables for preferred activity time today. On table 1 I have paper and crayons that I brought from home today. During the last month we have spent a great deal of time learning how to use adjectives to add color to our language. And we have tried to turn the images of our mind into verbal imagery in our poetry. Today I thought some of you might like to reverse the process and take the verbal imagery from some of your poetry and turn it back into visual imagery. The crayons are for anyone who would like to make a picture from one of their poems.

Where do you think three-quarters of the class was? The scene was a reenactment of a scene from my kitchen when six neighborhood kids are drawing with one box of crayons.

- Hey, can I borrow the red? Does anybody have red?
- Hey, pass the blue over here when you're done? Come on, you're hoggin' it.
- Hey, I need the orange. Why don't you break the orange in half so I can have some of it?
- Wait your turn! I'm not going to break the orange in half. That ruins the crayon.

Of course, the drawings that were done that day were high-school level drawings, and the banter was high-school level banter. The teacher even entered in and drew a picture while sharing in the banter. It was a blast. These juniors in high school had not had an opportunity to crayon a picture in half a decade. Was it fun and games or enrichment?

I had a teacher from an inner-city school, a macho type, who pooh-poohed the general notion of simple games in his class. He said:

> Hey, listen, these kids are laid-back and street-wise. I can't imagine them getting off on this kind of bull! If you ask these kids what they want to do, they'll say, "Smoke dope."

When I saw the teacher a month later for the second round of training, I asked him how preferred activity time had gone. He was amazed. He said:

> You won't believe the kinds of things they wanted to do for preferred activity time. It was easier than you said it would be. You know what they did three out of the first five preferred activity periods? They wanted to play Red Rover!

They would have probably liked playing Steal the Bacon as well if the suggestion had been made.

The only limitation to the use of fun and games, especially at the secondary level, is to make sure you start PAT with a clear precedent that PAT is for learning related activities of the teacher's choosing. After the pattern has been well established you can loosen up and have fun and games or even a party. But, if you start with fun and games, the students will take "kicking back" as their PAT birthright and resist any belated attempt to convert it into a learning-related activity.

OVERVIEW

Responsibility training is more than a single management procedure among other management alternatives. It is unique in its ability to use time as a reward and to use the real power of the classroom, the peer group, to guide the entire class toward constructive behavior at relatively little effort to the teacher. Using time as the universal medium of exchange in a general classroom management program is too simple and basic to permit too many alternatives.

Preferred activity time for many teachers is a golden opportunity. In the name of good discipline and time on task they can do all kinds of enrichment activities that they have always wanted to do but perhaps could not justify because of the press of subject material that just had to be covered. It comes as quite a release for them to know that they will not only recoup the time for such activities because of better discipline management, but also that they *must* set aside PAT in order to achieve cost-effective incentive management. They are "forced" to do what they always wanted to do, and they are given the means to buy the time in which to do it. Hurray!

For other teachers, however, PAT comes as a new and, therefore, foreboding experience. "How in the devil do you make studying for next Tuesday's history exam a reward? Lots of luck!" For this teacher PAT represents new learning fraught with the possibility of failure. "What if they think my PAT is dumb? What do I do then—crawl into a hole?"

Especially for the secondary teacher PAT must be part of a systematic training effort and, perhaps more important, part of a collegial support system. There are plenty of good PAT ideas in any department of any high school if only they are shared. But sharing must be made an integral part of professional life—planned for with time set aside and protected—or it remains only an idea. New PAT ideas need to be constantly supplied, and new games and activities need to be practiced so that teachers will feel comfortable enough with the rules and procedures to actually try them in their classes.

Additional input can be supplied by a wealth of preexisting educational materials or by books of learning games or by widely circulated magazines such as *Games*. As an aid to building a PAT "bank" at your school site, an appendix to this chapter is supplied which lists books of learning games and activities indexed according to appropriate grade level.

I am saddened as I travel to find many educators and school boards in their eagerness to get "back to basics" interpreting the concept of time on task as a mandate to maximize the time allotted to seat work and dittoed practice sets at the expense of enrichment and enjoyment. Such a simplistic approach to "squeezing more learning out of the school day" flies in the face of what is currently known about incentives. It is possible to have your cake and eat it too—to increase time on task while increasing enjoyment in the form of preferred activity time while generating good behavior.

To turn our backs on such advanced management procedures as responsibility training with its PAT can leave the classroom rather grim. In addition, the teacher is typically forced to rely heavily on negative sanctions for discipline because of lack of incentive alternatives. In the final analysis discipline management in the classroom must build relationship while it builds cooperation as a by-product of the "good time" inherent in advanced incentive systems. If not, it will probably destroy relationship as we are left by default to rely on negative sanctions as a primary means of discipline management. For this reason responsibility training often has the most dramatic effect on classroom atmosphere at the secondary level where teachers have all too little time to get to know the 150 or more students who troop through their class during any given day. Responsibility training would be worth the time and effort required for implementation in many classrooms if for no other reason than to reduce the anonymity of students and to break down the interpersonal distance between teacher and student.

APPENDIX

BOOK IDEAS

	Elementary	Middle grades	High school	Sponge ideas
Games of the World by Frederic Grunfeld: Ballantine Books	*	*	*	*
Thinking Games by Carl Bereiter and Valerie Anderson: Scholastic Book Services	*	*	*	*
Rainbow Activities—50 Multi-Cultural Human Relations Experiences: Creative Teaching Press	*	*		*
The Great Perpetual Learning Machine by Jim Blake: Little, Brown and Company	*			*

BOOK IDEAS (*continued*)

	Elementary	Middle grades	High school	Sponge ideas
Kid's Stuff, Math by Marjorie Frank: Incentive Publications	*			*
Bag of Tricks—Instructional Activities & Games by Janet Blake: Love Publishing Company	*			*
The Kid's Diary of 365 Amazing Days by Randy Harleson: Workman Publishing Company	*	*		*
Teacher's Gold Mine by Dorothy Michener: Incentive Publications	*			*
Word Games by Joanadel Hurst: Word Games	*	*		*
Mad Libs by Roger Price: Price, Stern, Swan Publishers	*	*	*	*
Frisbee by Stancil Johnson: Workman Publishing Company	*	*	*	
The Cooperative Sports & Games Book by Terry Orlick: Pantheon Books	*	*		*
Everybody's a Winner by Tom Schneider: Little, Brown and Company	*			*
The Spice Series: Educational Services Spice (Primary Language Arts); *Anchor* (Intermediate Language Arts); *Probe* (Science); *Plus* (Math); *Spark* (Social Studies); *Create* (Art); *Action* (Physical Activities); *Stage* (Dramatics); *Rescue* (Remedial Reading); *Pride* (Black Studies); *Launch* (Early Learning); *Flair* (Creative Writing); *Note* (Music); *Eco* (Ecology); *Prevent* (Safety).	*	*	*	*
The New Games Book by Andrew Fluegelman: The Headlands Press	*	*	*	*
Turn-Ons/185 Strategies for the Secondary Classroom by Stephen Smuin: Fearon, Pitman Publishers			*	*
The Great American Book of Games by Ferretli: Workman Publishing Company	*	*		*
Until the Whistle Blows by Hall, Sweeney & Esser: Goodyear Publishing Company	*			*
Skillstuff/Reading by Imogene Forte: Incentive Publications	*			*
Mathematics Games for Classroom Use by Norma M. Molina: Silver Burdett	*	*		*

BOOK IDEAS (*continued*)

	Elementary	Middle grades	High school	Sponge ideas
Games to Grow On by Carol Winner: National Institute for Curriculum Enrichment (Math)	*	*		*
Math Sponges: Enriching Ways to Soak Up Spare Moments by Leigh Childs and Nancy Adams: National Institute for Curriculum Enrichment	*			*
Big Book of Board Games by Laura Palmer: Troubador Press	*	*		*
Play the Numbers: Math Games of Chance by Kay Zmudka, Sharon Barr, Jean McDermott and Thomas Wickham: Shakean Station	*			
Teacher's Treasury of Classroom Reading Activities by Mary Jo Lass-Layser: Parker Publishing Company	*	*		*
Blackboard Games by Leslie Landin and Enoch Dumas: Scholastic Book Services	*	*		
Mathematical History: Activities, Puzzles, Stories and Games by Merle Mitchell: National Council of Teachers of Mathematics		*		*
The Wonderful Word Book by Don Wolfson: Xerox Education Publications		*	*	
Recyclopedia by Robin Simons: Houghton-Mifflin Company (how to make games, crafts, and science experiments out of recycled material)	*	*		*
The Beautiful Naturecraft Book (26 contributing authors): Sterling Publishing Company	*	*		*
The Kid's Arts and Crafts Book: Nitty Gritty Publications	*	*		*
A Handbook of Arts and Crafts for Elementary and Junior High School Teachers by Willard F. Wankelman, Phillip Wigg, and Marietta Wigg: Wm. C. Brown Company	*	*		*
Games by Frank W. Harris (49 games to encourage cooperation): Frank W. Harris, 14597 Warwick, Detroit, MI 48223	*	*		*

CHAPTER 12

OMISSION TRAINING AND PIGGYBACK PROGRAMS

What do you do for the alienated student with special needs? What do you do for the child who rejects responsibility training—who says, "I don't care if I lose all the preferred activity time. *You can't make me!*"

Our first reflex may be to think, "Oh, yes I can! If you don't, I'll . . .!" So much for rewards! This is where either student or teacher prevails: where force meets force. "No student of mine is going to tell me . . .!"

But *wait*. Relax. It has not come to force yet. We still have some *incentive* options up our sleeve, some very powerful ones. We need a special program for the individual child who is chronically provocative toward the teacher or toward peers.

This chapter describes incentive systems for tough kids and difficult situations. Of all the countless reward programs for students with special needs in the management literature, we will limit our attention to those few which we use regularly and on which we have come to rely. These programs are distinguished by being especially (1) powerful, (2) fail-safe, (3) cost-effective.

Of course, any individualized incentive program will be more cost-effective if it can function as an extension of a preexisting responsibility training program. We have found the most useful specialized program of this type to be omission training (OT).

OMISSION TRAINING

As mentioned previously, if responsibility training is going to need immediate help, it will occur when some student says, "I don't care if I lose time for the whole group. I'm not gonna, and you can't make me!" Take two relaxing breaths, walk slowly to the student, relax some more, and in a gentle, private tone say:

Billy, if you don't care about losing preferred activity time for the group, then responsibility training and preferred activity time do not apply to you, and you will not have to worry about them any more. At the break, I will talk with you about what we do next. For right now, I would suggest that you keep this problem of ours from getting bigger.

For now, let's get some work done. Here, continue this next sentence. I will be back in a minute to see how you are doing. [prompt]

If Billy wants to continue the confrontation at this point, he has just bought into the teacher's back-up system (explained in later chapters). The teacher will "put the lid on" regardless—even if it becomes quite costly for Billy. But in most instances Billy will cool it because:

1 The teacher is calmly using limit-setting.

2 Billy's lever for controlling the situation—the loss of PAT for the group—has just been taken from him.

3 The teacher has structured an alternative, face-saving course of action with a gentle prompt.

4 The moment of reckoning, in which Billy will be deprived of an audience, has been delayed and put in the background for the time being.

The teacher has sidestepped the win-lose confrontation for the moment in order to create a situation in which he or she can deal with Billy's upset more advantageously and at greater depth. Sometimes a heart-to-heart talk ensues. Sometimes the implementation of an explicit management program such as omission training ensues. But in no case will Billy have the power to destroy a program as beneficial for the rest of the group as responsibility training.

What is Omission Training?

Omission training (OT) is the generic name given to an incentive program system that rewards the *omission* of an unwanted behavior. It rewards cooperation by arranging the student's reality so that he is a hero within the classroom if he exerts self-control.

It is impossible, however, to reward a student in a classroom every time he *refrains* from doing something obnoxious.

Gee, Billy, I like the way you didn't hit Paul just now.

That sounds weird!

What do you mean, I wasn't going to hit Paul!

You do not know when students are exerting self-control. You only know when they are not. Consequently, since you cannot reward the exertion of self-control directly, you reward it indirectly. You reward the student for behaving appropriately for a certain period of *time*.

Billy, you have been doing a fine job for the past half hour.

Omission training, like responsibility training, is a time incentive. But OT is a specialized time incentive. The central calculation of omission training is: How long can Billy act appropriately on an average day? By focusing on the misbehavior of a problem student, we often *overlook* assets such as his or her capacity for self-control. A young student who hits other students several times a day, for example, may work or act appropriately for a half hour or even an hour on many occasions. In omission training we time the student's good behavior. If, for example, we judge the appropriate *time interval* for a particular student to be a half hour as in the example above, he would immediately rejoin responsibility training (RT) and participate in PAT as soon as he acted appropriately for a half hour. In addition he earns extra preferred activity time as a bonus which would be shared with the entire class.

> Group, Billy has been doing a good job here this morning, and he has just earned a bonus minute of PAT for the entire class. What do you think of that? Let's add that to our PAT tally on the board.

Omission training, therefore, is nothing more than a bonus clause grafted onto responsibility training at relatively little effort to the teacher. Billy is excluded from preferred activity time until he behaves himself for a predetermined time interval at which point he becomes a class hero by earning a bonus that is shared by everyone. Billy can then continue to earn bonus PAT for each additional time interval in which he behaves himself.

The whole program can be explained to Billy and implemented with the class in about 5 minutes! In fact, if you had designed an individualized behavior modification program for Billy alone, you would probably have invested more time than it would have taken to institute responsibility training for the entire class with omission training added on.

Does it work? In a regional special-education center in which most students were emotionally, behaviorally, and educationally handicapped, OT was about as far as we ever needed to go in managing negativistic and oppositional behavior, and that was only required in about one-third of the classrooms during an entire year! Limit-setting and responsibility training took care of the rest of the management problems with few exceptions. In *regular* classrooms OT is rarely needed. Many regular classroom teachers imagine upon first hearing about omission training that they might need several OT programs in their classrooms, but they have not experienced the combined power of limit-setting and responsibility training. By itself OT is good, but on top of everything else, OT is amazing.

Who Needs Omission Training

Perhaps the most common situation requiring a special OT program is coping with the oppositionalism of an emotionally handicapped (EH) student who is angry, negativistic, and continually provocative toward both teacher and peers. Think for a moment of the kind of student who says, "I don't care if I lose everybody's PAT!" One of the most predictable sociological characteristics of the negativistic and aggressive student who continually gets into trouble in the classroom is that he or she has *low peer status*.

On a sociogram these children are all by themselves at the periphery of the group. What other student would say, in effect, "I don't care if everyone hates me. I don't care about you either!"

But do they care? In most cases the one thing that low-status children want more than anything is peer status. In spite of their defenses that say, "I don't care about you guys because you don't care about me either," they care! They may not have the social skills to acquire peer status, and the peer group may have long since become callous toward them, but they care. If students have alienated themselves from both adults and peers by their own actions, they are alone, and children—even teenage children—have a very low tolerance for being alone in this world.

Therefore, most of the power of omission training comes from the peer group—the very people Billy repudiated when he said, "I don't care if I lose all of the PAT!" Only the peer group can give Billy the things he really wants most: acceptance, affirmation, status. Only the teacher can rearrange Billy's reality so that he is given the opportunity for peer approval instead of peer censure.

If a teacher ever needs OT, it will probably be in dealing with the single negativistic child who has dared to stand alone rather than back down in some self-generated, no-win power confrontation. Understanding the child's vulnerability may help us to relax and proceed slowly with OT rather than to overreact with punition as the child expects us to do.

Omission Training Procedures

Initiating Omission Training

Abort the Confrontation   Remove the student from the self-generated power confrontation by (1) removing him or her from responsibility training, and (2) deferring problem solving to a nonpublic place at a future time (see preceding example of teacher-student dialogue).

Estimate the OT Time Interval   Before your meeting with the student, estimate the maximum duration of time in which the student might reasonably be expected to act appropriately. Estimate conservatively thinking in terms of a typical day rather than a good day. The most common intervals are 15 minutes, 30 minutes, and 1 hour although a half day or a full day may sometimes be judged appropriate. This is the time interval of your OT program, the amount of time that the student must avoid any major hassle in order to earn reward.

Pinpoint Target Behaviors   Before your meeting with the student, give some thought to the types of behaviors you will want the student to omit as part of the OT program. Do not include minor disruptions such as talking to neighbors. Such a *broad* definition of appropriate behavior would require the student to be almost perfect and thereby render success unlikely. You do not, after all, dock time for such minor infractions on the part of anyone else in the class. Use omission training as a remedy for major confrontations, and use limit-setting for terminating lesser disruptions as it was designed.

On the other hand, do not define the problem too narrowly, for example, hitting.

Such a *narrow* definition excludes too many analogous behaviors such as pinching, ruining someone else's work, or being verbally cruel. Rather, define the target behavior as a class of behaviors—anything really severe or nasty including a confrontation with the teacher. Use recent problems as examples.

In effect you are asking the student to behave appropriately regardless of what the precipitating problem was. When viewed from this perspective, the program is focusing on both a specific objective (omitting specific problem behaviors that have occurred in the past) and a more general objective (being good, which implies the omission of *any* severe problem behavior). For this reason, the more technical name for omission training is Differential Reinforcement of Other behavior (DRO).

Conference with the Target Student   At the appointed time have a conference with the student and begin by explaining that your objective is to help her or him to get along not only with you, the teacher, but also with the other students. This is a natural time for the sharing of feelings, but beware the student's blaming and excuse making. If a heart-to-heart talk develops, it will be now. If the problem seems likely to recur, explain that you do not intend under any circumstances to tolerate such problem behavior or anything like it. Explain as well that omission training is only one option among many for dealing with the problem although it is by far the most pleasant.

The tone of the conference should be tolerant and patient yet firm, rather than harsh as in "laying down the law." Usually the student is quite aware of what he or she is doing as well as the effect that it is having on the class. The teacher must engage the student in a joint effort to make things better. A reconciliatory tone is consistent with the teacher's objective of eliciting the student's cooperation in carrying out the omission-training program.

Explain the process of earning bonus PAT to the student and explore those activities or opportunities that may be most meaningful as rewards. Be sure the student understands that you must briefly explain the program to the class.

Buying Back into Responsibility Training   If the student exhibits intolerable behavior again, the teacher will deal with it in any way necessary to put the lid on (see the chapters dealing with your back-up system). If, however, the student cooperates and behaves appropriately for *one* time interval, he will immediately be reinstated into RT since he has demonstrated a willingness to cooperate.

If, for example, PAT is 30 minutes and each OT time interval is worth 1 bonus minute, the first instance of cooperation gives the target student the 30 minutes of PAT *plus* 1 extra minute for the class. You have made an offer that the student cannot refuse.

Operating Omission Training

Timing the Time Interval   The timing or recording of time intervals must be *flexible* so that the target student can earn a bonus at any time that he or she is good for one time interval—in this case, 30 minutes. *Do not* ever lock yourself into a fixed time interval—a time that is defined rigidly on the clock, such as 9:00–9:30. A fixed time interval is treacherous since, if the student misbehaves at 9:05 and loses the bonus, you have no incentive system until 9:30.

Using a flexible time interval is greatly facilitated by the use of a simple kitchen timer. Set the timer for your time interval and forget it. When the timer dings, turn to the target student, praise her, and briefly announce to the group that the student has just earned everyone an extra minute of preferred activity time while marking it on the board. Applause usually ensues early in the program.

The teacher is now equipped with the two pieces of scientific apparatus required for state-of-the-art time incentives—a stopwatch (optional) and a kitchen timer (not optional). The kitchen timer has proved indispensable when implementing OT because, without it, the teacher soon stops watching the clock and teaches into the next time interval. The teacher has thereby put the student on an extinction program for being good. If you fail to catch the student being good, the student will certainly get your attention when he or she is being bad and it is too late to give past-due rewards. Thus, the kitchen timer is primarily a cue for the teacher that guarantees a consistent reward for the student while relieving the teacher from having to be a clock watcher. Explain the use of the kitchen timer to the student as a simple means of keeping you from blowing it, and he or she will be comfortable with it since it is seen as helping you give the reward rather than as timing the student.

Bonus Tally   The target student can earn a bonus for *each* time interval in which he or she exhibits no serious misbehavior. If, for example, each time interval of 30 minutes is worth 1 bonus minute, the student could potentially earn 5 bonus minutes between 9:00 and 11:30. If you decide on a 15-minute time interval, you may wish to adjust the value of the time interval downward to 30 seconds of bonus PAT to keep the total amount of bonus from becoming excessive. The length and worth of a time interval are teacher judgments. Record the bonus tally publicly with praise so that the target student experiences affirmation from both the teacher and the peer group.

If the target student should get into serious trouble at 9:15, the teacher would deal with it using whatever means necessary. When the student was back on task following the incident, the teacher would reset the timer and again encourage the target student to earn bonus time. With a flexible time interval made possible by the kitchen timer, the student always has a fresh start, and the system is always in operation.

If there are 18 minutes on the timer at the end of a class period or school day, carry it forward so that it is not lost. Tomorrow morning, for example, Billy would only have to be good for the first 12 minutes of school to earn his first bonus.

Explaining OT to the Class   You must explain omission training to the class so they will understand what is happening. You need not go into great detail about the mechanics of the program, and you may, if you wish, be fairly vague about the behaviors in question.

> Billy will earn a bonus minute for everyone if he can cooperate and keep from getting into trouble for half an hour.

You may wish, however, to initiate omission training with a class discussion in which the exact nature of the problem is discussed and the role of everyone in helping Billy is clarified. Such discussions usually focus on values clarification. You may wish to stress, for example, that the class members can help and encourage Billy while ensuring that they receive bonus time if they: (1) refrain from provoking Billy, (2) ignore his provocations, (3) report a problem rather than retaliating, and (4) encourage and praise Billy's success.

As you explicitly discuss Billy's problem, do not worry about labeling Billy. If you call Billy incorrigible or stupid, you are definitely labeling Billy. But if you talk candidly about hitting or hurting or profanity, the students you are addressing have been the victims of the problem and will learn nothing new as the result of a little candor.

Problems at the elementary level are often student-to-student problems and profit more from sharing and discussion. Problems at the secondary level are more often student-to-teacher problems, and most of the talking will be done in private.

Dealing with Small Disruptions   An omission training program would typically only be implemented for a problem that was severe or persistent and for a problem that had failed to respond to a combination of limit-setting and responsibility training. Omission training is not designed to function as a substitute for the consistent use of other management procedures for a given student. Consequently, if the target student engages in a low-level disruption typical of classroom disruptions in general, respond to it as you normally would with limit-setting or responsibility training and do not reset the timer.

Some few teachers use OT as a weapon by restarting the time interval at the drop of a hat. An incentive system is weakened by a reduced rate of reward. Do what you can to see that the target student wins—especially if this entails early intervention with a lesser consequence so that the giving of bonus PAT is protected. As usual, a sophisticated management procedure will place the teacher in a firm but protective role toward the offending student.

Never take bonus away from the target student as a penalty for anything. OT is a bonus system, and it loses its integrity as such when a teacher takes back what she has agreed to give.

The Nature of Reward

Positive Peer Process   By using group reward, the student who has made himself unpopular by obnoxious behavior can very rapidly be converted into the hero of the class. By appropriate behavior, he is earning a reward that everyone can share. In this fashion, a positive group process is set in motion that will maintain the student's appropriate behavior after omission training has been faded out. The student, having experienced popularity as a result of appropriate behavior, will usually not want to relinquish that popularity and will continue the appropriate behavior to assure himself of his new-found acceptance.

Omission training, by inducing the peer group to extend itself toward the low-status child, also helps compensate for the target student's frequent lack of the social skills required to gain popularity—skills that are so often lacking in emotionally handicapped children. Thus, one of the greatest benefits of OT, and one which is not immediately obvious, is the creation of a positive peer process in which the group's "enlightened self-interest" works to the great benefit of the target child. Omission training is the only management program I know of that can radically alter a student's peer status within a few days.

Maintenance of behavior change must eventually be transferred from the formal management program to "contingencies existing in the natural environment." The primary natural contingency of OT will be the peer approval and increased peer status that has been facilitated by the OT program itself. Continuing praise by the teacher will always be crucial, but it will typically be less potent than the supportive peer process that has been built.

Individualized Reward On occasion, target students will strongly prefer a reward activity that they do by themselves or that involves only a few students. To gain the benefit of positive peer pressure in this case, keep track of the total bonus time earned by the target student and give it to the whole group anyway. The fact that the target student wants to do his or her own thing is a trivial matter since many other students may have the same preference. Preferred activity time for the group does not imply that everyone must do the same thing. It only implies that everyone has the same total amount of preferred activity time which is spent or squandered jointly.

Eliminating Omission Training

Estimating Success The life span of an omission training program is highly variable. It can vary from 3 to 6 weeks in a special classroom with an emotionally handicapped student to less than a week in a regular classroom. The teacher must judge when to terminate the program on the basis of the *overall* behavior pattern of the target student. It is time to begin to dismantle OT if the student has (1) improved in cooperativeness, (2) been integrated into the larger peer group, and (3) shown pride in his or her improvement.

If in doubt, wait.

Methods of Terminating OT An OT program can be terminated once the problem behavior has disappeared in either of two ways:

1 Fading the program by gradually eliminating its functional components.
2 Extending the time interval so that more and more good behavior is required to earn bonus PAT.

Fading an OT program is accomplished in at least *three* steps. This fading process should be preceded by a conference with the target student in which he or she is praised for his or her accomplishments.

1 Keep the bonus tally privately. Keep the bonus tally at your desk rather than publicly on the blackboard where the tally serves as a visual prompt for good behavior. If the good behavior pattern maintains for a week, proceed to the next step of fading.
2 Sever the contingency relationship between earning bonus points and receiving the reward. Tell the target student and the class that this week, as an experiment, the class will receive the bonus preferred activity time in advance—guaranteed like an allowance—because the student has earned the full bonus consistently. Keep records

of bonus time earned at your desk as before to monitor maintenance of the program. If the good behavior pattern persists for a week, proceed to the next step of fading.

3 Discontinue record keeping. The OT program is over.

Fading will be accepted gracefully by everyone if:

1 Fading is done gradually: no more than one step per week in special classrooms.

2 The reward is retained as a permanent part of preferred activity time rather than being dropped (a penalty for success).

3 Praise of the target student for cooperation is maintained at a fairly high rate by the teacher.

If difficulty should be encountered (usually in the form of a gradual reappearance of the problem behavior) back up a step in the fading process and wait. The new behavior pattern apparently needs more time to become established as a strong habit.

Examples of Omission Training

Lamar the Terrible Lamar was a third grader at a regional special education center who had distinguished himself by being the most aggressive child in the building. He hit and kicked peers to the point where parents of classmates were complaining, and when he was on good behavior, he only hurt feelings with names and insults. Limit-setting and responsibility training had eliminated most of the teacher's ongoing management worries within the classroom except for Lamar. Lamar was not indifferent to responsibility training as hyperaggressive students sometimes profess, and, indeed, some reduction in hitting had been noted as a result of RT. But peer pressure did not carry the day when Lamar was aroused—which was a sizable portion of the time.

Since Lamar was in a special education setting, everyone appreciated the fact that his aggression had deep roots that went far beyond the classroom. He was in a foster home, and his natural parents had been reported for child abuse although not convicted. Support services were provided in the form of play therapy for Lamar and counseling for the foster parents, but additional "leverage" was obviously needed to help Lamar to stop aggressing against all his potential friends in the classroom.

As a result of omission training Lamar was free of peer aggression within 2 weeks although it had become rare by the third day. The program was faded out in 6 weeks. As is typical with omission training, the greatest gains were at the emotional-social level and occurred as a spin-off of group reward. Even on the first day of the program after the reward system was explained to the group, classmates were heard openly encouraging and praising Lamar after he had earned the class 2 bonus minutes during the first work period. The informal observation of a face that frequently smiled where it had previously frowned suggested that the behavioral program had also served as an efficient vehicle for achieving emotional and interpersonal therapeutic goals.

Pete the Profane The utilization of omission training at the secondary level is illustrated by a high school student in a special education classroom named Pete who frequently swore in class, particularly favoring the word "fuck." An omission training program was designed for Pete in which he could earn 1 minute of preferred activity time for the class for every half hour that he went without swearing. By this simple mechanism the function of swearing for Pete was reversed. Instead of it being a high-status event which enhanced Pete's reputation for being tough, it became a low-status event which signified Pete's failure to maximize rewards for the group.

The consultation to set up the program lasted not quite 5 minutes since the teacher had been previously trained and was already using RT, and the omission training program eliminated profanity (all forms) within 1 week. Only after the problem had been eliminated did several of his friends volunteer to Pete that they thought he had been a jerk for swearing.

High School Mouth   A high school teacher who recently went through training had a girl in his basic (i.e., remedial) freshman math class who was verbally cruel to certain classmates and was a master in the art of put-downs. Limit-setting produced flamboyant back talk to the teacher which was dealt with quite successfully using camping out as described earlier. But the attacks on classmates continued, and time loss as part of responsibility training did not help with this particular problem. The girl said, "I could care less."

The teacher had a heart-to-heart talk with the girl and suggested omission training—one of the few instances in recent years that I have observed OT being needed in a regular classroom with a trained teacher. I asked the teacher how long the program took to self-eliminate. He said 3 days.

Questions and Answers

1 Might some students cause trouble on purpose so that they could have an OT program of their own to earn extra PAT for the group?   This question is often asked and is certainly logical enough, particularly when you consider how an OT program elevates the peer status of the target student. Imagine that, if ten students could be bad enough to earn OT programs, they could all be heroes while the class spent most of the day in PAT.

In practice, however, I have never observed, as a result of systematic teacher training, a student being bad in order to get an OT program of his or her own although it is theoretically possible. Some of the reasons that OT does not spread are:

a Group reward   The target student is not getting an extra reward opportunity that might arouse envy. Rather, everyone shares the bonus PAT so that no one feels slighted. I have observed the spread of OT in a few cases years ago when *individualized* rewards were used.

b Getting in trouble   You have to stick your neck way out *repeatedly* even to be considered for an OT program. And, each time you stick your neck out, you get limit-setting or time loss in responsibility training or even a back-up response (discussed in following chapters). That is a high price to pay just to be a candidate.

c Countermoves   Should a student ever ask, "If I get in trouble, can I earn extra PAT too?", a well-trained teacher responds, "Perhaps, but then the bonuses are worth only half as much."

In fact, the question of other students wanting their own OT program is still hypothetical to the best of my knowledge. The cost-benefit ratio of a student's seeking to have an extra OT program of his or her own is horrendous. A student would have to be many times more brave and obnoxious than she presently is and get in trouble repeatedly to receive something she already has.

2 What if you need several OT programs? Might that get complicated?   The likelihood of needing several OT programs at the same time is extremely remote for a trained teacher; it's all but nonexistent in regular classrooms. It is easy for an untrained teacher to *imagine* needing several OT programs for the "incorrigibles" of his class, but such a fantasy exists without the experience of successfully implementing either limit-setting or responsibility training. Standing by itself OT might be called upon frequently. But, as part of a management *system* in which each technique is doing its job, multiple OT programs are conceivable in only the most difficult of special classrooms.

Should you wish to operate two or three OT programs simultaneously, either get another timer or, more likely, run the programs in succession rather than simultaneously. Do *not* simplify the mechanics of OT by using a *single* time interval for several participants. This backs the teacher into a *fixed* time interval.

3 You do not have baseline data or any formal record keeping other than a simple tally. How do you document success and monitor improvement?   I must admit that omission training as described in this chapter is an invention of my trainees, not me. Years ago in the height of my B-Mod days I used to have teachers take baseline data, etc. just as you might find the procedure described in an OT research protocol. I quickly discovered how much most teachers hate baseline data and the formal record keeping that goes with most behavior modification programs.

Rather than taking baseline data, the teachers, without telling me, simply offered the student a bonus for each time interval—cash on the barrelhead. Consistently the student went cold turkey in a day or two. Lamar the Terrible was our first example, and he demonstrated that even the most obnoxious kids are capable of controlling themselves quite well when the price is right.

Lamar and a succession of other "incorrigibles" have helped to show us the incredible power that *group reward* and peer approval add to an individualized program. When we saw OT and RT work together, we realized that individualized programs with special rewards for just that one student and the baseline data, progressively changing criteria of success, and complex record keeping that goes with them were obsolete.

4 Is OT your only answer to the highly disturbing and obnoxious student?   No. The very need for an OT program is symptomatic of a rather severe social-emotional problem. The need for an OT program, therefore, is diagnostically important and should impress upon the teacher the urgency of the student's need for help. Additional help could range from heart-to-heart talks on the one hand to a referral for special services such as psychotherapy on the other hand. Thus, the OT program should be regarded as a short-term remedy which may need to be followed by collaboration with other professionals.

5 What if OT is too slow, or what if it is insufficient?   Use your back-up system, which will be described in following chapters.

PIGGYBACKING

What is Piggybacking?

"Piggybacking" is the process of adding one management program on top of another preexisting management program at little or no cost. Adding program on top of program at little additional cost is made easy when *time* is the universal medium of exchange in your classroom management incentive programs.

Adding omission training on top of responsibility training is a classic example of piggybacking. Omission training could be fairly complicated if done as a separate program for a single student. But as an add-on to a responsibility training program, OT can be set in motion with a single 5-minute conference with the student. Not only is the piggybacked OT program easier to initiate than would be an individualized program, but it is also more powerful owing to group reward.

In the preceding chapters responsibility training was described as the basic or backbone management program for eliciting cooperation in any classroom. The reason for the special backbone quality of RT becomes more clear in the light of OT and the concept of piggybacking. RT is extremely powerful and flexible while it builds reward and enjoyment into the everyday life of the classroom. In addition, RT provides the basic time exchange system for the classroom: the PAT that can easily be augmented to serve special needs. Omission training is cheap and easy because it is nothing more than a specialized bonus added to a preexisting reward.

Extending Responsibility Training beyond the Classroom

Students can earn bonuses for preferred activity time by acting responsibly outside the classroom even when the teacher is not present as long as the teacher finds out about it. The key ingredients are (1) supervision and (2) feedback.

The Lunchroom   Making the lunchroom a civilized place requires intervention on many levels, but one of the simplest programs for the teacher of a self-contained classroom is to piggyback a lunchroom program onto responsibility training. If the class has good manners and does a good job of cleaning up, they could receive a PAT bonus.

If the teacher is in the lunchroom, supervision and feedback are taken care of. But if the teacher is absent and the lunchroom is being supervised by someone else, the teacher need only receive a note after lunch from the lunchroom supervisor to give the class a bonus or, in the case of extreme messiness or misbehavior, a penalty. Be leery of penalizing the class for something that happened in your absence, however, unless your source is unimpeachable, like the principal or another teacher.

The Playground   Bonuses can be given for many aspects of playground behavior in the elementary grades from lining up quickly to passing through the halls quietly to playing nicely. They can be given for the class as a whole, or they can be given for the behavior of an individual child. When given for the group, bonus is a simple extension of responsibility training. Individual bonuses represent an extension of omission training. A student who needs OT in the classroom for being aggressive, for example, will commonly need it during recess as well. Unless the OT program is extended outside, the problem student may ruin the games of younger children or hit with impunity. Rather than "benching" the problem student or sending him to the office, let your first lines of defense be (1) close supervision and (2) reward-based incentives.

Tattling   Most elementary teachers are plagued by tattling, especially following recess. Many secondary teachers get a stiff dose of it too, and it is a problem that is difficult to deal with. Most tattling is rewarded by the attention of the teacher as he or she listens to the tattle. Yet not to listen seems heartless to many teachers. What do you do?

A rather subtle and delicious remedy for dealing with chronic tattling is explained in the next chapter under the heading "Response-Cost Programs." Yet a far simpler approach than response-cost management may serve your needs better if your problems of tattling are not too chronic or severe. Simply piggyback a bonus onto responsibility training if the class can come in from recess without tattling. Respond to any of your regular tattlers with a hand gesture or brief prompt reminding them of the bonus. If you see blood, of course, dump the program and help the kid with no loss of bonus.

Extending Responsibility Training to Motivation

Omission training is the most common piggyback incentive program for discipline, but OT only scratches the surface of piggybacking possibilities. You can use piggybacking to deal with almost any tough case, both in the area of discipline *and* in the area of motivation and instruction. Some examples might help to flesh out the notion of piggybacking.

Silent Suzanne   Suzanne was an emotionally handicapped 9-year-old girl in a special classroom. She would never talk in a group. Although she occasionally spoke with friends, she was an "elective mute" during discussions, sharing, or small group instruction.

One day, after a brief meeting with Suzanne before a group discussion, the teacher announced:

> Class, as you know, Suzanne never speaks out when we are having a discussion. Today I would like to try something new. Whenever Suzanne participates in the discussion, she will

earn a star that will go on this star chart. Each star will stand for 1 minute of extra preferred activity time for the whole group! Let's help Suzanne as much as we can.

The class helped Suzanne. One child asked her a question, and several others said Yea! Suzanne stammered out a sentence, and the group cheered. She spoke twice more before the period was over, and the teacher reported 3 weeks later that the problem had disappeared. The star chart was a little extra visual goodie for Suzanne, but it was the group that took care of the problem.

Andrew Do-Nothing   Andrew was nearing the end of third grade and had distinguished himself by never yet having handed in an assignment since entering public education. The teacher who had been trained earlier in the year finally offered Andrew an incentive for doing school work known affectionately as "cash on the barrelhead." She said:

Andrew, I want you to try some of these math problems in this assignment. Every time you complete one problem it will be worth 30 seconds of extra PAT for the group. I will announce to the class as you earn them extra PAT. Let's see how much you can get!

The teacher utilized some instructional skills that are described in the volume *Positive Classroom Instruction* literally to teach Andrew through the first few problems, at which time she announced the bonus to the class. The group reacted with a moment of incredulous silence, and then someone said, "Hey, all right!," and applause ensued. The applause petered out in a week and a half, but the bonus PAT increased so that Andrew was handing in all his assignments by the beginning of the third week.

OVERVIEW

One of the beauties of piggybacking is cost. By using *time* as a universal medium of exchange in classroom incentives, a large number of management objectives can be attained at minimal cost. Begin with a well-planned preferred activity time and simply add or subtract from it according to the student's behavior. Thus, individual programs can be set up at the drop of a hat by adding a bonus clause or a combination bonus and penalty clause. In fact, all the variants and extensions of responsibility training are nothing more than the continual accumulation of bonus and penalty to be added or subtracted from a single PAT.

Omission training is the primary piggyback program for getting a student to *stop* an obnoxious behavior, but as the examples show, piggybacking can also be used to get a student to *start* a behavior. In fact, simple bonus clauses added onto responsibility training are one of the most powerful *motivational* tools in all behavior management. One of the practical advantages of responsibility training, therefore, is its capacity both to stop undesirable behaviors (discipline) and start desirable behaviors (motivation) simultaneously.

One of the strongest arguments for instituting responsibility training in the classroom is often its usefulness as a vehicle for piggybacking. I have trained teachers, for example, who have instituted RT quite apart from considerations of classroom discipline just so they could use group reward as a lever to get a particular student to do work.

In a sense piggybacking an individualized management program on top of responsibility training is no different than getting the class to be in their seats when the bell rings or to hustle during lesson transitions or to pick up papers off the floor. In both cases PAT is used as a lever to get the class to take responsibility for making something happen. The group will make good things happen when proper structure is provided whether the behavioral objective in question focuses on the group or an individual.

CHAPTER 13

BEHAVIOR MODIFICATION AND PARALLEL PROGRAMS

Where do most behavior modification programs fit into positive classroom discipline? What about the use of extinction in the classroom? What about the use of highly specialized management programs for students with special needs? This chapter attempts to bridge what educators may already know about behavior management with the methodology that has been presented as part of Positive Classroom Discipline thus far.

During training teachers and administrators often assume that whatever is not explicitly included in positive classroom discipline is somehow excluded. Quite to the contrary, positive classroom discipline is intended to supply a basic framework for understanding the management of classroom discipline. It focuses on group management procedures that are both basic and highly cost-effective. But it does not presume to be a summary of the entire technical literature, nor does it implicitly exclude any proven technique. If you are using something else that works, hang on to it. You may soon need it.

Parallel programs are simply incentive systems that do not fit within the context of time incentives. They must therefore be implemented *parallel* to and separate from responsibility training rather than being piggybacked on top of it as in the case of omission training.

Parallel programs are sometimes necessary, but they are always extra work. To the extent that teachers can solve a problem by some combination of limit-setting, responsibility training, and piggybacking, they minimize the cost of behavior management. When all else fails, however, the teacher may need to use either a specialized incentive system, perhaps a behavior modification program designed for a particular student with a particular problem, or a back-up response (negative sanction) to put the lid on. Incentive programs that are implemented separately from responsibility training are discussed in this chapter. Back-up responses and negative sanctions are discussed in the following chapters.

The final criterion for choosing any management technique is *cost*. The past two decades of research have produced a multiplicity of classroom management procedures that have proved effective in a wide variety of settings. When you examine the options for solving a problem, therefore, the critical question is not does the technique work but, rather, how much time and effort does it require. Cost will ultimately determine the number of problems a teacher can fix. This chapter may be considered a user's guide to behavior modification seen in the light of cost.

INDIVIDUALIZED INCENTIVES

Basic Design

The classic behavior modification program is the individualized incentive program for a behaviorally and/or educationally handicapped student. The objective of such a program is typically to replace problem behavior with appropriate behavior. The steps in implementing such a program serve as a model for contingency management in general.

1 Pinpointing the Problem   What behaviors do you want to change? Very often teachers and parents will have a vague and undifferentiated notion of the problem when pressed to describe it. They may describe the child, for example, as oppositional, nasty, lazy, or out of control. "Pinpoint interviewing" will help delineate the boundaries of the problem and will sometimes turn up surprises as the exact nature of the problem is explored. For example, one elementary teacher who requested a management program for a student who was described as incorrigible could not cite any instance of incorrigible behavior during recent weeks. When interviewed further the teacher was able to cite only one memorable experience—an instance earlier in the year when the student spat in her face during a tantrum. The incident was so disgusting to the teacher that it colored all subsequent perceptions of the child.

2 Pinpointing Behavioral Assets   Understanding a student's liabilities is only the first part of diagnosis. What are the strengths upon which you can build? Knowing that a student hits other students frequently is one thing, but knowing that he or she can often go all morning *without* hitting is quite another. A management program is not built around deficit behavior since a deficit provides no foundation for building. Rather, most management programs focus on *maximizing assets*. A management program almost always focuses on the simultaneous manipulation of a *pair* of behaviors— the one you want to eliminate and the one you want to build in its place. If you focus only on the elimination of problems, the building of appropriate behavior is left to chance.

3 Recording Target Behavior   You cannot assess improvement unless you have some notion of the rate of target behaviors (key problems and key assets) before and following intervention. The data from recording the rate of target behaviors before intervention is called "baseline data," and most behavior modification programs make their first appearance in the classroom with the recording of baseline data.

Baseline data can also produce some surprises of its own. Sometimes the problem isn't there, and often a discipline problem disappears as a result of baseline data, especially if the teacher is taking the data. When the problem disappears, it is typically because the teacher quit ignoring the problem and began looking at the offending student every time he or she misbehaved. Often the taking of baseline data by a teacher is more valuable as a means of training the teacher to track the problem behavior than it is as a source of data.

4 Pinpointing Critical Reinforcers A reinforcer is not necessarily a reward. A reinforcer is anything that anyone will work for. A reward offered by a teacher but spurned by an uninterested student is not a reinforcer. It is simply a waste of time—a false start.

A reinforcer is not necessarily pleasant either. It is axiomatic that children have a very low tolerance for being totally ignored. Children work for attention, and if they cannot get good attention, they will usually work for bad attention rather than accept no attention for a prolonged period of time. Consequently, children will at times provoke their teachers or parents when the only consistently observed consequence is criticism or scolding. Reprimands, scolding, criticism, and even receiving a beating can serve therefore as reinforcers in the course of human events.

When building a management program the reward must be potent enough that the student will *consistently* work for it. It must be of *critical* importance to students to induce them to forgo accustomed forms of reward that reinforce inappropriate behaviors. If you cannot find a *critical reinforcer,* you are up a tree.

5 Intervention Intervention typically focuses on changing any or all the following:

a *The setting.* The setting includes general contextual factors which may govern the occurrence of the problem, such as room arrangement, seating location, lighting, and the presence of distractions. The setting, however, can include almost anything the presence of which influences the occurrence of the problem. For example, "setting" may include the presence of certain people, expectations, or pressures to perform.

b *Events preceding the problem.* Preceding events include specific prompts or cues for the onset of the problem behavior. Such cues, which precipitate or trigger the onset of the target behavior, usually come from either the students or the teacher.

Rearranging the setting and the precipitating events (prompts) to alter the rate of a problem behavior is typically referred to as "stimulus control" since the intervention focuses on altering the stimuli that govern the onset of the behavior.

c *Events following the occurrence of the problem.* Events of interest which follow the occurrence of a problem include specific consequences of that behavior. These consequences or "contingencies" include both positive and negative events as well as no consequence at all. That portion of an intervention which focuses on altering the consequences of a target behavior is typically referred to as "contingency management."

Although "intervention" looks simple, it hides most of the technology, lore, and collective wisdom of behavior modification. It is the specific nature of the intervention program that will either work the teacher to death for limited results or produce widespread improvement at minimal effort.

6 Going Back to the Drawing Board   If (a) you know your behavioral management basics, (b) you know the ropes in your particular setting, (c) you have enough clinical savvy to deal effectively with the affective and interpersonal aspects of the situation, and (d) you have adequate control of the environment, you will *eventually* succeed with your behavior management program.

This likelihood of eventual success does not imply, however, that you will not fail a few times along the way or that you may not succeed at first with a program that is so expensive and impractical that no one will use it. If, for example, teachers whom you respect tell you that your beloved program is just too much trouble and effort for them to use, listen to them! Only they know how difficult the rest of their job is. Back to the drawing board!

This final step of program design implies the standard for behavioral management programs—*fix the problem!* Thirty percent improvement or change significant at the .01 level just doesn't cut it. In behavioral research there are two tests of significance for an intervention: statistical tests and the "so what" test.

Psychologist: We improved the problem by 25 percent!
Teacher: So what! The kid is still disrupting the class and driving me nuts!

Behavior management lives or dies by the "so what" test. As one prominent colleague of mine said (only slightly exaggerating) while reviewing the graph of data from a modestly successful intervention: "If you can't see the change from across the room, to hell with it."

Design Pitfalls

High Cost and Cutting Corners   It is obvious from a review of the basic design features of an individualized behavior modification incentive program that it is a lot of work! It also requires expert judgment, and consequently such programs often require special consultation from program design specialists as well as help with data taking. Such programs become more tricky and expensive the more disturbed the student. Consequently full-blown, individualized behavior modification programs are most common in special education where special funds can support the personnel needed to remedy truly tough situations.

Regular classroom teachers, however, have few resources available to help them with behavior management apart from their memories of an introductory college course in behavior modification, if even that. Yet the management of a regular class-room is a very complex—especially when it may contain a few "special" students who either never quite qualified for special education or who have been mainstreamed.

It's not surprising that regular classroom teachers frequently design reward pro-grams in an attempt to help their problem students. Under the pressures of dealing with the needs of the rest of the class and with no consultant or extra personnel to carry out the programs, many of the basic design features of an individualized behavior modification program are routinely violated. Programs are quickly put together, base-line data is almost never taken, and if the program doesn't work, either the teacher doesn't know it or the program is unceremoniously dumped.

When "quick and dirty" reward programs are instituted, quick and dirty results tend to occur. There is no such thing as a halfway incentive program. It either works or blows up in your face. If it just fails and dies with a whimper, you are lucky. The notion of offering rewards as a quick cure for problems in the classroom has been greatly oversold in recent years. Most teachers have not been adequately trained to recognize the pitfalls that accompany the offering of rewards. The most common ex-ample of counterproductive results with rewards is the offering of a reward for work completion without strict accountability for the *quality* of the work. Rewarding com-pletion without strict accountability for quality produces a speed incentive which con-tinuously reinforces fast and sloppy work. Accountability is always the most expensive and most commonly neglected part of a management program. In order to reward diligence and excellence the teacher must be able to monitor the quality of work being done as it is being done or very soon thereafter. If you cannot afford strict and accurate accountability, you cannot afford to offer rewards.

Fortunately, the failure of a reward program for a *discipline* problem is often less costly and counterproductive than failure of a reward program for work completion. When a quick and dirty reward program for a discipline problem fails, it usually pro-duces either no improvement or an obvious flare-up. Both are easy to see and produce a quick dumping of the program. Thus, as long as *negative sanctions* are *not* employed to cure a discipline problem, quick and dirty incentive programs tend to be costly but relatively benign. At least the teacher does not back into an escalating cycle of coercion and countercoercion with students as often results from the misapplication of punish-ment.

Seduction into Coercion   While the high cost of most individualized programs may lead to cutting corners with the resulting high risk of program failure, perhaps the greater risk of mismanagement comes, ironically, from simplistic incentive systems which lack well-designed penalties for goofing off. As mentioned earlier, in the be-havioral economy of the classroom the built-in rewards for goofing off are very likely to be stronger than the teacher's simple reward programs for shaping up. In frustration and without more sophisticated incentive alternatives such as responsibility training, many teachers are backed into becoming harsh as a means of finally putting an end to the problem. Once teachers opt to fight fire with fire, they have entered a hazardous arena in which they are ill-equipped to survive.

GROUP INCENTIVES

Since individualized behavior management programs are so expensive and potentially numerous in almost any classroom, the teacher may wish to implement a *group* management program that applies to everyone in the classroom. Without a single, simple universal medium of exchange for rewards such as time, however, the widespread use of rewards for the entire group may multiply the work (i.e., cost) of management.

Point Economies

A point economy is a management system that uses "points" rather than time as a universal medium of exchange. This simple difference in design, however, determines many other design characteristics of the management system which can greatly increase the cost and the headaches of implementation.

Token economies are perhaps the best known point economies although there are endless variations on the theme. For some strange reason point systems are almost always named after the way in which the points are given out, perhaps the least critical design feature of a point economy. Thus, token economies give plastic tokens or poker chips, check-mark systems give check-marks on a check-mark card, star programs put stars on charts, and bean or marble programs put beans or marbles in a cup or jar. In the final analysis a point is a point, and they are all fairly easy to give out—be it for individuals or for the group.

The real work of a point program begins when you start to *collect* and *exchange* the points once you have given them out. To appreciate the potential cost of such management programs let us examine one of the earliest and most straightforward point economies for individually rewarding everyone in the class—the check-mark system.

In a typical check-mark system each student has a 3 × 5 index card on the corner of his or her desk, and as the teacher passes by during seatwork, he makes a check on the card if the student is on task. The more check-marks a student accumulates, the bigger is the reward. Such systems have been used with considerable success in many special education settings, but their cost prohibits widespread use in regular classrooms. The cost immediately becomes apparent when you begin to collect the points. Imagine your effort as you carry out the following steps.

1 Point Tally   How many points has each student earned? You must tally them yourself or monitor the tallying so that students do not give themselves points.

2 Point Recording   You now record point totals on a score sheet to facilitate exchange for reinforcers and to provide a simple record by which you can monitor improvement.

3 Point Exchange   With point exchange you are up against the *real* cost of point economies. Since each student may have a different number of points, you must have *rewards of different sizes* to match the points earned or else the earning of points is meaningless. The process of exchange may easily consume a half hour, a cost in time which may nullify the gains in time on task produced by the program.

Elementary and special education teachers have tended in the past to use *tangible* rewards since they are concrete and since you can dole out more or less of them to match the point totals of the students. (Secondary teachers avoid the whole thing like the plague.) Matching point totals with tangible rewards locks you into operating a "general store"—a repository of enough different kinds of gee-gaws, goodies, and rubber spiders to allow you to act as point broker.

4 Buying the Rewards   Who buys the stock for the general store? You guessed it—the poor teacher who cares enough to go the extra mile. I have known many a teacher who has spent 10 to 15 dollars a week out of pocket to buy the behavioral and academic improvement that a point economy offers.

The cost of running such a so-called group management system comes largely from the fact that it is not group management at all. It is, in effect, an *amalgam* of many *individual* point economies. The use of point economies has, therefore, died of natural causes in regular education over the past decade owing primarily to the cost of point exchange. As one teacher remarked to me, "It is not the kids who are driving me nuts any more. It is those damn points and all that junk that I have to give out!"

Simplified Point Economies

The cost problems of point economies are sufficiently obvious to those using them that methods of cost-cutting have proliferated both in the field and in research. A quick look at the most straightforward methods may provide some needed perspective on point economies.

Reduce Target Behaviors   A point economy may cover many diverse types of behavior throughout the day so that the opportunity to earn points is always available. Or, you may retrench and offer points for doing only the six or eight major jobs that are the source of most nagging in the classroom. Post a chart of these basic responsibilities with a place to make a check by each student's name when he or she carries out the responsibility and you have a *responsibility chart* (columns are responsibilities, rows are students' names). Put pretty stars in the squares of the chart, and you have a *star chart*. Although responsibility charts may sound rather basic (for little kids only), many a high school shop teacher or home economics teacher has shaped things up with such a program.

Simplified Recording   If the point tally can be simplified, considerable time can be saved. If, for example, you were to use a card for your check-mark system with numbers 1 to 50 printed on one side, you could simply mark through a number rather than making a check, and you could instantly read your total.

Project Class at the University of Oregon has for years used a point card to be placed on the student's desk which is red on one side and green on the other with an easy-to-read point tally on each side. When students are on task, they earn points on the green side, but when they disrupt, the card is flipped over onto the red side. Continuing disruption or time off task earns more points on the red side. When the student has been on task for a while, the card is flipped over to green and the student can again start earning points on the green side. At the end of the period or day the cards are collected, and red points are subtracted from green to give the total earned. The teacher can therefore operate a *complex* point economy (bonus and penalty) with two simple tallies.

Activity Rewards vs. Tangible Rewards   A great many teachers and administrators have a strong distaste for incentive systems because of the kinds of rewards that have traditionally been associated with behavior modification programs. In a point economy students have typically worked for points or tokens which can later be exchanged for "back-up reinforcers." At the beginning of the evolution of the token economy, back-up reinforcers usually meant tangible reinforcers, a concrete, manipulable reward such as food, candy, trinkets, or some other nicknack.

The association of incentive systems in general with tangible rewards, usually referred to as "junk" by teachers, is unfortunate and largely a matter of historical chance. Most of the early money for behavioral research in classrooms was earmarked for retarded and multiply handicapped students. When casting about for effective rewards for a child with a mental age of 2 or 3, tangible rewards soon prove to be among the most effective options.

Most students, however, have mental ages and abilities which are far greater than those of the handicapped children who served as subjects for most of the early research. For most normal school children a tangible reward or junk is one of the *least* appropriate and efficient types of rewards. They are expensive and cumbersome, and they tend to produce boredom and rapid satiation. They also invite students to engage in upsetting behaviors such a hoarding, stealing, and counterfeiting which then become discipline problems in their own right. Consequently, for most regular and special classrooms the use of junk may be considered inefficient and obsolete, and the tendency of educators to equate incentive systems with junk is a dated stereotype.

The forms that rewards can take in incentive systems are potentially infinite. One of the major advances in understanding rewards occurred in the early 1970s when researchers found that *preferred activities* could serve as rewards in the place of tangible reinforcers. The earliest research with preferred activities tended to focus on fun and game activities. This was a logical step in research since fun and game activities were obviously desirable and provided a safe and straightforward test of the notion that preferred activities did, in fact, have enough clout to radically alter students' behavior (i.e., to function as critical reinforcers). Subsequent work with incentive systems has extended the boundaries of preferred activities as far as possible in order to maximize the range of activities, particularly learning-related activities, that might function successfully in classroom incentive systems.

Once teachers employ activity rewards in the classroom, they are one step away from a primitive form of time incentive. Each point earned by a student can represent a certain amount of time during which a student can have access to a preferred activity (PAT). If, for example, the last hour of Friday afternoon is PAT, and each point is worth 1 minute, a student with 25 points could have PAT for the last 25 minutes of the day. Many teachers hand out paper slips or monopoly money (Lucky Bucks) when students are helpful or on task, which can later be redeemed for PAT.

A management system which uses activity rewards instead of tangibles, although greatly improved, still leaves teachers with point exchange. They will get little done during PAT other than excusing students from work when their total of points permit.

Group Incentive Systems vs. Aggregate Systems   As mentioned above, a point economy in which students earn points individually is not really group management so much as it is an aggregation of individual programs that may simply involve every-one in the group. The expense of point exchange, no matter how streamlined, will always be a burden as long as different students can accumulate different point totals. In order to eliminate point exchange you must have a true group management system in which the *entire group receives one single point tally.* Everyone in the group there-fore receives the same amount of reward. When it is "one for all and all for one," the teacher finally has relatively simple mechanics.

A teacher can operate a simple group incentive system with a single point tally which can be recorded in any way she wishes from a hand-held tally counter to a star chart to marbles in a jar depending on how concrete and graphic she wants the accu-mulation of points to be. She can praise the group as points are earned by saying things like: "I like the way the class has quieted down," or "Thank you, Janette, for getting back to work."

As educators gain experience with point economies, they become more adept at streamlining the mechanics of the system and at developing worthwhile reward expe-riences. Yet no matter how well streamlined and enriched the point economy may become, it is still a relatively blunt instrument for dealing with most disruptions and most forms of dawdling and goofing off in the classroom. Point economies are chron-ically vulnerable to certain predictable pitfalls which are especially crippling to pro-grams designed to reduce classroom disruptions.

Point Economy Pitfalls

In practice the main pitfalls of point economies stem from the fact that they are (1) failure-prone, (2) weak, and (3) punition-prone. Enough experience with point econ-omies in the field will always supply you with plenty of reasons to go back to the drawing board.

Failure-Prone   When presented with a point economy, students sooner or later seem to learn almost all the ways of cheating with "money" that their elders have devised. Thus, as mentioned earlier, students will hoard, steal, cheat, and counter-feit—each instance of which produces your next time-consuming management di-lemma: "Hey! Somebody stole my Lucky Bucks out of my desk!"

Operating an aggregate point economy for an entire class is like trying to navigate a leaky old boat. Every time you think you have it going, it springs a new leak which you then have to fix. Pretty soon you realize that you are spending more time fixing leaks than sailing.

In addition, although a teacher can reward the group for the behavior of various individuals ("I appreciate your taking your seat, Robert"), it is treacherous to base group reward on the behavior of the group. The problem is that you cannot reward *anyone* until *everyone* cooperates. It takes only one goof-off out of thirty to prevent you from giving the reward ("I'm sorry that I cannot give you your point for getting back from lunch on time because one person was late"). Blocked from giving reward, you not only lose the power of your incentive system, but you also appear as withholding and negative to the students. Thus, your attempt to be generous with rewards may do more harm than good for technical reasons.

Weak Point economies, and especially *group* point economies, are notoriously weak in managing misbehavior. The students who respond most readily to points given to the group tend to be the nice students or the borderline nice students who can be co-opted into being good with a bit of reward. For your chronic goof-offs and troublemakers, you are driving a weak bargain. You are asking them to give up the joys of not working and of fooling around *right now* in order to receive some preferred activity promised later in the day. One of the major determiners of the potency of a reward for altering behavior is *immediacy of delivery.* They are taking immediate delivery of a reward of their own choosing (i.e., goofing off) as opposed to your promise of something nice for the whole group hours from now. Do not be surprised if your chronic goof-offs fail to rise to the bait.

Simple incentive systems in general, and simple *group* incentive systems in particular, therefore, tend to run out of gas just when you need them the most. Although they may increase the general level of cooperation in the classroom, most improvement comes from the middle third of the class, and most of the highly disruptive students continue as usual. You have lost out once again in the marketplace of the classroom, and you are left with most of the problems you started with plus the overhead of operating your management program.

As mentioned earlier (Chapter 8), simple incentives are most useful for increasing good work habits and least useful for increasing good behavior. In *discipline* the rule is: Simple incentive systems always help you most when you need them least, and they always help you least when you need them most.

Punition-Prone When your points or stars or marbles in the jar give out, where do you go? How do you get rid of those remaining obnoxious behaviors? The answer for most teachers is *punition*.

Because a simple incentive system, either individual or group, lacks an adequate means of suppressing disruptions, the disruptions from the biggest disrupters continue in spite of the offering of rewards. Consequently, simple incentive systems need backing up quite frequently with negative sanctions that can put the lid on when all else fails. Most classroom back-up systems, however, are simplistic and punitive, consisting in most cases of warnings and reprimands followed by time-out, detention, loss of privileges, or a trip to the principal's office.

While such a system may put the lid on in the class of a firm but warm primary or intermediate teacher with a fairly nice group of kids, it helps you least when you need it most. With a roomful of big kids (fifth grade and beyond), with a group of problem students, or with a punitive teacher, such a simplistic approach to back-up will stack kids up at the office day in and day out.

With point systems, furthermore, teachers will sometimes try to suppress obnoxious behavior and keep the system afloat not by using a separate back-up response as described above but by *taking points*. A punitive teacher can pervert a point economy unbelievably. I have been in classrooms where students were as often in the hole with their point tallies as they were ahead and where students had to buy the most menial privileges such as going to the toilet with their reward points. *Taking points* is such a straightforward and obvious notion that a great many teachers will employ it even though they were never taught to do so. This particular form of tinkering and abuse is so common that it must realistically be reckoned as an innate attribute of simple point systems as they occur in the field.

In the final analysis, most point economies are simply obsolete. The giving of rewards is a nice idea, but it has to be wedded to an extremely sophisticated delivery system or it can easily be more trouble than it is worth.

Raffles

One way to economize on both the cost of the reward and the accountability of a classroom incentive system is to have a raffle. A raffle is essentially a thin, random, intermittent schedule of reinforcement for cooperation. It gives the student something to work for at very little work to the teacher, and it is fun. Raffles have a limited range of power and effectiveness, however, so they will probably be used by the teacher only as a supplement to her normal classroom incentive program.

To operate a raffle a teacher needs raffle tickets and some simple prizes. Large rolls of raffle tickets are fairly inexpensive, and prizes can often be privileges or individualized PATs rather than tangible reinforcers. Status and affirmation incentive (see the following section), such as a special commendation or privileged role within the classroom, also work well for younger children.

Raffle tickets come in pairs—two tickets with the same number—so that the teacher can give one to each student while keeping the other to put into the raffle box. Students are responsible for putting their names on the raffle ticket immediately in case it is lost or stolen. The teacher can give out raffle tickets at any time for anything, but it is helpful for the students to know certain things that raffle tickets will be given for so that they can be prepared to earn one. For example, a teacher could give raffle tickets for clean desks in a self-contained classroom and then have "clean desk spot checks" once or twice a week at unannounced times. Every student with a clean desk "wins" in that they get a raffle ticket. Many teachers I have worked with have experienced a sudden upsurge in completed homework when each assignment turned in produced a raffle ticket for the student as well as praise.

A weekly raffle can easily be integrated with preferred activity time, and the drawing takes only a minute. Raffles are not only cost-effective in that they allow the teacher to reinforce frequently at little real cost, but they also produce relationship dividends by repeatedly placing the teacher in the role of affirming students where they might otherwise nag.

STATUS AND AFFIRMATION INCENTIVES

Rewards can be given in the form of special commendations that elevate peer status, affirm the student personally, or inform parents of special achievement. Such commendations are designed to make the students feel proud of themselves in the hope that such pride and good will then translate into improved participation at school.

Giving of such awards is fairly straightforward, but it is easy to overlook hidden costs in trying to assess the relationship between cost and benefit. The most common kinds of awards are (1) special awards given in awards assemblies, (2) commendations sent home, and (3) honors and awards within the classroom. These types of affirmation incentives correspond to the settings in which the student deals with adult caretakers; the school site, home, and within the classroom.

Award Assemblies

Awards assemblies in which students from each classroom or grade level are singled out for public recognition have become very popular in recent years. The value of such forms of recognition is difficult to formally assess, and their importance at the school site seems to vary depending on whom you talk to.

My experience indicates that if the awards are given for academic achievement, they can serve a potent incentive function while generating positive feelings in both students and teachers. An example of such an award might be a math honor roll in which students who miss no more than three or four problems on a comprehensive monthly math test receive a certificate to take home. Another example of such an award was provided recently by a junior high school in Wichita, Kansas, that began giving cloth "letters" just like letters earned in athletics as a reward for academic achievement. As a result of the program, the number of students making the honor roll has increased by 15 percent. Peer recognition within the relative anonymity of secondary education is always a potent reinforcer if we can figure out how to tap into it. As one student wearing his letter jacket said in a TV interview, "It is something you really want. People know who you are."

If, in contrast, commendations are given for good behavior and are nonspecific such as citizenship awards, my observation is that they tend to have relatively little immediate, observable effect. Principals, however, tend to rate citizenship awards highly because (1) it was their idea, (2) they get to play a benevolent role, (3) they are making a public show of helping with discipline, (4) they get to know some students, which may some day result in a smile, a hello, or a greeting by name in the hall, and (5) some kids even improve as a result of special recognition.

Teachers, on the other hand, tend to be lukewarm about citizenship awards assemblies because it is rare that a student changes markedly as a result. This is not too surprising since the moment-by-moment contingencies of the classroom are far more powerful and remain unchanged. And, teachers are also lukewarm because the citizenship awards assembly takes an hour out of the day, which leaves them behind. Although this sounds like petty complaining, this latter gripe has some substance when you consider that a 1-hour assembly for 700 students costs 700 hours of learning time. Was it worth the investment?

Commendations Sent Home

Commendations sent home have also become very popular ranging all the way from a personal letter sent by a high school teacher to a "happygram" for the parents of a third grader. Commendations sent home can be very important not only in building relationship between the teacher and parents but also in creating an atmosphere of reward at home for accomplishments at school.

Commendations sent home are most useful in the area of academic achievement and can often be part of a more complex management program involving both teacher and parents. Such cooperative programs may hold the student responsible for completing uncompleted school work and turning it in. The cost-benefit ratio of commendations sent home can be quite favorable if the teacher is operating a folder system (see Chapter 4). A brief personal note on a piece of work often accomplishes more in terms of relationship building with parents and affirmation of the child than a formal system of awards and commendations.

In the area of discipline the role of such commendations is more limited, since the teacher is primarily in control of the students' behavior in the classroom and must produce good behavior by good management before the commendation is earned.

Within-Classroom Honors and Awards

Within-classroom honors and awards have produced some surprisingly good results in certain settings that I have observed—settings in which awards assemblies and commendations sent home produced only marginal improvement.

One fifth grade teacher had a simple yet powerful award system in which up to five students per day could receive a special ribbon to wear on their shirt or blouse as a sign of special accomplishment. In addition, up to three students per week could earn a special arm band to wear for the remainder of the week in recognition of outstanding cooperation and achievement. Students were given awards for effort and improvement so that problem students were equally eligible and were, in fact, frequent recipients.

My impression was that these awards were doing as much for discipline, achievement, and general classroom atmosphere as were all the teacher's other management programs. I was also impressed by the teacher's enthusiasm, warmth, and skill in relating to students. All these students wanted very much to be recognized and commended by this particular teacher because of their respect for him. I have been in plenty of classrooms in which I cannot imagine such commendations being more than a matter of indifference. As with most programs which focus on personal affirmation, I suspect that relationship is carrying the technique rather than the technique carrying the teacher.

EXTINCTION

If you perform a behavior in order to get something, but the something never comes, you may sooner or later become discouraged, lose interest, and quit. As you perform the behavior over and over to no avail and your optimism begins to fade, you might be described as being "on extinction." The repetition of a behavior in the absence of reinforcement ultimately produces extinction—the cessation of the behavior.

The *first* thing to remember about extinction within the context of classroom discipline is that you cannot put a student's misbehavior on extinction unless you control the reward for the behavior in the first place. Only then can you withhold the reward. The *second* thing to remember about extinction in the classroom is that most classroom behavior is rewarded not by the teacher but by peers (talking to neighbors) or by the behavior itself (walking to the pencil sharpener instead of doing school work).

Thus, the *ignoring* of a misbehavior by a teacher rarely puts that behavior on extinction. Ignoring only puts a misbehavior on extinction if the teacher was reinforcing the misbehavior in the first place. Since most teachers in their right minds would not knowingly reward a *misbehavior,* it is safe to assume that either (1) they are not rewarding the misbehavior and cannot therefore put it on extinction or (2) they are rewarding the problem inadvertently. When a teacher inadvertently rewards some form of disruption, he or she may be said to have committed a *reinforcement error.*

Reinforcement errors almost always occur in the classroom when a teacher gets upset at a student's misbehavior. If, for example, a teacher is shocked or upset by an outrageous behavior, he or she may have already committed a reinforcement error by becoming upset. They have rewarded the student who was trying to gain fame or revenge by "grossing the teacher out." If, in addition, the teacher reprimands the student, he may commit a second reinforcement error simply by calling the attention of the entire class to the attention-seeking behavior. Reinforcement errors are common in the classrooms of teachers who criticize and reprimand frequently.

An Historical Overemphasis on Extinction

During the late 1960s, a series of classroom management experiments demonstrated the effectiveness of ignoring in conjunction with praise as a means of reducing classroom disruptions. In one such study[1] a boy who was chronically out of his seat before intervention was observed to have typically received a reprimand from the teacher as a result. The reprimand reinforced the student's being out of seat with attention. The intervention consisted of training the teacher to ignore the student when he was out of his seat and to attend to him and praise him when he was in his seat working. The study dramatically reversed the rates of "out of seat" and "on task" behaviors as the boy now received attention for being good.

Such studies were powerful in their demonstration that:

1 Discipline problems can be managed.
2 Teacher attention is critical in producing or remediating typical forms of misbehavior.

3 The ignoring of misbehavior can be more effective than most forms of reprimand when paired with teacher attention for appropriate behavior.

However, such studies produced several misconceptions among a great many educators new to applied behavior analysis including the notions that:

1 Ignoring is extinction. In fact ignoring may *possibly* produce extinction only if you were previously reinforcing the disrupting behavior (a reinforcement error) *and* if you have control over critical reinforcers (i.e., the disruptive student cannot bootleg reinforcement from somewhere else such as the peer group). In the study described above, the teacher was committing a reinforcement error by providing attention (reprimand) for the student's being out of seat, and the behavior was not outrageous enough to produce much bootleg reinforcement from peers in the form of laughter and attention.

2 Ignoring in conjunction with rewarding appropriate behavior is an "extinction program." In fact, ignoring a bad behavior while rewarding a good behavior is more complex than extinction and is typically referred to as a DRL program (Differential Reinforcement of Low-rate behavior). Most of the power of such programs comes from the *differential reinforcement* of appropriate behavior, and ignoring is primarily a device which is needed to eliminate the teacher's reinforcement error.

As a point of strategy, extinction programs by themselves are nearly worthless in the management of classroom discipline problems because they are usually contaminated by some form of bootleg peer reinforcement in any group setting. Some kid across the room giggles at the misbehavior that the teacher is trying to ignore, for example, thereby supplying bootleg reinforcement for the problem while undoing the extinction. In addition, as mentioned earlier, since most disruptions are self-rewarding, even differential reinforcement programs are often not strong enough to counteract the self-administered rewards of goofing off.

Nevertheless, early misconceptions regarding ignoring and extinction have produced a general overemphasis in the classroom management literature on extinction as being an effective discipline technique. For years student teachers have been told by their professors that if they ignore disruptive behavior, praise diligence, and have an interesting lesson, righteousness will prevail in the classroom. Those young teachers receive a rude shock when they enter the complex management milieu of the classroom.

What is Extinction Good For?

Extinction is good for denying a child the response from you that she is working for by being obnoxious—especially in a situation in which she is not amenable to differential reinforcement or to reason. Thus, extinction is the classic cure for a tantrum. Extinction also works well with students who play helpless to get your attention: "Mr. Smith, is this right?" It is not a bad initial response to low-level wheedling as well, although you may be forced to other means if the wheedling does not stop.

Extinction, however, does not stand by itself. It is slow and unreliable as interventions go. Rather, ignoring and extinction serve best as a strategic element in other more complex classroom management procedures. As such, extinction is almost always present to some degree in any management program. There is always a time when it is best to "cool it" and keep your mouth shut. Limit-setting, for example, uses ignoring most explicitly in dealing with student back talk as the teacher is taking relaxing breaths while waiting for the opportunity to differentially reinforce returning to task. Silence is golden in responsibility training as well if the student wheedles while the watch runs. In both limit-setting and responsibility training, relaxation training helps prevent teachers from opening their mouths at the wrong time and undoing themselves with a reinforcement error.

RESPONSE-COST PROGRAMS

Response-cost procedures are great for getting a child to quit a bothersome behavior when all the typical combinations of reward and punishment seem inadequate or awkward. In a response-cost program the teacher places a cost on the response that is too dear for the student to be willing to pay. Then you let human nature take its course.

Response cost is tongue-in-cheek management. It requires that you design a *due process* for dealing with a problem that is simultaneously both (1) completely fair and (2) a complete pain in the rear. It is important to keep a straight face while carrying out a response-cost procedure. Response-cost programs lie out of the mainstream of classroom management procedures, but occasionally they can come in handy. One particularly tricky problem which seems amenable to response-cost management is tattling.

Tattling and the Tattle Box

How do you eliminate tattling? Tattling is a headache that afflicts teachers from preschool to junior high, and it is as resistant to cure as almost any form of bedevilment. In dealing with tattling teachers are over a barrel. If they attend to the tattling, they reward it by providing attention to the tattler (perceived as sympathy). If they do not attend to the tattler, they may seem callous while failing to hear about real problems in need of attention. What to do?

One solution to tattling is the Tattle Box, a stratagem that was given to me full-blown by Carol Hatfield, a teacher in South San Francisco, California. The Tattle Box is a box for tattles (surprisingly enough)—a shoe box with a slit in the top which sits on the teacher's desk. When little Sammy comes in from recess complaining as usual that somebody did something terrible to him on the playground, look concerned and sympathetic and say:

> Sammy, I want to hear all about what happened to you on the playground. Here is a pencil
> and a piece of paper. I want you to describe exactly what happened to you. Describe it in at
> least one full paragraph and remember to put your name, date, and the time of day at the
> top. When you are done, I will check it for spelling and punctuation. Then we will put it in

the Tattle Box. You go ahead and start writing while I get things going with the rest of the class.

Most of the time Sammy will say, "Oh, that's all right" and sit down without writing his tattle. So much for that tattle. Mild protest and whining will be met with an understanding nod and a gesture that tells him to start writing. Get busy doing something else if Sammy persists, in order to put wheedling on extinction. He may, however, actually write a description of the crime. When he is done writing, have him place his tattle dutifully into the Tattle Box.

If Sammy cannot write yet, do anything to avoid committing the reinforcement error of giving too much attention to the tattle. Have him draw a picture or have him briefly tell you or preferably your aide what happened so you can jot it down while Sammy takes his seat. *Do not* start listening to the whole story.

On Friday we have *tattle time*. Solemnly take the lid off the Tattle Box and *turn it upside down* to empty out the contents. This puts Monday morning's tattle on the top of the heap. Pick it up and say: "Our first tattle is from Sammy on Monday morning. Sammy, do you remember what this tattle was about?"

Sammy cannot remember. So, you say, "Well, then it must have taken care of itself," and you drop the tattle into the wastebasket. Now you see why you turn the Tattle Box upside down before you start.

You may come to a tattle that is well-remembered.

Jo Ellen, do you remember what happened?

Yeah, I remember! Irene shoved me down on the playground, and it hurt!

Since the problem is obviously still a live issue, you have a perfect opportunity to deal with it. It is time for some "human development circle" or group problem solving. During group problem solving teach the students to talk to each other to solve problems. Don't allow them to start whining to you all over again. When the air is clear, proceed to the next tattle.

The duration of tattle time can be limited quite easily if you wish. Either limit it arbitrarily or start it 10 minutes before PAT with a hurry-up bonus thrown in: "If we get done with tattle time early, we can begin PAT early."

Naturally we will assume that you can tell the difference between a tattle and a child who needs immediate attention because he or she is hurt or severely upset. Do not respond to blood by having the child write a report about it. Within the limits of good judgment, however, the Tattle Box has a perverse beauty. It provides the rare thrill that comes from outwitting a flim-flam.

Abuse of the Office

The uses of response cost range all the way from dealing with tattling to dealing with secondary teachers who send a student a period to the office for disciplinary reasons. In a typical high school, 90 percent of the office referrals are produced by 5 percent of the faculty—the "bouncers" or "office junkies."

"This is the second time I've asked you to stop chewing gum, Janet. Here's a slip to take to the office."

The reinforcer for bouncing is that the teacher does not have to deal with the problem or have the offending student in his or her class for the remainder of the day. But the cost to the school is high. Abuse of the office in the form of irresponsible referrals, typically for minor offenses, will consume the efforts of one or two administrators for the entire year. More will be said about both the context of such abuse and the administrator's role in servicing teachers' disciplinary needs in the next section on back-up systems. For the time being, however, it will help our understanding of response-cost programs to consider a possible use of due process for bouncers.

Bouncers are responding to an implicit cost-benefit trade-off, an incentive system. If they bounce, the problem goes away for a while at little effort. If they do not bounce, the problem stays in the class, and they have to deal with it. Bouncing is the easy (and irresponsible) way out for the time being—a solution that never really solves anything.

The administration will have little success with bouncing until most of the faculty has been trained in discipline management so that they will understand the abuse of the office and be willing to work with their administrators in developing a response-cost program for bouncers—the new "due process." And, administrators will have little chance of success until their management skills and those of the majority of the faculty have been developed to the point where administrators have confidence that they will have the time to make the new policy work. Thus, this program will typically not be instituted until the end of the second year of work at a high school site. The new policy might sound like this:

> The office can help teachers in classroom management as part of the back-up system for dealing with crises and extreme behavior. Often, however, because we are overloaded, we have dealt with office referrals by simply talking to a student and then sending him back to class. If a problem is serious enough to require the removal of a student from the classroom, however, it is serious enough to warrant the collaboration of the teacher and administrators in developing a response to such a problem that can succeed in eliminating the problem rather than just reacting to its recurrence. This procedure must be thorough, systematic, and carefully implemented.

The new procedure is described in Chapter 16. The key issue as far as response-cost management is concerned, however, is that the new "due process" locks the referring teacher into a process of problem solving that is realistically thorough and systematic—thorough enough to represent a careful attempt to solve a serious problem. Such problem-solving efforts, almost by definition, require so much more time and effort than dealing with the problem in class that they form a natural incentive for taking responsibility for classroom management and a natural disincentive for bouncing.

OVERVIEW

As early as 1970, two experiences in my work caused me to seriously question the practicality of most behavior modification interventions that my colleagues and I were designing for students with special needs. The *first* experience that prompted my reevaluation of B-Mod was the development of an understanding of limit-setting. I soon realized that limit-setting was fixing more problems at less effort as a result of some skill training than the teacher and I could fix in a year with the type of B-Mod programs described in this chapter under "Individualized Incentives." Limit-setting opened my eyes to the possibility of *group* management of a broad spectrum of behaviors based on training teachers to use effective *interpersonal skills* as a primary means of classroom management.

The *second* experience which caused me to question the cost effectiveness of traditional behavioral approaches was frequently spending many hours in consultation with a teacher to implement a series of B-Mod programs to fix various students' behavior problems without having any great impact on the functioning of the classroom as a whole. We could make three or four disruptive students into angels without markedly improving the baseline rate of disruption for the group as a whole. In contrast, when this struggling teacher was finally trained to use limit-setting, the whole classroom changed and whole categories of problem behavior disappeared overnight.

The experience of leveraging some skill training into the effective management of many discipline problems simultaneously at little ongoing effort to either the teacher or myself was heady—a feeling of effectiveness multiplied. It allowed me to put the behavior modification revolution into perspective and to move on. I put individualized programs and point systems on the shelf as far as my research was concerned and set about developing a technology of *group* management for the classroom.

My early experiences with behavior management in the classroom impressed upon me the ultimate criterion for evaluating management program cost-effectiveness. Behavior management programs must do more than just succeed. Management programs must address multiple objectives while *reducing* both the work load of the teacher and the need for specialized consultation. Behavior modification might be thought of as the "first-generation" technology of classroom management. Although contingency management programs supply some of the pieces of any behavior management puzzle, classroom management must go further to be affordable.

In classroom management it is the *program,* the multifaceted management system with its multiple objectives, that is the final unit of consideration—not just the pinpointed behaviors with their functional analysis and contingency management. Programs are larger chunks of matter with both formal incentive procedures and subtle interpersonal skills that must be practiced and integrated to be fully successful. In order to achieve optimal results behavior management must analyze the classroom as a complex, interrelated social system, and interventions must be *systems interventions* if they are to produce widespread improvement in the classroom learning environment at an affordable cost.

REFERENCES

1 Becker, W. C., Madsen, C. H., Arnold, C. R., and Thomas, D. R. The contingent use of teacher attention and praise in reducing classroom behavior problems. *Journal of Special Education,* vol. 1, no. 3, 1967, 287–307. (Reprinted in O'Leary, K. D. and O'Leary, S. G. Classroom Management: The Successful Use of Behavior Modification, New York: Pergamon Press, 1972.)

BACK-UP SYSTEMS

14

THE NATURE OF BACK-UP SYSTEMS

- There are some kids in my class who just like to talk. They are not bad kids, and I don't like for them to get into trouble, but they are going to continue talking no matter what.
- I have a few students in my classroom who will push the system as far as it will go just as sure as you're born.
- Incentives are nice for students who care about PAT, and limit-setting is nice when it works. But some students just don't care about either. What are you going to do when they just defy you?

Up to this point *Positive Classroom Discipline* has stressed a combination of clear structure, relationship building, limit-setting, and responsibility training with piggy-back programs such as omission training to produce appropriate student behavior and active cooperation within the classroom. By this time any teacher who is skillfully and systematically using positive discipline within his or her classroom will typically have dealt successfully with almost any discipline problem that occurs on a predictable basis. The main area of discipline management that remains is crisis management—the teacher's response to repetitive or sudden problems of a rather high level of severity.

Yet no discipline management procedure comes with a guarantee. No matter how well designed a management system is, problems can persist, crises can arise, and outrageous behavior can sometimes come out of the blue. Teachers must know exactly what to do if they are to keep their balance at such times. To avoid punition, a teacher must know how to respond in a way that is:

- Low-keyed
- Easy to use

- Low stress to the teacher
- Protective of the student
- Self-eliminating

When upset or off-balance, unprepared teachers may act like a bull in a china shop in response to provocation: instinctively resorting to harsh punition when they feel their backs against the wall. But such responses rarely serve the best interests of either the teacher or the student. As usual, the student decides whether or not to initiate the problem, but the teacher's response determines whether the problem will get bigger or smaller.

So, what do we do when all else fails—when we have no choice but to put the lid on? The answer, of course, is that we put the lid on. But we will learn to put the lid on intelligently and carefully so that the cost to everyone involved remains minimal.

WHAT IS A BACK-UP SYSTEM?

We now come to the systematic use of *negative sanctions* in discipline management— negative sanctions that go beyond the mild social sanctions of limit-setting and the penalty component of responsibility training. How and when should negative sanctions be used to serve the best interests of teacher and student in discipline management?

Although the use of negative sanctions is not incompatible with a positive approach to discipline, we must understand how to use them properly. Before examining specific back-up responses within the classroom, therefore, it will be important for us to understand what a back-up system is, what it is good for, and how it can fail. Back-up systems are good for far less than we typically imagine, and as used in the field, they frequently fail. When they fail, however, rather than being discarded, they are typically overused. Such overuse when chronic constitutes abuse. Thoroughly understanding the nature of back-up systems is one of the only available antidotes to their abuse.

A Hierarchy of Consequences

A back-up system is an organization of negative sanctions to suppress severe disruptions. It is designed (1) to keep the size of the negative sanctions minimal and (2) to self-eliminate. To be more specific: A back-up system is a systematic, hierarchic organization of negative sanctions (from small to large) which has as its function rendering the escalation of unacceptable behavior futile.

Upon first reading the definition of a back-up system within the context of positive discipline, many people are most struck by the term "negative sanction." In fact, the key term is "futile." To put it more simply: A back-up system is a series of responses designed to meet force with force so that the uglier the student's behavior becomes, the deeper he or she digs his or her hole with no escape.

Once again, when people first read this definition of a back-up system they are typically struck by the words "force with force." In fact, the real key words are "no escape."

All classrooms and all schools have a back-up system whether effective or ineffective, systematic, or "catch as catch can." When a situation becomes intolerable, teachers and principals will do what they have to do to put the lid on. Whatever a particular teacher does under stress as a last resort (be it foolish or wise), as long as it is a negative sanction rather than an incentive system, constitutes the beginning of his or her back-up system. Obviously, some back-up systems are more systematic than others.

A back-up system is composed of a series of discrete procedures or responses arranged in ascending order so that at some point, it is to be hoped, the adult authorities on the scene can put a stop to the problem. Back-up responses, however, are not delivered by teachers alone. All adults who take responsibility for the caretaking of a child can be part of the school's back-up system. In education the person most *likely* to deliver a negative sanction is, of course, the teacher. But the administration has negative sanctions to back up the teacher, and the police have negative sanctions to back up the administration, and parents may also be enlisted to deliver negative sanctions once the child gets home.

A back-up system is designed to deal effectively with a wide range of unacceptable behavior in the classroom and at the school site. The use of the back-up system begins potentially the first time a student does something intolerable in the classroom, and it ends potentially with the involvement of the police and juvenile authorities—and it includes anything in between.

A back-up system *should* be carefully constructed—an interlocking system of negative sanctions that provides a rational and constructive plan of action for dealing with tough situations of all sizes. A back-up system meets force with force, but a *good* back-up system is designed to use minimal force (typically the force of enlightened self-interest and steadfast resolve on the part of responsible adults) and it is designed to provide the student with maximal opportunity for constructive decision making.

Obviously, teachers with a sophisticated management system at their disposal will rarely be in a position in which they are forced to use their back-up system. However, teachers with only a rudimentary understanding of management may frequently find themselves relying on the use of negative sanctions even though they may find it distasteful.

Anatomy of a Typical Back-up System

A back-up system might best be thought of as being constructed in layers. Each layer is a different stratum of the adult world as it relates to a student who is about to get into trouble, and each layer serves a specific function. These layers are:

Level 1   Classroom Policy   Classroom policy is the teacher's first line of defense. If a problem is going to be handled while it is still small, it will be handled by the teacher as the problem is unfolding. The teacher's response may be *private,* in which case the student shapes up and hardly anyone in the classroom is made aware that anything took place. Or the teacher's response may be *public,* in which case the teacher must deal not only with the immediate problem but also with its aftereffects such as embarrassment, resentment, and revenge. When at all possible a wise teacher will use all his or her skills to prevent *going public*.

Level 2   School Policy   A school discipline policy spells out the due process for dealing with discipline problems that must be handled by teachers and administrators working together. School discipline policies range from the sublime to the ridiculous, and at worst there is no formal schoolwide policy beyond the shared understanding that teachers are not supposed to send kids to the office unless they really have to. This, for all practical purposes, represents no school policy at all.

A well-developed school policy typically consists of a clearly defined hierarchy of negative sanctions for dealing with severe or recurring behavior problems. Such policies tend to be far more explicit at the secondary level than at the elementary and are typically referred to as a "school discipline code" or a "hierarchy of consequences."

A typical hierarchy of consequences at the secondary level might include something like the following:

- Warning
- Conference with student
- Time-out, being sent to the office, detention
- Conference with parent
- Conference with teacher, parent, and principal or vice principal
- In-school suspension
- Suspension (1 day)
- Suspension (3 day)
- Expulsion and/or a special program such as "continuation school"

The back-up system at the school site implements district policy on a day-to-day basis. Problems that go further run a high risk of involving the police and the juvenile court system. Consequently, most large school districts, in an effort to avoid being forced to involve the law in issues of school discipline, have constructed a buffer in the form of a review board between the school system and legal authorities. Such review boards consider problems of a severe nature occurring on school property— usually violence, vandalism, chronic truancy, extortion, and drugs. These review boards have many names such as the "School Attendance and Review Board" or the "Attendance and Discipline Committee." They are typically staffed by a fairly small group of select individuals from the school and the local community. Recommendations may include expulsion, restitution of some form, testing or therapy, enrollment in a remedial program, placement in "continuation school," or referral to social services, family court, or even prosecution.

Level 3   Law Enforcement and the Juvenile Justice System   Many teachers do not think of the juvenile justice system as having anything to do with school much less classroom management and would not initially think to include such sanctions in *their* back-up system. Yet legal sanctions are there in any case as part of the back-up system.

If, for example, a student knifes another student, who do you call? If a student punches out a teacher, where do you go? In most states these behaviors constitute assault, and failure to report them to legal authorities is against the law.

By defining the hitting of a teacher as assault and battery, most states have removed the consequences of hitting a teacher from the discretion of school authorities—largely because school authorities have historically failed to provide meaningful consequences. In a regional special education center where I consulted to a population of over 300 emotionally and behaviorally handicapped junior high and high school students, the passage of a state law the year before my arrival defining hitting a teacher as assault reduced the number of such incidents from being regular weekly occurrences to zero. Indeed, the students could control themselves when the price was right.

In an attempt to construct a second buffer between the school system and legal authorities, many larger communities have developed a special court, often referred to as family court, which attempts to deal with the context of juvenile offenses rather than with the single issue of guilt or innocence. Children from disorganized homes who suffer some form of neglect or abuse are routinely referred to family court. The judge's recommendations might include psychological testing or therapy, a special remedial program, attending a rehabilitation program, referral to county agencies such as child protection or social services, some form of restitution to the plaintiff, or even prosecution in juvenile court. In many communities the functions of family court are a part of the juvenile justice system itself rather than being a separate agency.

Although the back-up system is a three-layered structure when viewed from the outside (i.e., classroom, school and district, and law enforcement) such a perspective misses much of the subtlety of a back-up system visible from the teacher's perspective within the classroom and the administrator's perspective in the office. In fact, large problems usually come from small problems that have been mishandled. Teachers' and administrators' reactions to provocations often make the problems worse. The handling of the problem when it first occurs before the teacher goes public may, therefore, be the most crucial part of the back-up system. From the perspective of the classroom and school site, therefore, it might be most useful to regard back-up response options as coming in four basic sizes like underwear—small, medium, large, and extra large. They are:

1 *Small.* Quick and relatively easy-to-use responses by the teacher which involve only the teacher and the offending student(s) in a private or semiprivate interaction.

2 *Medium.* Negative sanctions involving the teacher and the student(s) which are explicit, public, and typically represent extra planning and effort to the teacher.

3 *Large.* Negative sanctions which involve school personnel *outside* the classroom and therefore represent a considerable cost in time to several people. A large back-up response usually involves sending a student to the office.

4 *Extra large.* A major confrontation of the teacher *and* administration with the student and/or their parents which requires backing at the district level and which may involve the law. Such sanctions include suspension and expulsion and often obligate school personnel to the management of an ongoing program such as "continuation school" in lieu of expulsion.

WHY BACK-UP SYSTEMS FAIL

A back-up system may be designed, or it may just evolve over the years. It may be planned, or it may be a hodgepodge. It may succeed, or it may fail miserably. Most back-up systems in most classrooms and at most school sites are poorly designed and fail with unnerving regularity. Though often providing immediate relief, they tend to be self-perpetuating rather than self-eliminating. They fail for a variety of reasons, but they fail in most cases because they are designed only to respond to crisis and because they are harsh. They are reactive rather than proactive, and, consequently, they respond too late, off-balance, and punitively. They lack well-defined management options when the problem is small, and they inadvertently make the problem worse thereafter.

In order to understand why back-up systems so consistently fail, we must understand how back-up systems function in the first place and how they become self-perpetuating rather than self-eliminating. They typically fail whether the back-up response is small, medium, large, or extra large. We will leave law enforcement out of the picture for the time being and look at the top half of the back-up system—large and extra-large back-up responses—and the failure of the typical school discipline code. Our microcosm will be the office at a high school.

The Office and the Failure of Large and Extra-Large Back-up Responses

In a typical high school, teachers will send students to the office on a daily basis, and suspension will be a part of school life year after year without anybody asking, Why do we have to do this year after year? But have you ever heard of a junior high or high school where any of the following have self-eliminated?

- Detention
- Being sent to the office
- Parent conferences
- Suspension
- Expulsion

Quite to the contrary, they so thoroughly fail to self-eliminate that we have come to regard them as part of the necessary, everyday fabric of social life at a school. Many teachers and administrators, in fact, become disoriented and mildly upset at the notion that we would expect them to go away.

However, before we can understand the office at a typical high school, we must understand a semiesoteric topic in behavior theory—"schedules of reinforcement." Pay close attention to this digression for until you understand schedules of reinforcement, you will never really understand why our time spent with the hard-core kids seems to get us nowhere.

Schedules of Reinforcement   Schedules of reinforcement is a story of mice and men. Perhaps it will be best for us to learn about schedules of reinforcement by learning something about why mice behave the way they do.

Let's imagine a mouse who lives in a learning laboratory and partakes of the good life. Several times a day the mouse is put at one end of a maze, and as soon as the mouse gets to the other end of the maze, it pulls a lever and gets a food pellet. The mouse has been trained to run the maze on a "continuous" or 1:1 schedule of rein- forcement. That is, when the mouse runs one time, it gets reinforced one time. Life is easy in the lab. Relatively little work satisfies all the mouse's needs and it cannot lose. A mouse just cannot beat a deal like that.

Then one day in an act of perversion, the experimenter turns off the feeding ma- chine to see what the mouse will do. The mouse enters the maze full of optimism expecting that, once again, it will saunter down the path to pull the food lever and eat a food pellet. But today when the mouse pulls the lever nothing happens. The mouse looks around somewhat surprised and pulls the lever again. Nothing happens. The mouse imagines that something is temporarily wrong with the lever and pulls it several more times. Nothing happens, and the mouse becomes increasingly agitated and ner- vously sniffs the corners of the maze while frequently returning to pull the lever. The mouse works all the harder because it knows that the machine *should* work. Besides, it's hungry.

Does the mouse conclude that the machine is turned off? That would be a pretty fancy inference for a mouse. Rather, it concludes that this experience is simply a weird exception to reality, and it pulls the lever all the harder to *make* it work. How different are mice and men? Have you ever seen somebody banging on a candy machine that just took his or her money?

The mouse is put in the maze several more times and, as hunger increases, it runs the maze more swiftly and pulls on the lever more feverishly hoping against hope that the machine may still work. At last, however, the truth begins to dawn. In successive trials the mouse shows increasing apathy and discouragement. Why, after all, should a mouse run down a maze for nothing? The mouse is on extinction. Finally the day comes when, as the mouse is placed at the top of the maze, it just sits there. It doesn't give a damn anymore. It just plain quits. Maze-running behavior has fully extin- guished.

Extinction takes place more rapidly on a continuous or 1:1 schedule of reinforce- ment than any other schedule because the mouse can discriminate most rapidly that the machine is not working. Let us imagine that we have a very bright mouse and that it was able to figure out in five trials that it would no longer get fed for running down the maze. Its extinction curve might look like that of Figure 14-1. Note that in a classic extinction curve the rate of behavior always increases immediately after the machine is turned off as the mouse frantically tries to make the machine work. Only later does the rate drop off. This is very important for a parent to know who is trying to extinguish the tantrum behavior of her 3-year-old. It will always get worse before it gets better. Many parents, not knowing this, scrap the extinction program that the therapist has so carefully designed just before the rate starts to go down.

Now let us imagine a different mouse on a different schedule of reinforcement. This mouse gets fed *every fifth time* it runs down the maze like clockwork. This schedule of reinforcement is known as 1:5FR or "one-to-five fixed ratio." Since the ratio is fixed at 1:5, the mouse knows that even though it has not been fed for the last four times, it should keep running because success will come eventually. In the terminology

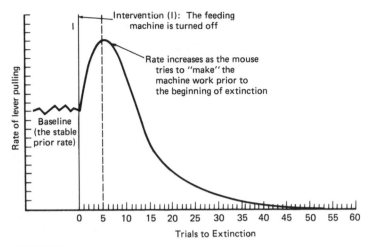

FIGURE 14-1
A classic extinction curve with extinction beginning on trial number 5.

of learning theory a 1:5 schedule of reinforcement is much "thinner" than a 1:1 schedule of reinforcement. Thin schedules of reinforcement are very slow to extinguish. They teach mice to have *hope!* If at first you don't succeed, try, try again! Mice on 1:1 schedules of reinforcement are quitters by comparison. They have never been taught that persistence pays off.

How many times will the mouse on the 1:5FR schedule of reinforcement have to run the maze in order to gain the same amount of experience with a turned-off machine that the first mouse got in five trials, assuming that the second mouse had a perfect memory? You probably guessed it. If it takes a mouse on a 1:1 schedule of reinforcement five trials to figure it out, it will take the second mouse on a 1:5 schedule of reinforcement 5 × 5 or 25 trials to begin extinction. The rate of extinction relative to the first mouse is so slow that it would seem to an impatient experimenter that extinction will just never happen. On paper it looks like Figure 14-2.

Life rarely provides us with fixed-ratio schedules of reinforcement. Quite to the contrary, life tends to be rather random. Although a mouse might be on a 1:5FR schedule of reinforcement in the laboratory, a human being in everyday life might be on a 1:5 variable ratio (1:5VR) schedule of reinforcement. On a variable ratio schedule of reinforcement, the ratio of reinforcement to work *averages* one to five, but on any particular occasion the mouse might be fed on the eighth run or the second run or the fifth run or the tenth run. Variable ratio schedules of reinforcement train both mice and men to have even *more* hope and resistance to extinction than those on a fixed-ratio schedule of reinforcement. This mouse has learned that when the going gets tough the tough get going. It might take a mouse several times as long to reach extinction on a 1:5VR schedule of reinforcement than on a 1:5FR schedule of reinforcement, assuming that it had a perfect memory.

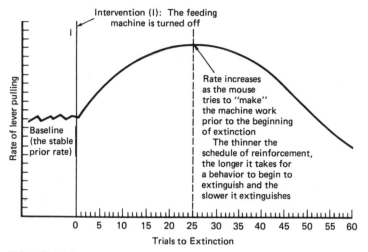

FIGURE 14-2
An extinction curve with a 1:5 fixed-ratio schedule of reinforcement and a mouse with a perfect memory.

What does all this talk about schedules of reinforcement have to do with back-up systems and why they fail? To bridge the gap we need to know just a little more about a topic that is basic to child rearing: consistency.

Consistency and Inconsistency   Have you heard a friend say something like,

- I think I'm pretty consistent in dealing with my kids.
- I'm consistent most of the time.
- In dealing with little Ricky, there are times when I'm consistent, and there are times when I'm not.

To someone who understands schedules of reinforcement, all three of these statements contain a sad element of humor. What these parents don't know is that there is no such thing as "pretty consistent" or "consistent most of the time." Consistency is like style—you either got it or you don't!

We all know that in some homes no means *no*. And in other homes no doesn't mean much of anything. Can you tell the difference when you are around the children? How do some parents inadvertently make their kids into brats? Imagine a situation in which a child comes in from play at 4 o'clock wanting some cookies and milk. Let's also imagine that this child, like all children, does not like to take no for an answer.

Child: Ma [or Dad as the case may be], may I have some cookies and milk?
Parent: No, dear. I'm going to have dinner on the table in 40 minutes.
Child: But, *mom*, I'm *hungry*! Can't I please?
Parent: No, dear. I don't want you to ruin your appetite.
Child: But, *mom* . . .

At this point in the conversation the parent usually either sets limits on the child's nagging or fails to do so. If she fails to do so, she gets more of it.

Child: But, *mom,* the other kids are getting a snack.
But, *mom,* it's not fair.
But, *mom,* just a little bit?
But, *mom . . .*
But, *mom . . .*
But, *mom . . .*

Let us imagine that, finally, under the pressure of the child's persistent whining and nagging, the parent cracks.

Parent: All right! Take a cookie out of the jar and *leave*! I'm tired of listening to your yammering!

In the home as in the classroom, everything the parent does teaches a lesson and creates an incentive system. What lesson did the parent just teach?

You can have anything you want. But first you have to punish me in order to get it.

The parent held out for a long time, but then she cracked. And when she cracked, she created a thin variable-ratio schedule of reinforcement for her child's never taking no for an answer. The parent is training her child to be a nagger and whiner—to hold out until the child wins. The parent has just committed a "reinforcement error." The reinforcement error is inadvertent reinforcement of the problem behavior, thereby making it worse. Giving a cookie to a nagger and whiner creates an incentive for nagging and whining incessantly. This example illustrates why there is no such thing as "consistent most of the time." You are either consistent or you create a thin schedule of reinforcement for the problem behavior itself.

Yet, while some children become naggers and whiners as a result of their parents' management errors, other children learn that you have to *escalate the intensity* of nastiness in order to get your way. Some parents hold the line pretty well with nagging but crack when the child screams or throws tantrums. Some children, in turn, learn to be nasty and profane, and other children learn to be physically abusive. There is a continuum of intensity in parent abuse just as there is in child abuse. And, at the end of that continuum of intensity one usually finds alienated children living in a home of punitive parents who are engaged in a sad form of domestic warfare.

The children from the more dysfunctional homes have learned to play a rather brutal game in order to get their way. If at first you don't succeed, escalate! If persistence doesn't make it, get loud, get nasty, get physical—escalate, escalate, escalate until you blow the management system away and get what you want. The lessons learned at home will come to school.

Reinforcement Errors in the Office   Any teacher or administrator will tell you that 95 percent of the severe discipline problems in a high school come from 5 percent of the student body. These are typically the angry, alienated kids who combine a general dislike of rules, structure, and public education with a pattern of escalating the intensity of confrontations with adult authority figures. What lesson will the school back-up system teach these students? Can they get away with the strategy of "escalate, escalate, escalate?"

In effect, the school's back-up system conducts the following behavioral dialogue with chronic and severely disruptive students:

> Kid, if you gross out a teacher, do you know what we are going to do? The teacher is going to give you a reprimand, and we know how much respect you have for those. And, kid, if you do it again, we are liable to involve your parents, and you know how supportive they usually are. And, kid, if you gross out the teacher again, do you know what we are going to do? We are going to send you to the office! And you know what happens down there? Well neither does anyone else. But wait a second, kid! If you persist in this behavior and gross out another teacher again, do you know what we are going to do with you? We are going to have no choice but to suspend you for a whole day. You will have to give up learning in favor of hanging around the streets, playing video games to your heart's content, and perhaps making some money on the side. But wait a second, kid! That's not the end of it. If you keep up this behavior, do you know what you are going to force us to do? You are going to force us to give you 3 days off! Do you hear that? For 3 solid days you will be denied access to your math class, your English class, your social studies class, your science class and all study halls. Our ultimate weapon is to force you to go out and have a good time.

For these students, the management system at school is a bizarre mirror image of the mismanagement system at home. We are teaching the child a lesson, as always. Escalate, escalate, escalate, and you can get out of this place. If you want out of school, however, there is only one ticket. Gross out a series of teachers so badly and so often that you leave us no choice but to suspend you. If, on the other hand, we want to keep the kid in school, we had better manage the provocation right or we will pay.

To put it bluntly, most school-site back-up systems are a grandiose and quite painful series of reinforcement errors. I am surprised that more kids don't have the insight and candor to simply say, "Listen, let's just stop this cycle and either let me out for the asking or tell me who to punch." The kid would be asking an incisive and straight-forward question regarding your incentive system: What is the price? What do I have to do to get out? Just tell me so that I can do it. Year after year we send thousands of kids to the office, and suspend them, and suspend them again, and expel them only to have the pattern repeated year after year with no change. It makes one wonder who the slow learners are.

A successful discipline management technique is one which *self-eliminates*. There is a reason why this definition of a successful discipline management technique is the only functional definition of success. For a behavior to persist, it must be reinforced or else it will be on extinction and decrease over time. The only way to maintain a behavior is to reinforce it, and the only way to maintain an inappropriate behavior is to commit a reinforcement error. Discipline techniques that do not self-eliminate over time fail to do so because they embody reinforcement errors.

Once we understand how reinforcement errors perpetuate the severe behavior problems which are dealt with repetitively in most back-up systems, we can see why the key words in our definitions of a back-up system were "futile" and "no escape." If you are going to implement a back-up system, make sure that it does in fact contain the behavior in question. If it fails to contain the behavior, it will reward the behavior by supplying the obvious reinforcement—escape.

Although it should not be harsh, a back-up system must be *tight*. We must eventually bring the intolerable behavior to a halt. Since a back-up system is brought into play only when everything else fails, it must succeed, for if it does not, what else is left? A back-up system that fails only teaches an unruly student that unruly behavior succeeds and that the most effective response when blocked is to escalate.

The Failure of Small Back-up Responses

Back-up systems typically fail at the top because they reward the escalation of obnoxious behavior with freedom. Unfortunately, they also fail at the bottom end, at the very beginning of escalation. Why do back-up systems typically fail the teacher at the beginning of the process of escalation when problems are small and already contained within the confines of the classroom?

Imagine how many different answers you would get from fifty different teachers if you were to ask the following question:

> Exactly what is the first thing you would do in response to a behavior in your classroom that you never wanted to see again? What would be your body language, the first words to leave your mouth, your agenda? How would you get in and how would you get out in such a way that would produce a minimum likelihood of repetition or escalation of the problem?

How many answers would you get from fifty teachers? You would get at least fifty different answers, probably more. What does this teach us? It teaches us that there is no methodology.

Consequently, when the obnoxious behavior originally occurs, before it has recurred and grown into a real management dilemma, teachers are winging it with their favorite home remedies without the aid of a sophisticated plan. Home remedies often fail—nagging and threatening are the most common—and before you know it the problem has grown, the size of the negative sanctions has grown, and the teacher has been backed into an adversary relationship with the most difficult-to-manage student.

The time to deal most easily with unacceptable behavior is at the beginning of the process of escalation before it has gotten out of hand. Only then can your response be relatively small, low key, and therefore cheap. The further the escalation goes, the more stressful and risky will be the teacher's response to the situation no matter how well he or she performs.

Yet, it is exactly at the beginning of the process of escalation when it is still possible to nip it in the bud that the teacher is most thoroughly without direction as regards the use of the back-up system. The formalized back-up system at most school sites does not even begin until a problem has become repetitive or obnoxious—with a parent conference or with a warning or detention or sending the student to the office. By that time the problem has gone beyond the point where quick, simple, low-key cures can do their job.

This lack of definition and consistency at the *bottom end* of the back-up system forces educators to continually go higher up the back-up system to use larger negative sanctions than would otherwise be necessary. Unfortunately, as you go up the back-up system two things occur to varying degrees no matter how well the system is designed and implemented. As you go up the back-up system from small to larger sanctions, the sanctions inevitably become more *costly* and more *failure-prone*.

One of the key objectives of the back-up system in Positive Classroom Discipline is to supply teachers with some highly specific response options for unacceptable behavior when it *first* occurs so that the teacher can succeed in the containment of a behavior problem while it is still easily containable. Our objective, as usual, is to keep it simple and keep it cheap—both for the teacher in terms of stress and effort and for the student in terms of humiliation and resentment. Until we know exactly what to do at the beginning of the back-up system, we have a high likelihood of using the rest of the back-up system far more often that we would like.

The Failure of Medium Back-up Responses

Medium back-up responses include most of the old favorites of the discipline business. Medium back-up responses differ from small back-up responses in that, rather than being private or semiprivate, they are public. The last thing teachers want to do with their back-up system is to go public. When they go public with negative sanctions, teachers usually humiliate a student in front of his or her peer group. For that, teachers pay, usually before the day is over.

Medium back-up responses include such things as a public warning, a threat, loss of privilege, detention, time out, sending a student to the hall, and many parent conferences. The worst form of medium back-up responses, of course, is to lower grades or to give the student extra work. The teacher thereby clearly conveys his or her opinion of formal education to the student; it's pure punishment. Medium back-up responses exemplify very clearly the principle that as we go up our back-up system it becomes more expensive and more failure-prone.

To provide a simple example of the cost escalation that accompanies medium back-up responses, consider the price of a simple parent conference—a very common element in any school discipline hierarchy. How much does it cost and what does it achieve?

Escalating Cost

Time   To appreciate how fast the cost of back-up responses increases as you go up the back-up system, compute the potential cost in time of a simple parent conference—one of the most common back-up responses near the bottom of a typical school's hierarchy of consequences. First, let's calculate how long it takes a teacher to leave the classroom, walk to the office, wait for a phone line out, call a parent to have a brief conversation, return to the classroom, and resume instruction. Teachers generally estimate the cost of such a phone call on a good day when you do not have to wait for a phone line out at about 10 to 20 minutes with an average of 15 minutes.

Call 1 Nobody home.

Call 2 You leave a message with the sitter or with Aunt Erma to have Mrs. Schwartz call you back. Does Mrs. Schwartz call you back? Do you think Mrs. Schwartz is eager to talk to Billy's teacher? She has been getting calls from Billy's teachers since Billy entered first grade, and it has yet to be a gratifying experience.

Call 3 You call late in the afternoon or in the evening and you catch the Schwartz family at home. You set up a conference for next Monday after school. The father can't make it. Unfortunately, Mrs. Schwartz doesn't make it either.

Call 4 You listen to excuses about Monday and schedule a second conference for Thursday. This time Mrs. Schwartz shows up.

At 15 minutes per phone call you have already invested nearly an hour in this parent conference (not counting the time you spent waiting after school on Monday) and the conference has not yet taken place! If you think this represents an atypical investment, ask a teacher. If you are a teacher, you won't need to ask.

Now the parent conference takes place. How long does it take? It usually lasts about an hour before it is all wrapped up. You already have an hour on the meter from four 15-minute phone calls, and now the price has risen to *2 hours* total (1½ hours in the best of circumstances). Now ask yourself the critical question: Is the problem fixed? Can you rest assured that, as a result of your conference, the problem will not recur in your classroom? Are you kidding? Instead, you get this kind of response:

> You know, I can't do a thing with Billy either. He just won't do a thing I say, and some days he almost drives me nuts, especially when he's around his little brother. And his older sister is even worse. Boy, if you come up with anything that works, please let me know. As far as I'm concerned, the real problem is Billy's father. Do you want to hear about my husband?

For this you spent 2 hours?

I have yet to meet a teacher who has any feeling of assurance whatsoever that the problem will not recur as a result of a parent conference. What have you accomplished with your typical parent conference? You have spent 2 hours *not fixing a problem!* That is expensive! And, that is failure-prone! And is it self-eliminating?

Alienation   The cost of a back-up response must be calculated for the student as well as for the adults at the school site. The stress experienced by teachers and administrators in delivering the negative sanctions is typically mirrored as upset on the part of the student. The further up the back-up system the problem goes, the more deeply student and adult are locked into an adversary relationship—into prosecutor and defendant roles.

If the relationship between teacher or administrator and student is allowed to degenerate and polarize into an adversary relationship, then a war of attrition develops between punitive adult authority and revengeful child. As already noted in this chapter, at most school sites 95 percent of the serious grief is in fact generated by 5 percent of the student body. Who do you think is paying more dearly in stress, upset, and time away from things that need to be done, the professional educators or the 5 percent?

Failure-Prone

The second unavoidable liability of going up the back-up system in addition to cost escalation is the tendency of negative sanctions to become more failure-prone no matter how well they might be delivered. Take, for example, detention after school—a time-honored remedy if there ever was one. Who shows up at detention? Is it the hard-core problem student who earns detention regularly and is a candidate for continuation high school? Are you kidding? That kid often doesn't even show up to fifth period. Do you think the kid is going to come back to serve time? The kid that shows up is the fairly nice kid—the one who needs the back-up system the least—who just happened to screw up today. Welcome to the most perverse rule of back-up systems: Back-up systems usually affect the students most who need them the least, and they usually affect the students least who need them the most.

Medium back-up responses are less reliable than smaller back-up responses because the ramifications of going public are hard to predict and because an adversary relationship has been initiated. In addition, when you rely on other people, they often prove unreliable, as in the case of the parent conference. And finally, if smaller back-up responses have not been employed effectively, there are only a limited number of things that you or anyone else can do to fix the situation.

A BACK-UP SYSTEM AS PART OF A LARGER MANAGEMENT SYSTEM

Any back-up system will be overstressed if it stands by itself. It cannot serve as a teacher's accustomed response to hassle. Thus, for a back-up system to serve its proper function, it must be embedded within a context of effective management. That context has been carefully described in previous chapters.

As you go up the back-up system, the stakes get higher as the intensity of the student's testing of the system increases. In addition, the likelihood of serious reinforcement error increases rapidly since if the teacher cannot contain the problem in the classroom, it is unlikely that the administration can magically contain it in the office. What then is the proper function of the back-up system? The back-up system has only two proper functions: (1) put the lid on and (2) buy time.

Putting the lid on is the straightforward objective of any back-up system. But buying time? Buy time for what? The answer is to buy time to consult with colleagues, think it over, get additional help if you need it in order to come up with a plan to change the student's behavior using *incentives*. You must ultimately manage the extremely alienated student's behavior with incentives or you will never manage the behavior at a price you can afford. If instead of dealing with incentives you deal in punition, beware! You are entering into a war of attrition with a student who may have very little to lose when you begin and nothing to lose by the time you are done.

Can you ever reach angry, alienated students using punition? Remember, that is the home environment in which they grew up. For them the power struggle with you is a crucial event in their battle with unreasonable adult authority. For you it is just another kid in another class period who is giving you a hard time. If you wish to enter into a war of attrition, you will lose. They have a far greater vested interest in persevering. Rather than backing yourself into a war of attrition in which you use larger and larger negative sanctions to deal with larger and larger behavior problems, stop and review your management options.

To state it somewhat differently, a back-up system is:

1 A stopgap measure
2 A short-term solution
3 A temporary containment of a sudden crisis or a repetitive provocation

The back-up system provides a quick remedy, but it does not provide a permanent remedy. To put it simply: You can visit your back-up system, but you cannot live there.

OVERVIEW

A back-up system must be constructed with the same care as the rest of your management system, and it must sit squarely on the rest of the management system as its foundation. A back-up system cannot function constructively by itself. Negative sanctions, when they exist in the absence of effective limit-setting and responsibility training, tend to be overused. The overuse of negative sanctions constitutes the abuse of negative sanctions.

Yet, most teachers do not have a management system on which to base their back-up system, and most school sites do not have a management system that is free of major reinforcement errors. In the classroom and at the school site, therefore, education tends to rely on negative sanctions for discipline to a far greater degree than is either necessary or productive. Rather than having a mature technology at its command, education tends to stagger and stumble in the dark, relying repetitively on its time-honored home remedies, perpetually off-balance and perpetually unprepared.

Negative sanctions, therefore, rather than being the exception in discipline management as they should be, tend to be the rule. The result is a counterproductive cycle in which punition destroys relationship, which is the basis of cooperation. Inadvertently, therefore, we back ourselves into a management corner which ultimately makes educational casualties out of a predictable minority of the student body.

To put it bluntly, the use of negative sanctions is *dangerous*. They can be destructive and often are. Unless carried out with a high degree of caring and sophistication, the back-up system of a classroom and school site may easily do more harm than good. Negative sanctions can alienate. They can be destructive of caring, respect, and the motivation to learn. And they can generate a desire for revenge that will guarantee the recurrence of the problem.

We must, therefore, take a fresh look at back-up systems in an effort to understand how to make them work for us rather than against us and for the student rather than against the student. We must become familiar with the terrain that the potential use of negative sanctions presents to us so that, with due respect but without undue fear, we may learn to respond effectively when all else fails.

When we describe a back-up response and its uses in the following chapters we assume that the teacher's rules and management system are clearly spelled out, that the teacher is well-trained in limit-setting and responsibility training, and that she or he is humane and effective at relationship building with the parents early in the school year as well as with the students. Thus, we will focus on the *appropriate* use of back-up responses assuming that the students' behavior rather than the teacher's misman-agement is the sole reason for going up the back-up system.

CHAPTER 15

BACK-UP RESPONSES WITHIN THE CLASSROOM

Even though we understand from the preceding chapter that entering your back-up system also means entering treacherous waters, we still must learn to navigate those waters. Crises can occur, and we must know what to do. If we are ill-prepared and winging it, we will probably get ourselves into difficult situations in which we resort to crude and sometimes harsh countermeasures.

We will describe small back-up responses which are powerful, low-key, and semi-private, and we will then proceed to medium back-up responses. We will also examine an incentive system that can keep us from having to make the transition from small to medium back-up responses should members of the class repeatedly give us a hard time. But first we will take a look at the decision to use our back-up system in the first place and the clinical judgment that is sometimes required.

BEGINNING TO USE NEGATIVE SANCTIONS: CLINICAL JUDGMENT AND ROOM TO MANEUVER

When to Begin

Knowing the boundaries of your back-up system is crucial to its proper use. When do you jump in? Overuse of your back-up system often means jumping in too soon, usually in lieu of knowing what else to do.

Sudden Problems   Sometimes disruptive situations develop very fast. Students may provoke each other to produce a "flash crisis" such as a fist fight. Or, early in the school year before you have gotten to know the class well, *you* may make a demand on a student that he or she cannot tolerate. You walk into the crisis and then have to do something quickly to put the lid on. When students are coming unglued, with limit-setting out of the question and no time to implement an incentive procedure, you may reach for your back-up system.

Recurrent Problems   Limit-setting may only temporarily succeed with a student who is sly enough to fold early but who then begins disrupting as soon as your back is turned. When you see the disruption being repeated, you have two choices.

1 Try limit-setting one more time, but up the ante and stay at palms or camping out for a while.

2 Drop limit-setting immediately and go to another technique. You drop limit-setting if you judge it to be futile.

If you have done limit-setting twice within a fairly *short time span,* it is definitely not working. You may decide it is futile after the first time. Using limit-setting repeatedly is simply bad tactics—an inappropriate use of limit-setting. By giving a child five warnings you only define the first four as hot air. If it is not working, take a hint! Use limit-setting once, maybe twice, before dumping it in favor of another technique.

Clinical Judgment

Beginning to use your back-up system is a more serious step than most untrained teachers realize. You are signaling the end of any attempt to use reward to co-opt the student into cooperation for the time being, and you are moving instead to containment without structured offsetting reward. If limit-setting has preceded the decision to enter your back-up system, you are already using a negative sanction, albeit a subtle and forgiving one. Either sudden crisis or repeated rule breaking may cause you to scrap limit-setting for the time being. You will use limit-setting once, maybe twice. But why once and why twice?

A Well-Behaved Student   If a student is typically well-behaved but is feeling rambunctious one day, you may give her a second chance on the gamble that she will "cool it" if you stay at palms or camp out a while longer for emphasis. Upping the ante by prolonging close physical proximity is a message that most well-behaved students will read: That is far enough!

A Repeat Disrupter   If a student is typically one of your troublemakers, you may give limit-setting only one chance. Using the repetition of the disruption following limit-setting as a sign that the student is "jerking you around" as usual, you might judge a repetition of limit-setting as a waste of time. It is often a better tactic to give the repeat disrupter a shorter rope.

Beware, however, if you have not been carefully trained to use limit-setting properly. Without such formal training, attempts to use limit-setting typically have only a fraction of the power that they have in the hands of a well-trained teacher. Untrained teachers trust limit-setting less and tend to do it too rapidly with only partial relaxation at best. As a result, they go to their back-up system prematurely.

Not Him- or Herself Today   A student may provoke the teacher on a given day in such an uncharacteristic way that the teacher is taken aback. The student is simply "not him- or herself today." Should you go to your back-up system as you typically might?

Please keep in mind that nothing in this book is intended to force you to go against your good judgment and sense of the situation. Only the teacher in the classroom who knows the students intimately can make the judgments and trade-offs that lead to a final choice of technique. If your clinical judgment tells you that something is amiss, dump discipline management if you feel that you should. If the student seems to be angry or hurting, feel free to respond to the feelings and put behavior management on the shelf for the time being.

Many times the best prompt for the student opening up with the hurt inside is the calmness and slowness of responding typical of limit-setting accompanied by the words:

> You seem upset. [pause]
> Can I help? [pause]

Moving from a standing to a kneeling position, with perhaps some touching, typically signals to the student that this is nurturance instead of a negative sanction. If the student clams up, set a time aside to talk in the near future.

Room to Maneuver with "Quiet Time"

When a not-too-severe problem has recurred in spite of proper management, a teacher can jump one of two directions; (1) think and talk or (2) warn and deliver. Warn and deliver refers to the straightforward use of a negative sanction. If the problem is sufficiently great, this may be the teacher's only meaningful response. If, however, the problem is of lesser magnitude, the teacher may try a little "think and talk" before it comes to warnings.

"Quiet time" is a particularly gentle and low-key response which is most applicable to a young student who is having a struggle keeping her act together. Elementary teachers often have a "quiet place" such as a table, rocking chair, or study carrel where students can go to work by themselves. For situations such as that described above the teacher may send the student to the quiet place to reflect on her behavior instead of employing a negative sanction. The teacher might say:

> Kathy, it seems as though you are having a particularly hard time leaving your neighbor alone this morning. In order to keep this from becoming a bigger problem, I want you to go over to the quiet place to think about the way you have been bothering Randy. When you have decided what you plan to do about it, I want you to come to me, and we'll talk.

A few minutes to reflect often produces an apology as part of a brief talk with the teacher. If the behavior recurs, you can always go to a warning and beyond. But quiet time has the beauty of keeping the responsibility for what happens next with the *child* in conjunction with some time and space to get her act together. Better that students decide to behave than that the teacher warn them that they must. Quiet time is a particularly nurturant way of conveying to a child that something *has* to change.

SMALL BACK-UP RESPONSES

Small back-up responses are the part of a school's "hierarchy of consequences" that is usually left out. They represent the cheap part of the back-up system—the small, quick, semiprivate, and relatively safe things that a teacher can do to "rein in" a squirrelly situation before anyone sticks his or her neck out too far. Small back-up responses should represent the *beginning* of the teacher's use of the back-up system.

The characteristic of *small* back-up responses that distinguishes them from *medium* back-up responses is that they are private or semiprivate, whereas medium are public. Thus, a warning given in a whisper to a student without the rest of the class being aware of it would be a small back-up response. A warning given publicly would be a medium back-up response, which would involve the whole class.

Going public with your back-up response is a tactical move to be avoided since peer involvement at such a time is rarely to your advantage. If the student is embarrassed, you will be the object of his revenge or efforts to save face. If the student is a clown, you have just provided an audience. Whichever response you produce, revenge or show business, it will no longer be simple or cheap. Rather, by going public teachers usually lay the foundation for their next discipline problem.

Rather than beginning the use of your back-up system by creating a public forum from which it is difficult to extricate yourself, it is to your advantage to create a situation in which the student decides to "rein it in" with a minimum of fanfare. As always, it is the student who decides to start the problem, but it is the teacher's response which will determine whether the problem gets larger or smaller.

Small Back-up Response Options

Small back-up response options are simply private or semiprivate messages that let students know in no uncertain terms that they are near the end of the line. The smart gamblers will fold if they already perceive the teacher as meaning business.

There is no best set of small back-up response options. Your choice will be governed to some degree by the age of the students you are dealing with. For example, I have had elementary teachers succeed in putting an end to a recurring problem by simply placing a 3 × 5 card on a student's desk with a picture of a telephone drawn on it. Sometimes catching a student's eye and writing her or his name in your grade book will suffice. Sometimes a teacher will simply whisper in the student's ear "That's one" or "That's two" or, if the signal is understood, give the same message from across the room with one or two raised fingers.

Whatever the mechanics which appeal to you, the small back-up responses will constitute a *graded series of two or three private or semiprivate messages* to students that give them a chance to buy out cheap. If they take the hint and fold, management has remained simple and cheap for everyone. Typically the student will experience a sense of justice and of having been protected by the teacher—the opposite emotions from those typically generated by the teacher's going public. Indeed, if the small back-up response is given with some finesse while the teacher "works the crowd" or moves from student to student giving corrective feedback, it would be impossible for anyone other than the teacher and student to know that the use of the back-up system had begun.

There is no telling how many effective small back-up response options may exist out there in the classrooms of clever teachers. Here are a few of the best ones I have found, arranged in the order in which they might typically be employed. They are (1) warning, (2) pulling the card, and (3) letter on the desk.

Warning   Everyone knows what a warning is, right? Wrong. A warning can make a problem better or worse depending on how it is delivered. The effective delivery of a warning is highly related to the skills of *limit-setting*—so closely related that it might be thought of as a variation on the limit-setting sequence.

A warning may either employ the formal limit-setting sequence as outlined in Chapters 5 and 6 or, more likely, appear as simply whispering with the students as you "work the crowd." During seat work, other students couldn't discriminate this interaction from work check or corrective feedback. Take plenty of relaxing breaths as you go and look at the students for a few moments before speaking. Then in a low tone of voice audible only to the student say something like:

> I am sorry that I have had to deal with this behavior yet another time. [pause, eye contact] If I have to return again, something very different than this little conversation of ours will take place. [pause] Do you understand?

or

> This is the second time I have seen this behavior today. I will have to begin thinking seriously about putting a stop to it should I see it again.

or

> Do you think you can take responsibility for controlling this behavior, or will I have to do something about it? I will be watching carefully, and I hope that I will not have to come over here again.

After the warning has been delivered (which is not terribly specific about what will happen next), relax, prompt the students back to work, take two more relaxing breaths, thank them, and stand up slowly. Stand looking at the students for at least two more relaxing breaths to observe them working and then slowly return to where you started. Turn and take two more relaxing breaths while looking at the offender(s) and then return to instruction—exactly as with limit-setting.

You have informed the students that they have just crossed over a threshold into back-up systems. The students will know exactly where they stand if you thoroughly explained your management system at the beginning of the school year. This warning echoes the timeless reminder: A word to the wise should be sufficient.

Following a demonstration of the giving of a warning during teacher training, I will turn to the group and ask, "Do you know what I just said to these two students?" The group responds, no, and I say, "Good, because it is none of your business." The physical proximity of limit-setting and the quietness of speech make the warning an intimate and private communication. It lets the students know enough is enough without going public. It thereby protects the dignity of the students by avoiding any public challenge or embarrassment.

What if, instead, the warning is public: some nagging from across the room or a name written on the chalkboard?

> Janet! Robert! This is the second time I've looked up to see you talking and out of your seats. Now, if I see any more of that, I'll . . .

Sound familiar? It's a classic job of pheasant posturing coupled with (1) public embarrassment and (2) a public challenge. The teacher has done everything possible to precipitate the next disruption. Only the well-behaved students will fold under these circumstances. More disruptive students are almost duty bound to take the next step—if not for revenge, at least to save face. Such clumsy discipline management will tend not to self-eliminate, and it will tend, therefore, to draw the teacher deeper into punition.

Going public defines a medium back-up response as opposed to a low-key, semi-private, small back-up response. By going public so quickly and clumsily, the teacher has just leapfrogged over his small back-up options—the cheap, low-risk ones—and has blundered into a public confrontation. Remember, the student decides to disrupt, but the teacher's response determines whether the disruption will get larger or smaller.

Pulling the Card   A word to the wise should be sufficient, but not everyone is wise. So, what do you do in those remaining instances in which the students disrupt one more time? The second small back-up response is called "pulling the card." Here are two variations.

Recall those 3 × 5 cards with names, addresses, home phone numbers, parents' work addresses, and their work phone numbers that you had the students fill out during the first hour of the first day of school (Chapter 3). Now you will discover one more reason to have the students fill out those cards.

Imagine a repeat disruption following the warning—more talking to neighbors since it is the most common example. Imagine also that you wish to give the disrupters a very good reason to stop disrupting that is not much effort for you but goes well beyond the warning that has just proved ineffective.

Turn, take two relaxing breaths, establish eye contact, say the students' names, and take two more relaxing breaths. They are looking at you, and you are looking at them, so far so good. Walk slowly to your desk, pick up your card file, turn, and look at the students for two more relaxing breaths. Then slowly pull each of their 3 × 5 cards. Lay them on the corner of your desk, gently put the file box down, and look at the offending students for two more relaxing breaths. They will not need an interpreter to figure out whose cards have been pulled and whose parents' addresses and phone numbers are lying face-up on the teacher's desk. A prompt with your finger from where you stand is usually enough to get them turned around and back on task.

Variation two combines warning and pulling the card into one operation in a case in which you are dealing with particularly squirrelly individuals who need to be reined in more definitively. Give the warning exactly as described above, and as you walk away from the students, walk to your desk. Pick up the card file, turn, and pull the card.

Any student who does not get the notion that something serious is about to happen is fairly dense! For most students most of the time the price of playing poker has just gotten too high, and they will fold. If so, your effective use of a small gesture signifying a large consequence has prevented the problem from getting bigger and your response from getting more expensive.

Letter Home on the Desk　As mentioned before, no discipline management technique comes with a guarantee. So, what if the disruption continues even after you have pulled the card? How can you still stop the disruption without taking on the cost and risks of medium back-up responses? The final response in your hierarchy of *small* back-up responses is to write letters home to the students' parents. Then tape the letters onto the students' desks with an appropriate warning. The procedure goes something like this:

1 Turn, say the students' names, relax, etc., walk slowly to the students' desks, pause with eye contact for three relaxing breaths and slowly go to palms exactly as with the warning.

2 Say, after a pause, "I am sorry that this has happened again." Pause and look at them for a moment. Say nothing more. Remember, slowing down adds forcefulness to your body language.

3 Stand, turn, and walk to your desk. Turn to look at the students, then sit down, take out pen and paper, and begin to write.

4 Write a brief letter home for each of the offending student(s). Describe the nature of the behavior and the student's persistence in disrupting. Request the parents' assistance in dealing with the behavior in order to "prevent it from becoming a serious problem." Tell them that you will be calling within the next day or two.

Write a separate letter for each student if two are involved. Make them brief and to the point (four or five sentences) so that each letter takes only a few minutes to write. You can write two letters in less time than it would take to make one phone call home (usually under 5 minutes). This is cheap compared to the alternatives.

The school may have a form for such correspondence which will produce a copy for your files (NCR paper). A record of persistent discipline problems has saved many teachers from being on the defensive should a student have a hearing for a severe behavior problem. If no such form is available, however, the teacher's personalized stationary is a nice touch. Put the note in an envelope, address it (using the information in your handy card file), and seal it.

5 Stand slowly and walk back to the students' desks as in limit-setting with the letter(s) in your hand and a piece or two of tape on your fingers. Lean over slowly and tape the first letter to the corner of the first student's desk.

6 Go to palms and calmly say:

This (pointing) is a letter to your parents telling them exactly what I have had to put up with from you today. If I see no more of this kind of behavior for the rest of the week (or day for primary students), then at the end of school on Friday afternoon *with* my permission *and* in front of my eyes, you may tear this note up and throw it into the wastebasket. If, however, I see *any* more of this kind of behavior, this letter will *immediately* go home, even if I have to mail it, accompanied by a *phone call.* Do you understand? Personally, I would like to have you tear it up. *But,* the choice is *yours.*

Stay at palms until the student acknowledges that he or she understands. Take two relaxing breaths, prompt the student back to work, thank him or her, take two more relaxing breaths and move to the next student. Repeat the message to each of the offending students. Then stand slowly, take two relaxing breaths, and pull out as usual.

7 Leave the letter taped to the desk if you teach a self-contained classroom. If, however, you teach in a departmentalized setting, remove the letter at the end of the period. Tape the letters on the desks again without comment at the very beginning of the same period tomorrow before you have said anything to the rest of the class.

A student has to be a little dense, self-destructive, or spoiling for a fight to continue the disruption at this point with the note already halfway home. Most of the time the disrupters will decide that the time has come to fold. If so, the teacher has succeeded in terminating the problem while keeping the cost relatively low for everyone involved.

Keep in mind, however, that the small back-up responses described in detail above are options rather than prescriptions. Many successful alternatives exist. A look and a brief notation in your grade book may suffice. Just keep it small and keep it cheap for everyone.

Preventing the Transition to Medium Back-up Responses

The effective use of small back-up responses will have eliminated the need to go further in all but a few rare cases. You must experience the effect that the letter home taped to the desk of your most bothersome student has before you can fully appreciate how unlikely it will be that you go further up your back-up system.

Yet everything is possible in the classroom, and some student may up the ante further by some form of recurrent or sudden misbehavior. When it happens to you the first time, you jump to medium back-up responses or beyond if necessary to put the lid on. But as soon as you spot a pattern—a situation that calls for the repetitive use of medium back-up responses or larger—stop what you are doing and step back from the situation. It is time to think of prevention, which is cheap, rather than remediation, which is costly. Medium back-up responses represent a dramatic increase in both cost and risk to the teacher.

Omission Training for the Group with Penalty   Before we make the transition to medium back-up responses, we will insert an incentive system to reduce the likelihood of this situation's continuing. We will offer a reward for self-control, and we will offer it to the *group* in order to enlist the power of peer pressure to help induce the problem students to rein it in.

The simplest, cheapest, and most powerful incentive system for use in this situation is an old friend—omission training. But rather than using it for an individual we will institute it as part of classroom policy. And rather than being a simple bonus program, it will be a complex incentive system with both bonus and penalty. As usual, penalty puts teeth into the system. Omission training for the group can be implemented in about a minute when piggybacked on top of responsibility training by giving the following speech:

> Class, I want to talk to you about some behaviors that have occurred in the classroom over the past week and a half that I would like to see stopped. As you know, several times during the last week and a half I have had to deal with fairly severe misbehavior. On two occasions I had to give students warnings, on one occasion I had to tape a letter home on someone's desk, and in one instance I even had to go to the office with the student.
>
> I think that we can be together in school without such problems. Most of the time we get along just fine, so I know that you can control such behavior when you choose to. If we all work together, these problems will be eliminated.
>
> Let me suggest a program that might help us think of others before we cause problems. To begin with I will give you a bonus of 5 minutes of PAT just to signify that the objective of this program is to give, not to take away. But, every time I must give someone a warning or pull their card or place a letter home on the desk or worse, we will also *lose 3 minutes* from our PAT. Thus, if we have one major problem, our bonus will be reduced to 2 minutes. If we have two problems, we will go into the hole by 1 minute. If, in contrast, we get through the entire week with no such severe problems, I will double your bonus to 10 minutes. So, the first severe problem is especially costly since it loses 3 minutes plus the special 5-minute bonus for a perfect week. Ask yourself, "Is my causing a problem worth 8 minutes of PAT?"
>
> Any questions? Now let's see how much bonus we can keep by watching how we act.

The Dynamics of Group OT with Penalty Omission training for the group with penalty when used as part of our back-up system provides an incentive for trying to avoid major problems and a strong disincentive for the escalation of disruption. The penalty clause, however, not only puts a price on disruption which is important if we want to suppress unwanted behavior, but it also allows us to graduate our response. A modest penalty in conjunction with a large bonus allows us to reduce the bonus *by degrees,* and it thereby maximizes our ability to end the week with a net bonus.

More important, the incentive system changes the interpersonal nature of the disruptive transaction completely. A back-up response is a negative sanction which is delivered by an adult authority figure. To some students this is like waving a red flag in front of a bull. If the student is not responding to negative sanctions from an adult, it may indicate that the reinforcement inherent in provoking an adult exceeds the size of the penalty of the small back-up response. Such a trade-off is not uncommon among angry, alienated children. Read the message and respond with the management system that avoids the power struggle with adult authority. Enlist the power of the peer group before you increase the size of the negative sanction. Let peer pressure provide an added reason to rein it in without your even targeting a particular individual as the cause of the problem.

Now, when a student considers continuing with his disruption, he must not only consider the teacher as an authority figure, but he must also consider his standing among peers. Does he want to be regarded as a jerk by everyone for his misbehavior? You have just robbed provocation of its hero value, and in the process you have given the obnoxious student an overwhelmingly good reason to fold. There is no longer any real or imagined gain for the student's doing battle with adult authority.

MEDIUM BACK-UP RESPONSES

Medium back-up responses are for more difficult management situations, and they are therefore more public than small back-up responses. They usually represent significantly greater cost in terms of planning and follow through, and they always involve significantly increased risk of failure as the teacher becomes involved in a public confrontation. Medium back-up responses, however, are still carried out primarily by the teacher in the classroom and deal with problems of lesser magnitude than might require the added back-up of school administrators.

Medium back-up responses include those negative sanctions most widely known among educators. They typically constitute much of the teacher's "bag of tricks" rather than being part of a systematic discipline management system. Consequently, although "tried and true," they are commonly overused or misused by teachers and therefore fail to self-eliminate. Medium back-up responses include techniques such as:

1 Time out in the classroom
2 Time out in a colleague's classroom
3 Public warning
4 Threat
5 Being sent to the hall
6 Detention after school
7 Loss of privilege
8 Parent conference

or at worst:

9 Lowering a student's grade
10 Extra homework

Each of these methods sounds familiar and easy to do, but in fact each method is daily abused in countless different ways. In order to use them correctly, several would need to be the subject of training programs in their own right.

Medium Back-up Response Options

Time Out in the Classroom

Mechanics of Time Out   Time out is a prime example of a simple-sounding technique which is often misused and for which full-blown training programs have been described in the research literature. Stated most simply, time out in a classroom consists of the temporary removal of a student from an activity as a consequence of inappropriate behavior. The duration should not exceed 5 minutes. The negative sanctions are simply social isolation and the loss of access to a desirable activity. The place to which the student is sent should be neutral, often a chair in an out-of-the-way area.

Simple enough? Not exactly. Proper execution of this "simple" technique (just like benching a kid for running at a swimming pool if you're a lifeguard, right?) requires the careful execution of at least the following steps:

1 Rules and expectations spelled out clearly in advance

2 Consequences for unacceptable behavior described and demonstrated in advance

3 Selection of an appropriate time out place that denies the student substitute means of reward

4 Early response to the problem behavior with limit-setting followed by a warning which is also delivered with effective body language as described earlier (i.e., slow, relaxed, deliberate, and intimate—no reprimanding, yelling, or threatening)

5 Follow through the *next* time the behavior occurs by sending the student to time out—once again with effective body language, little talk, and *no* anger

6 Effective prompting in the delivery of time out such as walking students to time out if they are resistant

7 Effective responding to problems that may arise during time out such as the student's making noise, calling out, or leaving the time out area

As with any skill, results come from the effective execution of specific response components rather than from a general understanding. And, effective execution comes from thorough input, good modeling, and practice, practice, practice! No discipline technique, even one that "everyone has been doing since time began," should be assumed to be in every teacher's behavior repertoire in an acceptable form without specific training. Research has shown that interventions as simple as increased praise for good work often prove ineffective without modeling and practice of the specific occasion, form, and timing of the teacher's response.

Uses of Time Out   Time out is relatively flexible and effective in a wide variety of situations from preschool through high school. It has become particularly prominent in the past 10 to 15 years since it is one technique that is taught in almost any course on behavior modification. It has provided a great many teachers and parents with a negative sanction that is relatively mild, matter of fact, and emotionally low key. The use of time out, therefore, has tended to reduce the risk of harsh punition and emotional polarization between adult and child. This procedure, consequently, has replaced more primitive and destructive negative sanctions in many settings such as criticizing, yelling, sarcasm, or even physical abuse, and it is generally regarded as an "enlightened" technique of classroom management. Time out helps students cool off and take responsibility for their own behavior with a minimum of humiliation and resentment.

On the *negative side,* however, time out is often used too early and too often as a primary means of classroom management rather than as a back-up response of fairly large magnitude. It cannot be used as an alternative to effective limit-setting in most settings without being overused. And, it cannot be used as an alternative to behavioral incentives since it does not systematically provide motivation to cooperate. It works better the younger and "nicer" the students are. Cost can quickly escalate by the fourth or fifth grade as students get large and occasionally resistant going to time out. By junior high it has become a risky and questionable strategy in most classrooms, and in emotionally handicapped secondary classrooms any success at all requires considerable nerve and ironclad back-up by the principal.

Time Out in a Colleague's Classroom　If a student at the elementary level continues to disrupt after being sent to time out, an alternative form of time out can be employed which typically puts an end to the problem and helps keep the cost within the medium price range. If students will not behave themselves during 5 minutes of time out within their own classroom, they may be obliged to accept a longer time out in another teacher's classroom with a folder of work since they will be staying a while (15 to 30 minutes). This program is often affectionately referred to as the "lend-louse program."

The following fine points should be observed to ensure consistent success:

1 The colleague must thoroughly understand and approve of the program, must not feel put upon, and must feel free to send a student to you under similar circumstances. Usually your partner is a friend with whom you see eye to eye on discipline.

2 The colleague must put the child to work—usually facing the wall—and *not* include him or her in class games and activities.

3 The colleague should give academic help periodically in a brief, matter-of-fact way.

4 Finally, separate the disruptive child from his or her peer group *by as many years as possible*. For example, send a first grader to a fifth or sixth grade classroom and a fifth or sixth grader to a first grade classroom.

This last condition is perhaps the most important since it leaves the child feeling a bit like a fish out of water without anyone to entertain. It is this last condition which is most often violated since the colleague you share the most with and see eye to eye with on discipline is likely to be at your grade level conveniently located in the same hall. But, if you send students to their own grade level, they still have their peer group to show off to.

Trained teachers with even the most unruly little critters in their classrooms have typically reported that "lend louse" was the end of the line in their use of their back-up system and that it only had to be used once. It is a wise teacher, however, who takes out some insurance against the student becoming a "runner" by escorting the student to the colleague's classroom. If this precaution is not possible and if the student is at risk for turning into a runner, provide him or her with a "time out card" on which both teachers write the exact time of leaving and arriving.

Time out in a colleague's classroom is less readily available to secondary teachers in a departmentalized setting, but when applicable it is generally superior to sending a student to the office. The variant most useful is to send an unruly student in a basic level class to an advanced class within the same department. Thus, a general science teacher might send a student to the physics class down the hall or a first year French teacher might send a student to the fourth year French class next door. Once again, the student is denied peer approval for goofing off since advanced classes tend to be very achievement-oriented. The student can cool his or her heels in the achievement-oriented environment until the end of the period at which time the first teacher is at liberty to discuss the matter with the student.

Public Warning and Threat   Public warning and threat have been discussed earlier. In general they represent a clumsy and counterproductive public confrontation—a classic example of nagging and pheasant posturing from across the room.

Being Sent to the Hall   Being sent to the hall is simply a variation on time out which removes students from the action within the classroom without sending them to a colleague's classroom. While it is time-honored and can work, it is a gamble. This technique is recommended only for "nice" elementary students whom the teacher can trust to sit and work in the hall rather than talking to passers-by and wandering about. One might well wonder how a student who would get to medium back-up responses, given all the management technology that has been described so far, would qualify. Typically this option is used unsystematically and simply represents "bouncing" as an act of exasperation by the teacher. In any case, liabilities of this technique include:

1 The child's being rewarded by events in the hall like talking to other kids or just seeing people come and go

2 Turning into a "runner" and disrupting other classrooms, hiding, or leaving the grounds

3 Being forgotten until the next time the teacher leaves the room ("Oh, my goodness! Are you still here?")

At the secondary level, sending students to the hall invites further problems due to the public humiliation. It also signals the teacher's inability to cope more effectively and often represents a teacher's abdication of responsibility for dealing with a discipline management situation. This pattern of abuse can become exaggerated in schools which employ adult hall monitors. In such settings I have repeatedly observed teachers bounce a student out of their class and then 5 minutes later stick their head out of their door to criticize the hall monitor for all the noise in the hall which is being generated by the kid they just bounced. To put it bluntly, at the secondary level this technique usually represents mismanagement.

Detention after School   The cost of detention varies widely from the elementary to the secondary levels. At the elementary level the teacher *also* has to stay after school—a cost which most teachers will quite sensibly avoid. Since the cost to the teacher is high, detention is rarely abused at the elementary level. The cost of detention to an elementary teacher may, however, be minimized in many cases. Holding a student 5 minutes after school with a bit of values clarification before dismissal may be plenty of time since the student's friends will have gone off without her or him.

A teacher can, however, subvert the intent of detention either by making it highly unpleasant and generating resentment or by making it pleasant with talk and chores to do. Like time out, it is enough if it is simply *boring*. Sometimes, however, any form of detention will be preferred by a student who has only an empty house to go home to. If detention provides company to a lonely child, it is also a reinforcement error.

At the secondary level the cost of detention is radically different than it is at the elementary level—no more effort than issuing a pink slip. This reduction in cost produces a corresponding increase in abuse as some teachers simply "zap" a student to detention rather than engaging in more sophisticated and demanding management procedures.

Will the most unruly students at the school site voluntarily show up to a detention room in order to lengthen their school day? Are you kidding? Half the time they split before school is out. Do you think they will return from the video game parlor to serve time? As is usually the case with medium back-up responses, detention always works best for the students who need it least, and it works least for the students who need it most. Perhaps for this reason I have never heard of the use of detention ever having self-eliminated at a school site.

Loss of Privilege   Although this technique may seem to work in the short run, it runs a high risk of generating resentment on the part of the student. If so, the teacher will pay.

Parent Conferences   The cost-effectiveness of most parent conferences has already been described in the preceding chapter, and in general it is quite low. Sometimes, however, it is your best bet. The commitment and social competence of the parent are prime determining factors.

Conferencing is a skill which deserves separate training in its own right, and the communication skills needed are not included in this discussion of parent conferencing. Neither will I describe all the ways parents can be involved in a school-based contingency management program. Most such programs come under the heading of "individualized behavior modification" programs and have been dealt with thoroughly in the technical literature. Training parents to get their child to do homework without having a nightly battle over it is also a special topic in its own right which frequently comes up as part of a parent training program.

A note of caution is appropriate, however, regarding parent conferencing. The more sophisticated teachers become in managing the behavior of students, the less they need the parents' help and the more they will be sought out by the parents who need *their* help. You may soon be perceived as an expert in child management by parents who are at their wits end in managing the child at home. Almost any well-trained teacher could end up running a small child outpatient clinic from his or her classroom every day after school if he or she were so inclined. Beware lest your good intentions consume you.

Get what you can out of a parent conference and keep you hopes modest. In most cases it is cheaper to fix it yourself.

Lowering Grades and Extra Work   I will say little about either lowering grades or extra work as medium back-up responses apart from the fact that they are unfortunately very common. They condition students to hate schoolwork (extra work) and resent the teacher (lowering grades).

Once a student's grade is gone, so is the incentive function of working for grades.

If the student cares about grades, lowering the grade gives him or her nothing to lose and nothing to work for. And, if the student does not care about grades, lowering the grade is a useless, impotent gesture.

Both these responses, therefore, are akin to a teacher's shooting him- or herself in the foot. These responses can only work effectively for a conscientious, highly motivated student who is mortified at the thought of lowering his or her grade or of displeasing the teacher. Why would you be using medium back-up responses with such a student?

Warnings for Medium Back-up Responses

Issuing warnings for the use of medium back-up responses is a tricky topic. If a teacher is going up the back-up system in an orderly way, the natural warning for the use of a medium back-up response is the prior use of a small back-up response.

In practice when untrained teachers give explicit, public warnings, it usually means that they have jumped over small back-up responses entirely. The most common form of warning apart from a verbal reprimand is putting the student's name on the board. Such a public warning is quick and easy. It requires none of the finesse of a private warning which uses the body language of limit-setting acquired during systematic teacher training. Though consistent with the conventional folk wisdom of discipline, in practice the use of public warnings is usually symptomatic of a highly simplistic and punishment-oriented back-up system.

A more constructive warning for the use of a medium back-up response can be given to an individual, however, in the form of a serious talk in private with a student who has been recurrently difficult. A serious talk as a means of preempting the use of medium back-up responses for an individual is analogous to the use of "quiet time" (think and talk) as a means of preempting the use of small back-up responses. It may be preferable to group omission training with penalty when a single individual is the main problem. One particularly effective strategy for doing this at the secondary level is to call the student out of *another* class period to have your serious talk. High school students are usually very impressed that you would look into their schedules to find out where they were during another period of the day, and they therefore perceive you as extremely serious in your intent to follow through in dealing with the problem.

Preventing the Transition to Large Back-up Responses

As with small back-up responses, the transition to the next larger class of back-up responses will be wisely avoided through the use of incentives. First, however, a careful *reexamination* of your entire management system with perhaps some help from a friend or a specialist would be most appropriate, since if you get this far in your management system very often, you are probably "blowing it."

The incentive system of choice is group omission training with penalty as described in the previous section. If you need it and have not instituted it yet, now is the time. At this point in the management hierarchy, however, you may consider a specialized behavior management or behavior modification program. Although expensive, such a custom-built program may be cheaper, more effective, and far more positive than continuing up the back-up system.

OVERVIEW OF BACK-UP SYSTEMS WITHIN THE CLASSROOM

A back-up system is designed to deal with severe or persistent disruptions of any magnitude. The bottom half of the back-up system consisting of small and medium back-up responses is primarily in the hands of the classroom teachers. It is their responsibility to put the lid on as early and as gently as possible in order to keep the problem from growing and continuing. When teachers do their job quickly and effectively, they protect the student from getting into any big trouble by their calm and by their constructive use of negative sanctions.

It is easy to imagine being in a situation in which a small back-up response might need to be used, but it is difficult to imagine being in the same situation in need of a small back-up response *repeatedly.* The first or second time it happens to you, chalk it up to experience. The third or fourth time it happens to you, chalk it up to ineptitude or inaction.

A successful back-up system will be self-eliminating because it works—it consistently raises the cost of intolerable behavior above any possible benefit. But a total management system that is successful will also eliminate its back-up system by design—by *quickly* implementing an incentive to remedy any problem which recurrently calls forth the use of the back-up system. In an analogous fashion when the bottom half of the back-up system is used appropriately within the context of effective limit-setting and incentives, the remainder of the back-up system is rarely needed. When teachers use negative sanctions ineptly, however, they all but guarantee the frequent use of the top half of the back-up system.

Obnoxious behavior is frequent enough to require the use of small and medium back-up responses from time to time in many classrooms. Ugly behavior can occur suddenly and throw the teacher into using large and extra-large back-up responses on rare occasions. But if the teacher is using positive discipline properly, such blow-ups will typically be between peers rather than between student and teacher. The main determiner of whether most obnoxious behavior turns ugly is, as usual, the teacher's initial response to it. Consequently, the frequency of teachers' need for help with discipline from outside their classroom serves as a barometer of the effectiveness of their management within the classroom.

CHAPTER 16

BACK-UP RESPONSES BEYOND THE CLASSROOM

That portion of the back-up system that lies outside the classroom, the top half, consists of large and extra-large back-up responses. Large back-up responses are for the most part equivalent to sending a student to the office, whereas extra-large back-up responses include follow-up sanctions such as in-school suspension, suspension, and expulsion. Large and extra-large back-up responses when used properly involve the collaboration of a team of professionals to solve an extremely difficult problem. When used improperly, however, the top half of the system can represent nothing more than one person dumping a problem into someone else's lap.

LARGE BACK-UP RESPONSES

Large back-up responses require that the administration directly help a teacher in dealing with a management problem that began in the classroom. Whereas a wide variety of things might happen to students once they are sent to the office, a watershed step in management has irrevocably occurred. The teacher has passed the primary responsibility for solving the problem to someone else.

Large back-up responses involve an immediate and dramatic cost escalation insofar as any such response requires the time and attention of several professionals. This cost escalation may be entirely justified as the only sufficiently powerful way of responding to any ugly situation. However, the *repeated* use of the office for back-up by a teacher usually signals an unwillingness or inability to manage behavior within the classroom by any more effective means.

The Problem with the Office

The office is in deep trouble when students are "bounced" there for moderate-size offenses. When a student is bounced to the office, everybody loses. The teacher, in spite of any pheasant posturing or bravado, has made a public demonstration of his or her inability to deal successfully with the student within the classroom. In most cases the teacher has gotten upset, has felt stymied, and has finally had to pull rank to get back on top.

The student has, most likely, upset the teacher even if the teacher remains stone-faced. The student has thereby controlled the situation, since in body language calm is strength and upset is weakness. The student has probably also made a successful show of bravery and prowess relative to the teacher. And, in addition, the student has gotten revenge for any public humiliation that may have occurred during the preceding escalation. The student, therefore, is rewarded for provocative behavior within the first few seconds of the confrontation, a reinforcement error that cannot be undone by subsequent events in the office. The outrageous student has no doubt also been re-warded by the attention, laughs, and "oohs and ahs" of the peer group.

The office also loses because it has no effective cure for ineffective classroom man-agement that can be reliably brought into play after a student has arrived with a pink slip. When several students are waiting to be seen, administrators can usually only afford to admonish the students and send them back to class—the old revolving door policy. Yet teachers keep complaining that the office doesn't help them while contin-uing to send kids to the vice principal as though he or she were an exorcist.

Consequently, although sending a nice kid to the office may occasionally produce repentance, in most cases sending students to the office produces a no-win manage-ment situation for teachers and administrators alike—one which is self-perpetuating rather than self-eliminating. Indeed sending a student to the office may have the du-bious distinction of being the most overused and overrated discipline technique in education.

Since using the office for back-up can be an expensive and seductive trap, we will examine its use carefully. We will attempt to understand how and why it so predictably malfunctions as an agent of discipline enforcement. Since the magnitude of the failure of the office in eliminating behavior problems is most blatant at the secondary level, we will begin with a careful examination of the way in which the office at a large high school functions and malfunctions as part of the school-site back-up system.

The Office at High School

The typical large high school has, on the basis of my conversations with administra-tors, between 2500 and 5000 referrals to the office per year for discipline problems that occur within the classroom, including tardies. This astronomical total, which re-mains fairly constant from year to year, stands as a testimonial to a management method that does not self-eliminate.

Bouncing by "Office Junkies"   The majority of referrals at a school site (omitting tardies) are made by a handful of teachers. The most competent teachers at a typical school site will not only rarely make a referral to the office but will also be totally unaware of the people who are making the referrals, the number of referrals being made, and the reasons for their occurrence. These referrals will consume the time of half the administrative staff of the school site—usually two people high on the salary schedule. The remaining administrators will often have forgotten about the nature and extent of the referral problem until some event forces the issue into their consciousness.

Sometimes the event that causes a principal, for example, to take a fresh look at office referrals is the illness of a colleague. As one principal confessed to me:

> I had forgotten what is was like to be a vice principal until I had to pinch-hit for Herman. I think I wanted to forget. I spent the whole day dealing with one referral after another and didn't get a damn thing done! And most of the referrals were bullshit! I couldn't believe it! So-and-so was late to class. So-and-so was chewing gum. So-and-so kept talking after I asked her to stop. So-and-so forgot his book again. And the referrals that really were big problems were in most cases made into big problems by the way the teacher dealt with the kid!

Teachers, however, have a different point of view, and their point of view is often not heard until the entire school staff has suffered long and hard at the hands of a minority of the student body. At such times teachers, administrators, and even parents may be forced to take a new look at the way in which discipline is being managed at the school site. In times of great stress all parties involved may join to form a "discipline task force."

The Discipline Task Force   I will tell a story of my involvement with a particular discipline task force at a large inner city high school that highlights the key problems of dealing with discipline in the office. You must realize, however, that for a high school task force on discipline to resort to calling in an outside consultant, they must be suffering. The task force is at loggerheads over how to deal with kids for at least a year, and everyone hates everyone.

The Teacher   If you talk to the teachers about the problem, they say:

> We don't get any support! I have kids in my classroom who try to get away with murder, and they know that the worst that can happen to them is that I will send them down to the office. Do you know what happens then? In 10 minutes they're back! It's a big joke! And when I want some real help down at the office, they give me the message, "What's the matter, can't you handle the problems in your classroom?" or "Don't send your problems down here because we can't fix them any better than you can." The message over and over again is you're on your own kid. Lots of luck. Some of these students are a foot taller than I am—tough, street-wise, big-mouthed kids—and being on your own leaves you pretty damn vulnerable! Listen, I want some *real help* when I need it!

The teacher's complaint seems all the more plausible when you know the statistics on teacher assaults and injury at such school sites to say nothing of burn-out. So I ask the administrators what it looks like from their angle.

The Administrator The administrators that I deal with in such situations are usually vice principals. Few principals in their right minds would place themselves on the discipline task force. A typical dialogue with a vice principal goes something like this.

VP: Do you see that bench outside my office?

Me: Yeah.

VP: You know what that's for?

Me: Yeah. That's where kids sit while they're waiting for you to see them.

VP: Right! Now, school opens up here at 8 o'clock in the morning. Do you know when the first kid is on that bench?

Me: Eight o'clock in the morning.

VP: No. 7:50! The kid got into a fight while waiting at the door. I talk to the kid for 20 or 30 minutes because he's one of my regulars. He's all bent out of shape about something. When I open the door to let him go to class, how many kids do you think are on the bench now?

Me: How many?

VP: It could be five or more, but on a good day let's say its only three. So I see the next kid, and when I open my door the next time there are five or six kids on the bench for sure. At that point counseling is all over for the day. I mean, if I don't speed things up, we're all gonna *die!* The kids will be shoving each other off the bench and making noise and hassling the secretary. The last two secretaries we had quit within 6 weeks. Then somebody's mother walks in, and some kid calls her a choice name. She goes to the principal, and then we have an irate parent to deal with. I mean, if I let those kids stack up out there in the office, it will turn into a zoo! So, what do I do? Get 'em in, and get 'em out. Hell, I know it's not helping very much, but it's better than instant chaos! What are my choices?

Since chaos is clearly intolerable, most VPs and counselors settle for survival. Yet, the revolving-door policy, perhaps unavoidable under the circumstances, is neither good counseling nor good discipline. The counseling is so superficial, in fact, that it amounts to a parody on counseling—and most VPs and counselors are well enough trained to know it. But when the students begin to stack up outside, what indeed are the choices?

And after the lecture on good citizenship is over, does Bill walk back to class muttering "mea culpa" to himself? Are you kidding? As he swaggers into the teacher's class, someone whispers "How was it?," and Bill says "Shiiit!" as he puts his feet up on the table. And now what is the teacher going to do? And what is she going to do tomorrow when the same problem recurs?

The Parent Once I've gotten the administrator's perspective, I ask to talk to the parents. The parents say:

> My child was doing just fine until I sent him up to that school, and now they tell me he's having problems. I think it's the school's fault. He was a perfectly wonderful child before he went up there. He tells me the classes are boring!

The kid may have a dossier 5 inches thick that goes back to kindergarten, but who's counting. Satisfied parents don't volunteer for a discipline task force.

Proper and Improper Use of the Office   I have one piece of advice to give to teachers about using the office to solve their classroom discipline problems: *don't!*

The reason I say don't is not because I think that teachers shouldn't send students to the office. That is not the point. I don't deal with "shoulds" or "shouldn'ts." I deal with the lessons of the school of hard knocks. The reason a teacher is better off not relying on the office is because the office is *inherently unreliable!*

The office is unreliable not because people in the office do not want to help teachers. That attribution by teachers, no matter how true to their experience it may be, misses the reason the office continually lets them down. The office is inherently unreliable because its capacity to help was never that great to begin with. As soon as there are three students on the bench outside the vice principal's office, counseling is done for the day, and the revolving-door policy begins. The office *can* help teachers with discipline management. The problem is that the office cannot help them *very often.* As soon as the demand for service exceeds the supply, the entire system *jams* and become useless! At a typical high school the office becomes jammed by 9:30 a.m. What happens for the rest of the day is simply a matter of survival.

And how many bouncers or office junkies do you think it takes on a faculty to keep the office permanently jammed? Any faculty of sixty to eighty teachers will have *at least* a half-dozen bouncers, and that is *more* than enough. Owing to their ineptitude or irresponsibility in classroom management, they will jam their colleague's access to the office for back-up all year long. The bouncers' more competent colleagues will not understand why the office can never serve them. They typically have no idea of the chronicity of bouncing among a minority of their colleagues, much less who the bouncers are. All they know is that when they need help it's not there—just as their bouncer colleagues keep saying in the teacher's lounge. Such topics are not well understood much less candidly discussed at most school sites.

In short, the notion that teachers as a group can send students to the office as a common means of fixing classroom discipline problems is one of the most long-standing myths in education. In spite of the daily evidence delivered in overwhelming quantities that the practice does not work, nearly everyone—teachers and administrators and parents alike—seem unalterably convinced that it *should* work.

Reinforcement Errors That Feed the Problem

The Teacher   For the bouncer, sending an obnoxious kid to the office is instant relief. Never mind that they will be back tomorrow, at least they are gone today. Immediate relief rewards the act of bouncing, and the long-term consequence—the repetitiveness of the problem—is most logically misattributed to the students. They keep disrupting because it is their nature. They are "rotten kids."

The Principal   If the administration were to attempt to stem the flow of referrals by closing the door and refusing to receive students, they would be met by a blistering accusation of nonsupport, *especially* from the bouncers. If the office does its best to respond to the constant stream of referrals, even if it is just with the revolving door, at least they are trying. When you don't know what else to do, doing your best is certainly more rewarding than being hung in effigy.

The Counselor Most VPs and counselors at most high schools have little time to use their higher level job skills that qualified them to be a counselor in the first place. If they do have the luxury of adequate time to do some real counseling, however, they must beware of committing a reinforcement error in the process.

What is the incentive for lonely and troubled students to work hard and act appropriately in class when an exhibition of inappropriate behavior gets them some counseling? Since the luxury of real counseling is in short supply in regular education settings, the extent of such a reinforcement error is correspondingly limited. But it can be rampant in special education settings where there are more counselors and fewer students. In many cases the availability of one-to-one TLC (tender loving care) is the primary reinforcer for periodic outbursts in the classroom, especially during difficult subjects. By delivering counseling as a reward for having a severe problem, the hapless counselor can collect a clientele of chronics, just like the nurse.

For counseling of a severe behavior problem to produce the intended result, the time and place must be chosen carefully. In training educators to deliver counseling in conjunction with a back-up response, there is a rule of thumb that spells out when it is OK to talk with a student about his or her problem. The rule is: First you pay. Then we talk.

Until students have experienced the appropriate consequences for their actions, a heart-to-heart talk is impossible. Before the delivery of the negative sanction, a student's *vested interest* is typically to wheedle his or her way out of the consequence that she or he has earned by some form of blaming and excuse making: *not* by joining the teacher in clarifying values, feelings, and motivations.

The Student The rewards available for a student's getting the teacher's goat have already been described. They are entertainment, control, and revenge. Additional reinforcement errors can occur as TLC is delivered in the counselor's office as we have just discussed. As a result of being outrageous, a student can talk to someone who listens, rather than having to learn algebra.

The cycle is therefore complete—everyone is inappropriately rewarded to some degree for using the office to solve discipline problems—everyone, that is, except the poor, hapless *competent* teacher who only needs the office once or twice a semester and cannot understand why it is not there when he or she needs it. Were the faculty to attack the administration for nonsupport, the best teachers would join the bouncers based on their disappointing experience with the office.

Reducing Abuse of the Office

A Response-Cost Program for Bouncers In Chapter 13 a response-cost program for reducing abuse of the office was briefly mentioned. To review, a response-cost program requires the construction of a due process for dealing with a problem that is costly enough to induce someone to take care of the problem in order to avoid the due process. Response-cost programs are ideal for suppressing irresponsible behavior in a situation in which direct suppression via negative sanctions is awkward or inappropriate.

The repeated bouncing of students to the office for minor offenses is a classic management dilemma calling for response-cost management. If an administrator said, "Don't send them to the office," he or she would generate intense faculty resentment for lack of support. If they bend to the unreasonable demands of the bouncers, however, administrators commit a reinforcement error by acceding to their demands while removing any reason for the bouncer to learn better methods of coping.

A response-cost program to eliminate bouncing, however, will not be a live option for an administrator until the majority of the faculty (at least two-thirds) have been thoroughly trained in effective methods of classroom management so that they understand and support the administrator's goals and strategy. Thus, the following program is usually not instituted until the second or third year of involvement with a school site.

As mentioned earlier (Chapter 13), the administrator approaches response-cost for bouncers from the perspective of doing a more thorough and conscientious job of dealing with problems severe enough to warrant an office referral. Far from being a ruse, this commitment to dealing thoroughly with tough management problems is not only appropriate but long overdue at most school sites. Most administrators shy away from such a large commitment to adequate follow through because they do not have time for it. Being able to afford the due process of the response-cost program, therefore, is a luxury that only appears as affordable after most of the faculty have stopped making office referrals and are standing squarely behind the new policy.

The new policy is simple:

1 If a discipline problem is too big to handle within the classroom, it is serious enough to warrant a systematic plan to solve the problem developed by the teacher in conjunction with key administrators.

2 When a student is referred to the office, the teacher must fill out an incident report (one full page) and describe those management methods that were used before the office referral. (A check list can be provided on a separate page with room for explanation.) The incident report must accompany the student to the office so that administrators may know in adequate detail what has happened.

3 A planning conference of at least a half hour must be held with the referring teacher and key administrators after school on the *same day* to plan a future course of action in dealing with the problem. This plan should focus on prevention as well as remediation.

For the bouncers, the days of the quick, cheap, short-term solving of classroom management dilemmas by simply issuing a pink slip are over. They will either have to handle it themselves within the classroom or become involved in a careful, systematic, and therefore relatively costly problem-solving process.

Most bouncers will experience anxiety and will often express anger. If, after all, they had adequate classroom management skills, they wouldn't be bouncing. They are frequently burned out and want to leave school as soon as possible. They see the incident report and the planning meeting as a burden. So, what are they to do? First they may try to gather support in opposition to the new policy: "We get no support. That's their job, isn't it?"

A naive, untrained faculty may well rally around the complainers, the negative leaders of the faculty. But a trained faculty will stand firmly behind the new policy. The bouncers must now cope within their classrooms or spend a lot of time picking up the pieces after school. At this point many of the teachers who had been negative toward classroom management training finally see the light and volunteer to learn new skills. Indeed, the upgraded due process for handling office referrals is the final mechanism whereby burned-out teachers are provided incentives for actively participating in professional growth.

Keep Adequate Records Although the careful problem solving of the new due process confronts the bouncers most directly with a new set of responsibilities, in fact, almost all school sites need to do a more thorough job of keeping track of serious behavior violations. In all but a relatively few secondary sites, no permanent records are kept of severe or recurrent behavior problems. This sloppy record keeping can cost a teacher or a school district dearly if a chronic troublemaker finally gets into serious trouble with the law (violence, vandalism, drugs, etc.). The parent can deny either any prior record of serious misconduct or any attempt by school authorities to help the child. With no record of serious incidents and attempts at management, the educators in the room look like a bunch of dummies.

Although an incident report should always be filed for major "altercations," any secondary teacher should keep a log which records in simple terms the student's work habits and noteworthy behaviors. A piece of notebook paper with three headings is sufficient: (1) date, (2) work, and (3) behavior. The work column can simply record assignments turned in and not turned in although the log sometimes replaces the gradebook with notations for quality of work and extra-credit work. The entries in the behavior column should be brief but can be exceedingly revealing, for example:

9-15 Hits, gets surly, takes seat.
9-17 Nasty back talk—call parent and leave message.
9-18 Parent doesn't return call. Call again. They blame me. Set up conference for 9-22.
9-22 Parent doesn't show.
9-23 Call parent. He is surly ("Get off our kid's back.") Conference reset for 9-30.
9-25 Uses profanity in class.
9-30 Parent doesn't show.

Getting Out of the Office At those school sites in which the demand by teachers for help from the office finally reaches a low level, options open up to the vice principals and counselors that were not possible before. They not only have time to devote to students who really need special help with their lives, but they can also deal with discipline referrals in a completely different way. When the number of daily discipline referrals to an administrator becomes moderate, it becomes more cost-effective for the administrator to *leave the office* and go to the student rather than having the student come to the office.

The advantages that accrue to going to the student's classroom quickly become apparent when the administrator sees the gratitude on the face of teachers as they come to the door. The administrator is obviously going out of his way to help. Students are more impressed by a vice principal at the door than they are by a pink slip. The teacher also remains more credible as a discipline manager to the students since, at least to a degree, the problem is still being handled within the classroom. And the opportunity for goofing off on the way to the office and in the office while waiting to be seen has been eliminated. Finally, there is much less wasted time not only for the students but for the administrator as well. An administrator can often have four or five quick conferences with students outside their classrooms in a single period while monitoring the halls and school grounds in the process. In addition, the continual presence of administrators in the halls can suppress a lot of out-of-classroom problems. Simple mobility or MBWA (Management By Walking Around) has proved to be one of the most effective ways for executives in both industry and education to stay on top of things.

The Office at the Elementary School

All problems of relegating discipline management to the office at the secondary level apply to the elementary level as well. Abuse takes roughly the same form for roughly the same reasons.

Yet the problem of bouncing seems to be less extreme at the elementary level. Owing to the structure of the self-contained classroom, elementary teachers face a different set of contingencies for bouncing. *First,* in self-contained classrooms all students are well known. It is naturally easier for a secondary teacher to bounce a relatively anonymous student who is with them only one period a day and in no way distinguishes him- or herself apart from getting into trouble. *Second,* in a self-contained classroom there is no such thing as bouncing a kid and not having to see him or her for the rest of the day. These kids always come back to you wearing whatever chip on their shoulder you helped put there, and you must live with the consequences of your own discipline practices for the rest of that day. And, *finally,* elementary teachers quite naturally tend to see their students as children rather than as young adults. Consequently, elementary teaching is more strongly infused with the parent role. When students are sent to the office at the elementary level, it is more often because they have done something terrible for which sitting in the presence of the "supreme authority," the principal, seems to be the only sufficiently awesome thing to do.

One dilemma at the elementary level that is unique to small school sites with only one administrator, however, is that the principal is not there half the time! She is at a meeting at the district office or with some planning committee or parent group. If I had to rely for back-up on someone who was not there half the time, I would look for good alternatives.

Why Use the Office   At the elementary level one more often thinks of taking students to the office rather than sending them to the office. A teacher at any grade level typically *takes* the student to the office not only to make sure he or she gets there but also to confer with the principal about a plan of action. One might, on the other hand, imagine a bouncer *sending* a student to the office to get the problem out of his or her hair and to make someone else responsible for dealing with it. This contrast between taking versus sending a student to the office shows the difference between responsible and irresponsible use of the office in dealing with a discipline problem.

Irresponsible use of the office, whether at the elementary or secondary levels, signals an abdication of management, an attempt to give the problem to someone else rather than to seek the other person's collaboration in a joint effort at problem solving. Implicit within an understanding of the responsible use of the office in problem solving lies a criterion for when to use the office: *There is no reason to bring a problem to the office unless it requires the professional judgment of at least one additional colleague* (the principal, for example) *in order to figure out what to do next.*

Smooth Moves

Collaboration with the Principal   A teacher who is effective in managing classroom discipline typically needs to come to the office only with something that was sudden and unforeseen—usually injury or fighting. After the teacher explains the incident to the principal, he or she will often stand there expectantly waiting for a remedy to be instantly coughed up. The teacher apparently does not know what is going through the principal's mind at this moment. To clarify, the principal is thinking, "What the hell do you expect me to do about it?"

The choreography in this situation is for the principal to take two relaxing breaths, stand slowly, look the student in the eye, take two more relaxing breaths, and say

> Billy, I want you to sit in this chair and look at the wall. We will return in a minute, and when I walk through that door, I will expect to find you looking at the wall! Do you understand?

Then the principal and teacher leave together. They close the door behind them and keep walking. When teacher and principal are out of earshot of the student, the principal turns to teacher and says, "What the hell do you think we ought to do about this?" If you are not sure what to do next, at least have the sense not to debate it in front of the kid. If solving the problem does not require the combined judgment of two professionals, the teacher has no business in the office.

Phone Calls   Question: If you decide to call the parent, who explains what happened over the phone? Answer: The kid.

The principal rings the parent and explains the situation before turning the phone over to the student to fill in the details as the principal and teacher look on. Once the student commits himself to a story over the phone with the latitude to lie removed by the presence of the principal and teacher, he can't lie and alibi so easily after he gets home. Many a fruitful collaboration with a parent has been aborted at the beginning by the child going straight home and lying in order to get a somewhat blind or gullible parent to side with him or her against an "unfair teacher."

Transition to Extra-Large Back-up Responses

The issue of sending or taking a student to the office brings into focus a watershed event in the teacher's management of a discipline problem within his or her classroom—seeking the direct aid of someone else (a school administrator) in solving the problem. Upon this event hang three issues:

- The size of the problem
- The teacher's competence in classroom management
- The teacher's taking responsibility for classroom management

Once the administrator accepts responsibility for fixing the problem by dealing directly with the student, all three issues have been resolved for all practical purposes. The administrator has implicitly acknowledged that (1) the problem is sufficiently large, (2) the teacher knows what to do before coming to the office, and (3) the teacher has done all that he or she can. If any of these implications is not accurate, the administrator is responding to the wrong issue.

Consequently, before going further up the back-up system, we will insert an additional step: *Reexamine!* The teacher and administrator should reexamine the whole situation together to reassess the nature and source of the problem. A sudden or violent situation can force the teacher and the administrator beyond large back-up responses on rare occasions. But if a situation is at all repetitive, the mere repetitiveness of the problem should serve as a red flag to all involved. Most students who repetitively get to the office or beyond do so as a result of mismanagement.

EXTRA-LARGE BACK-UP RESPONSES

The treatment of extra-large back-up responses will be brief. We are now well beyond the confines of the classroom and beyond the normal applications of positive classroom discipline. The topic of extra-large back-up systems is potentially immense: it covers the management of delinquent populations and the involvement of education, both regular and special, with the juvenile justice system and the families of court-referred youths.

For our purposes it will be most useful to restrict our focus to those management procedures which are commonly known and in use at many school sites. These procedures might well be considered by a faculty and administration as they go about constructing or reconstructing their school discipline policy.

Common Procedures

In-School Suspension   In-school suspension is a variation on time out which has received much attention in the past few years, especially at the secondary level. In-school suspension is time out for an extended period, usually a half day or full day, in a private study area with a folder of assigned work and academic supervision.

For the extremely or chronically provocative student, in-school suspension offers an alternative to suspension from school which keeps the student in a learning environment. The negative sanction is social isolation. The message quite clearly is: You are going to attend school. You can study one of two ways—either with your friends or by yourself. The choice is yours. When applied conscientiously, in-school suspension can be extremely effective.

The primary liability of in-school suspension is cost. The first two prerequisites of operating such a program are (1) a private room, and (2) someone qualified to supervise the room and offer academic assistance at least once every 15 minutes. The first two problems typically encountered by a staff considering the use of in-school suspension, of course, are a lack of space and supervisory personnel.

If adequate space and supervision are provided, the cost of operating the system for a year can be high indeed since it preempts the use of a much-needed room and adds at least part of a salary to the payroll. If adequate facilities and supervision are not provided, the school not only risks a lawsuit with strong legal precedents supporting the student's "right to treatment," but the school also risks doing a botch job, which will make the problem worse. The following conversation with a junior high school principal provided a timeless example of how not to do in-school suspension for cheap.

Principal: Hello, Dr. Jones. I'm glad you could come out here today to speak. Of course, we don't have any *serious* discipline problems at this school site. We have been using a discipline management program here for quite some time.
Me: Oh, really? What kinds of programs do you use?
Principal: Well, in-school suspension mainly.
Me: Oh, where do you hold it?
Principal: Well, there's this room down by the lunch area that used to be for storage.
Me: How big is it?
Principal: Oh, about 14×20.
Me: Who do you get to supervise it?
Principal: Are you kidding? We're short one secretary and three teachers today. I'm going to have to cover two periods. Besides, even at best, there's nothing in the budget to provide for supervision.
Me: How many kids are typically down there?
Principal: Oh, it depends. Maybe five or six. Sometimes up to eight or nine.

By doing a half-baked job of in-school suspension, the school had in fact designed an incentive system to set up five or six or sometimes eight or nine first-hours teachers to be faced with an intolerable discipline problem. The reinforcement error offered for outrageous behavior was the opportunity to be bounced to in-school suspension. Any junior high student who not only hates school but is also capable of being thoroughly obnoxious who cannot make it down to the in-school suspension room by 9:00 a.m. to join the gang is definitely off his form. Indeed, that is exactly how I found the system to be working when I later consulted to the school.

Saturday School   Saturday school as a means of dealing with cuts and tardies can not only prove effective in suppressing poor attendance, but it can often recoup a large portion of its cost by generating the state aid for attendance that was previously lost by cuts. Administrative costs are high, however, and the concept must have parental support. Thus, any school considering in investment in Saturday school should also consider an investment in teacher training as well as a more sophisticated school-site management system for preventing cuts and tardies in the first place.

Suspension   Suspension is fairly well understood by educators. Rarely is it seen as fixing anything permanently. More often it is simply regarded as the only thing left. Administrators generally appreciate as well the frequency with which the intent of suspension as a negative sanction is totally undermined by rewards available outside school. These rewards range from watching TV at home to hanging out at the local computer game palace to dealing a few hundred dollars worth of drugs on the street.

With suspension, as with most extra-large back-up responses, frequent experience with them reduces their effectiveness. They probably carry far more weight as a possibility for a fairly good kid than as a common reality for a chronic troublemaker.

Suspension depends heavily upon parental support and follow through consistent with the intent of the school. If, for example, caring parents express their concern to the child in an intelligent fashion and carefully monitor the child's doing schoolwork at home with no play until the normal school dismissal time, then suspension has a chance. It succeeds, however, more as a vehicle for communicating a need for involvement to parents than as a one-shot cure in its own right. To the extent that the parents do not cooperate, the method is crippled.

More Extreme Procedures

Delivering a Student to a Parent at Work   Dad or mom may well become more involved in supporting management effort when their little darling is delivered to them at the office or construction site at 10:00 a.m. with the accompanying message:

> Harold has done X, Y, and Z for the nth time today. For him to be readmitted into the public (private) educational system, we require that you bring Harold to school personally and stay for a conference on _____ day.

The need for such a radical cure may not be within the experience of most regular classroom teachers and may therefore sound extreme or bizarre. But it is not at all far-fetched for those who deal with delinquent students, court-referred students, juvenile-hall school students, or severely emotionally and behaviorally handicapped students. The objective of the intervention is parental involvement in an effort to help the child. The first response of the parents will probably be one of rage, and you have to be willing to take the heat.

Accompanying the Student to School   A sanction which ranks on a par with the preceding one for involving the parents of an incorrigible student, usually against their wills, involves the school's requiring that, as a condition for readmitting the student to school, the parent(s) must accompany the child throughout the school day, including sitting next to her at all times and riding next to her on the bus. The message conveyed by the school is that, since their child cannot or will not govern her own behavior at school, she will need adult supervision. Since the school has no staff for such purposes, the supervision will have to be supplied by the parents.

Naturally the student hates it, and the parent isn't too fond of it either. But as a last resort it can work.

Call the Police   Calling the police typically involves felony or assault although it may be used for theft or drugs. We are fast running out of options.

Expulsion   In a sense the issue of expulsion is the issue underlying all the more extreme back-up procedures. The question raised by their use is: Are we going to pull out all the stops to keep this student in public education, or are we going to call it off?

Administrative Commitment to "Hang Tough"

Extra-large back-up responses should be extremely rare and usually represent an attempt by school personnel to get some kind of responsible action from the parents of an incorrigible student. Often such a student would be in a special education class, but not often enough. Parents of such students sometimes covertly support the deviant behavior and usually say to the school, "It's your problem, not mine."

Before attempting to use a more extreme back-up procedure, the school administration should make several key decisions:

1 Are we going to take a united stand to keep this student in school? If a parent can eliminate the program with an angry call to the superintendent or a school board member, forget it.

2 Are we willing to upset our schedules for a while to see this thing through to the end?

3 Would we all feel better if the kid disappeared? Are we really going to see it through?

Obviously, commitment is the main ingredient. The education system is making its last stand to keep a student from washing out. Options available to teachers and administrators vary from state to state.

More extreme back-up options will provoke a mild to major family crisis as well as a confrontation with the school system in most cases, and such a confrontation can be quite stressful to everyone involved. Such a crisis, however, is sometimes the first painful step toward change. The cost is obviously high by this time, but the potential results may well justify the investment.

BACK-UP SYSTEMS IN RETROSPECT

A back-up system is a carefully designed hierarchy of negative sanctions which is designed as part of a larger management system to be used as infrequently as possible and for as brief a period of time as possible. A back-up system exists to put the lid on a nasty situation and to buy time for the implementation of more sophisticated, incentive-oriented interventions.

A back-up system in using negative sanctions is relatively dangerous because negative sanctions when misused can be destructive. A back-up system when abused is ultimately most destructive to the alienated students—the big disrupters who have long since expended any store of sympathy they may have had with their elders. They are the ones who are locked by reinforcement errors into a pattern of behavior that is ultimately maladaptive and self-defeating. They ultimately lose out on their education.

A successful back-up system is designed and implemented from the bottom up as well as from the top down. The heart of an effective back-up system is in the teacher's initial responses to unacceptable behavior, which renders its recurrence increasingly unlikely. Effective discipline must, of course, be supported from the top down, and administrators must play their role. But administrators can impose effective discipline on a school site neither through a series of policies and directives nor by the adoption of a tough hierarchy of consequences. Such a hierarchy, though perhaps part of an effective back-up system, is too little and too late. By itself it will never self-eliminate and it will always tend to overload. Yet it will, in a perverse and empty way, tend to please everybody by creating the illusion that something "tough" has been attempted without requiring real change from anybody.

As we get into large and extra-large back-up responses, we get the sense that we are now only picking up the pieces rather than preventing problems. Indeed, an analysis of the function of administrators in responding to crisis in this chapter in conjunction with the section "Why Back-Up Systems Fail" from Chapter 14 will probably face principals and vice principals with a clear look at a no-win situation that is only too familiar. If these descriptions have destroyed the illusion that administrators could and should carry out a major back-up role for classroom management on an hour-by-hour basis, then we are all better off. As long as teachers expect the impossible from the office and as long as administrators attempt to supply it, nobody will be in the market for either a serious reevaluation of discipline management or a serious training program for teachers and administrators.

CHAPTER 17

SCHOOL-SITE DISCIPLINE MANAGEMENT PROCEDURES

Discipline management at a school site can be divided into two domains:

1 *Classroom discipline management.* The management of discipline problems within the classroom where the teacher can structure the learning environment more or less unaided.

2 *School-site discipline management.* The management of discipline problems outside the classroom where the teacher is highly dependent on the collaboration and support of colleagues for success. School-site discipline management includes the management of noise in the halls, noise and mess in the cafeteria, cuts and tardies, yard duty, bus duty, smoking in the lavatory, and conduct in assemblies to name but a few.

Our analysis of discipline management in this volume has concerned itself primarily with classroom discipline management. The use of large and extra-large back-up responses, however, draws the teacher into collaboration with administrators to solve management problems that have now spilled out of the classroom. Since large and extra-large back-up responses delineate school-site policy rather than classroom policy, the topic of back-up systems places us at the point of transition between classroom discipline management and school-site discipline management.

The purpose of the present chapter is to flesh out to a greater degree the interface in discipline management between teachers and their colleagues, both fellow teachers and administrators. This topic, of course, is worthy of a separate volume, so the treatment here will be brief. It will focus only on selected topics that may help us to see key elements of the teacher's and administrator's roles in discipline management out-

This chapter was written in collaboration with Thomas H. DeBolt, Principal, Hermitage High School, Richmond, Virginia. In 1985, Hermitage High School was cited as one of the 100 top high schools in America by the U.S. Department of Education.

side the classroom. It is hoped that this discussion will help prevent some common miscalculations that often cripple a faculty's efforts to deal effectively with discipline problems at the school-site level.

WHERE TO BEGIN?

If we were to take a poll of teachers concerning the most pressing discipline problen.. at their school sites, most would top their list with discipline problems *outside* their classrooms.

- If you could just get rid of the noise in the halls, I could teach.
- It's the cafeteria! That's the most obnoxious part of my entire school day.
- The kids get into hassles with each other in the yard, and then they bring the bickering and fighting into the classroom.
- Attendance and tardies! That's what drives me up the wall! I don't get anything taught for the first 5 or 10 minutes just because I have to deal with all those pink slips and kids wandering in late!

And, just as with teachers, if we were to ask administrators what was needed to improve discipline at the school site, most would also cite discipline problems *outside* the classroom. Perhaps because of its apparent (and illusory) scope and simplicity, school-site discipline policy tends to be seen as the most direct route to an improved work environment by teachers and administrators who share the misplaced notion that major improvement can be achieved by mandates in conjunction with more severe negative sanctions for offending students.

In fact, beginning to improve the discipline at a school site by focusing on school-site discipline policy—regardless of its degree of sophistication—rather than classroom management is a tactical choice that usually produces meager results because:

1 Faculty consensus and commitment are required to deal with most problems of school-site management.

2 *Consensus* as to what to do and how to do it and *commitment* from everyone to follow through are extremely hard to reach with an untrained faculty. See how many faculty meetings you can waste discussing the simple issue of who is responsible for the noise in the halls.

3 Successful management of behavior outside the classroom does not increase *time on task* and learning within the classroom nearly as dramatically as does classroom management.

4 Success with classroom management reduces teacher *stress* more than does success with management outside the classroom.

5 Many problems outside the classroom can be managed through the extension of classroom management programs such as responsibility training (see Chapter 9). Thus, it is usually more cost-effective to begin within the classroom.

6 Unless sophisticated classroom management programs are in place which can deal effectively with most severe or recurring behavior problems, administrators' time will be consumed operating relatively simplistic back-up programs based on punition which do not self-eliminate. Such programs consume much of the time and energy needed for effective school-site leadership while structuring an adversarial relationship between administrators and chronic troublemakers.

As a majority of teachers on a faculty become trained in the use of effective classroom management techniques, however, a consensus grows regarding:

• *Method.* The faculty now shares a common language and technology for talking about and dealing with management problems. Methodological sophistication produces a shared understanding of which method is best for which problem.

• *Confidence.* Once success has been experienced in classroom management as a result of affordable methods, a confidence grows among trained teachers that management problems outside the classroom can be dealt with successfully and straightforwardly. In fact, the faculty gets impatient to collaborate in order to eliminate chronic school-site headaches.

• *Responsibility.* Trained teachers now know what the office can do for them and what it cannot do for them. And they know what management options are available to administrators as well as the cost. If administrators want to deal with the issue of bouncing, for example, they can usually muster faculty support for a response-cost program to deal with it (see Chapter 16) rather than precipitating faculty resentment. And if the administration needs full faculty involvement and support in developing new procedures, teachers are more likely to work together out of enlightened self-interest since they have no illusions about the cost of not working together.

As a faculty reaches a shared, well-developed understanding of discipline management, they will come to appreciate more how dependent they are on each other for success outside the classroom. With confidence up and blaming and defensiveness down, a faculty, with some guidance, can grow to accept the single, simple principle which underlies any successful attempt to implement improved school-site behavioral standards: *Every student belongs to every teacher all the time.*

Without this cohesion plus a well-developed management plan which involves faculty and administration working together in each management situation, a school site is usually doomed to repeat the errors of the past. Weak faculty members abdicate responsibility for management while demanding continual support from the administration, and the rest of the faculty concurs. Administrators respond with policy mandates while squandering their time and energy accomplishing very little in the office (see Chapter 16), and everyone agrees that kids have certainly changed for the worse over the years.

ADEQUATE STRUCTURE PREVENTS EXPENSIVE REMEDIATION

School-site discipline management procedures, like classroom rules, routines, and standards, describe the "how to" of carrying out basic jobs at the school site. As with rules, routines, and standards within the classroom (see Chapters 3 and 4), school-site discipline management procedures are the *preventive medicine* of discipline management for student behaviors outside the classroom. If done properly, school-site discipline management will *prevent* much of the use of the school site's back-up system.

Whereas classroom rules, routines, and standards focus on the responsibilities of *students* within the classroom, school-site discipline management procedures focus on the responsibilities of the *faculty*. As with classroom structure, however, school-site structure is often designed and implemented on a "quick and dirty" basis. In order to succeed, school-site discipline management procedures and responsibilities that have been carefully organized and practiced need to be detailed and shared.

Instituting school-site discipline management procedures puts into bold relief a dimension of the principal's role as instructional leader that is rarely appreciated. In developing and implementing school-site management procedures, the principal's role in relation to the faculty is highly analogous to the teacher's role in relation to their students in classroom discipline management. In the teacher/leader role it is the principal's responsibility to establish the priority of working together to carry out basic routines involving the student body, to set time aside for procedural development and values clarification, and to teach the performance of the various procedures as a series of structured lessons.

As with classroom management, the ownership of the values, rules, and procedures of school-site discipline management will be much greater if the people responsible for implementing them are enfranchised in the process of development. School-site leadership, therefore, puts a premium on skills of consensus building and team building—higher level facilitation and negotiation skills that are not always present in the skill repertoire of the principal. To the extent that these skills are absent, mandates will be substituted for rule building, obedience will be substituted for ownership, and the irresponsible behavior of individuals will be substituted for faculty cohesiveness.

SAMPLE PROCEDURES

What are some successful procedures for school-site discipline management? Are they elaborate, subtle, and tricky? Quite to the contrary, they tend to be simple, straightforward, and commonsensical. However, they often fly in the face of existing practice. Above all they require a clear and effective plan and the expenditure of effort by everyone to achieve effective supervision as a means of preventing student unruliness.

We will examine several management settings in order to observe effective school-site management up close. The pattern of school-site faculty and administrative cohesiveness will emerge quite naturally for the reader as it did for me in observing many school sites and talking with their administrators and teachers over the years. We will look primarily at secondary schools since problems of school-site discipline management are more complex and more acute there. We will look at elementary schools separately when the nature of implementation changes form, but for the most part what works at the secondary level works at the elementary level.

We will begin with all-school assemblies at a high school. Such assemblies have grown so disorderly in recent decades that they have been discontinued altogether in many school sites. Principals and teachers in these schools throw up their hands at the idea of reinstituting that obnoxious ritual mindful of the rowdiness that caused such "cultural events" to be discontinued. A study of successful all-school assemblies, however, provides a paradigm of effective school-site discipline management and faculty cohesiveness.

All-School Assemblies

> I can usually tell within 2 minutes after I enter a high school who runs the place. I simply stop by the boys' lav on the way to the office and take a look around—especially at the floor. If it is clean, I know that the adults run the school. If it is dirty and there are cigarette butts, I know the kids run the school.

This casual but revealing remark was made by a member of a theater group that frequently performs at all-school assemblies in high schools throughout the southeastern United States. Litter and cigarette butts on the lavatory floor mean a long, difficult afternoon in front on an unappreciative audience.

In high schools where all-school assemblies have fallen into disrepute, teachers will often fight the idea of having all-school assemblies because of the rowdiness. "Let's forget the whole thing" is, however, a decision that robs students of many valuable learning experiences. The overriding rationale for having all-school assemblies is that you can do things in an assembly that you cannot do in the classroom. Musicals, theater, special speakers, and presentations that are too large and expensive for small groups can only be presented in assemblies. And learning how to behave in an assembly is as much a part of the students' socialization as is learning how to behave in a classroom.

All-school assemblies, like any large group gathering of students, warrants the coordinated effort of administrators and the entire faculty because of the sheer numbers of students needing supervision. A common assumption among faculties who have severe management problems with all-school assemblies is the notion that managing large-group settings is not part of their job. Such an assumption turns a blind eye to the fact that the students are in the building and, by definition, under supervision of the staff. In schools where all-school assemblies have degenerated into blatant rowdiness, typically few teachers and administrators are on the scene managing the situation. Most have dumped the kids and left for the lounge. So, the kids raise hell, predictably. Rowdiness in unsupervised large group settings is not a strange happening among adolescents. What is strange is the lack of adequate adult supervision.

The following procedures for managing an all-school assembly are not etched in stone. They simply add up to the success of some exceptional high schools with which I have worked. It is hoped that these guidelines can provide direction to faculties as they work out the details at their various school sites. Take these seven guidelines as an example rather than as a prescription, but keep in mind that compromises which omit basic pieces of the puzzle may carry a disproportionate cost in terms of ensuing management problems.

1 *High-Quality Programs with Variety.* Having a thousand students watch a 1-hour presentation is 1000 hours of time on task. The program should be worth the time. And since you cannot please everyone, variety is the spice of life.

2 *Seating According to a Plan. Absolutely avoid open seating.* Anonymous seating produces a zoo in which various groups and cliques (the bikers, the jocks, the freaks, the four-wheelers, the greasers, and the "students") sit together and show off for each other through heckling and outrageous behavior. Instead, seating is by *small groups* supervised and monitored by a regular teacher (usually the homeroom teacher or the first period teacher).

3 *Teachers Responsible for Supervision.* Teachers are responsible for their students' behavior in an assembly just as they are in the classroom. Teachers sit where they can see all their students. Thus, if a teacher has rows six through nine, the teacher sits in row nine where she or he can watch the students. If someone is out of line, the teacher sends a message down the row and deals with the behavior afterwards. Teachers are also responsible for making sure the troublemakers are not sitting next to each other. In some cases the teacher may even have a seating plan for assemblies with specific students sitting next to the teacher. In addition, teachers are responsible for getting their students quiet as they enter the auditorium and are seated.

4 *Clear Expectations.* Behavior appropriate to all-school assemblies should be clearly reviewed and discussed at the beginning of the semester, and basic rules should be reviewed before each assembly.

5 *Consistent Beginning Format.* The principal opens the assembly in an upbeat fashion, typically sharing some form of good news with the student body. It is the principal's responsibility to make sure that everything is "cool" before the assembly proceeds. Movement is extremely valuable to the principal at this time, and a lavaliere microphone is nearly a necessity. The principal is, in effect, limit-setting on the wing as he or she walks part way up the aisles in order to address the students personally. He or she does not stand on the stage behind a podium like a statue. When the tone of the assembly has been set, the principal turns the microphone over to the student-body president, who introduces the assembly program.

6 *Dismissal by Plan.* Management of the student body by small groups continues through dismissal. Dismissing everyone at once is an invitation to chaos. Typically the assembly is dismissed by rows or by teachers' names so that only three or four classrooms are standing to leave at any one time.

7 *Fixed Time Frame.* The next period of the school day should start immediately after the assembly with attendance and tardies strictly monitored. A clear focus on immediately getting back to work greatly reduces dawdling, tardies, cuts, and a "school's out" attitude that makes for rowdiness in the halls.

Graduation ceremonies are simply all-school assemblies to which the parents are invited. Although graduation has become an outrageous "happening" at many schools in recent years, the guidelines stated above plus a few special rules should infuse the proceedings with an appropriate degree of orderliness. Special rules for graduation include:

1 *No babies.* To be more specific, no one under 4 years of age.

2 *Admission by ticket only.* Unless admission is by ticket only, the school is leaving itself wide open for the staging of a carnival rather than a graduation ceremony. Anyone who cares to show up does so in any imaginable condition. Boyfriends and girlfriends from different school sites and different parts of town drop in along with a few local bikers, drunk uncle Barney, and a bunch of drop-outs complete with six-packs. Someone can be counted on to yell at the most inappropriate moment, "Fairfield sucks!" (this is Fairfield's graduation), or "Central High is number one!" (Fairfield lost to Central in the big game). If the administration is lucky, the fights will take place *under* the grandstands.

3 *Careful rehearsal.* In many schools, it is amazing that people are simply told to show up. In order to avoid the obvious, rules and procedures need to be clarified with students in conjunction with several rehearsals, which include a rehearsal of checking in and checking out gowns and caps.

4 *All faculty and administrators help with supervision.* Graduation is a school function, not an optional event. If everybody helps, there may be one supervisor for every twenty to twenty-five students. As usual, as in any all-school assembly, seating and supervision will be by small groups with a faculty member responsible for each group of students.

Halls and Lavatories

School-site discipline management procedures in the halls and lavatories are related issues which focus on passing between classes in a departmentalized setting. Although many highly specific procedures may be instituted at any given school site, the following general guidelines convey the tone and nature of effective supervision.

Monitoring the Halls   Monitoring the halls is a classic example of management by walking around—the administrative equivalent of limit-setting on the wing. Halls need to be monitored at all times, and all administrators and teachers need to help. The following policies give a rough outline of a successful management procedure.

1 Two teachers are on hall duty during every period.

2 Administrators are in the halls frequently, ready to deal with whatever they find (see Chapter 16).

3 Additional teachers and administrators are in the hall while students are passing between classes.

4 No student is in the hall without a pass during class periods.

5 Hall passes are written so that they are not easy to issue (a response-cost management system for issuing hall passes).

6 Teachers keep a log of hall passes in each class (including the time of going and returning) as a check against abuse of the hall pass privilege (if there is such a thing as hall passes at the school site).

Monitoring the Lavatories   As the member of the theater troupe was well aware, lavatories provide a most sensitive indicator of who runs the school building. If adults stay out of the lavatory, it belongs to the students. If it belongs to the students, then the lavatory is the logical place to smoke, deface property, deal drugs, have fights, and get outrageous. Perhaps as important, a lack of adult supervision establishes the precedent by default that students can do what they please on school property regardless of what the rules say. The following guidelines are designed to make the lavatory a part of the school that is managed just as any other part:

1 Faculty members on hall duty spot-check each lavatory repeatedly during each class period as do administrators who are out and about.

2 Faculty members have specific assignments for monitoring lavatories during breaks.

The objective of supervision of the lavatories, like all management of large group gatherings outside class, is to provide an adult presence in a systematic and predictable fashion to make students accountable for their behaviors. The goal is to keep the "bad-ass" 5 percent of the student body from pulling the "turkey" 15 percent into taking over the place. The vast majority of the student body will be most grateful for the faculty assuming its proper leadership role since it is no fun to be intimidated as the price of going to the bathroom.

Managing Behavior in the Cafeteria

At the secondary level management of behavior in the cafeteria is, for the most part, a variation on the theme of management by walking around, monitoring by moving continuously among the students, conversing with them comfortably and keeping an eye on things. As always, the key ingredient is the presence of an adult for purposes of accountability within a pleasant context.

The open seating and free conversation of the cafeteria make a "hang loose" attitude among adults most appropriate. Diplomacy is the key as opposed to an authoritarian attitude. Effective cafeteria monitors typically know the students by name, engage in informal conversation and kidding with them, are regarded by the students as a friend, and deal with minor problems through physical proximity and simple prompts which are often nonverbal. In the case of a confrontation, if monitors can simply remember the golden rule of limit-setting (when in doubt do nothing), and if they relax, shut up, retain eye contact, and simply wait after having given a prompt, the student will usually fold rather than continue the incident.

Supervision of the cafeteria at the elementary level follows the same principles as at the secondary level with the exception that it has a larger element of instruction concerning appropriate cafeteria behavior—especially in the primary grades. Thus, teachers typically accompany their young students to the cafeteria and eat with them.

Many teachers find this notion of eating with their students a noxious intrusion into their free lunch period, but there is no quick, easy, and effortless way to train students to use good manners and clean up after themselves. If the teachers pay their dues up front, however, by carefully supervising lunchroom behavior early in the school year, the ratio of monitors to students can be thinned as good eating habits and good cleanup habits become established. Lunchroom monitors hired from the community can be gradually substituted for the teacher's supervision in many cases so that the teachers can eventually have their free lunch period.

The efforts of the faculty in behavior management in the cafeteria must be matched by the administration, particularly at the elementary level. The one major correlate that I find between a trouble-free cafeteria and administrator behavior as I travel is that the principal is present in the cafeteria. Many principals will throw up their hands in revulsion on first hearing this news, but these are the same principals who describe their cafeteria as a zoo—as though the situation were both natural and irremediable. In well-managed cafeterias the principal typically talks with the students as they enter, kidding them and conversing with them by name, and walks among the tables during lunch giving praise and gentle reminders.

An active administrator role during the lunch period pays dividends not only with the student body but with the faculty as well. Help by the administrator in cafeteria supervision helps free teachers from cafeteria monitoring so that they can have their free lunch period earlier in the school year. In this way the principal is seen as paying his or her dues with a direct benefit to the faculty for which the teachers are usually quite grateful.

Supervision of the Yard and/or Playground

At both the secondary and elementary levels most fights take place on the playground as does most intimidation, extortion, and other assorted maladies. As in the supervision of all other large group settings, the main tool still seems to be responsible adult supervision and management by walking around. The administrators, in particular, pay their dues by supervising the yard or quad at the junior high or high school, but their efforts need to be supplemented by teachers who have specific supervisory assignments.

The behavior of the yard supervisors should be low key as it is in the cafeteria, with a maximal use of body and a minimal use of mouth for dealing with unpleasant situations. As in any form of supervision, accountability is the key objective and, consequently, knowing the students by name is critical. For this reason alone, the hiring of outside personnel for supervisory duties can help only up to a point. It does little good, for example, to hear from a playground monitor at an elementary school:

> Some big kid from the fourth or fifth grade punched out one of the little kids and took his ball. I don't know who it was, but he had sandy brown hair.

If the playground supervisors know the students by name, however, so that strict accountability for inappropriate behavior is a possibility, then management can often be a simple extension of the homeroom teacher's responsibility training program (see Chapter 10). The playground supervisor may wish to "bench" the student temporarily, but a note routed promptly to the teacher after recess can be translated into a loss of PAT which encourages the peer group to set limits on their own behavior during play.

A more difficult problem at the secondary level on some campuses is verbal abuse, verbal threat, and physical threat to faculty who attempt to intervene in an unacceptable situation. Teachers who have not been trained in the skills of limit-setting will tend to be confrontational when dealing with outrageous behavior. They may as well wear a sign on their back that says "I'm a jerk," or "crucify me."

> Kid, what's your name!
> George Washington.
> Oh, yeah? Listen, you can't talk to me that way!
> I just did.

It is downhill from there, and the macho teacher is probably in for more abuse if he continues to up the ante with pheasant posturing. Often a heavyhanded teacher turns a relatively innocuous situation into a painful if not dangerous one. Usually physical proximity, relaxation, a respectful prompt, eye contact, and closed mouth will produce the desired result. If, however, a student should threaten the adult, the faculty member or administrator must make a tactical decision. Is it a bluff or is this for real? Am I in physical danger? Usually the cardinal rule of "when in doubt do nothing" will provide the best rule for action in the heat of the moment—or inaction as the case might be. Should the situation become dangerous, the adult simply excuses him- or herself respectfully and leaves peaceably. It is time to get help.

PLANS, PRIORITIES, AND LOGISTICS

Cohesiveness and Commitment

Many attempts to manage behavior fail owing to the simple lack of a plan. An all-school assembly with open seating is a classic example of a large group gathering without a plan of management. It therefore becomes mismanagement by nonmanagement. The absence of continual supervision of the lavatories and halls is another common example. Unless there is a specific, highly detailed plan with well-understood assignments for all administrators and faculty members, there is no reason to expect a large gathering of young people to be anything but a picnic.

Quite often a faculty's first experience with a well-planned group activity comes as something of a revelation. As one teacher commented to me regarding the school fire drill:

> Our fire drills were always the same, a mass of confusion. The kids would be told how to walk through the halls and where to meet outside the buildings. But when the bell rang, we always ended up with the whole student body milling around on the playground. Following training I decided, as you had suggested, to treat the fire drill as I would any other structured lesson with explanation, modeling, and practice. I took my students through a dry run complete with the verbal commands that I would be giving, walking through the halls properly, finding the place where we are to line up outdoors, and reentering the building. Sure enough, when we had the fire drill, it all went according to plan. It was embarrassingly straightforward. Students weren't unruly at all once they knew exactly what to do, especially with me being there the whole time.

Yet the notion of a plan carries with it the notion of faculty commitment to carrying out the plan. It must be an important faculty activity which is acknowledged by everyone and shared by everyone. Consensus and commitment are the ingredients by which school-site discipline management lives or dies.

As in all discipline management, we are up against a classic case of "pay me now or pay me later." A faculty that does not want to be bothered by management will be bothered by an endless stream of obnoxious behavior. The resulting reliance on enforcement rather than prevention will be more stressful and costly in the long run—a series of failure-laden run-ins with lippy kids convincing many on the faculty that discipline management outside the classroom is rightfully somebody else's job. When faculty and administration share this perception they will simply pass mandates directly to the students with no meaningful plan of implementation whatsoever. Students, in turn, frequently screw up—as is predictable in lieu of structures that spell success—while adults and young people back ever deeper into mutual resentment.

As I talk with teachers and administrators about effective school-site discipline management, I get two distinctly different types of responses—a bimodal split with not much in between.

The *first* response, typically given by faculty and administrators at effective school sites, is: Of course! That's obvious. The *second* response is: Are you kidding? You're out of your mind if you think we are going to go to that kind of trouble. What goes on outside my classroom is not my problem. Faculties with the second attitude are, predictably enough, the faculties that are suffering most from obnoxious and unruly behavior.

A lack of faculty cohesion is most commonly evident in a simple unwillingness of faculty members to deal with problems outside their classrooms. I have worked with high schools, for example, who had as many as forty hall monitors on salary only to find out that this massive expenditure was to no avail. Hall monitors simply became plainclothes Keystone Cops who provided the student body with a new indoor sport while issuing pink slips that were never processed in the office. Even the good students took great delight in sneaking past the hall monitors to get to their lockers that were off limits during their lunch breaks. At this same school site I saw, as mentioned earlier, teachers bounce students out of their classrooms for misconduct and then, minutes later, open their doors to criticize the hall monitor for the noise being made by the kids they had just bounced.

At another school site the faculty fretted about profanity toward faculty members and the riding of bicycles and skateboards on campus when, in fact, almost nobody was willing to come out of the classroom to do anything about it. They wanted a foolproof school policy—namely, a back-up system that would give the kids a good reason to shape up. Harsh measures were proposed which were always strangely separated from any meaningful system of supervision and accountability. The predictable result, I attempted to point out, would be an increasing number of suspensions with no noticeable impact on student behavior.

When faculty-administrative cohesiveness deteriorates past a certain point, the few teachers who are willing to take responsibility for school-site management are finally made to feel like fools. "Why should I be the only one to bust my behind around here when no one else cares?" is a common complaint of the effective teacher. Or, as one disillusioned teacher confided:

> I quit caring when I found a student vandalizing a drinking fountain one day while I was walking to the office during my break. I stopped to deal with the incident. It was obviously

vandalism because the drinking fountain was halfway out of the wall and the kid was giving me lip. The vice principal walked around the corner, looked at me, and just kept walking. I thought to myself, "What do you need, a neon sign on the wall that flashes the word 'dummy'?" That's the last time I ever personally intervened in a discipline situation outside of my classroom. If the administration can pretend that they don't see, so can I. I'm not going to be the only one out on a limb.

If the planning and time commitment necessary for effective school-site discipline management strike the faculty as outrageous, chances are that this very perception is a clear-cut symptom of the low faculty morale that comes from poor school-site leadership. Sometimes we simply have to acknowledge that a social institution is moribund. It will not change without a massive infusion of help.

The Logistics of Success   All the plans and good intentions in the world will eventually fail if they are at cross purposes with logistical realities. A great many high school districts, for example, have negotiated themselves into a six-period day with five teaching periods and one prep period. What seemed to slip away without anyone's noticing it was a duty period in the teacher's schedule which provides the manpower for school-site discipline management. Teachers often regard this as some kind of negotiated victory, whereas it usually represents their having shot themselves in the foot. If the school district hires outside personnel to man the cafeterias and halls, the money siphoned away for such salaries will be unavailable for teachers' salaries. And, if additional personnel are not hired, the school goes unmanaged and deteriorates into a depressing place to work. Added to this, adequate administrative staff to coordinate the supervisory effort has also been cut by many school boards in the belief that somehow a school site with over 1000 young people and tens of thousands of square feet can be managed by two or three executives.

Where there is no manpower there is no management, and where there is no time there is no management. If local educators and school boards express their priorities through such self-defeating scheduling and staffing procedures, then they may as well also recognize that effective schools are for them simply not worth the price.

OVERVIEW

The more that I have examined and compared the school-site management policies of effective schools, the more impressed I have become by how simple, clear, straightforward, and similar they all are. There is no quick cure or free lunch through policy or mandate. There is no discipline code or increase in the severity of punishment that can bring order out of chaos. Nor is there any substitute for faculty cohesiveness and shared responsibility in the business of operating every aspect of school-site life. Rather, there is the unavoidable necessity of clear, sensible plans conscientiously carried out.

In the language of operant conditioning, effective school-site discipline management procedures are primarily a matter of stimulus control rather than contingency management. It focuses on structure versus consequences, prevention versus remediation, effective procedure versus crisis response, faculty cohesion versus edict. It views policy as proper process rather than ultimate consequences. Effective school-site discipline management, therefore, is one of the most important ways in which a school site systematically avoids the built-in shortcomings and abuses of its own back-up system so carefully described in the preceding three chapters. It is the principal's and vice principal's contribution to their own job satisfaction—the chance to get out of the crisis mode and *lead*.

Most effective school-site management procedures are direct analogs of classroom management procedures. The principal's role is highly analogous to the teacher's role in the clarification of expectations with their faculty, the continual supervision of the faculty, and the follow through that is needed to make rules into realities. The principal is, in effect, the teacher of teachers when it comes to school-site discipline management.

The specific skills of management are also analogous from classroom to school site. The most common management technique is limit-setting on the wing—an adult presence which constantly monitors student performance and unobtrusively enforces rules through management by walking around (MBWA). Most effect school-site management, like most effective classroom management, is low key, unobtrusive, warm, personal, and continuous—a by-product of the physical proximity, accountability, and relationship building that comes from effective supervision.

The use of incentive systems on a schoolwide basis, however, is in its infancy relative to its use in the classroom. There is a scanty research literature on school-site incentives for such things as attendance, picking up trash, noise in the cafeteria, etc. But the state of the art would have to be categorized as rudimentary. The development of incentives for use in large group gatherings will, it is hoped, develop in coming years so that it approaches the cost efficiency of responsibility training in the classroom.

SECTION **SIX**

SYNTHESIS

CHAPTER 18

DISCIPLINE MANAGEMENT AS AN INTEGRATED SYSTEM

Positive Classroom Discipline has described in considerable detail a series of management procedures for dealing with classroom disruptions of almost any shape and size. These procedures have been presented as an integrated management system: a technology based on fundaments which are simple, powerful, and adaptable to the wide range of management dilemmas that characterize a typical day in the classroom. The present chapter attempts to describe more fully the interrelationships between the parts of positive classroom discipline, a careful organization of fundamental skills and procedures rather than a "bag of tricks."

THE BAG OF TRICKS

The way teachers talk about solving discipline problems reveals much about our traditional frame of reference for discipline management.

- What do you do when a student . . .?
- That's a neat idea. I can add that to my bag of tricks!
- Just show me briefly how it's done.

These statements, so common to my ears after years of teacher training, reveal with elegant simplicity the dominant notion held by most educators about how classroom management techniques are mastered.

- A discipline technique is a reaction to a problem situation.
- The management of discipline consists of the collection of as many remedies for as many problem situations as possible. You are better off the bigger your bag of tricks.

• Techniques are simple notions about what to do that can be quickly and easily conveyed by a few words or a quick demonstration.

Such a simplistic view of discipline dooms teachers to be perpetually overwhelmed by the complexity of the task. A roomful of students will always have more tricks up their sleeves than you will have in your bag of tricks. In a week in the classroom any teacher will be faced with a thousand "what do you do if . . .?" situations. Even if the prescriptions existed, who could learn them all and keep them all straight?

As the years go by, I have developed an increasing aversion to the term "bag of tricks." It characterizes the management of discipline as a hodgepodge of home remedies—a catch-as-catch-can collection of cures for the dilemmas of everyday life in the classroom. When teachers refer to their bag of tricks, they acknowledge that they are out there winging it with anything that they have been able to beg, borrow, or steal over the years.

Unfortunately the term bag of tricks describes rather accurately the lack of any systematic methodology for discipline management in education. Bag of tricks represents to me the antithesis of a modern profession with an empirically based technology of professional practice. A professional, most simply, is a person with highly specialized skills, skills taking years to master which equip that person to do a difficult job that is far beyond the capability of untrained laypeople. For having these much-needed and difficult-to-master skills, professionals charge and receive a high price for their services. Teachers refer to each other as professionals, but the general public more frequently thinks of teaching as glorified baby-sitting. Until teachers are masters of a repertoire of specialized, professional-level management skills that clearly set their competencies apart from those of the average parent, teachers will be neither regarded highly nor paid highly by the general public.

Rather than being a bewildering array of home remedies, Positive Classroom Discipline clarifies fundamental vectors of management and defines high level yet basic professional skills and competencies. From this organization of skills and competencies comes the ability to choose between potent management options on the basis of cost-effectiveness rather than perpetually running through the bag of tricks for yet another quick cure or bail-out.

LEVELS OF MANAGEMENT

Differential Reinforcement

Most effective behavior management programs must deal with *pairs* of behaviors. You must systematically strengthen the behavior you want while systematically weakening the competing behaviors that you do not want. A discipline program, for example, should not only eliminate problem behavior, but it should also systematically build the positive behaviors that you want to replace the problems. If problem behaviors are simply eliminated, whatever replaces them will be left to chance. It could be dawdling, or it could be another discipline problem.

Discipline management, therefore, is more appropriately viewed not as the simple suppression of problems but rather as the differential reinforcement of appropriate behaviors, often in conjunction with suppression of the problem. Since most problem behaviors in the classroom are self-rewarding, some suppression is usually needed to eliminate the reinforcement generated by the problem itself, which then competes with the differential reinforcement of appropriate behavior.

Each level of discipline management, therefore, should ideally have both reward and penalty components. The more explicit the reward component, the more predictably positive will be the outcome of an intervention.

The Three-Tiered Management System

Positive Classroom Discipline is composed of three different management methodologies which are integrated to form a three-tier approach to discipline management.

- Limit-setting
- Incentive systems
- Back-up systems

Each of these three methodologies, however, can be properly understood only within the context of the differential reinforcement of appropriate behavior.

Limit-Setting   Limit-setting is mild social punishment, and as such it is incomplete. For limit-setting to be in balance, there must be reward. The reward would, of course, be social reward—the positive social interactions between teacher and student that create an informal incentive system. The natural counterpart of limit-setting, therefore, is relationship. Together, *limit-setting* and *relationship building* form a tier of the management system which we might best describe as the *interpersonal-interactive* level of management.

In the interpersonal-interactive level all sanctions, both positive and negative, are delivered as part of the fleeting interpersonal interactions between teacher and student. The teacher's success at the interpersonal-interactional level depends on the *social competence* of the teacher—his or her accurate assessment of interpersonal situations and spontaneous and effective use of a broad range of social skills and emotions with students of all kinds moment by moment throughout the day.

The effective juxtaposition of positive and negative sanctions during the social exchanges of teacher and student requires a much higher level of precision than we have any right to expect from an untrained teacher. And they require the consistently supportive and successful helping interactions to be described in *Positive Classroom Instruction*.

Incentive Systems   Incentive systems make the exchange of positive and negative sanctions prearranged, explicit, concrete, and public. It is the formalized counterpart of the interpersonal-interactive level of management with positive and negative sanctions being juxtaposed in an analogous fashion.

Incentive systems can be so formalized as to be written in the form of a contract. "Contingency contracting" is a type of individualized behavior modification program in which the quid pro quo of the behavioral exchange is both negotiated and set down in writing. Incentives in business and industry are typically negotiated and written down in the form of a contract, but in education the cost of the negotiation and the giving of individualized reinforcement limits their use to special settings in most cases.

With responsibility training the only thing that may need to be written down is the tally of accumulated PAT. This simple tally, however, is a kind of written contract that keeps the system honest by making the size of the reward accurate (fair) and public. It is axiomatic in parent and teacher training that the first person to break a contract between adult and child is almost always the adult who fails to deliver the agreed-upon reward. It is often innocent: for example, losing track of time while teaching so that there is no time left for PAT. A public record, however, will almost always ensure that PAT happens on schedule. The class will see to that.

One might, therefore, consider incentive systems as the *incentive-contractual* level of management. Training in the proper use of incentives can be more "bookish" than training at the interpersonal-interactive level. Yet a basic technical understanding of incentive systems is indispensable for teachers, along with a thorough familiarity with the mechanics of some of the more important classroom management procedures. Social skills for implementing responsibility training focus primarily on relaxation and the issue of having fun—especially fun with learning.

Back-up Systems   Back-up systems break the pattern of differential reinforcement. Back-up responses are negative sanctions, and the reinforcement of appropriate behavior is left to chance.

The smaller the back-up responses, the more likely it is that differential reinforcement will take place. In the classroom of a nurturant teacher, for example, the use of a small back-up response might be juxtaposed and balanced with warmth and approval for good behavior. Relationship therefore provides the balance for small back-up responses just as it does for limit-setting.

The larger the negative sanction, however, the more difficult it will be to offset penalty with reward. Thus the higher up the back-up system you go, the more unbalanced the management system will become. The more unbalanced the system, the more likely you will be to generate resentment, resistance, and revenge.

Teachers frequently use threat of impending punition, such as the loss of a privilege, to "control" their students.

> All right, class. If you don't settle down and take your seats right now, we are going *nowhere* when the recess bell rings! Do you understand!

Almost any social exchange between people creates some kind of incentive system. When threat and loss of privilege are used by themselves, however, they typically signal a teacher who is off-balance and struggling to regain control of a situation that is unraveling. Such attempts at management are shortsighted, and their results are short-lived. Without clear differential reinforcement of appropriate behavior, there is no systematic behavior building, and no answer to the question, "Why should I?" that would produce lasting cooperation. Incentive systems based on punition alone are incentive systems gone awry—stripped of their incentive function. To avoid confusion

TABLE 18-1
LEVELS OF DISCIPLINE MANAGEMENT

---

1. Interpersonal-interactive

+ Informal incentive systems (relationship which includes positive instructional inter-actions)
- Limit-setting

2. Incentive-contractual (formal incentive systems)

A. Simple incentive systems
B. Complex incentive systems
+ Reward/bonus
- Penalty

3. Back-up and containment

Punishment, suppression (disincentive systems—penalty only)
+ (Nothing)
- Negative sanctions

---

we will refer to such unbalanced contingency exchanges which focus on penalty alone as "disincentive systems."

Back-up systems, especially those negative sanctions going beyond the relatively innocuous exchanges of small back-up responses, are exercises in disincentive management. The lack of differential reinforcement dooms them to rarely self-eliminate if used repetitively since there is no systematic mechanism to build cooperation and thereby reduce the ongoing reliance on negative sanctions.

Medium back-up responses are an in-between zone in which a nurturant teacher with an effective classroom incentive program can still match penalty with reward to an acceptable degree. A less nurturing teacher who has established little relationship with his or her students will already be "in the hole." By the time large back-up responses are being used with a student on a regular basis, the management system will most likely have become counterproductive.

The differential reinforcement for back-up responses will in most cases have been borrowed or "bootlegged" from level 1 or level 2 (see Table 18-1). To the extent that you use your back-up system, therefore, you are living on credit. We may only hope that you have plenty of relationship "money in the bank" and that you draw out no more than you have put in. The economics of cooperation, therefore, dictate that you cannot live permanently within your back-up system. You may only visit while you buy time to develop a balanced, reward-based management system.

To a greater or lesser degree the decision to use negative sanctions signals the boundary between generating cooperation and achieving containment at any cost. The most appropriate term for level 3 of discipline management might, therefore, be *back-up and containment* level of management.

The three levels of management might be characterized as shown in Table 18-1.

DEALING WITH ESCALATION

Avoiding Negative Sanctions

In a sense *positive classroom discipline* can be divided into only two parts:

1 Everything you can possibly do to avoid the use of your back-up system
2 Back-up systems

This division of positive classroom discipline accurately reflects the ambivalence and therefore the caution that any educator should have toward the use of negative sanctions in management. The repeated use of negative sanctions in discipline management places all teachers, who continually need the students' cooperation in both behaving properly and learning, into double jeopardy. One of the sad but predictable ironies of discipline management is that the more teachers rely on their back-up system for managing discipline, the less likely they are to effectively build relationship. Not only does the repeated use of negative sanctions kill relationship, but people who naturally favor punition also tend, obviously, to value relationship less and to build and preserve it less. Thus, as negative sanctions are used more often, balance becomes less likely and student resentment overwhelms the will to cooperate.

Most people, however, assume that discipline means punishment and that a bigger discipline problem deserves a bigger punishment. Never mind that the vast majority of the severe discipline problems at any school site are generated by that small minority of the student body that has been the recipient of the largest negative sanctions. Never mind that this pattern perpetuates itself year after year. If something is not working, more of the same must be the cure.

Saving the Loser

The progression in the management of discipline problems from mild negative sanctions for common disruptions to a preference for positive sanctions for extreme disruptions was as much a product of the school of hard knocks as it was a result of theory or values. Classrooms full of emotionally, behaviorally, and learning-handicapped teenagers comprised the crucible in which the ideas of Positive Classroom Discipline were formed.

With regular elementary and secondary students and with behaviorally handicapped elementary students we learned about the incredible power of limit-setting. With behaviorally handicapped secondary students we learned that limit-setting was not enough, even with both the back-up of negative sanctions and the aid of individualized incentive programs. We learned that most alienated teenagers have a life or death commitment to winning any battle for behavioral control waged by adult authorities. In addition, they possess the jaded cockiness of a seasoned veteran in matters of discipline that produces a willingness to "high roll" in the classroom discipline poker game until the stakes are driven to dizzying heights. We learned that we would either come to understand incentive systems well enough to generate *cooperation* consistently among our alienated teenagers or we would burn out teachers faster than we could matriculate our problems.

The Negative Deadlock What kind of home do you think produces an angry, alienated child? The modal pattern is not as mysterious as one might think. Aggression produces counteraggression—a continued reliance on management by negative sanctions in conjunction with a shortage of nurturance produces anger and alienation.

To raise a truly angry child, parents must usually start early. Slap the hands of a 9-month-old for picking up forbidden objects. Swear in exasperation when the baby spills or smears or drops food on the floor. Admonish your 2-year-old through clenched teeth to "act your age!" when he or she fusses and whines in public. Threaten that things will get worse if the child does not learn his or her lesson. Meet the child at *his or her* emotional level so that you will be able to finally get through to him or her.

The dialogue of force progresses over the years from the terrible twos to the miserable threes to the abominable fours. It is a home where discipline all too often means nagging, threatening, yelling, spanking, criticizing, hitting, demeaning, and endlessly revoking privileges.

- Get down off that counter top! How many times do I have to tell you before you'll listen! If you don't get down this instant, I'm going to warm your little bottom!
- Would you shut up when I'm on the phone! I said shut up! Can't you see I'm trying to talk!
- You get up those stairs right now or I'll give you a reason to move that you'll remember!
- This damn kid of mine won't do a thing I ask.

When you grow up with negative sanctions, you grow immune to them through repeated exposure. Your skin is thick, your feelings are defiant, and you take pride in your capacity to absorb punishment and prevail. Therapists often refer to this pattern as the "burned child" syndrome. You learn to *fight* force with counterforce, and you learn to *frustrate* force with noncompliance. You master the art of passive resistance. Cooperation means capitulation, and you resist that humiliation as long as possible out of resentment and pride.

When these children finally enter the public education system, they will be seasoned veterans in the politics of power—their "school of hard knocks." They have been trained to regard adult authority as arbitrary, capricious, and unjust. And now you, the teacher, are going to ask these children to cooperate and go along with the demands for conformity with the multiplicity of rules, structures, and routines required for organized group activity. You will make more demands for both work completion and rule compliance before lunch than the parents would dare make in an entire day. And we are surprised at the response of a predictable minority?

- You and your stupid rules!
- Gimme a break! You're always pickin' on me!
- This is unfair, I'm not going to do it!
- Get off my back!

How are we going to cope with their provocations and oppositionism? We are obviously going to have to "use discipline." Use discipline—our age-old stereotype of discipline sneaks up on us again. We will have to get rid of these intolerable behaviors—suppress them—put the lid on. See how easy it is to reach our back-up system in one easy step? When pushed, most teachers and parents instinctively turn to negative sanctions.

Can you ever make it with "burned children" while relying primarily on negative sanctions? Can you ever reach them or turn them around or shape them up using the same control techniques that they grew to hate and learned to overpower? To try to do so produces the same conflicts at school that characterize the home, an endless exchange of force and counterforce, a war of attrition characterized by coercion.

And who are the casualties? Will you absorb the stress and punishment endlessly, or will you at some point simply "bounce"? "It's them or me, and it sure as hell isn't going to be me!"

Oh yes it is. Our alienated, burned child has already extracted his or her pound of flesh from you and from a succession of your colleagues. As long as we meet negativism with negative sanctions, force with counterforce, we will pay the price of our folly until either these children drop out or the public education system spits them out.

A Philosophy of Punitive Parenting

"That damn kid won't do a thing I ask!" says the distraught, angry parent at his first family therapy session. "The only thing he understands is when I take off my belt!"

"Does it work?," I ask.

"It's the only damn thing that works!"

"It's the only thing that works!" I wonder how many times I have heard that sentence from a parent while wondering each time how they could say it out loud without hearing its sad irony. Things that work solve problems. Things that do not work perpetuate problems. "If it works so well, what do you think has brought you to therapy?" I think to myself.

If I have found any one predictable feature about parents who are deeply locked into a cycle of coercion and countercoercion with their child, it is a marked failure to appreciate the role of reinforcement—either formal or informal—in generating behavior. It is a lacuna—a blank space in their understanding, a circumscribed ignorance that in many cases is nearly complete. In its more extreme forms it is encased in a series of attributions and rationalizations that form the punitive parent's philosophy of child rearing.

> Hey, listen, I don't buy this reward stuff! You're telling me I'm supposed to give them some kind of payoff or bribe just to get them to do something? Listen, I *expect* them to do things that I ask them to do because I *say so*. They're living in my house, eating off my table, and I'll be damned if I'll kiss their behinds to get them just to agree to do a few things around the house! Nobody ever offered me any rewards for doing what I was supposed to do when I was growing up!

Indeed, nobody probably ever did, nor are those parents offering any now, nor in all likelihood will their children when they become parents. It is hard to give what you never got. You must be raised with nurturance, approval, and reward to understand

and appreciate them. If you were raised by the scruff of the neck, the notion of reward does not compute, and the feelings and spontaneous responses of nurturance are withered and small. You are doomed to repeat the past to one degree or another because it is you.

And some of these burned individuals become teachers and some become principals. And some are more burned than others, and we are all burned to some degree. If an angry, withholding child meets a teacher cut from the same cloth, we will surely have a "personality conflict." And if an angry, withholding child meets a warm and nurturing teacher, he or she will frustrate that teacher to death. The child will continue to play the "you can't make me" game until the child's game extinguishes or until the teacher's patience runs out or until we somehow skillfully *teach* that child about nurturance and reward, about giving and receiving.

Lesser Degrees of Oppositionism

But these alienated students are the few, not the many. They are the lower 5 percent. They are not typical. Most of the discipline problem kids are not "at war."

True, not many students qualify as severe cases. But a great many are mild to moderate cases. A few hate school from the beginning and fight authority all the way, but many others will be passive resisters who distinguish themselves by tuning out most of the time with occasional outbursts of squirrelly behavior. Some lose their education with a flourish, but most of the walking wounded lose it by inches.

Yet the lessons learned in the crucible of secondary special education apply to all. A class of alienated teenagers will give you only two choices, learn how to generate cooperation or struggle with enforcement until you burn out. Yet the choices are the same in any classroom. Only the rate of burn-out is different. You cannot write off the lower 5 percent without blinding yourself to the needs of the middle 50 percent. You cannot turn your back on the basic imperative of discipline management to deal constructively with students' negativism. Cooperation based on reward will always be the central issue of discipline management, and limit-setting and penalties will always serve only as a means of allowing appropriate rewards to operate.

Most of us want to give and need only a sophisticated technology to set us free from the continual struggle for control. Some of us only understand control and will struggle with the notion of discipline based on reward. Most of our students want to respond with cooperation based upon affirmation and reward. Some of them respond only to threat and punishment.

For all the students we must learn the lessons of Positive Classroom Discipline. But we must learn our lessons especially well for the sake of the burned child. We must teach such children about rewards and cooperation and nurturance from scratch. Patience and sweetness are not enough—the negative transfer from home is too strong. They will fight us and they will wear us down. We must know our craft well enough to succeed at a price we can afford in spite of their resistance. For these burned students in particular but for all students to some degree we must either master the skills of limit-setting and the technology of incentive systems or be doomed to fight an eternal battle of containment that no one can win.

Escalation and Reward-Based Discipline Management

Before proceeding to an examination of Positive Classroom Discipline as a whole, it will be useful to examine the way in which limit-setting and incentive systems as used in Positive Classroom Discipline systematically fly in the face of the timeless notion that discipline is punition and that bigger problems call for bigger negative sanctions.

Limit-Setting   In dealing with the *typical* classroom disruption—the small, everyday disruption that accounts for most of the teacher's stress and most of the students' time off task—the most cost-effective way of responding will usually be limit-setting. Limit-setting, as part of the teacher's normal classroom demeanor, not only terminates disruptions effectively in those few instances when part of the limit-setting sequence is used, but it also trains the class that you mean business. Once a teacher's capacity to respond effectively to disruptions has been firmly established, his or her mere presence in the classroom serves as a discriminative stimulus for the continual presence of rule enforcement through limit-setting, which subsequently acts to prevent most disruptions from occurring.

Limit-setting, however, is *mild social punishment*. When given skillfully it is low key and gentle, and it minimizes the likelihood of a power confrontation between teacher and student. It saves the student from the consequences of his or her own foolishness as in the case of back talk and is therefore actively protective of the student. Nevertheless, from a scientific standpoint limit-setting is a mild aversive social consequence for an unacceptable behavior which suppresses the rate of that behavior: punishment as defined in any learning textbook.

Responsibility Training   As a teacher attempts to deal with more difficult or off-balance management situations in the classroom—the repeat disruptions, dawdling, noise level, coming to class without necessary materials, time wasters, and chronic nuisance behaviors such as pencil sharpening and hall passes—responsibility training becomes the most cost-effective technique. Responsibility training, however, is a *complex* incentive system with explicit reward and penalty components. In responsibility training reward is built in rather than being unstructured for the teacher to supply through relationship as in limit-setting. And penalty is peer-based rather than residing solely in the person of the teacher.

Omission Training   Finally when we must deal with one of the most difficult of our management situations—the angry, alienated student who turns his or her back on both relationship and formal rewards and locks him- or herself into a "you can't make me" power struggle with the teacher—omission training is the technique of choice. Omission training is an entirely reward-oriented management system, a bonus clause pure and simple.

Counteracting Escalation   Ironically, the more difficult and negativistic the student's behavior becomes, the more *reward-oriented* is the teacher's response. As the teacher progresses from limit-setting (mild social punishment) to responsibility training (reward plus bonus and penalty) to omission training (bonus only), Positive Classroom Discipline progresses from mild social punishment to pure reward. The tendency of

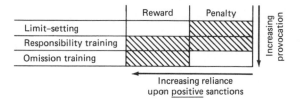

FIGURE 18-1
The relationship between an increasing level of provocation and a reliance upon positive sanctions.

Positive Classroom Discipline to become *less* punitive under conditions of increasing provocation is graphically represented in Figure 18-1.

This progression from negative sanctions to positive sanctions in coping with discipline problems of increasing magnitude flies in the face of what most people would expect from a discipline management system: that meeting a bigger provocation dictates the use of a bigger negative sanction. This age-old stereotype of discipline, which we have attempted to overcome with Positive Classroom Discipline, is not only harsh but counterproductive in the long run.

POSITIVE CLASSROOM DISCIPLINE AS AN INTEGRATED SYSTEM

The Discipline Decision Ladder

Informed Judgment versus Rigid Prescription   Positive Classroom Discipline has evolved over the years into an orderly process of problem solving. As teachers are forced to deal with discipline problems of increasing severity, they can proceed from one management strategy to the next in an ordered sequence that combines management power and cost-effectiveness with gentleness and protection of the student.

Yet each management technique has its strengths and limitations, and each management situation has subtleties known only to the teacher. Thus the decision-making process is ultimately a matter of informed judgment rather than rigid prescription. Prescriptions are doomed to failure in far too many cases because they lack the flexibility to adapt to the specific situation. Only a well-trained teacher with mastery of an adequate repertoire of responses—an integrated system of successful skills and procedures—can gamble well enough in the moment to consistently make the problems go away.

Figure 18-2 represents the full range of CMTP discipline management options as they would be considered chronologically in dealing with a discipline problem of increasing severity. Management options are arranged along two dimensions, (1) reward and (2) penalty. Ironically, the age-old adage about the carrot and the stick accurately describes the basic polarity underlying the response options available for discipline management. Together reward for appropriate behavior and minimal penalty for inappropriate behavior produce the most efficient discrimination learning for the student.

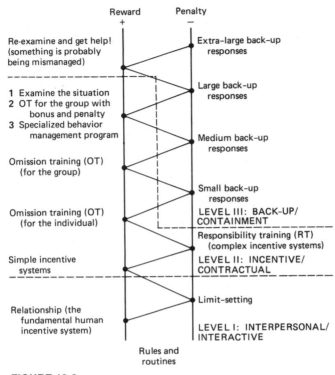

FIGURE 18-2
Positive Classroom Discipline as an integrated system.

Response options to be used early in discipline management are placed at the bottom of the diagram.

Of course, this diagram represents an idealized management progression for a hypothetical problem, and certain liberties will be taken at the discretion of the teacher. The cardinal error, however, is to jump rapidly from the bottom toward the top in anything but a crisis situation. This pattern, which we refer to as "leapfrogging," usually represents a *primary* reliance on negative sanctions by the teacher rather than a reliance on smaller, more subtle, more reward-based sanctions toward the bottom of the decision ladder.

Judgments and Trade-Offs   Relationship is the beginning of management, the informal yet fundamental human incentive system. Yet, relationship is not enough. The job of any student is to test limits—to find out what is real and what is not. With relationship students learn that you care. With limit-setting they can encounter firm boundaries without getting bruised.

Relationship is built spontaneously as a caring, loving teacher interacts with students on a moment-by-moment basis. Relationship is also built systematically as a byproduct of effective limit-setting, which is protective of the student, and as a by-product of responsibility training as well, which structures fun with learning into class-room life as a means of getting necessary jobs done. Relationship is also built as a by-product of effective instructional technique as the teacher learns to have more frequent and more positive helping interactions with students. Thus, effective instructional tech-niques are an integral part of the interpersonal-interactive level of discipline manage-ment. We will learn much more about relationship building in *Positive Classroom Instruction,* the companion volume to this work, as we integrate discipline and instruc-tion into a cohesive approach to classroom management.

Formal incentives, the incentive-contractual level of management, pick up where the interpersonal-interactive level of management leaves off. Incentives give us a pre-dictable and affirmative way of answering the student's eternal "Why should I?" Sim-ple incentives bring us back to the reward side of our decision ladder, but simple rewards are only occasionally useful for discipline. They lack the power to suppress the disruptions of the few so that the teacher will have the opportunity to reward the many. To put teeth into *group* incentive management we must cross over to the penalty side where responsibility training, a complex incentive system, gives us the capacity to suppress goofing off. With an extremely negativistic and oppositional student, how-ever, we may need to cross back to the reward column as we use omission training.

Our back-up system picks up where the major portion of the incentive-contractual level of management leaves off. However, even in the lower half of the back-up con-tainment level of management, incentives and negative sanctions continue to be inter-spersed as a means of juxtaposing peer sanctions with adult sanctions and reward with penalty. Small back-up responses are followed with group omission training before the transition to medium back-up responses is made. Medium back-up responses are also followed by a reward phase which may include omission training or any imaginable type of custom-built incentive program.

With further progression up the decision ladder, however, comes the obligation to stand back, to get help if necessary, and to examine how you got this far. Only large and extra-large back-up responses remain at the top of the decision ladder along with an exhortation to reexamine what you are doing and seek help. With repeated use of large and extra-large back-up responses the management system becomes increasingly unbalanced, and the likelihood of generating alienation and a cycle of coercion mul-tiplies.

Basic Strategies

As positive classroom discipline evolved over the years into a tight system that could cope with the full range of discipline problems that a teacher might face, a simple problem-solving strategy emerged which is most graphically represented in Figure 18-2: When rewards prove ineffective, go to penalty. When penalty proves ineffective, go to reward.

Added to this strategy is a second strategy of equal simplicity: Proceed up the management system one level at a time. Jump a level only in the face of severe crisis.

Though simple enough as strategies go, both of these statements fly in the face of conventional wisdom. Most people will respond to the failure of a negative sanction by reaching for a larger negative sanction. And most people will jump rapidly to their back-up system on the basis of internal upset or inexperience rather than proceeding on the basis of systematic problem solving.

Added to these two basic strategies is a third which defines our long-range objective in discipline management. Our long-range objective is to *work our way down the management system*. Over time the use of the back-up system should self-eliminate so that we are handling almost all discipline problems at the incentive-contractual and interpersonal-interactive levels. With the passage of more time the penalty component of responsibility training should self-eliminate until only PAT is left.

Over time, therefore, the size of negative sanctions steadily decreases while the reinforcement components of the system remain constant or, as in the case of PAT, even grow. In the end almost all management takes place at the interpersonal level with limit-setting on the wing preventing even the use of the mild social punishment inherent in the limit-setting sequence.

When effective discipline management in the classroom can take place almost entirely at the interpersonal-interactive level of management, discipline management has finally become extremely cheap, easy, and positive. But this goal will elude us unless specific, advanced *instructional* skills are employed in conjunction with effective discipline management. Lessons which produce confusion, boredom, or discouragement for certain students will always produce enough goofing off and fooling around to force us up the management system toward a stronger reliance on punishment. The instructional skills so important to completing the interpersonal-interactive level of classroom management are described in *Positive Classroom Instruction,* the other volume of this comprehensive treatment of behavioral management in the classroom.

Simplistic Discipline

Can a teacher have good discipline without all this technology? Haven't good teachers achieved good results in the past with a far simpler approach?

Well, yes and no. I have known many excellent teachers who had "no discipline problems to speak of" who reduced their disruptions by 80 percent and doubled their time on task as a result of systematic teacher training. And I have known teachers whose methods served them well in the past who nevertheless suffered painfully at the hands of a particularly difficult class. I have also seen the best teachers use much of Positive Classroom Discipline instinctively without realizing that they were using any special technique at all. And I have seen rather crude management techniques succeed beautifully with a fairly nice kid who wasn't all that much of a problem to start with. But more than anything I have observed that teachers who do not labor hard at a high level of stress in a classroom full of young people are few and far between.

A teacher can sometimes manage with clear rules, clear warnings, and a handful of negative sanctions. But if they succeed with little stress they must (1) have a nice group of youngsters, (2) have a fairly young class in most cases, preferably fourth grade or below, and (3) have superb skills of relationship building. Yet even when these conditions pertain, effective teachers who are adequately trained typically ex-

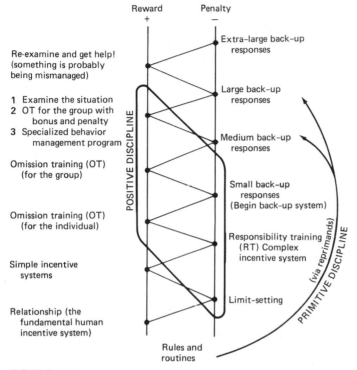

FIGURE 18-3
A comparison of positive discipline and primitive discipline.

perience (1) a rapid reduction of stress and exasperation, (2) a rapid increase in academic learning time and time on task, and (3) an elevation of standards.

Primitive Discipline

The problem with simplistic discipline is that very few teachers can get away with it for long, and almost no one can get away with it forever. For the vast majority of teachers simplistic discipline becomes primitive discipline under pressure.

Primitive discipline is discipline management that goes from rules to reprimands to the back-up system. Primitive discipline begins with a warning or reprimand and has names on the board right away with the threat of worse to follow. It is the "three strikes and you're out" school of management which creates a semblance of order at the price of a high casualty rate. Most of the casualties are children, especially the losers who could have been saved, and the rest of the casualties are teachers.

Primitive discipline is the norm. It is the embodiment of our folk wisdom concerning discipline. At a relatively high price to the teacher it holds in check those students who are fairly easily controlled. But for the burned child it holds out no hope of learning to cooperate.

Positive classroom discipline, as it has grown over the past decade and a half, has sought to discover a better way. From observation, I have attempted to construct a management system that provides as much management power and flexibility as a teacher will ever need before the use of the back-up system. If primitive discipline leaps to medium, large, and extra-large back-up responses, positive classroom discipline does as much as possible to keep from getting there.

The contrast between positive classroom discipline and primitive discipline can be quickly seen by contrasting those procedures which have been either developed or refined as parts of positive classroom discipline over the years with those which are currently the mainstay of discipline for most classrooms and school sites. See Figure 18-3.

OVERVIEW

It was impossible for me to see classroom discipline as an integrated system so neatly arranged until the pieces had been developed. Only then was there a real sense of coherence—a sense that the major questions had been addressed, the major needs met, the major loopholes plugged. Only then was the full pattern clear.

Discipline dilemmas in the classroom, however, do not always lend themselves to the following of a management system in a neat, step-by-step progression. Yet the steps of the Positive Classroom Discipline decision ladder define the path and make the next step more sure. When teachers have mastered their basic discipline management skills, they are well equipped to make the necessary trade-offs and fine adjustments.

Until a teacher has been adequately trained, however, he or she has only a bag of tricks at best, and he or she must settle for partial results and a relatively greater reliance on negative sanctions. Since negative sanctions destroy relationship and since relationship is the basis of cooperation, such a simplistic system will rarely self-eliminate. In the final analysis the only alternative to punition and stress is finesse. And the only means of acquiring finesse is through careful and extensive training.

CHAPTER 19

PATTERNS OF COERCION
AND COOPERATION

Perhaps the best final integration of classroom discipline might take the form of a review of some of the scientific underpinnings of behavior management. This grounding in the basics of the science of learning is often lacking in the background of practicing teachers. But more important, it can serve as an aid to discrimination between productive and counterproductive modes of discipline management.

BASICS OF BEHAVIOR CHANGE

Objectives

There are two fundamental objectives in behavior management, (1) starting or strengthening a behavior and (2) stopping or weakening a behavior. If you can start the behaviors that you want and stop the behaviors you do not want, you will be a very successful teacher. Behavior management programs, therefore, will simultaneously manipulate a *pair* of incompatible behaviors, the one that you want to start or strengthen and the one that you want to stop or weaken.

In addition, there are only *two* ways to *start* a behavior, and there are only *two* ways to *stop* a behavior. You will, therefore, be able to understand the nature of almost any behavior management program by thoroughly understanding the subtleties of these four basic ways of changing the *rate* of a behavior.

Starting Behavior   Both of the ways of starting or strengthening a behavior are labeled *reinforcement*. You might think of the term "reinforcement" as an attempt to create a technical term for "strengthening" that is close to common usage and understanding—like reinforcing a weak fence or reinforced concrete.

The two types of reinforcement are labeled *positive* reinforcement and *negative* reinforcement. Positive reinforcement can be pleasant or unpleasant, but negative reinforcement is almost always unpleasant.

Stopping Behavior   The two ways of stopping or weakening a behavior are (1) extinction and (2) punishment. Extinction occurs when a purposeful behavior is consistently followed by no meaningful consequence. The behavior weakens gradually as it is repeated in the absence of any payoff. The behavior in question dies slowly as it comes to be regarded as nonfunctional or worthless.

Punishment is suppression. It actively eliminates a behavior rather than passively ignoring it to death. Consequently, it has the potential for acting faster than extinction.

MEANS OF BEHAVIOR CHANGE

I Starting behavior (strengthening)
  1 Negative reinforcement
  2 Positive reinforcement
II Stopping behavior (weakening)
  1 extinction
  2 punishment

We will examine each means of behavior change as well as the relationships between them so that we may better understand the fundamental processes of both discipline management and discipline *mis*management. Our focus will be the misuses and abuses of each of these four basic means of behavior change in relations between adults and children so that we may better discriminate the constructive means of management available to us in the classroom.

Starting Behavior

Negative Reinforcement   Negative reinforcement is perhaps the most commonly misunderstood means of behavior control, often being confused by educators with the term "punishment." Negative reinforcement and punishment are, in fact, functional opposites. Negative reinforcement starts behavior whereas punishment stops behavior. Both are often unpleasant in the course of human events, but there the similarity ends.

The Negative Reinforcement Chain   Negative reinforcement is a bit complicated—not a simple contingency as is implied by its typically being included among methods of contingency management. Rather, negative reinforcement is a more complex sequence of events, a behavior chain which typically has the following active steps when used by one person on another:

1 Tell the other person what you want her or him to do.
2 Inflict pain on the person until he or she complies. This may be accompanied by

warnings or threats which serve as prompts so that the recipient may understand what is expected of him or her and when.

3 Terminate the pain as soon as the other person complies.

As you can see, negative reinforcement does not paint a pretty picture. It is the unpleasant way to start a behavior. It may conjure up a picture of torture during war-time. But we all practice little tortures. The most common everyday example of negative reinforcement is *nagging*.

Negative Reinforcement Addiction   Unfortunately, negative reinforcement is *addictive* in addition to being unpleasant. In fact everyone involved in the negative reinforcement chain is reinforced in a perverse way. Nagging, being a common experience of us all, might provide the most useful example of the seductiveness of using negative reinforcement on those around us.

Imagine that you want your son to set the table before dinner, and imagine that he is slow to get off his duff because he is watching a television show in the next room.

Billy, it's time to set the table. [no response]

Billy, I said it is time to set the table! Now this is the *second time* I've had to ask! [no response]

Billy, do you *hear me!* I said it is time to set the table, and I'm tired of telling you. Now get in here! [no response]

Billy, so help me, if I have to come in there to get you, I am turning that TV off, and it is going to stay off! Now I'm not just talking to hear myself talk! You get in here right now! Do you understand? [no response] I said, do you understand? [no response] Damn that kid!

[Parent walks into the next room, and Billy disarmingly stands up.] OK, dad.

What is the parent's reward for nagging and threatening? Billy finally got up and got moving! What was Billy's reward for getting up and getting moving? Dad quit nagging! And what was Billy's second reward for procrastinating as long as possible? He got to watch TV longer, a PAT for procrastination. The person inflicting the pain is rewarded when the other person capitulates, and the victim is reinforced by the cessation of pain. Everybody wins!

Resentment and Passivity   Such tactics do not engender a spirit of cooperation in the victim. Billy learns not to respond to simple requests for two reasons. *First,* the longer Billy delays, the longer he avoids work while doing some preferred activity. *Second,* Billy resents being nagged, and passivity frustrates the nagger. What could be easier—temporary victory by doing nothing more than sitting on your duff and watching TV.

Billy has long since learned to tune out the nagging to reduce the pain. Besides, it interferes with TV. The only meaningful cue to action is the *final threat.* Then you cut your losses if you're smart by acting pleasant as you stand up and do the inevitable. Meanwhile, the parent feels victorious in a hollow sort of way while getting high blood pressure and ulcers. With repetitions a pattern is established in which the child never does what he is told until forced. Consequently, over time the child tends to learn a peculiar form of passivity in which *only* intense nagging serves as the effective cue for the onset of the desired behavior. Now the parent is doubly addicted. Negative reinforcement has become the only way to get him to do anything!

Pain Control Behavior management which uses pain as a primary means of control has been labeled coercion or "pain control" by Gerald Patterson,[1] one of the pioneers in the study of behavior management interactions in family and school life. Negative reinforcement explicitly uses pain to manage behavior—not as a mistake or as an unintended by-product but, rather, explicitly and purposefully. Though never part of a condonable classroom management program, negative reinforcement is no stranger to the classroom.

Positive Reinforcement Positive reinforcement is a consequence of a behavior that strengthens that behavior and maintains its rate or increases its rate over time. In the absence of positive reinforcement, extinction begins.

Positive Reinforcement Can Be Unpleasant Positive reinforcement is frequently misunderstood insofar as it is equated by many educators with the term "reward" which implies something necessarily pleasant or nice. Reinforcement, however, can be both nasty and nice. As was mentioned in an earlier chapter, children love attention, need attention, and will get attention by one means or another. If they cannot get attention by being good, they will get it by being bad.

When it comes to adults giving attention to children, it is definitely a "pay me now, or pay me later" situation. We will either choose to be with children during time which we structure as "good time," or they will take our choice away from us and coerce us into giving them attention by being obnoxious. In the absence of *positive reinforcement from us,* they will learn to use *negative reinforcement on us.* They will nag and badger us or make a mess or get into some kind of trouble in order to force us through pain control to attend to them. At such times the attention they get will be positive reinforcement that is unpleasant—a reprimand, a threat, or even a hit.

Thus negative and positive reinforcement can represent two different forms of pain control in human interactions that have gone awry. In *negative reinforcement* pain plus a request for behavior is the *prompt* for compliance, and the cessation of pain is the consequence that reinforces compliance. In *positive reinforcement* pain can be the *consequence* of a behavior that is prompted by extreme physical or psychological need. If, for example, you must endure pain to get food and thereby avert starvation, you will suffer the pain as a necessary means to an end. And, if you must endure humiliation to avert psychological starvation, you will do that too and learn to be a masochist in the process.

Positive Reinforcement, When Unpleasant, Is Addictive When adults use a reprimand, a threat, a hit, or some other means of pain control to stop the child's obnoxious attention-seeking, they typically see themselves as *punishing* or suppressing the behavior rather than as rewarding it. This unpleasant attention, however, may *positively reinforce* the deviant behavior because the obnoxiousness has produced at least *some* kind of attention—a reinforcement error.

The adult's use of pain control produces a quick fix as the child temporarily shapes up to minimize the pain and thereby cut losses. Thus the adult is hooked on a perception of success. But soon the cycle beings again as the child seeks more attention. The *adult,* however, is now addicted to the use of *harsh reprimands* and other negative sanctions toward the child (which function as positive reinforcement but which appear to punish or suppress the unwanted behavior in the short run). The child, in contrast, is now addicted to the use of any convenient form of obnoxious attention-getting toward the adult (which not only functions as part of the negative reinforcer for the harsh reprimands, but which also produces a quick fix for social deprivation). In this way adult and child back into a form of reciprocal coercion or pain control that is self-perpetuating. When one considers child beating as positive reinforcement in an extreme version of this process, the tendency to equate positive reinforcement with "pleasant" disappears.

We can already discern a pattern. Pain control is always *addictive.* It tends to seduce and then lock people into forms of pain control that become self-perpetuating. When it comes to "giving yourself to children," adults pay their dues in *time* sooner or later. It will either be good time of your choosing or bad time of their choosing. For this reason alone good behavior managers are proactive rather than reactive in giving their time to children.

Positive reinforcement might be represented as varying along two major dimensions: *quality* (pleasant or unpleasant) and *quantity* (plentiful or scarce). See Figure 19-1. As we can see, unpleasant and scarce go together to form a most destructive adult-child interaction pattern whereas pleasant and plentiful go together to form effective caretaking. Reinforcement strengthens behavior for good or for ill. Reinforcement errors almost always strengthen negative behavior and thereby both reinforce and produce pain.

FIGURE 19-1
Dimensions of positive reinforcement.

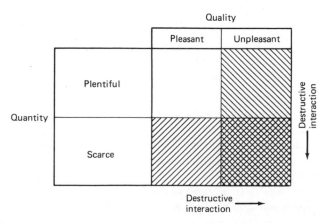

Stopping Behavior

Discipline is commonly and erroneously associated with simply stopping unwanted behavior. Yet, while building cooperation is central, stopping unacceptable behavior is nevertheless crucial. When we examine the methods of stopping behavior, we will be able to see more clearly additional perennial miscarriages of discipline management.

Extinction   Extinction, the decrease in the rate of behavior over time that results from an absence of reinforcement, has been discussed relatively thoroughly in Chapter 14. The nature of extinction as it relates to discipline gained added dimension, however, when we considered the topic of *consistency*. The exhortation to be consistent is like the exhortation to lose weight—perennially true and perennially boring. The awesome power of teachers and parents to self-destruct over the use of consistency, however, is hard to appreciate without some understanding of *schedules of reinforcement*. Let us imagine again the example from Chapter 14 of the child who nagged mommy for a cookie until mommy finally gave in. Mommy held out for a long time, but then she cracked and thereby put her child on a lean, intermittent schedule of reinforcement for nagging. Of course, mother will hold out for different lengths of time on different days depending on her patience. She will therefore put her child on a variable ration schedule of reinforcement for nagging that approaches randomness. She taught a lesson: You can have anything you want, but you will have to inflict pain on me for a long time before you get it. The mother committed a reinforcement error, inconsistency you might say, and thereby trained her child to use negative reinforcement and to use it relentlessly and without pity.

The mother's reinforcement error has not only taught the child to use pain control to start a behavior (giving the cookie), but it has also set the stage for the mother to commit a second management error. How will she get rid of that incessant nagging? You know enough about schedules of reinforcement by now to write off extinction. That leaves suppression. The adult may eventually use *harsh* measures such as yelling, threatening, or hitting in an attempt to eliminate the nagging—pain control to cope with pain control. Another cycle of coercion has been created. It is no accident that nag, threat, and punish go together.

This coercive cycle is, of course, not extinction at all. It is described under the topic of extinction because it represents the type of coercive cycle that is produced when extinction fails through inconsistency. As you can see, extinction is an all or nothing proposition which, when mismanaged, produces its own form of addiction.

Punishment   The term "punishment" has two meanings, one technical and one nontechnical. Technically punishment is a consequence of a behavior that *reduces* the rate of that behavior over time. Technically punishment is suppression.

Punishment in everyday speech, however, simply means a painful consequence or negative sanction given to someone who is doing something you dislike in the hope that they will stop. The only problem is that sometimes the negative sanctions stop undesirable behavior and sometimes they don't. Why? Was it just that the size of the negative sanction was not big enough?

As we have seen in our examination of the painful forms of positive reinforcement, reinforcement error is one likely explanation. Peer or "bootleg" reinforcement for the problem is another explanation since the joys of goofing off may exceed the pain of the negative sanction. Ineptitude in using negative sanctions is a third explanation. There is no guarantee, therefore, that a negative sanction will function technically as punishment. Whether our attempts at suppression succeed or fail usually depend on (1) how it is done, and (2) the context in which it is done.

How It Is Done   If you know how to do limit-setting, you are extremely sophisticated in the proper implementation of a very effective negative sanction—mild social punishment. It is calm, slow, gentle, polite, and protective of the child. More to the point, it self-eliminates. It self-eliminates when done properly not only because it conveys interpersonal power effectively, but also because it is free of the reinforcement errors that often undo our attempts to mean business. The primary reinforcement errors which threaten limit-setting are (1) getting upset, (2) moving too fast, and (3) talking too much—all of which put the student in control of the situation. Most of these reinforcement errors are "built out" by the teacher's calmness, slowness, effective use of body language, and knowledge of when to shut up. The relaxing breath is the natural enemy of the reinforcement error. Failure is almost unavoidable as soon as the teacher becomes upset.

Success with negative sanctions, to put it bluntly, requires finesse: fine points of execution which one must both learn to appreciate and learn to perform. Clumsiness will produce the reinforcement errors that sustain a pain control cycle between teacher and student.

The Context   Sometimes a moderate level of punishment will succeed for a teacher in suppressing a given student's undesirable behavior, and sometimes it will *not* although the implementation may be identical. For example, giving a warning to a particular child might prove effective for the first period teacher of a problem student but ineffective for the second period teacher even though the technique was carried out proficiently in both instances.

If one holds the mode of implementation constant with a given student, the main determiner of success will probably be the availability of reward for appropriate behavior. In one classroom being good may be richly reinforced whereas in the next it may be on extinction. The success is being determined not by the punishment technique but by the availability of *differential reinforcement for appropriate behavior.* The system that failed was out of balance.

Nevertheless, the failure of a small negative sanction usually leads to the use of larger negative sanctions. Not too surprisingly, punishment-oriented adults tend not to be reward-oriented adults. Thus, a scarcity of positive reinforcement often coexists with harsh negative sanctions in unhappy classrooms, unhappy schools, and unhappy families.

Unfortunately, harsh negative sanctions when used by themselves to suppress unwanted behavior within a context of inadequate differential reinforcement tend to be *addictive.* Wielding a big stick produces quick short-term results. Obnoxious kids may be resentful and uncooperative, but they are not stupid. They cool it to avoid immediate pain. Quick short-term success, then, reinforces the use of harsh negative sanctions, and the strength of the addiction increases.

COERCIVE SOCIAL SYSTEMS

As we come to understand more intimately the workings of positive and negative reinforcement as well as extinction and punishment, we gain added insight into the hidden pitfalls of discipline management as well as avenues to success. The pitfalls are treacherous because they always seem to delude us into a perception of success while they addict us to the repetitive use of coercion.

Negative reinforcement and harsh negative sanctions, for example, are addictive because they get quick results by forcing immediate compliance. They are counterparts of sorts, with negative reinforcement being the addictive quick fix for attempting to *start* a behavior and harsh negative sanctions being the addictive quick fix for attempting to *stop* a behavior. They are the fraternal twins of pain control and coercion.

Negative reinforcement and harsh negative sanctions all too frequently become the primary means of behavior control for a person with a fairly primitive response repertoire, especially under stress. Not too surprisingly, adults who rely heavily on pain control or coercion to force compliance from children teach the children to do the same. And leaders of an organization who rely heavily on coercion train other members of the organization to do the same. The result is a social system that is highly coercive: pain control is used repetitively by various members of the group to start and stop each other's behavior.

This two-way reliance on pain control by members of a group produces a super cycle of coercion, the "reciprocal coercion cycle." Pain control may ultimately come to characterize behavioral management within a given classroom, family, or organization. I am indebted to Dr. Gerald Patterson[1] of the University of Oregon for first describing the process of reciprocal coercion which allowed many other aspects of discipline management to fall into place.

By-products of Coercive Cycles

Behavior management which relies heavily on coercion creates relationship by-products that eventually touch every major dimension of the immediate social system. These by-products are as counterproductive as they are inadvertent. They are the price we pay for the quick, short-term results characteristic of pain control. The major by-products are (1) destruction of relationship, (2) resentment and withholding, (3) irresponsibility, (4) dependency, and (5) countercoercion. Those that have been discussed previously will be mentioned only briefly. Taken together, however, they create patterns of dysfunction commonly found in working groups that range from families to corporations.

The Destruction of Relationship Frequent reliance on pain control reduces the subsequent potency of the approval and reward given by the persons relying on pain control. Thus, when people opt to rely on pain control, they immediately begin to burn their bridges behind them. Ultimately there may be nothing of relationship left. Such people's time and attention and even their gifts are no longer valued or appreciated. In terms of differential reinforcement and relationship, they are broke. They are alone with their coercion: addicted, embittered, and fully convinced that nothing else works.

Resentment and Withholding Coercion and cooperation are incompatible behavior management opposites. Coercion is control by force. Cooperation, on the other hand, is by its very nature an act of volition or free choice. Most people resent being forced, and their anger kills the desire to give. Thus, force can produce compliance, but it cannot produce cooperation. Since cooperation can always be withheld at will, it *will* be withheld out of resentment.

The destruction of cooperation leaves the controller with only force. He or she may now have compliance, but he or she will have to accept *minimal* compliance—the least that can be given by the victim without triggering the renewed use of force. Thus, coercion produces *withholding*. In contrast, building patterns of cooperation necessitates *giving* in order to produce *mutual giving*.

Irresponsibility People tend to take responsibility for behaviors that they *chose* to perform. They tend *not* to take responsibility for behaviors that they were *forced* to perform. The natural and obvious attribution of responsibility by the recipient of coercion is to the person or agency that coerced them and that controls the use of pain. If the locus of control is external, the responsibility is external and the blame for any resulting misfortune is external. Thus a police state creates an irresponsible population, a coercive parent creates an irresponsible child, and teachers who respond to back talk by opening their mouths create students who do not accept responsibility for the argument that results. It is always someone else's fault as far as the recipient of coercion is concerned. So, it's "Get off my back," and "You fix it," and "It's not my problem."

One common by-product of coercion by adults toward children, as mentioned earlier, is that peculiar passivity of the children toward doing what they are "supposed to do" until forced that drives parents and teachers to rage. The "do nothing" passivity and irresponsibility of the child then create the occasion for the next round of coercion which then further fuels resentment.

Dependency The fourth by-product of coercion is *dependency*—dependency on the very authority figure(s) that the victim has grown to resent. Owing to a lack of experience and skill and, therefore, confidence in being responsible, the victim will eventually "need" the authority to take responsibility for making the decisions that govern his or her life. This need, however, is a bitter emotion, a love-hate combination of dependency and resentment. For someone not accustomed to taking responsibility for managing their own affairs, the sudden requirement to do so is truly difficult and frightening—even an unreasonable request under the circumstances.

Countercoercion A natural outgrowth of the resentment endemic to coercion is an attempt by the victim to end the coercion. Since sweet reason typically fails, the obvious methods of control for the victim are the tactics of coercion being modeled all around him or her. Counterforce may, of course, be passive resistance: the joys of frustrating the authority that comes from indulging your feelings of resentment by withholding and irresponsibility. But in other circumstances force will produce counterforce. Violence is the most blatant symptom of a social system that has failed. As the system deteriorates, the options narrow to force and counterforce.

The long-term effects of people management via pain, therefore, produce a social system bound together by the circular forces of coercion and irresponsibility, demanding and withholding, dependency and resentment, need and fear. Social maturation beyond a certain point is blocked.

Corporal Punishment

If the technology of discipline management could be likened to an animal, then corporal punishment would surely be its ass end. Of all the discipline techniques in existence, corporal punishment distinguishes itself as having the fewest assets and the greatest number of liabilities. In terms of locking adult and child into a series of coercive cycles, it is the all-time champion. Those who rely on it swear by it—a testimonial to the addictive properties of quick short-term cures.

It would be nice to be able to say that the research overwhelmingly shows that corporal punishment does not work. Unfortunately the research shows nothing.[2] It would seem as though the topic has been singularly unattractive to professors and their graduate students. Thus, there is no scientific literature of consequence to serve as the basis of scientific debate.

Perhaps it is just as well that we are spared the debate. I have never thought of corporal punishment as a management technique anyway, although I know that many people do. I am, in fact, frequently asked what my "stand" is on corporal punishment. What miserable terrain on which to make a stand. The question is usually asked as if it were some kind of litmus test regarding my being strict with discipline as opposed to soft and permissive.

Within the context of a systematic understanding of discipline management, corporal punishment has always stood out to me as the most blatant example of mismanagement—primitive discipline, coercion, pain control in its purest form. Except for its ethical dimension, corporal punishment is a dead topic as far as the technology of discipline management is concerned. It is dead not only because of a lack of merit but also because of irrelevancy. If teachers have their backs against the wall with severe discipline problems, then I can perhaps understand the attractiveness of corporal punishment as a quick cure with retribution as a bonus. But when they are armed with a high-powered technology for getting kids to "eat out of their hands" such as positive classroom discipline, who would be drawn to use or rely on or even defend corporal punishment?

The fact that many educators stoutly defend the use of corporal punishment can only be taken as further evidence of the fact that they do not know anything better to do and that coercion is addictive. In an insightful article describing the corporal punishment cycle, Terry Rose describes the multiplicity of reinforcers and reinforcement errors that cause many educators to be consistently deluded into thinking that corporal punishment has caused something effective to happen in discipline at their school.[2] The bogus reinforcers occur during the four phases of a typical student's trip to the office to receive corporal punishment: (1) disruption in the classroom, (2) the trip to the office, (3) arrival at the office, and (4) return to class. A brief catalogue of reinforcement errors or bogus reinforcers for everyone involved is enlightening.

1 Disruption in the classroom
Student
- Admonishment from the teacher delivers the full attention of the group to the offender.
- Description of the offense during admonishment provides status among friends whom the disrupter may wish to impress by being "bad"—which in slang means "good."
- Removal from class rewards many students, especially if they hate the class or are doing poorly in the class.

Teacher
- Removal of a bad actor rewards the teacher by the removal of the problem.
- Catharsis of some internal upset through public admonishment of the student feels righteous.

2 The trip to the office
Student
- Opportunity is provided for verbal exchange and a chance to hassle the teacher further (revenge) if he or she accompanies the student.
- Attention from other teachers and students in the halls may produce attention and status ("Hey man, what did *you* do!")
- If the teacher does not escort the student, the student is free to talk to peers, go to the bathroom, heckle a friend in another classroom, or have a quick smoke.

3 Arrival at the office
Student
- The student receives attention from office staff, usually in the form of mildly shocked admonitions. ("Oh, Kate, what did *you* do?")
- Waiting to be seen provides opportunities to talk with peers who are in the office (especially if they are waiting to be seen too), to talk with office staff (the sympathetic secretary), to read a magazine, or to gripe out loud about the bum rap the student just got. Of course these opportunities for reinforcement are much greater if the teacher bounces the student than if the teacher accompanies the student to the office.
- The office may be the only air-conditioned place in the building.
- Individualized attention from the principal is provided as he or she lectures on the virtues of virtue. Upsetting the principal may add a special bonus.

Principal
- Apparent contrition by the student makes the principal feel effective.
- Approval from the teacher and the staff in general for backing them up affirms the principal's leadership role and avoids any teacher complaints concerning lack of support which therefore buttresses staff morale.
- An apology accompanied by a (very) short-term reduction or elimination of the problem provides further evidence to the administrator of his or her efficiency.

4 Return to the classroom
Student
- All the rewards of passing through the halls are once again available.
- On arrival peer attention is immediately focused on the disrupting student. Peers

are eager to know what happened, what was said to the principal, whether it hurt. The student now wears an invisible badge of courage. He or she is now *really* bad.

Teacher

- The student cools it for a while thereby providing final confirmation to the teacher that the great effort expended by everyone was worth while since it "got results."

As can be seen, the corporal punishment cycle is simply an exaggerated form of "bouncing" in terms of the web of reinforcement errors inadvertently generated. These reinforcers enmesh student, teacher, and administrator in an increasing dependency on coercive back-up for discipline problems.

Corporal punishment adds a new level of intensity to the use of pain control, however. With every escalation the management system becomes more unbalanced, and the probability of cooperation becomes more remote. With every escalation the likelihood of counteraggression, often in the form of vandalism, or of leaving the situation, perhaps in the form of dropping out, becomes more likely. In a perverse fashion the final or terminal event of this "problem student's" checkered academic career, dropping out of school, provides the last bogus reinforcer for educators addicted to pain control.

COOPERATIVE CYCLES

Reinforcement-Based Decision Making

Cooperation is based on *free choice*. A simple and useful definition of free will might be the luxury of basing one's choices on the relative desirability of competing reinforcers.

Reinforcement-based decision making is typically seen as belonging to us because we have had control over it. We got to choose what we wanted most. We naturally tend to take responsibility for behaviors and their consequences which we view as ours. This sense of responsibility is maximized when, as we learned earlier, (1) the reinforcer is a finite resource, (2) we have control over its consumption, and (3) we have to live with the consequences of our decisions regarding the consumption of the resource.

In cooperation, as with coercion, a recognizable constellation of management procedures tend to go together to produce cooperative, responsible behavior. They are not too mysterious; pleasant and plentiful reward for appropriate behavior given in conjunction with both extinction (consistent ignoring) for goofing off and gentle, effective, and consistent negative sanctions to suppress inappropriate behavior when needed. Within this context strictness means high standards rather than harshness. In such a classroom environment children quickly and pleasantly learn to work hard and follow basic rules. These classrooms are dynamite!

The Basics of Successful Management within Us

Some of the characteristics of discipline management are so basic as to govern the behavior of large corporations as well as your cat and dog. We prefer pleasure over pain, and over time we can come to trust and care for those who consistently give us pleasure in the absence of pain. We acquire trust gradually, and consequently we build cooperation gradually. Though a slow process, it is the only road to a pleasant work or family environment characterized by responsible behavior and reinforcement-based decision making.

The dual curse of cooperative cycles are that (1) they are relatively slow and (2) you must pay. The world wants quick, cheap cures for knotty interpersonal dilemmas—simple cures that can be summarized in a sentence. But what appears quick and cheap? The answer, of course, is coercion. But is it really cheap considering that it does not self-eliminate and it does not build a responsible, cohesive work group? Yet if your perspective does not extend beyond the present, you will be blind to these flaws.

However, people and all other animals, by their very nature, will teach us the same lessons of behavior management over and over again until we finally get them right. Only reinforcement-based social systems remain happy and productive in the long run. Only discipline done positively will enhance the building of a happy and productive work group—such as a classroom, family, shop, corporation, or government.

When we finally understand how human social systems work, we will learn to make people happy and productive in their work. The path to success is built into the animal since nothing else will work to the same degree in the long run. Our happiness and the happiness of those around us will be greatly increased as we acquire the new skills that will allow us to manage social situations positively. And, our happiness and the happiness of those around us will be hastened by our gaining enough sophistication to avoid being seduced by the kinds of quick yet painful "fixes" that are achievable in the short run.

OVERVIEW

Many topics could be added to enrich Positive Classroom Discipline, but at least the fundamentals have been set forth. It is to be hoped that discipline management is out of the woods by this point. Positive Classroom Discipline, however, has three aspects, only one of which can be covered in a book. The three are (1) what to do, a matter of information, (2) how to do it, a matter of thorough teaching and practice, and (3) how to produce deep and lasting growth and change among the faculty and administrators at a school site and within a school district. How to do it is a matter of skill practice which rests on a highly developed training program. How to produce deep and lasting change rests on equally sophisticated methods of "systems intervention" which structure a broad-based, shared, long-term staff development and professional growth effort that pervades the life of the school and/or district.

Throughout Positive Classroom Discipline it has been impossible for me to avoid repeated reference to trained teachers. The difference in skill proficiency between a trained and an untrained teacher is as different as day and night. And the difference in depth and longevity of a change effort that is well supported and incorporated into the life of an institution as opposed to a fleeting in-service experience is also as different as day and night. You can learn about teaching from a book, but you can't learn how to teach from a book—any more than you can learn how to ski from a book. Please let this book serve only as a beginning.

We must, however, still attend to a great deal of unfinished business. It would seem as though the topic of classroom discipline has been well mapped out. Actually, it has been only *half* mapped out. Only when our technology of Positive Classroom Discipline had been defined could we see the full nature of the teaching errors inherent in most classrooms that could hobble an excellent discipline management program and squander many of its promised gains in time on task. Once we had learned about positive classroom discipline we had to learn about instructional skills that would serve as the *primary prevention* component of a comprehensive classroom discipline program. Those instructional skills are described in *Positive Classroom Instruction,* the other volume of this two-volume treatment of classroom management.

REFERENCES

1 Patterson, Gerald R., *Coercive Family Process,* 1982, Castilio Publishing Company, Eugene, Oregon.

2 Rose, Terry L. The corporal punishment cycle: a behavioral analysis of the maintenance of corporal punishment in the schools. *Education and Treatment of Children,* 1981, 4, 157–169.

BIBLIOGRAPHY

GENERAL REFERENCES

Alschuler, A.S. The discipline game: playing without losers. *Learning Magazine,* August–September 1974, 80–86.

Alschuler, A.S. School discipline through social literacy. In D.C. McClelland (Ed.), *Education for values.* New York: Irvington, 1980.

Alschuler, A.S. *School discipline: a socially literate solution.* New York: McGraw-Hill, 1980.

American Friends Service Committee. *Creative discipline: searching for the better way.* Newsletter Series. Columbia, SC: Southeastern Public Education Program, 1977–1978.

Bayh, B. *Challenge for the third century: education in a safe environment.* Washington, DC: U.S. Government Printing Office, 1977.

Bayh, B. Seeking solutions to school violence and vandalism. *Phi Delta Kappa,* January 1978, *59,* 299–301.

Brenner, B. *Love and discipline.* New York: Ballantine Books, 1983.

Brodinsky, B. *Student discipline: problems and solutions.* Arlington, VA: American Association of School Administrators, 1980.

Canter, L., and Canter, M. *Assertive discipline: a take charge approach for today's educator.* Los Angeles: Canter and Associates, 1976.

Carter, R. *Help! these kids are driving me crazy.* Champaign, IL: Research Press, 1972.

Charles, C.M. *Building classroom discipline.* New York: Longman, 1985.

Children's Defense Fund. *School suspensions: are they helping children?* Cambridge, MA: Washington Research Project, Inc., 1975.

Cuban, L. *To make a difference: teaching in the inner city.* New York: The Free Press, 1970.

Curwin, R.L., and Mendler, A.N. *The discipline book: a complete guide to school and classroom management.* Reston, VA: Reston Publishing, 1980.

Dodson, J. *Dare to discipline.* Wheaton, IL: Tyndale House, 1972.

Dollar, B., *Humanizing classroom discipline: a behavioral approach.* New York: Harper and Row, 1972.

Dreikurs, R., and Cassel, P. *Discipline without tears.* New York: Hawthorne Books, 1974.

Dreikurs, R., and Gray, L. *A new approach to discipline: logical consequences.* New York: Hawthorne Books, 1978.

Dreikurs, R., Grunwald, B.B., and Pepper, F.C. *Maintaining sanity in the classroom.* New York: Harper and Row, 1971.

Duke, D.L. How administrators view the crises in school discipline. *Phi Delta Kappa,* January 1978, 325–330.

Duke, D.L. (Ed.). *Classroom management.* The seventy-eighth yearbook of the National Society for the Study of Education. Chicago, IL: University of Chicago Press, 1979.

Epstein, C. *Classroom management and teaching: persistent problems and rational solutions.* Reston, VA: Reston Publishing, 1979.

Ernest, K. *Games students play.* Millbrae, CA: Celestial Art, 1972.

First, J.M., and Mizell, M.H. (Eds.). *Everybody's business: a book about school discipline.* Columbia, SC: Southeastern Public Education Program, 1980.

Gordon, T. *Teacher effectiveness training.* New York: Peter H. Wyden, 1974.

Grantham, M.L., and Harris, C.S. A faculty trains itself to improve student discipline. *Phi Delta Kappa,* June 1976, 661–663.

Gray, J. *The teacher's survival guide. How to maintain classroom discipline and live to tell about it!* Belmont, CA: Fearon, 1974.

Hammill, D.D., and Bartel, N.R. *Teaching children with learning and behavior problems.* Boston, MA: Allyn and Bacon, 1978.

Handbook for developing schools with good discipline. The Phi Delta Kappa Commission on Discipline. Bloomington, IN: Phi Delta Kappa, 1982.

Howard, E.R. *School discipline desk book.* West Nyack, NY: Parker, 1978.

Johnson, L.V., and Bany, M.A. *Classroom management: theory and skill training.* New York: Macmillan, 1970.

Jones, V.F., and Jones, L.S. *Responsible classroom discipline: creating positive learning environments and solving problems.* Boston: Allyn and Bacon, 1981.

Kauffman, J.M., and D.L. Clayton (Eds). *Teaching children with behavior disorders.* Columbus, OH: Charles Merrill, 1974.

Kounin, J. *Discipline and group management in classrooms.* New York: Holt, Rinehart and Winston, 1970.

Kounin, J., and Gump, P.V. The ripple effect in discipline. *Elementary School Journal,* 1958, 59, 158–162.

Maggs, M.M. *The classroom survival book: a practical manual for teachers.* New York: New Viewpoints, 1980.

Martin, R., and Lauridsen, D. *Developing student discipline and motivation.* Champaign, IL: Research Press, 1974.

National Institute of Education, *Violent schools—safe schools: the safe school study report to the Congress.* U.S. Government Printing Office, Washington, DC, 1978.

Silberman, M.L., and Wheelan, S.A. *How to discipline without feeling guilty.* New York: Hawthorne Books, 1980.

Tanner, L.N. *Discipline for effective teaching and learning.* New York: Holt, Rinehart and Winston, 1978.

Wallen, C.J., and Wallen, L.L. *Effective classroom management.* Boston: Allyn and Bacon, 1978.

Welch, D.I., and Hughes, W. *Discipline: a shared experience.* New York: Hart, 1977.

Wolfgang, C.H., and Glickman, C.D. *Solving discipline problems: strategies for classroom teachers.* Boston: Allyn and Bacon, 1980.

TIME ON TASK

Anderson, L.W. Student involvement in learning and school achievement. *California Journal of Educational Research,* 1975, *26,* 53–62.

Anderson, L.W. Learning time and educational effectiveness. *NASSP Curriculum Report,* December 1980, vol. 10, no. 2.

Arlin, M. Teaching transitions can disrupt time flow in classrooms. *American Education Research Journal,* 1979, *16,* 42–56.

Berliner, D.C. *The beginning teacher evaluation study: overview and selected findings, 1974–75.* San Francisco, CA: Far West Regional Laboratory for Educational Research and Development, 1975.

Berliner, D.C., Fisher, C.W., Filby, N., and Marliave, R. *Executive summary of beginning teacher evaluation study.* San Francisco, CA: Far West Regional Laboratory for Educational Research and Development, 1978.

Bloom, B.S. Time and learning. *American Psychologist,* 1974, *29,* 682–688.

Brophy, J. Teacher behavior and student learning. *Educational Leadership,* 1979, *37,* 33–38.

Brophy, J.E., and Evertson, C.M. *Process–product correlations in the Texas teacher effectiveness study: final report.* Austin, TX: University of Texas, 1974.

Davidson, C., and Bell, M.L. Relationships between pupil-on-task performance and teacher behaviors. *The Southern Journal of Educational Research,* 1975, *9,* 225–235.

Denhan, C., and Lieberman, A. (Eds.). *Time to learn: a review of the beginning teacher evaluation study,* National Institute of Education, 1980.

Fisher, C.W., Filby, N.N., Marliave, R.S., Cahen, L. S., Dishaw, M.M., Moore, J.E., and Berliner, D.C. Teaching behaviors, academic learning time and student achievement: final report of phase IV-B, beginning teacher evaluation study, technical report V-1. *Beginning teacher evaluation study.* San Francisco, CA: Far West Laboratory for Regional Educational Research and Development, 1978.

Fisher, C., Marliave, R., and Filby, N.N. Improving teaching by increasing academic learning time. *Educational Leadership, 37,* 52–54.

Frederick, W.C. The use of classroom time in high schools above or below the median reading score. *Urban Education,* 1977, 459–464.

Gage, N.T. *The scientific basis of the art of teaching.* New York: Teachers College Press, 1979.

Good, T.L., and Beckerman, T.M. Time on task: a naturalistic study in sixth-grade classrooms. *The Elementary School Journal,* 1978, *73,* 193–201.

Guthrie, J.T., Martuza, V., and Seifert, M. *Impacts of instructional time in reading.* Newark, DE: International Reading Association, 1976.

Harnischfeger, A., and Wiley, D.E. Exposure to schooling: method, conclusions, policy. *Educational Researcher,* February 1976, 5.

Harnischfeger, A., and Wiley, D. The teaching-learning process in elementary schools: a synoptic view. *Curriculum Inquiry,* 1976, *6,* 5–43.

Medley, D.M. *Teacher competence and teacher effectiveness: a review of process-product research.* Washington, DC: American Association of Colleges for Teacher Evaluation, August 1977.

Rosenshine, B.V. *Academic engaged time, content covered, and direct instruction.* Unpublished paper, University of Illinois.

Smyth, W.J. Pupil engaged learning time: concepts, findings and implications. *The Australian Journal of Education,* 1980, *24,* 225–245.

Stallings, J. Allocated academic learning time revisited, or beyond time on task. *Educational Researcher,* 1980.

Stallings, J.A., and Kaskowitz, D. *Follow-through classroom observation evaluation, 1972–73.* Menlo Park, CA: Stanford Research Institute, 1974.

Stanford program on teacher effectiveness. A factorially designed experiment on teacher structuring, soliciting, and reacting. Stanford, CA: Stanford Center for Research and Development in Teaching, 1976.

Welch, W.W., and Bridgham, R.G. Physics achievement gains as a function of teaching duration. *School Science and Mathematics,* May 1968, *68,* 449–454.

Wiley, D.E., and Harnischfeger, A. Explosion of a myth; quantity of schooling and exposure to instruction, major educational vehicles. *Educational Researcher,* 1974, *5,* 7–12.

APPLIED BEHAVIOR ANALYSIS

Arnold, J.H., and Clement, P.W. Temporal generalization of self-regulation effects in under-controlled children. *Child Behavior Therapy,* 1981, *3,* 63–68.

Averill, J.R. Personal control over aversive stimuli and its relationship to stress. *Psychological Bulletin,* 1973, *80,* 286–303.

Ayllon, T., Garber, S., and Pisor, K. The elimination of discipline problems through a combined school-home motivational system. *Behavior Therapy,* 1975, *6,* 616–626.

Ayllon, T., Layman, D., and Burka, S. Disruptive behavior and reinforcement of academic performance. *Psychological Record,* 1972, *22,* 315–323.

Ayllon, T., and Roberts, M.D. Eliminating discipline problems by strengthening academic performance. *Journal of Applied Behavior Analysis,* 1974, *7,* 71–76.

Azrin, N.H., and Lindley, O.R. The reinforcement of cooperation between children. *Journal of Abnormal and Social Psychology,* 1956, *52,* 100–102.

Baer, A.M., Rowbury, T., and Baer, D.M. The development of instructional control over classroom activities of deviant preschool children. *Journal of Applied Behavior Analysis,* 1973, *6,* 289–298.

Baer, D.M. A case for the selective reinforcement of punishment. In C. Neuringer and J.L. Michael (Eds.), *Behavior modification in clinical psychology.* New York: Appleton-Century Crofts, 1970.

Bailey, J.S., Wolf, M.M., and Phillips, E.L. Home-based reinforcement and the modification of pre-delinquents' classroom behavior. *Journal of Applied Behavior Analysis,* 1970, *3,* 223–233.

Bandura, A. *Aggression: a social learning analysis.* Englewood Cliffs, NJ: Prentice-Hall, 1973.

Barrish, H., Saunders, M., and Wolf, M. Good behavior game: effects of individual contingencies for group consequences on disruptive behavior in a classroom. *Journal of Applied Behavior Analysis,* 1969, *2,* 119–124.

Becker, W.C., Madsen, C.H., Arnold, C.R., and Thomas, D.R. The contingent use of teacher attention and praise in reducing classroom behavior problems. *Journal of Special Education,* 1967, *1,* 287–307.

Bijou, S.W., and Sturges, P.T. Positive reinforcers for experimental studies with children—consumables and manipulatables. *Child Development,* 1959, *30,* 151–170.

Bolstad, O.D., and Johnson, S.M. Self-regulation in the modification of disruptive behavior. *Journal of Applied Behavior Analysis,* 1972, *5,* 443–454.

Braukmann, C.J., and Fixsen, D.L. Behavior modification with delinquents. In M. Hersen, R.M. Eisler, and P.M. Miller (Eds.), *Progress in behavior modification,* vol. 1. New York: Academic Press, 1974.

Broden, M., Bruce, C., Mitchell, M.A., Carter, V., and Hall, R.V. Effects of teacher attention on attending behavior of two boys at adjacent desks. *Journal of Applied Behavior Analysis,* 1970, *3,* 199–203.

Broden, M., Hall, R.V., Dunlap, A., and Clark, R. Effects of teacher attention and a token reinforcement system in a junior high school special education class. *Exceptional Children,* 1970, *36,* 341–349.

Broden, M., Hall, R.V., and Mitts, B. The effects of self-recording on the classroom behavior of two eighth-grade students. *Journal of Applied Behavior Analysis,* 1971, *4,* 191–199.

Brown, D., Reschly, D., and Sabers, D. Using group contingencies with punishment and pos-itive reinforcement to modify aggressive behaviors in a Head Start classroom. *Psychological Record,* 1974, *24,* 491–496.

Brownell, K., Colletti, G., Ersner-Hershfield, R., Hershfield, S.M., and Wilson, G.T. Self-control in school children: stringency and leniency in self-determined versus externally im-posed performance standards. *Behavior Therapy,* 1977, *8,* 442–455.

Burchard, J.D., and Barrera, F. An analysis of timeout and response cost in a programmed environment. *Journal of Applied Behavior Analysis,* 1972, *5,* 271–282.

Burka, A.A., and Jones, F.H. Procedures for increasing appropriate verbal participation in spe-cial elementary classrooms. *Behavior Modification,* 1979, *3,* 27–47.

Campbell, D.P., Adams, R.M., and Ryabik, J.E. Group-contingent time-out and behavior on a school bus. *Psychological Reports,* 1974, *34,* 883–885.

Carden Smith, L.K., and Fowler, S.A. Positive peer pressure: the effects of peer monitoring on children's disruptive behavior. *Journal of Applied Behavior Analysis,* 1984, *17,* 213–227.

Chomsky, N. The case against B.F. Skinner. In F.W. Matson (Ed.), *Without/within: behaviorism and humanism.* Monterey, CA: Brooks/Cole, 1973.

Christie, D.J., Hiss, M., and Loganoff, B. Modification of inattentive classroom behavior: hyperactive children's use of self-recording with teacher guidance. *Behavior Modification,* 1984, *8,* 391–406.

Church, R.M. The varied effects of punishment on behavior. *Psychological Review,* 1963, *70,* 369–402.

Clement, P.W., Anderson, E., Arnold, J., Butman, R., Fantuzzo, J., and May, R. Self-obser-vation and self-reinforcement as sources of self-control in children. *Biofeedback and self-regulation,* 1978, *3,* 247–268.

Cohen, H.L. Programming alternatives to punishment: the design of competence through con-sequences. In S.W. Bijou and E. Ribes-Inesta (Eds.), *Behavior modification: issues and extensions.* New York: Academic Press, 1972.

Cossairt, A., Hall, R.V., and Hopkins, B.I. The effects of experimenter instructions, feedback, and praise on teacher praise and student attending behavior. *Journal of Applied Behavior Analysis,* 1973, *6,* 89–100.

Cowen, R.J., Jones, F.H., and Bellack, A.S. Grandma's rule with group contingencies—a cost-effective means of classroom management. *Behavior Modification,* 1979, *3,* 397–418.

Danaher, B.G. Theoretical foundations and clinical applications of the Premack Principle: re-view and critique. *Behavior Therapy,* 1974, *5,* 307–324.

Deitz, S.M., and Repp, A.C. Differentially reinforcing low rates of misbehavior with normal elementary school children. *Journal of Applied Analysis,* 1974, *7,* 622.

Devine, V.T., and Tomlinson, J.R. The "workclock": an alternative to token economies in the management of classroom behaviors. *Psychology in the Schools,* 1976, *13,* 163–170.

Doleys, D.M., Wells, K.C., Hobbs, S.A., Roberts, M.W., and Cartelli, L.M. The effects of social punishment on noncompliance: a comparison with time out and positive practice. *Journal of Applied Behavior Analysis,* 1976, *9,* 471–482.

Drabman, R.S., Hammer, D., and Rosenbaum, M.S. Assessing generalization in behavior modification with children: the generalization map. *Behavioral Assessment,* 1979, *1,* 203–219.

Drabman, R.S., and Lahey, B.B. Feedback in classroom behavior modification: effects on the target and her classmates. *Journal of Applied Behavior Analysis,* 1974, *7,* 591–598.

Drabman, R.S., Spitalnik, R., and O'Leary, K.D. Teaching self-control to disruptive children. *Journal of Abnormal Psychology,* 1973, *82,* 10–16.

Drabman, R.S., Spitalnik, R., and Spitalnik, K. Sociometric and disruptive behavior as a function of four types of token reinforcement programs. *Journal of Applied Behavior Analysis,* 1974, *7,* 93–101.

Eitzen, D.S. The effects of behavior modification on the attitudes of delinquents. *Behavior Research and Therapy,* 1975, *13,* 295–299.

Fixsen, D.L., Phillips, E.L., and Wolf, M.M. Achievement place: experiments in self-government with pre-delinquents. *Journal of Applied Behavior Analysis,* 1973, *6,* 31–47.

Forehand, R., Roberts, M.W., Doleys, D.M., Hobbs, S.A., and Resick, P.A. An examination of disciplinary procedures with children. *Journal of Experimental Child Psychology,* 1976, *21,* 109–120.

Fowler, S.A., and Baer, D.M. "Do I have to be good all day?" The timing of delayed reinforcement as a factor in generalization. *Journal of Applied Behavior Analysis,* 1981, *14,* 13–24.

Glynn, E.L., and Thomas, J.D. Effect of cueing on self-control of classroom behavior. *Journal of Applied Behavior Analysis,* 1974, *7,* 299–306.

Glynn, E.L., Thomas, J.D., and Shee, S.M. Behavior self-control of on-task behavior in an elementary classroom. *Journal of Applied Behavior Analysis,* 1973, *6,* 105–113.

Gordon, J., and Bostow, D.E. *Lunch room noise management in an inner city public elementary school.* Paper presented at the annual meeting of the Florida Association for Behavior Analysis, Orlando, September 1981.

Grandy, G.S., Madsen, C.H., Jr., and De Mersseman, L.M. The effects of individual and interdependent contingencies on inappropriate classroom behavior. *Psychology in the Schools,* 1973, *10,* 488–493.

Graubard, P.S., Rosenberg, H., and Miller, M.B. Student applications of behavior modification to teachers and environments or ecological approaches to social deviancy. In R. Ulrich, T. Stachnik, and J. Mabry (Eds.), *Control of human behavior,* Vol. 3. Glenview, IL: Scott, Foresman, 1974.

Greene, B.F., Bailey, J.S., and Barber, F. An analysis and reduction of disruptive behavior on school buses. *Journal of Applied Behavior Analysis,* 1981, *14,* 177–192.

Greenwood, C.R., Hops, H., Walker, H.M., Guild, J.J., Stokes, J., and Young, K.R. Standardized classroom management program: social validation and replication studies in Utah and Oregon. *Journal of Applied Behavior Analysis,* 1979, *12,* 235–253.

Hall, J., and Baker, R. Token economy systems: breakdown and control. *Behaviour Research and Therapy,* 1973, *11,* 253–263.

Hall, R.V., Axelrod, S., Foundopoulos, M., Shellman, J., Campbell, R.A., and Cranston, S. The effective use of punishment to modify behavior in the classroom. *Educational Technology,* 1971, *11,* 24–26.

Hall, R.V., Axelrod, S., Foundopoulos, M., Shellman, J., Campbell, R.A., and Cranston, S.S. The effective use of punishment to modify behavior in the classroom. In K.D. O'Leary and S.G. O'Leary (Eds.), *Classroom management: the successful use of behavior modification.* New York: Pergamon Press, 1972.

Hall, R.V., Fox, R., Willard, D., Goldsmith, L., Emerson, M., Owen, M., Davis, F., and Porcia, E. The teacher as observer and experimenter in the modification of disputing and talking-out behaviors. *Journal of Applied Behavior Analysis,* 1971, *4,* 141–149.

Hall, R.V., Panyan, M., Rabon, D., and Broden, M. Instructing beginning teachers in reinforcement procedures which improve classroom control. *Journal of Applied Behavior Analysis*, 1968, *1*, 315–322.

Hayes, L.A. The use of group contingencies for behavioral control: a review. *Psychological Bulletin*, 1976, *83*, 628–648.

Herman, S.H., and Tramontana, J. Instructions and group versus individual reinforcement in modifying disruptive group behavior. *Journal of Applied Behavior Analysis*, 1971, *4*, 113–119.

Homme, L. *How to use contingency contracting in the classroom.* Champaign, IL: Research Press, 1972.

Hundert, J. The effectiveness of reinforcement, response cost, and mixed programs on classroom behaviors. *Journal of Applied Behavior Analysis*, 1976, *9*, 107.

Iwata, B.A., and Bailey, J.S. Reward versus cost token systems: an analysis of the effects on students and teacher. *Journal of Applied Behavior Analysis*, 1974, *7*, 567–576.

Jones, F.H. The gentle art of classroom discipline. *The National Elementary Principal*, 1979, *58*, 26–32.

Jones, F.H., and Eimers, R. Role-playing to train elementary teachers to use a classroom management "skill package." *Journal of Applied Behavior Analysis*, 1975, *8*, 421–433.

Jones, F.H., Fremouw, W., and Carples, S. Pyramid training of elementary school teachers to use a classroom management "skill package." *Journal of Applied Behavior Analysis*, 1977, *10*, 239–253.

Jones, F.H., and Miller, W.H. *The Laurence School socialized study, a preliminary report.* Paper presented at the annual meeting of the American Orthopsychiatric Association, Washington, DC, March 1971.

Jones, F.H., and Miller, W.H. The effective use of negative attention for reducing group disruption in special elementary school classrooms. *Psychological Record*, 1974, *24*, 435–448.

Kaufman, K.F., and O'Leary, K.D. Reward, cost, and self-evaluation procedures for disruptive adolescents in a psychiatric hospital school. *Journal of Applied Behavior Analysis*, 1972, *5*, 293–309.

Kazdin, A.E. Response cost: the removal of conditioned reinforcers for therapeutic change. *Behavior Therapy*, 1972, *3*, 533–546.

Kazdin, A.E. The effect of vicarious reinforcement on attentive behavior in the classroom. *Journal of Applied Behavior Analysis*, 1973, *6*, 71–78.

Kazdin, A.E. The token economy: a decade later. *Journal of Applied Behavior Analysis*, 1982, *15*, 431–445.

Kirschner, N.M., and Levin, L. A direct school intervention program for the modification of aggressive behavior. *Psychology in the Schools*, 1975, *12*, 202–208.

Kubany, E.S., Weiss, L.E., and Sloggett, B.B. The good behavior clock: a reinforcement/time-out procedure for reducing disruptive classroom behavior. *Journal of Behavior Therapy and Experimental Psychiatry*, 1971, *2*, 173–179.

Kuypers, D.S., Becker, W.C., and O'Leary, K.D. How to make a token system fail. *Exceptional Children*, 1968, *11*, 101–108.

Litow, L., and Pumroy, D.K. A brief review of classroom group-oriented contingencies. *Journal of Applied Behavior Analysis*, 1975, *8*, 341–347.

Long, J.D., and Williams, R.L. The comparative effectiveness of group and individually contingent free time with inner-city junior high school students. *Journal of Applied Behavior Analysis*, 1973, *6*, 465–474.

McAllister, L.W., Stachowiak, J., Baer, D., and Conderman, L. The application of operant conditioning techniques in a secondary school classroom. *Journal of Applied Behavior Analysis*, 1969, *2*, 277–285.

McLaughlin, T.F. A review of applications of group-contingency procedures used in behavior modification in the regular classroom: some recommendations for school personnel. *Psychological Reports,* 1974, *35,* 129–133.

McLaughlin, T.F. The applicability of token reinforcement systems in public school systems. *Psychology in the Schools,* 1975, *12,* 84–89.

MacMillan, D., Forness, S.R., and Trumbull, B.M. The role of punishment in the classroom. *Exceptional Children,* 1973, *40,* 85–96.

MacPherson, E.M., Candee, B.L., and Hohman, R.J. A comparison of three methods for eliminating disruptive lunchroom behavior. *Journal of Applied Behavior Analysis,* 1974, *7,* 287–298.

Madsen, C.H., Becker, W.C., and Thomas, D.R. Rules, praise, and ignoring: elements of elementary classroom control. *Journal of Applied Behavior Analysis,* 1968, *1,* 139–150.

Madsen, C.H., Becker, W.C., Thomas, D.R., Koser, L., and Plager, E. An analysis of the reinforcing function of "sit down" commands. In R.K. Parker (Ed.), *Readings in educational psychology.* Boston: Allyn and Bacon, 1968.

Marholin, D., II, Steinman, W.M., McInnis, E.T., and Heads, T.B. The effect of a teacher's presence on the classroom behavior of conduct-problem children. *Journal of Abnormal Child Psychology,* 1975, *3,* 11–25.

Mattos, R.L., Mattson, R.H., Walker, H.M., and Buckley, N.K. Reinforcement and aversive control in the modification of deviant classroom behavior. *Academic Therapy,* 1969, *5*(1).

Medland, M.B., and Stachnik, T.J. Good-behavior game: a replication and systematic analysis. *Journal of Applied Behavior Analysis,* 1972, *5,* 45–51.

Morgan, R.R. An exploratory study of three procedures to encourage school attendance. *Psychology in the Schools,* 1975, *12,* 209–215.

Murphy, H.A., Hutchinson, J.M., and Bailey, J.S. Behavioral school psychology goes outdoors: the effect of organized games on playground aggression. *Journal of Applied Behavior Analysis,* 1983, *16,* 29–35.

O'Leary, K.D., and Becker, W.C. The effects of a teacher's reprimands on children's behavior. *Journal of School Psychology,* 1968, *7,* 8–11.

O'Leary, K.D., Kaufman, K., Kass, R.E., and Drabman, R. The effects of loud and soft reprimands on the behavior of disruptive students. *Exceptional Children,* 1970, *37,* 145–155.

O'Leary, K.D., and O'Leary, S.G. (Eds.). *Classroom management: the successful use of behavior modification.* New York: Pergamon, 1972.

O'Leary, K.D., and O'Leary, S.G. (Eds.). *The successful use of behavior modification.* New York: Pergamon, 1977.

O'Leary, S.G., and Dubey, D.R. Applications of self-control procedures by children: a review. *Journal of Applied Behavior Analysis,* 1979, *12,* 449–465.

Osborne, J.G. Free time as a reinforcer in the management of classroom behavior. *Journal of Applied Behavior Analysis,* 1969, *2,* 113–118.

Packard, R.G. The control of "classroom attention," a group contingency for complex behavior. *Journal of Applied Behavior Analysis,* 1970, *3,* 13–28.

Patterson, G.R. The aggressive child: victim and architect of a coercive system. In L.C. Handy and D.J. Marsh (Eds.), *Behavior modification and families: theory and research,* Vol. 1. New York: Brunner/Mazel, 1976.

Patterson, G.R. A three-stage functional analysis for children's coercive behaviors: a tactic for developing a performance theory. In D. Baer, B.C. Etzel, and J.M. LeBlanc (Eds.), *New developments in behavioral research: theories, methods, and applications. In honor of Sidney W. Bijou.* Hillsdale, NJ: Lawrence Erlbaum Associates, 1977.

Patterson, G.R. A performance theory for coercive family interaction. In R. Cairns (Ed.), *Social interaction: methods, analysis, and illustrations.* Hillsdale, NJ: Lawrence Erlbaum Associates, 1979.

Patterson, G.R. *A social learning approach,* Vol. 3. *Coercive family process.* Eugene, OR: Castilia, 1982.

Patterson, G.R., and Cobb, J.A. A dyadic analysis of "aggressive" behaviors. In J.P. Hill (Ed.), *Minnesota Symposium on Child Psychology,* Vol. 5. Minneapolis: University of Minnesota Press, 1971.

Patterson, G.R., Cobb, J.A., and Ray, R.S. Direct intervention in the classroom: a set of procedures for the aggressive child. In F. Clark, D. Evans, and L. Hamerlynck (Eds.), *Implementing behavioral programs for schools and clinics.* Champaign, IL: Research Press, 1972.

Patterson, G.R., and Moore, D. Interactive patterns as units of behavior. In S.J. Suomi, M.E. Lamb, and G.R. Stephenson (Eds.), *Social interaction analysis: methodological issues.* Madison, WI: University of Wisconsin Press, 1979.

Patterson, G.R., and Reid, J.B. Reciprocity and coercion: two facets of social systems. In C. Neuringer and J.L. Michael (Eds.), *Behavioral modification in clinical psychology.* New York: Appleton-Century-Crofts, 1970.

Robertson, S.J., Simon, S.J., Pachman, J.S., and Drabman, R. Self-control and generalization procedures in a classroom of disruptive retarded children. *Child Behavior Therapy,* 1979, *1,* 347–362.

Rose, T.L. The corporal punishment cycle: a behavioral analysis of the maintenance of corporal punishment in the schools. *Education and Treatment of Children,* 1981, *4,* 157–169.

Rosenbaum, M.D., and Baer, D.M. Self-control training in the classroom: a review and critique. *Journal of Applied Behavior Analysis,* 1979, *12,* 467–485.

Sajwaj, T., Culver, P., Hall, C., and Lehr, L. Three simple punishment techniques for the control of classroom disruptions. In G. Semb (Ed.), *Behavior analysis and education.* Lawrence: University of Kansas, 1972.

Sallows, G.O., Strickarz, B.A., and Reutlinger, J.L. *Effectiveness of two group contingencies with emotionally disturbed elementary students.* Paper presented at the meeting of the Association for Advancement of Behavior Therapy, New York, December 1976.

Schmidt, G.W., and Ulrich, R.E. Effects of group contingent events upon classroom noise. *Journal of Applied Behavior Analysis,* 1969, *2,* 171–179.

Shutte, R.C., and Hopkins, B.L. The effects of teacher attention on following instructions in a kindergarten class. *Journal of Applied Behavior Analysis,* 1970, *3,* 117–122.

Solomon, R.W., and Wahler, R.G. Peer reinforcement control of classroom problem behaviors. *Journal of Applied Behavior Analysis,* 1973, *6,* 49–56.

Stevenson, H.C., and Fantuzzo, J.W. Application of the "generalization map" to a self-control intervention with school-aged children. *Journal of Applied Behavior Analysis,* 1984, *17,* 203–213.

Sulzbacher, S.I., and Houser, J.E. A tactic to eliminate disruptive behaviors in the classroom: group contingent consequences. *American Journal of Mental Deficiency,* 1968, *73,* 88–90.

Thomas, D.R., Becker, W.C., and Armstrong, M. Production and elimination of disreceptive classroom behavior by systematically varying teachers' behavior. *Journal of Applied Behavior Analysis,* 1968, *1,* 35–45.

Thomas, J.D., Presland, I.E., Grant, M.D., and Glynn, T.L. Natural rates of teacher approval and disapproval in grade 7 classrooms. *Journal of Applied Behavior Analysis,* 1978, *11,* 91–94.

Turkewitz, H., O'Leary, K.D., and Ironsmith, M. Generalization and maintenance of appropriate behavior through self-control. *Journal of Consulting and Clinical Psychology,* 1975, *43,* 577–583.

Van Houten, R., Nau, P.A., MacKenzie-Keating, S.E., Sameoto, D., and Colavecchia, B. An analysis of some variables influencing the effectiveness of reprimands. *Journal of Applied Behavior Analysis,* 1982, *15,* 65–83.

Varni, J.W., and Henker, B. A self-regulation approach to the treatment of three hyperactive boys. *Child Behavior Therapy*, 1979, *1*, 171–192.

Walker, H.M., Hops, H., and Fiegenbaum, E. Deviant classroom behavior as a function of combinations of social and token reinforcement and cost contingency. *Behavior Therapy*, 1976, *7*, 76–88.

Walker, H.M., Hops, H., and Johnson, S.M. Generalization and maintenance of classroom treatment effects. *Behavior Therapy*, 1975, *6*, 188–200.

White, M.A. Natural rates of teacher approval and disapproval in the classroom. *Journal of Applied Behavior Analysis*, 1975, *8*, 367–372.

Wilson, C.W., and Hopkins, B.L. The effects of contingent music on the intensity of noise in junior high home economics classes. *Journal of Applied Behavior Analysis*, 1973, *6*, 269–276.

Winett, R.A., and Winkler, R.C. Current behavior modification in the classroom: be still, be quiet, be docile. *Journal of Applied Behavior Analysis*, 1972, *5*, 499–504.

Wolf, M.M., Hanley, E.L., King, L.A., Lachowicz, J., and Giles, D.K. The timer-game: a variable interval contingency for the management of out-of-seat behavior. *Exceptional Children*, 1970, *37*, 113–117.

Worland, J. Effects of positive and negative feedback on behavior control in hyperactive and normal boys. *Journal of Abnormal Child Psychology*, 1976, *4*, 315–326.

MISCELLANEOUS

Antonovsky, A., *Health, stress and coping*. San Francisco, CA: Josey-Bass, 1979.

Dohrenwend, B., and Dohrenwend, B.S. *Stressful life events: their nature and effects*. New York: Wiley, 1974.

Emmer, E.T., Evertson, C.M., and Anderson, L.M. The first weeks of class . . . and the rest of the year. Paper presented in symposium, *Perspective on Classroom Research*. Annual meeting of the American Education Research Association, San Francisco, CA, April 1979.

Evertson, C.M., and Anderson, L.M. Beginning school. *Educational Horizons*, Summer 1979, 164–168.

Freudenberger, H.J. The staff burn-out syndrome in alternative institutions. *Psychotherapy: Theory, Research and Practice*, 1975, *12*(1), 72–83.

Freudenberger, H.J. Burn-out: the organizational menace. *Training and Development Journal*, July 1977, 27–29.

Hall, R., Gardner, C.W., Perl, M.S., Stickney, S., and Pfefferbaum, B. The professional burn-out syndrome. *Psychiatric Opinion*, April 1979, 12–17.

Mahingly, M. Sources of stress and burn-out in professional child care work. *Child Care Quarterly*, 1977, *6*(2), 127–137.

Maslach, C. Burned out. *Human Behavior*, September 1976, 16–18.

Russell, D., and Hunter, M. Planning for effective instruction. *Instructor*, September 1977.

Swent, B., and Smelch, W. Stress at the desk and how to cope creatively. Eugene, OR: Oregon School Study Council, University of Oregon, 1978.

Sylvester, R. Stress. *Instructor Magazine*, March 1977, 72–76.

PREFERRED ACTIVITY TIME (PAT)

See Chapter 11.